How & What to Pursue in Life

5 Pillars of Mind: On HOW to Live /
9 Absolute Values of Chakras: WHAT
We Should Live For

How & What to Pursue in Life

5 Pillars of Mind: On HOW to Live /
9 Absolute Values of Chakras: WHAT
We Should Live For

Yoon-Jeong Kim

BOOKS

Winchester, UK
Washington, USA

JOHN HUNT PUBLISHING

First published by O-Books, 2024
O-Books is an imprint of John Hunt Publishing Ltd., 3 East St., Alresford,
Hampshire SO24 9EE, UK
office@jhpbooks.com
www.johnhuntpublishing.com
www.o-books.com

For distributor details and how to order please visit the 'Ordering' section on our website.

Text copyright: Yoon-Jeong Kim 2022

ISBN: 978 1 80341 409 6
978 1 80341 410 2 (ebook)
Library of Congress Control Number: 2022917926

A CIP catalogue record for this book is available from the British Library.

Design: Lapiz Digital Services

UK: Printed and bound by CPI Group (UK) Ltd, Croydon, CR0 4YY
Printed in North America by CPI GPS partners

The author of this book does not dispense medical advice or
prescribe the use of any technique as a form of treatment for
physical, emotional, or medical problems without the advice of a
physician, either directly or indirectly. The intent of the author
is only to offer information of a general nature to help you in
your quest for emotional and spiritual well-being. In the event
you use any of the information in this book for yourself, which is
your constitutional right, the author and the publisher assume no
responsibility for your actions.

We operate a distinctive and ethical publishing philosophy in
all areas of our business, from our global network of authors to
production and worldwide distribution.

How and What to Pursue in Life
Part I

5 Pillars of Mind
On How to Live

Contents

About the Author:

Yoon-Jung Kim's curiosity about humans grew the more she studied Korean medicine. That is why when she became a doctor of Korean medicine, she focused more on individual constitution rather than the disease, and felt strong curiosity when she received an unfamiliar proposal regarding the origin and growth of an existence. All unconventional methods accompany clear light and darkness. She was overwhelmed by joy while learning the growth methods of unconventional existences, and experienced strong pain by failing to fully understand such methods. She thoroughly reflected on why such pain had to be caused, in terms of philosophy and Korean medicine. Now, here is the result of the reflection of how she was able to heal herself from such pain and expand her practices of healing patients based on such experiences.

Prologue

Before getting into this book I want to introduce myself to readers to whom I am a total stranger, to help in understanding and using this book.

I am a 41-year-old woman who practices Korean medicine in South Korea. I work in an ordinary Korean medicine clinic in an ordinary neighborhood, and the clinic being a primary care provider, I spend most of my work hours examining and treating patients who visit the clinic with a wide variety of symptoms. If there is a part of my life that has a particular significance with regards to the contents of this book, I never really had any vision or plan for my future, near or distant. In my childhood, grown-ups would ask me what I wanted to become when I grew up, and I thought it was just a very absurd question. But since I was expected to answer the question one way or another, I would emulate my friends and say, "I want to become a teacher," or even lied and said, "I want to become a pianist," even though I hated going to the piano lessons.

But that doesn't mean I didn't have any childhood dream. I had childhood dreams all right, but they were not about the future; they were about the present. Some of my childhood dreams included becoming the best hopscotch player in my neighborhood, or creating my own hopscotch moves to the song that I liked. There was also a time when I dreamt of becoming a child actress. My mom told me that I should become an actress when I grew up if I really wanted to, but being a child who did not dream of the future, I refused to agree with her. But eventually, I gave up on that dream when she told me that I would not be able to play hopscotch as much as I wanted to if I became a child actress. Then when my cousin, who was a college student at the time, told me that college students could pick and choose what they wanted to study, I asked him if there was a college that offered a hopscotch major. I was not the best hopscotch player in my neighborhood in my childhood, but, given that I was one of the best and my childhood friends would use the moves I'd created when we played hopscotch together, I think I fulfilled my dreams in my childhood.

In my high school senior year, when it was time to decide which college to apply to, I chose to go for a science major in accordance with my aptitude instead of thinking of a specific major or dream for the future. Since my father knew me well, he encouraged me to read the novel version of the Principles and Practice of Korean Medicine and suggested I apply to a college of Korean medicine, and, being a person who tended to make decisions spontaneously, I agreed without hesitation because I was captivated by the novel. I even studied another year after graduating high school and applied for the college of my choice the second time around until I was admitted, all because I was so captivated by the novel. I was also the kind of person who had to get what I set my mind to. While in college, I studied just hard enough to get the credits I needed to graduate, and after I graduated the college and became a Korean medicine doctor, I enrolled for – and graduated from – a graduate school with a major in Korean medical rehabilitation studies with a focus on pain treatment, so that I could learn what I needed to learn for my medical practice. I am the kind of person who applies myself to what I need or what I want here and now, and for everything else that I don't need or want right now, I don't think about how that will affect my future, am not interested, and don't care.

Then in early 2013, I was introduced to a life solution called AGD (accumulation of good deeds). AGD was sort of a character-building program and some of my friends who were studying Korean medicine with me had joined the program. The program presented two directions we were supposed to follow in life: one was the contemplation of ourselves and the other was love for others. These two directions were the keys to bringing about changes in ourselves and our lives. It was not much different from other character-building programs, but the essence of AGD was that the results of our contemplation of ourselves and love for others could be instantly verified in numbers. Perhaps many readers might find it strange and absurd to hear that you can confirm changes that happen within you in numbers. It's understandable, because it struck me as absurd at first as well. At any rate, I will explain about this numerical confirmation in detail later. I was intrigued by the program, and I thought I had nothing to lose considering how most other Korean medicine doctors who were studying with me had joined the program. So I decided to join the program and give it a try, because it didn't cost me any money. All I needed was the courage to ask and regularly check my inner progress in numerical scores.

The numerical scores of my progress that I could confirm changed me greatly. I had been someone who had lived life in the present moment only, but the program made me realize how the consequences of what we do in our lives is reflected on the present moment instead of appearing in the distant future, and that realization encouraged me to try harder. Other Korean medicine doctors and I shared tips on good contemplation methods, prayers for others, and stories about the changes that we noticed in the attitudes of our patients, and we took actions on what we shared and learned. This created a significant synergy effect. The internal progress we could sense within ourselves was confirmed in numbers, and we experienced dualistic verification in which we could tell how the progress confirmed in numbers was happening in our inner selves. I became less afraid when faced with life problems, I became more patient, and I had more energy to express gratitude. After having personally experienced the changes that happened in my present life, I enjoyed this personal growth more than before, and when asked the reason I was into accumulating good deeds, I would answer that I was doing it because I wanted to be happy.

At this stage, I was not really interested about how others were making more progress than I was. I thought it had nothing to do with my present life, and I did not have dreams for the future that I wanted to make come true by making big progress. As always, I was only interested in my present life, and as long as I was happy now, that was all that I needed.

About a year-and-a-half later, the collective liaison of this AGD started to break down. What happened was, when I think back, the breakdown started from the twisted concept of life being a war between evil and good. This twisted concept effectuated the diminished significance and nature of love, and the growing delusion about evil being something that has to be avoided and cut off. As a result, the leaders of this solidarity hurt the feelings of many people that they cared about, and regretfully, the love, which should have been the most important element in the AGD, started to disappear. But I could remain on this path longer because, even while this was going on, I was more interested in my present moment than anything else and I didn't care much about the future. It was because there were not many wounds I could inflict on others or others could inflict on me after my bond with others started thinning out, and while continuously growing at a slow pace, I experienced changes in which I found it easier to find my own way of loving others and standing a little stronger in the face of life problems. When I saw people in pain, I could not find any other way to reach out to them except feeling a little pain in my heart, because the only thing that mattered to me was building my own happiness.

And I drifted away from my peers who had stayed with me till the end and continued this journey alone. I chose to leave my peers who had stayed with me till the end at a time when we were just about getting close and building bonds. But the departure was not meant to be a closure; it was meant to be a waiting. I felt sorry that I was no longer able to share truth with them, but during the eight months that followed my departure from the group, I was able to learn many truths while building my love for them and blessing them. These truths have been a way that explains and guides the growth I've been making for three-and-a-half years. And it is also a way to build a happy life on my own without having to rely on others. This book will guide readers to the growth and the truth of happiness I've experienced.

I came upon numerous pains and difficulties on my journey to attain these truths. I was able to personally experience those truths and became free from those pains and difficulties after I acknowledged that those pains were of my own making. I wondered how many people who had taken the journey ahead of me had to suffer from pain like I did. This book is my homage of solace and appreciation for them. This book is also a letter of apology I send to numerous people who had to endure passive wounds that they'd sustained during the changes whereupon the AGD fell to pieces. And this book is my greeting of love for my old peers who are still entrapped in the twisted concept of war between good and evil.

Lastly, the most important people I want to dedicate this book to are none other than my readers – readers who wish to do their best in the present, and readers who wish to make this very moment a little happier. The truth of happiness I've experienced is something that has to be shared with all instead of keeping it only to myself. It belongs to all souls. Since the contents of this book are the results of my personal experience, I am presenting specific methodologies as well. The essence of the contents of this book is credited to the AGD that I've experienced, in addition to the books titled *Conversations with God*[1] and *Power vs. Force*[2] and Carl Gustav Jung's psychology. The book *Conversations with God* helped me find the true meaning of the AGD program, and the theory behind the book *Power vs. Force* made me convinced of some of the specific methods that I present in this book. And I was able to complete the creative integration of light and darkness with the help of Carl Jung's theories. For that reason, I am indebted to Neale Donald Walsh, who wrote *Conversations with God*, Dr David Roman Hawkins, who wrote *Power Vs. Force*, and the psychiatrist and psychoanalyst Carl Gustav Jung.

This is a series of two books. The first volume of the series is about the human mind, and I introduce and explain the nature and functions of the five energies found in all human psyche: Hon, Baek, Shin, Ui, and Ji. These five energies, which I will collectively call "Hon-Baek-Shin-Ui-Ji" in this book, are used in Korean medical practice, and once you understand the system that commonly applies to all human psyche, you can understand "how we should live" and will find ways to help your mind to harmoniously communicate with the world. The second volume of this book is about chakra, and I will introduce the will and choice of our soul in that volume. Answers to questions, such as "For what are we living as humans?" and "What should we seek in life?" can be found in our chakra. I will help readers remember the objectives of life by introducing absolute values found in chakra.

I am still living engrossed in the present time. My dreams are grounded in the present and I always try to seize it, and that is enough to make me happy. But I am engrossed in my present moment not because I am not interested in my future as I had been in the past. Now, I know by experience that the happiness I have today is encompassing my past and future. For that reason, I recommend my readers to dream the happiness of the present, because for those whose dreams are grounded in the present, the truths introduced in this book will materialize into reality.

Kim Yoon-jeong
March 2018

Endnotes

[1] *Conversations with God* by Neale Donald Walsh

[2] *Power vs. Force* by Dr David Roman Hawkins

On Being a Human

For a long time, I thought I was just "I." Just a simple totality called "I." Then I looked into myself more carefully and came to realize that I was not just a simple "I." I found my actions were very different from my mind. I would act out like a brave person even though I was intimidated in my mind, and sometimes I would act as if nothing was happening and I was an emotionless person when in fact, in my mind, I was really happy and excited. Sometimes I was deeply hurt inside and wanted to cry, but I forced myself to smile and continued to work as if nothing was bothering me. These are some examples that proved how my behavior does not always match with what is going on in my mind. I cannot say with confidence that my mind and my actions have been in sync more often than they haven't been. Since what I have in mind is different from how I act, I can say that within one existence that I call "I," there are two separate leagues: my mind and my behavior. In other words, I can say that "I" is the sum of the mind and the behavior.

Yet, there is another part of me within me. My mind and behavior will end after my life expires upon my death, but I cannot bring myself to believe that my existence itself will perish for good upon my death. I cannot tell for sure whether I will go to hell or heaven, or even reincarnate, but I am certain that I will exist even after I die. In fact, I've met numerous people in my life, and I hardly remember anybody who believed that they would perish forever once they died. They came from many different religious backgrounds, but most of them said things like, "You will go to hell if you act like that," "You must have saved your country in your previous life," "I will do everything I'd like to do in my next life," or "I am determined to go to heaven once I die." And nobody that I'd met said, "I will perish completely once I die." Probably, deep under their subconscious, they share the same belief as mine and think their existence will continue to exist even upon death.

If we indeed don't perish upon our death, the part of us that exists even after our mind and body are gone is our soul. Those who had near-death experience often describe how they felt themselves having turned into a free and wondrous being – a feeling that they'd never experienced while they were alive. Since it is not a feeling that we can experience in our ordinary lives, we can only assume that the feeling is attributed to the experience of our death-defying soul. Therefore, we can conclusively say that "I" am the sum of three entities: my soul that is an entity that remains even after death; my mind that is an entity that manifests itself as emotions and thoughts in everyday life; and the body that demonstrates our behaviors which sometimes match with what I have in mind, and sometimes the opposite of what I have in mind. We humans are an existence that is consisted of soul, mind, and body. I came to realize that I was the sum of these three entities. Since childhood, I've been going to a Catholic church and making the sign of the cross in the name of the Father, the Son, and the Holy Spirit, and now I wonder if the sign was a constant reminder that we humans are an existence consisting of three consubstantial beings.

Of the three beings of which we consist, the soul is the biggest frame. It is bigger than our body and even our mind. Since it is the biggest and the greatest being of all three, it remains even after death without perishing. And since the soul is immortal, it is the most perfect and sacred being of all three as well, because it would be impossible for an imperfect being to exist forever. Secondly, the mind is the fastest and the strongest energy of all three beings. We can tell how fast and strong our mind is from the fact that our mind can change in an instant, and it can also remain unchanged under any pressure. Therefore, the mind is the origin of our creative energy. Lastly, our body is the heaviest being of all three. We experience how it is difficult to express our thoughts in word, and how difficult it is to move our body to act on our plan. Since body is the smallest yet the heaviest part of our existence, it takes tremendous efforts to achieve the things that we set our mind to, even at a slow pace.

It is very important to understand that we humans are a three-layered being. Once we realize this truth, we can understand that our body naturally needs to take time to get anything done because it is the heaviest part of our existence and we can stop getting frustrated about it needlessly. Once we realize that what we have in mind can be different from what is indicated by our behavior, we can put our efforts to match our mind and behavior. Once we do that, we can liberate ourselves from all those uncomfortable and unpleasant feelings that we experience when our mind is not in sync with our actions. Once we acknowledge that our mind and our soul are two different entities, just like our mind and our action are two different things, we can understand that our mind is not what defines ourselves and we will be encouraged to change our mind. It will be very difficult to liberate ourselves from emotions and thoughts we wish to shake off as long as we believe that our present emotions and thoughts are the final destinations. We can think and ask ourselves if the current emotions and feelings are what our soul is wanting us to feel, try to find the path and direction that we truly want, and then we can change our mind to direct it to our true wishes.

We have to understand and take good care of all three beings. We humans cannot exist if we miss any of those three beings, and it is truly uncomfortable if any one of the three is not in sync with others. We are all aware of those uncomfortable feelings we get when our mind and our actions are not in sync. When our soul is far off from our mind and body, we develop a condition that is truly hard to handle on our own. Therefore, we have to ensure our soul embraces and looks after our mind and body; ensure our mind keeps our soul and body connected;

and our body to do what it is supposed to do without having to go through too much trouble by keeping our mind and soul in sync with each other. In fact, our body is the easiest of the three to handle. It is easiest to handle because it is slow and heavy. But mind is not easy to control because it is too fast and strong. And we don't even need to talk about how difficult it is with our soul, since it is difficult even to notice it. Therefore, I am going to explain and guide readers about the mind and the soul, and not about the body that is the easiest to handle.

There are numerous theories that explain the human mind. They are all excellent references and grateful guides for us. Psychoanalysis that studies subconsciousness can guide us to understand the causes of deep emotions and thoughts so that we can cope with them better, and the results of psychiatric researches are a great help for us to build better relationships with others and society by raising our awareness of the influence we have on each other and avoid misunderstandings. This book adds another theory about the human mind to these existing theories, and it is a theory based on Korean medicine. The essence of this theory is Hon, Baek, Shin, Ui, and Ji, which refer to the five major pillars that constitute our human mind, according to Korean medicine. This book is a guide to life found through the most fundamental structure of our conscience that is consisted of these five energies of Hon, Baek, Shin, Ui, and Ji.

Soul has been the domain of religion. Religion has been guiding us to the direction and path of our lives and the destinations, while telling us what to seek and what not to seek. But these days, religious teachings are growing less relevant to us. Religion surely provides us with great words that we can believe as the truth, but those teachings became irrelevant to the reality we live in, and such destinations as heaven and nirvana only feel too absurd for us to put our faith in them. Therefore, this book tries to make readers understand the soul so that we can narrow the distance between us and the teachings of existing religions. By understanding our soul with the chakra that all humans have within, this book introduces how the teachings of religions can influence everyone through chakra. And it will also make readers realize how important those teachings are. Readers are sure to find joy when they experience changes in chakras that happen when we satisfy our soul, and how practicing religious teachings are something that we must do without it having to feel unfair.

Soul can draw a blueprint for us to decide what to choose and what to achieve, while the mind creates everything with fast and strong energies we experience as thoughts and emotion, and the body manifests the outcome of our creativity in behavior. If I may describe it in a slightly different way, the soul is in charge of helping us make choices, the mind, to decide how to live, and the body, the manifestation of the results. If we realize what to choose in life through our soul, we will be able to accomplish the ultimate objectives of our life and existence while reducing the pain that results from confusion and misunderstanding. And if we realize how to do things through our mind, we will be able to lead a life that corresponds to our will and wishes more easily and conveniently.

If you think about the times when our mind and body were in sync, you realize how comfortable you felt with yourself at the time. Your action does not leave you with any frustration or regret. Therefore, you don't have to make unnecessary efforts to narrow the difference between the two. You don't have to feel anxious and nervous while worrying about having your hidden intention being disclosed. When your mind and action are in sync, you don't need to worry about uncomfortable consequences. And we feel happiness when our mind and action are in sync. The moments you truly felt happy in your life are the moments when your mind and soul were in sync. Happiness blooms with satisfaction when you have your mind and soul in sync because it means you made up your mind to make it accurately align with the objectives of life that your soul is seeking.

Therefore, we experience comfort when our mind and body are in sync; we experience happiness when our mind and soul are in sync; and eventually we feel joy and bliss when we reach the moment of trinity in which we become a being where the body, the mind, and the soul are all in sync. The smile of the Buddha that happiness brings will appear on our faces, our hearts become filled with satisfaction over the actions we take, and we experience the bliss when the electrifying joy is added to those as the signal that resonates with God. The objective of this book on Hon-Baek-Shin-Ui-Ji and chakra is ultimately to help readers experience the bliss of life by making all three entities be in sync with each other. It is truly regretful and unfortunate to live a life without having the experience of the joy of reaching the state of trinity. Since we will be left with no regret after we fully enjoy the bliss of the Trinity, and since the fate that we are supposed to enjoy to the fullest is given to us, I begin the book with a sincere hope for you to realize your own trinity in which you are simply a one being instead of a one being with three separate entities.

Hon-Baek-Shin-Ui-Ji (魂魄神意志): On How to Live

I wonder if you reflect on your mind as you lead your life. To be honest, I rarely reflected on myself, looked into my mind and thoughts, and observed them before I reached my 30s. There were times when I reflected on major events that had happened in my life and thought about their significance years later, but I rarely tried to figure out the reason I was feeling certain emotions and thoughts at the present moment, or their significances. I thought all that mattered was the raw feelings and emotions that I was feeling at the present moment, and I did not find anything wrong about it.

Then I read the psychoanalysis book *Human Landscape* by Kim Hyung-gyung[3] at age 30, and I started wondering why I was the way I was and reflected on myself. When I looked into my consciousness and subconsciousness, all of which consisted my mind, I realized that, at age 30, I was still having the separation anxiety that nearly smothered my mother when I was an elementary student. Having been the youngest daughter who received more than my fair share of love from my family and even my relatives, I tended to make friends only with some of the oldest kids of the families who liked me because they were trained to yield and sacrifice for others, and I also realized that it was really difficult to develop meaningful friendships with some of the oldest kids of families because they have been respected as the oldest kid and trained to be respectful. Even though deep reflection on myself did not relieve my separation anxiety or eliminate the characteristic traits of a youngest child, I was able to sense that the anxiety that I felt when I was troubled was the same anxiety experienced by a 3-year-old. I was also able to realize that I should be grateful for the favor and consideration my friends made for me instead of taking them for granted, and that I should try to show my appreciation by giving more of my love to them. That's how I moved on from the mentality of a 3-year-old and found the energy to lead a life more courageously and confidently, and to share more love with those who are dear to me.

Looking into our mind is really important in creating a life that we want. Our mind that mills out our emotions and feelings is so fluctuating that it can boil up at any moment and it can also quickly cool down for any reason. It is all because our mind is a very fast and powerful energy. It is so capricious that at one point our mind makes us fume with anger and then quickly start giggling while watching a TV variety show. Our mind can also remain stubborn for a long time and then quickly drop the stubbornness at an instance. It is because our mind is a very slow and gentle energy. It is to the point where people like myself hang on to the separation anxiety that had developed when they were a 3-year-old until they are in their 30s, and hold hatred toward someone and then completely drop the hatred when they find out what trouble the person is going through. We fill our lives with the energy of this fluctuating mind that is sometimes very fast and powerful and sometimes very slow and gentle.

This is the primal source of energy that creates our life. Therefore, we have to diligently and devotedly look into our mind. Instead of remaining at a stage where we rely on spontaneous feelings and thoughts, we have to keep asking why we felt and thought that way. "Why did I get so frustrated today? What should I have done to calm down my frustration? Why was it particularly hard for me today? What should I do to cope with this lethargy?" If you don't look into your mind and care about it constantly, whatever goes through your mind is left unattended without anybody noticing it. It is too pitiful to be so negligent of your mind. Therefore, we have to attend to it affectionately and attentively, and constantly look after it. We can make good decisions on what we need to do later on only when we demonstrate sincere affection for our mind and discover what is being created in our mind.

With regards to the methods of observing your mind, anything would work. The method is only of secondary importance because what matters is what you choose your mind to be: Do you choose to become the master of your life as an awakened person, or let your spontaneous feelings take control of your life? There are numerous possible methods: you can simply apply the psychoanalysis that I was introduced to first; psychological observation method; meditation that soothes you; writing about your days in journals; or religious repentance and contemplation. None of these methods is better or worse than others. Each method has its own advantages and disadvantages. Therefore, the best bet will be to try all these methods as you lead your life. Once you master diverse methods of observing yourself, you can look into your mind more easily and conveniently. Therefore, when it comes to the technique of looking into your mind, the more is the better. Instead of favoring one over the others, it is better to choose more paths and obtain more methods. For that reason, I am introducing one more technique of observing your mind: Hon(魂), Baek(魄), Shin(神), Ui(意) and Ji(志), which is collectively called "the five spirits" and used as the classification of consciousness in Korean medicine.

However, when you think about it, we all manage to lead our lives even if we don't make resolutions or determinations on what to do with them. We can manage to lead a decent life without having to think hard about what to do with our life because we all have the basic energies that guide us through our lives. We are not thrown into this world without any preparation at all. We exist here and now after being bestowed basic energies that are necessary to create our lives. And those basic energies that are necessary for humans to live are Hon,

Baek, Shin, Ui, and Ji, which are collectively called the "five spirits" in Korean medicine.

For a human being to live a life, he or she requires five fundamental elements: life (time and space), God (Creator), world (universe), I, and others. We have to fill the time and space given to us with our own energies, and we need to achieve the objective of our life through our relationship with our Creator. We have to follow the natural law as an existence that exists in the world and universe, we must know our own existential values, and we have to know the significance of our relationships with others. We can lead our lives only when we have the basic energies to support these five elements and become the Creator of our own lives. The five spirits of Hon, Baek, Shin, Ui, and Ji are the mental pillars that support these five elements, and they are the classification of consciousness that is necessary to support an existence.

Before explaining where the Hon, Baek, Shin, Ui, and Ji energies are found in us, I want to ask readers: Where do you think our mind exists? In general, people often think that our mind is in our heart or brain, because brain is where all our thoughts originate from, and heart is the organ that responds most sensitively to feelings. However, brain is an organ where the mind is converted into electric signals and generates thoughts, instead of being the organ that houses our mind. When our brain stops functioning, our mind still exists, even though brain cannot convert our mind into electric signals any longer. And heart can express our feelings outwardly with its beat, and it does not enclose the entire mind.

Then, let me ask this question: Where is our mind in us? According to the author of *Conversations with God*, our mind exists in every cell throughout our body. The author claims that there is no cell in our entire body including organs such as brain and heart that does not contain our mind.

Since the author claimed our mind exists between all cells throughout our body, we can say that our mind is the energy that embraces each cell in our body. Mind is also the energy that gives off creativity sometimes fast and powerfully and sometimes slowly and gently. The cells in our body generate energy through a complex organic chemical called ATP (adenosine triphosphate). That means all cells that generate energy are beholding our mind. The energy created by those cells shelters those cells and turns into thoughts and feelings to demonstrate creativity.

Ultimately, the entire energy that all cells in our body make is our mind. The mind is divided into consciousness and unconsciousness, with consciousness referring to the thoughts that can be perceived because it is formed into electric signals in brain cortex, while unconsciousness refers to the areas that belong to our mind but are not perceived. Psychoanalysis proved that the unperceivable energy of unconsciousness is much bigger and more critical than the perceivable energy of consciousness. The consciousness that we have in our mind is only a partial energy created at the brain cortex. The energy generated by all other cells is the mind of unconsciousness, and this unconsciousness is accounting for the majority part of our mind.

Hon, Baek, Shin, Ui, and Ji are the five pillars that support the mind that is present in all our cells. Hon, Baek, Shin, Ui, and Ji are situated at the central parts of our body beginning from the bottom of our feet to the crown on our head as they support our mind. Hon is present in the pineal gland of the brain, Baek in the cochlea of both ears, Shin in the heart, Ui in the ovary or testicular, and Ji on the soles of our feet.

The soles of our feet are there to support our whole body, ovary, and the testicular contains our genetic information and releases it to blend with other genetic information, and the heart is the organ where the vein of blood – our source of life

– starts. Called the third eye due to its structure that is similar to our eye, the pineal body of the brain is the channel through which we communicate with the universe, and our ears are the organ that receives information about the world. As we can see, Hon-Baek-Shin-Ui-Ji functions as the main pillar of our mind that exists in all our cells as well as its master because, in terms of their locations, they span from top to bottom of our body, and also in terms of their significance, because they create a balance. Since the mind that exists in all our cells is under the command of Hon, Baek, Shin, Ui, and Ji we can build the power to control our mind once we get to know Hon, Baek, Shin, Ui, and Ji.

Hon, Baek, Shin, Ui, and Ji are a group of energies that act as if they are independently alive. If you want to understand it more easily, you can think about the Pixar animation *Inside Out*, where the unconsciousness of the hero is descried in characters. In the movie *Inside Out*, the process of feelings being generated within a child is described in five characters that represent Joy, Sadness, Anger, Disgust, and Fear. Activities of Joy become the engine for the girl to lead a pleasant life, the activities of Sadness make her realize what is precious to her, and the activities of Anger help her learn how to protect her domain from injustice. The activities of Disgust make her establish her identity, and the activities of Fear keep her from danger. When I watched this animation for the first time, I thought it was created by a production crew that had a good understanding of Hon, Baek, Shin, Ui, and Ji.

Like the characters in *Inside Out*, Hon-Baek-Shin-Ui-Ji act as individually independent energies while playing the roles of generating and driving energies that are stronger than their surroundings. The difference from the animation is that the energies are spread out throughout our body and bring out energies of the entire cells instead of clustering them in the brain.

Ji, the energy found on the soles of your feet, is there to keep your existence standing in life, and it determines how you fill the life, which is time and space that was given to you. Hon, the energy found in the pineal body of your brain, communicates with the universe, and determines your perception of God the Creator and how to achieve the objective of having created you. Baek, the energy found in the cochlea of both ears, is where you receive the logics of the world, and determines how to accommodate and explore the logics of the world and the universe. Shin is the energy that pumps out life in your heart, and it determines how to define yourself. Ui, the energy found in the ovary or testicular, integrates your genetic information with that of others, and determines how to interact and build relationships with others. If you surgically remove these sources of energies, they find other parts of your body to settle.

Definitions of Hon, Baek, Shin, Ui, and Ji

Ji(志): Energy that determines how to fill life, which is the sum of time and space given to you.

Hon(魂): Energy that defines your relationship with the Creator and how to achieve the goal of your life.

Baek(魄): Energy that determines how to accommodate and explore logics of the world and the universe.

Shin(神): Energy that determines how to define yourself.

Ui(意): Energy that determines how to interact and build relationships with others.

If I may describe the definitions of Hon, Baek, Shin, Ui, and Ji in terms of the positive power that we know as love, Ji is the power to believe in your efforts and love the life that is given to you; Hon is the power to believe in the love of God and be faithful to the objectives of life; Baek is the power to love the world and experience love in the world; Shin is the power to believe in yourself and love yourself; and Ui is the power to trust and love others. Those are the positive and physiological powers of Hon, Baek, Shin, Ui, and Ji.

When you love your life, it is easier to accept the tasks that are given to you in life and become more devoted to life. And you can also make your dreams and hopes come true little by little. When you believe in the fact that you are being loved by the Creator and the Creator's almighty power, you can achieve the objectives of life while having the sense of dignity for your existence. When you trust and love the world, you can explore and cultivate your life to experience love through the world while accepting results that are given to you more easily. When you trust and love yourself, you can enjoy the pleasure of realizing yourself with confidence and self-assurance. When you love others and realize how others are the same existences as you, you can expand your self to become one with others. When you build the physiological powers of Hon, Baek, Shin, Ui ,and Ji, their energies also expand. In other words, you can build the mind's power to create with love.

Physiological Powers of Hon, Baek, Shin, Ui, and Ji

Ji(志): The power to love your life. Belief in realizing dreams and hopes while consenting to life and fulfilling your duties.

Hon(魂): The power to believe in the almighty power of God and keep you moving forward toward the ultimate goal of life. Belief in being loved by God and being connected with God as one.

Baek(魄): The power to believe in the fairness and logicalness of the law of the universe and to love the world and the universe. Belief in the complicated affairs of the world being there only for the goal of experiencing love.

Shin(神): Power to believe in and love one's self. Belief in one's precious and great existential value and offering one's self.

Ui(意): Power to believe and love others. Belief in the goodness of others and that others are one with one's self.

Hon, Baek, Shin, Ui, and Ji also forms healthy creativity with which you can satisfy primal desires that are necessary to lead your life. These primal urges are given to all human beings and individuals' lives, and the world as a whole can grow and develop thanks to these urges. Ji brings out the urge for sleep and rest that is necessary to lead a life diligently, and Hon brings about and fills the heathy urge to keep and acknowledge one's dignity. Baek brings about and satisfies the urge to build assets (wealth) that is necessary for life; Shin brings about the urge to keep one's body healthy and the sexual urge necessary for reproduction; and Ui satisfies the healthy urge for food and the urge to seek enrichment and comfort of livelihood. The healthy urges of Hon, Baek, Shin, Ui, and Ji are the fundamental creativity that has been developing human civilizations.

We tend to guard ourselves against our urges and even feel ashamed about them because the urges easily degenerate into desires. But without these urges, humanity would not have been realizing the prosperity that we have today, and the world would not have been able to develop. Therefore, our urges are the objects that we should love and bless. Our life and the world as a whole can grow more enriched and diversified if we know how to love and satisfy our urges appropriately. The three stages of truly loving our urges are about acknowledging one's urges, appreciating and faithfully answering to the healthy urges, and sharing and blessing the outcomes with others. When you love the urges of life appropriately, you can ensure stable and enriched life with the support of the creativity of Hon, Baek, Shin, Ui, and Ji. On the contrary, if you disapprove of your healthy urges, or insist on restricting everything only to yourself while degenerating urges into ungrateful desires, the creativity of Hon, Baek, Shin, Ui, and Ji creates sufferings and losses.

Satisfying Healthy Urges of Hon-Baek-Shin-Ui-Ji

Ji(志): Urge to sleep – Fills life with sleep and rest that is necessary to lead a diligent life

Hon(魂): Dignity – Fills the power to keep and acknowledge one's dignity

Baek(魄): Wealth -- Fills the power to earn money that is necessary for stable and healthy life

Shin(神): Sexual desire – Fills the power to build healthy body and reproduce

Ui(意): Appetite – Fills the power to ensure enrichment and comfort of life and appetite

Hon-Baek-Shin-Ui-Ji also has pathological powers that are antithetical to love and healthy urges as well. Ji harbors the pathological power of indifference that makes you become negligent of your life; Hon the power of inferiority complex that harms the dignity you have been bestowed by the Creator; Baek the power of anxiety that makes you become distrustful of the world; Shin, the power of disappointment and self-loathing that prevents you from realizing self-satisfaction; and Ui, the power of concerns that makes you distrust and be suspicious of others. These are the negative and pathological powers of Hon-Baek-Shin-Ui-Ji.

If you are indifferent to your own life, you find it hard to live with hope and the sense of achievement, and you become prone to become depressed, irresponsible, and indulge yourself in stimulating pleasures only. If you are unaware of the dignity the Almighty Creator has bestowed on you, you become prone to the sense of inferiority, and easily become angry and hateful because you let yourself become blinded by jealousy and honor. If you cannot trust the world, you might become too sensitive about others because you are nervous, and fear might drive you to become obsessive to money and hostile to the world. If you don't know self-satisfaction, you become easily disappointed and snappy over trivial things, and the self-loathing might drive you to disapprove your self-worth and become obsessive about physical body. When you cannot trust others, you subject yourself to all sorts of unnecessary concerns because you suspect everything; complain about and dislike others; obsess over materials instead of people; and find it easy to lie. When the pathological powers of Hon-Baek-Shin-Ui-Ji become dominant over your energies, it results in the weakening energies themselves and it becomes difficult to create love.

Pathological Powers of Hon-Baek-Shin-Ui-Ji

Ji(志): Indifference that hinders efforts to live life diligently.

Indifference gives birth to depressive lethargy, urge to find quick fix to problems, pursuit of hedonism, and irresponsibility.

Hon(魂): Sense of inferiority that disapproves of the dignity bestowed by the Creator.

Sense of inferiority gives birth to jealousy, anger, greed for honor, and hatred.

Baek(魄): Anxiety that hinders trust of the world.

Anxiety gives birth to excessive sensitivity to others, fear, greed for money, and resentment.

Shin(神): Disappointment and self-pity(loathing) that hinders self-satisfaction.

Disappointment gives birth to frustration, sadness, greed for physical body, and the denial of existence.

Ui(意): Suspicion and concerns that hinder trust of others.

Suspicion (concerns) gives birth to complaints, hatred, obsession to materials and lies.

The energies of Hon-Baek-Shin-Ui-Ji grow bigger when you build their physiological powers and weaken their pathological powers. Therefore, what you need to do is mindfully focus on your physiological mind and keep contemplating. You can also have a careful observation on yourself to identify negative consciousness and contemplate on it again. Developing this routine as a habit is the key to self-analysis that can help you build the energies of Hon-Baek-Shin-Ui-Ji. If I may introduce some examples of this way of thinking, you can tell yourself: "I snapped at my child for not listening to me, but I see it was just an anger whose origin is the sense of inferiority. My child didn't mean to ignore me, and she was just acting on her urge to do what she wanted to do. My anger was not called for. I see she's grown up so much to tell from the way she tries to make her own decisions." In this way, you can tell where your burdensome thoughts and mind originate from – the sense of inferiority, anxiety, disappointment, suspicion, and indifference – and think twice about them. Thinking twice about your thoughts is the process through which you transform negative energy into positive energy. Therefore, just because your initial thoughts are not positive doesn't mean you have to throw your hands up. All you have to do is to think twice about them. You can transform your mind's energy into positive energy by thinking about your thoughts again later on.

For my example, I said to myself: "I did a great job on examining my patients. I love my life that is dedicated to providing my services to patients"; "I came upon numerous complicated situations today, but I eventually resolved them all one by one. I will continue to resolve the rest patiently as well. I am so proud of myself being able to handle this"; and "I was able to be understanding to my child and what was going through her mind all because of the power of my prayer to become a good mother. I am grateful for God for having answered to my prayer." In this way, you can intentionally think twice and contemplate on the physiological mind of Hon-Baek-Shin-Ui-Ji. You can grow positive energy exponentially by thinking twice within the context of the physiological power instead of letting things follow their courses and pass.

"I love my life through this moment and this role that are bestowed upon me."

"My existence is blessed and loved by God, and I also love back God."

"My existence belongs to the just and logical universe, and I am determined to love the world as long as I live."

"I am a precious, great, and beautiful existence. I believe in the divine nature of myself and I also love it."

"I believe that others are just the same good existences as myself and I naturally love them."

We are all born with both the physiological power and negative power of Hon-Baek-Shin-Ui-Ji. And those powers are determined by how much more we discover as we live. That means, our mind can change depending on the difference between being able to discover the physiological power that rests within Hon-Baek-Shin-Ui-Ji and not being able to do it. Therefore, we have to willfully make efforts to discover the physiological power that we have within. And we have to fully acknowledge the fact that we have that power within us in order to discover it.

In general, we only acknowledge the existence of something when we discover it. You are right to acknowledge something only after its discovery, if it is something that some people have and some others don't. But if that something is universal in nature, we all have the opportunity to discover it when we have the awareness of it and acknowledge it. The physiological power of Hon-Baek-Shin-Ui-Ji being a universal power that is given equally to everybody, it is there to be discovered by anybody who acknowledges its existence. Therefore, you have to determinately acknowledge it and find the opportunity to discovery it, even if you haven't discovered it yet. The self-analysis of Hon-Baek-Shin-Ui-Ji begins with the acknowledgment of your own power and competes with the confirmation of that acknowledgment.

Those who are not used to reflecting on, contemplating, and analyzing themselves might find it tiresome and awkward. I was the same. When I saw people who contemplated on themselves, I would tell myself, "Why do they have to bother with that? They are being so weird." But it all changed when I read the book *Human Landscape* and started looking into my mind. Once I started practicing it, I realized that it was the difference between living with eyes closed and living with eyes open. In the past, I was living with my eyes closed, but once I started looking into myself, I was the one with open eyes.

As long as you are here to live, you cannot live blindly and randomly. You have to live with a consciousness that is awakened to yourself at least. When you analyze yourself with an awakened consciousness, you will realize that this is far from being a tiring and peculiar task. Rather, you will find it a rather comfortable and natural thing to do. And I strongly suggest the analysis of Hon-Baek-Shin-Ui-Ji as a way of self-analysis.

The larger the energies of Hon-Baek-Shin-Ui-Ji are, the stronger your power to control your mind as you please. In fact, most of us are struggling with our lives because we cannot control our mind as we wish to. Too often, we are suffocated by the pain we wish to be done with, and we fail to realize our wishes in ways we hope and desire. When you become skilled at analyzing Hon-Baek-Shin-Ui-Ji, you notice your power to control your mind growing stronger, and you become farther away from the thoughts and emotions that you don't want to keep in your mind. At first, certain negative emotions transform into positive emotions after you calm them down, but once you develop the habit of analyzing yourself, you can transform negative emotions into positive emotions faster than before, and the negative emotions become more and more scarce.

In the meantime, once the commanding cells of Hon-Baek-Shin-Ui-Ji become expanded, they guide the metabolism of all other cells to become more harmonious and active. In other words, you become physically healthy. The biggest advantage of using Hon-Baek-Shin-Ui-Ji as a way of mainlining health is that it brings you both efficient physical strength improvement and harmonious balance. Health supplement pills and workouts alone cannot bring you harmonious advancement. Rather, you run into the risk of unbalanced lopsided improvement at the cost of money and efforts. In fact, I come across numerous patients that prove it in my medical practice.

But expanding Hon-Baek-Shin-Ui-Ji can guide you to harmonious improvement in itself, and it becomes the foundation of all health management efforts. In fact, Korean medicine uses the Hon-Baek-Shin-Ui-Ji spots on the body suitable for acupuncture as an effective treatment for numerous chronic and hard-to-cure illnesses. I had suffered from persistent allergic rhinitis for 15 years, but started feeling a lot better once I developed the habit of analyzing Hon-Baek-Shin-Ui-Ji while getting treatment to tune them up. For all living humans, expanding Hon-Baek-Shin-Ui-Ji is an absolute necessity for physical health.

All answers to the question of how to live our lives can be found in Hon-Baek-Shin-Ui-Ji. We have to live while trusting our life, God, the world, our selves, and others. That trust gives us the energy to lead our lives and open the path to life as well. And all answers to the question of how we should create the world can also be found in Hon-Baek-Shin-Ui-Ji. We have to create the world by loving our lives, God, the world, our selves, and others, because the world created with love will return our efforts in the form of love as well. Therefore, we have to trust, and we have to love. There is no other way to live the right way other than trusting and loving them all. Surely, I am aware that it is not easy to trust and love all of them. For one thing, I've personally experienced how much hardship I have to endure to trust all of them, and how much pain I had to overcome until I was able to love them all.

However, we don't necessarily have to endure and overcome hardship and pain in order to grow. We can grow with minimal hardships once we put our efforts into discovering the physiological energies of Hon-Baek-Shin-Ui-Ji. Now, let me introduce the physiological energies of Hon-Baek-Shin-Ui-Ji that I've discovered through personal experiences. It is my sincere hope that you will grow with minimal hardships by accepting my experience-based accounts of them with love.[4]

Endnotes

[3] Kim Hyung-gyung: She is a Korean novelist and has written several psychoanalytic essays.

[4] Author's note: It was in the Lecture on the Practical Application of the Longevity and Life Preservation in Eastern Medicine (2015, held in Daejeon) for Eastern medical practitioners that Hon, Baek, Shin, Ui, and Ji were perceived to be the five fundamental elements of life and research results were reported for the first time. Based on the lecture, I carried out in-depth research on Hon, Baek, Shin, Ui, and Ji, and built a clinical treatment system while systematizing them into the definition, physiological force, desire, and pathological force.

1. Ji (志): I Love My Life

Among the five Hon-Baek-Shin-Ui-Ji energies, Ji is the energy that determines how we should fill the life that is given to us. In order to fill our lives, we have to think about "What should I do today?" Then you have to speak and act in accordance to your answer. That's how we fill each day of our lives. Simply put, Ji is about thinking about your choice of what to do in life, and it is also the will power that drives you to take direct actions. And if I may explain the will of life in terms of its results, it means creating a life in accordance to your thoughts and actions. The power to create a life is the definition of Ji. Therefore, Ji rests on the soles of our feet and is there to raise and support our mind and actions. Ji is the main engine that allows us to stand straight and strong on two feet as we lead our lives. Therefore, of all energies of Hon-Baek-Shin-Ui-Ji, Ji is the energy that starts all creations. Since we are living existences, we have the power to create, and since we are living, we are given opportunities to create things. Therefore, Ji the will of life is the beginning of all creations, and that's the reason I choose Ji out of the five energies of Hon-Baek-Shin-Ui-Ji as the first energy to explain.

Before I begin, let me ask you a question: Do you believe in the truth that you are the Creator of your own life? Perhaps some of you might think you are, and some of you think you are not. You might think you cannot say you can take the whole credit to the creation of your own life because there are things that happen purely by chance in life, and you might think you can take the whole credit because you reap what you sow in life as well. In our life, there exists a sort of predetermined destiny. However, it is always in this very present moment that the destiny unfolds for us, and its significance is determined. The thought we have, the emotion that we feel, the word we speak, and the action that we take in this very moment are what determine the destiny that will unfold in the next moment. Therefore, the destiny that is given to us now was created by ourselves at some point in our lives. It could be a year ago, or even 20, 100, or 1000 years ago. We don't know exactly when, but it was created by ourselves at some point in the past. The truth about life being your own creation seems obscure only because it is a truth that applies to multiple lives instead of just one.

But the important point to remember in creating your own life is that, no matter when your destiny was created, it is the present moment that is changing your destiny. Your destiny changes little by little in the direction that you intend it to be. Your destiny changes little by little in accordance to the actions you take in this very moment. Since the destiny that we will encounter is not a pre-fixed event, it goes through a continuously changing process. Whatever our destiny has for us, it happens at the most appropriate time after going through that changing process. Therefore, we are always in the process of creating our lives with the thoughts, emotions, and actions of this very moment. In the most fundamental level, therefore, everything that happens in our lives is attributed to nothing else but ourselves.

Then one might wonder why the life is not changing in the way we want it to be. Regretfully, we don't always think what we want in our life. We think more about the things that we don't want. We think about all sorts of illnesses while thinking that it would be nice not to be sick and die in pain. The more we worry about illnesses, the more we wish to avoid getting ill. We all wish to become rich, but we worry more about having no money or not having enough money. Probably, you will think about running out of money more than ten times before you think about the fact that you actually do have money. Our thoughts and emotions are all energies. Our destiny changes little by little depending on which sum is bigger between the sum of energy generated from the thought of running out of money and the sum of energy generated from the thought of being fortunate to have money. If you add to it the smoking habit that increases your chance to get ill and the actions that are at odds with your wish, such as maintaining the shopping habit that is sure to make you spend more money, you become more entrapped in the process of creating a life that you don't want.

In the book, *Conversations with God*, the author encourages readers to acknowledge that whatever we wish to have, we already have enough of it already, because that acknowledgment creates new satisfaction. In the book *The Secret*[5], the author tells us to stop thinking about the things that we don't want, because what we have in our thoughts are being attracted into our lives. The author kindly explains to us that we think hard about the things that would and should happen so that what we truly want would be attracted to our lives. In the book *Watching*[6], the author explains how the minute particles that constitute the world vibrate in accordance with our thoughts and mind and how the vibration brings about changes. Therefore, the author stresses, we have to let those minute particles vibrate in accordance to our wishes, if we want the life that we truly want.

The energies of the thoughts and emotions that we have today cause the particles that surround us to vibrate without the slightest error, and that vibration brings about changes in materials and affects the life of tomorrow. If we feel satisfaction and are enriched today, that energy vibrates our surrounding particles, and the satisfaction and prosperity become the reality tomorrow. The changes that happen day after day accumulate until they bring about important changes in fateful events. That fate happens in the most appropriate time either as an event that is more likely to bring me satisfaction and prosperity, or less obstructive to bringing them to me. The truth about our own mind and actions being the Creator of our own lives has now become such a universal wisdom that it doesn't even strike us as wondrous. There are numerous books and lectures that bless our Ji, and all we have to do now is to apply the wisdoms addressed in those books and lectures in our lives.

We have to narrow the gap between our wishes and reality in order to apply those wisdoms in our lives. To make that happen, we first have to love our lives. We have to appreciate and love the space where we stand today, and treasure and love the time that is given to us now. We have to love our wishes and hopes for the things that we want to happen, while loving the responsibilities that are given to us. The key to becoming the master of our own lives with the physiological energy of Ji is to love our lives. By loving the lives that we have today, we can open a road where our reality and wishes would become one.

We love our lives not because we love the satisfaction and happiness we find in our lives. We love our lives because, even though everybody is leading a life that is laden with one after another mountain to pass, we all know that we have the energy within us to cross those mountains. We love our lives because we acknowledge that this hardship is our own making; we understand the process is for the sake of ourselves; and we grow and become strong through a life laden with hardships. Therefore, those who are full of the energy of Ji do not flee from the hardships of life. Rather, they devote themselves to fulfilling the tasks that are given to them, thinking about what they have realized after experiencing hardship, cherishing new hopes and willingly putting more efforts into making their dreams come true. Even if their dreams don't come true, they continue to dream new dreams, take up new challenges, and fill their lives with hope persistently. That's the kind of people who truly love their lives.

Love is good only when it is practiced. Now is the time to take action with the love for your life in mind. Ji is also the will power to take actions on your love for life. You may have numerous grand visions and plans for your life, but they will not bring you anything if you don't take actions on them. That is what the proverb that says "the beginning is the half of the whole" is all about. Once you do the beginning, the rest is so easy that the beginning is the half of the whole, according to the proverb.

Whatever you try to do, there is the resistance in the initial stage of beginning. Since we humans are subject to the law of inertia, we tend to want to retain the status quo. Therefore, you are destined to require more energy than usual when you try to start your engine and take off. You have to start your engine with the firm conviction that you can do it, dauting courage, and passion for change in the beginning. Therefore, when you choose to be a person of courage, passion, and conviction, you are demonstrating the power of your Ji, while at the same time choosing to grow that power.

Ji is the beginning of all creations, and Ji is enfolding your will to start something. Taking the first step to begining the process of achieving something is truly important in our lives. The movie *Martian* eloquently speaks volumes about this importance. The movie is about a man who is left alone on Mars and eventually returns to Earth successfully after going through numerous trials and tests. It is essentially describing the importance of the power of Ji that sets the wheel in motion at the starting point.

The question I was asked the most after returning to Earth was, "'When you were stranded and alone up there... did you think you were gonna die?'" Of course, yes. It's space. It's filled with chance, circumstance, and bad luck. It doesn't cooperate. At some point, I promise, at some point every single thing is gonna go south on you, and you'll think: this is it. This is how I end. And you can either accept that... or you can get to work.. I had. There is nothing in the universe that works as you wish. That's all it is. You simply begin. Solve one problem. Then the next one, then the next. Then, you solve enough problems... and you get to come home."

Of course, this is just a movie that is based on a fiction, but it teaches us a powerful lesson: even though it may look impossible to survive on Mars and return home alive, you just start solving one problem and then the next one until you get what you want. "That's all it is. You simply begin." Like this dialogue tells us, it is the power of Ji that makes you begin and take actions and take up a challenge – any challenge – and simply beginning is how you make the energy of Ji grow stronger.

It is also the will of life that makes you persist with something you've started. "You simply begin. Solve one problem. Then the next one, then the next. Then, you solve enough problems. And you get to come home." To accept all the resistance and bad luck that accompanies the work you started, and to just keep going persistently – these efforts and commitment are what makes your energy of Ji grow stronger. These kind of efforts and commitment can be most frequently found in sports players. Since the players of sports where winning and losing is determined by the record or scores have to constantly battle against their limits, they show particularly good examples of efforts and patience to overcome their limits. Some of the most notable sports players who continue to push their limits by putting themselves through a lonely training process include the mechanical gymnast player Yang Hak-seon[7], weight-lifter Jang Mi-ran[8], figure skater Kim Yuna[9], rhythmic gymnast Sohn Yeon-jae[10], and swimmer Park Tae-hwan[11].

The Korean medicine clinic where I have my office being near the Han River, I often have students who belong to rowing sports team visiting me for treatment. I am amazed at these young students who put themselves through training in spite of pain. It isn't restricted to sports only; whenever we try to achieve something, we all find ourselves going through the process where our limits are tested. When it comes to limits, you can rarely push and pass your limits at the first try. More often than not, you can pass your limits only after you refuse to give up and make repeated attempts with perseverance. In the movie, the main character solved problems one at a time and came home alive, but in reality, you can expand your energy of Ji.

In my case, among the five energies of Hon-Baek-Shin-Ui-Ji, the energy of Ji is the weakest. Perhaps for that reason, I've always liked sports where the players take the challenge of pushing their limits, and I've always admired them. That was my subconscious response to the fact that my energy of Ji was weak. I was seeking vicarious satisfaction from their tireless efforts, devotion, and their accomplishments. However, when this vicarious satisfaction remained just vicarious satisfaction itself, it hindered the growth of my Ji energy. When you admire others and seek vicarious satisfaction from them, it makes you develop a perception that they are completely different existences from yourself. The more you admire them, the bigger your subconscious thoughts grow about them being special and you being not able to become somebody like them.

I still love individual sports games and great sports stars, but now I consciously block my subconscious urge to seek vicarious satisfaction through them. Instead, I appreciate and admire the hard work and industrial training these sports players demonstrate and celebrate their accomplishment, while telling myself over and over that I have the same great will power within me. I cheer and root for me while believing that the same will power is found within me in the most appropriate form for my life and in the most uniquely my own way, waiting to be revealed in me. And I bravely took up the challenge to write this book now, diligently writing it little by little in every early morning hour, with the support of my will power that I've been growing with that belief. We all have the will power similar to that of such great sports players as Kim Yuna and Park Tae-hwan in our own unique form. I recommend you bringing it out and using it to get your hands on the work you wish to do. I cheer you to start it with the love for your life and keep pushing forward to your goal. The process will expand the energy of Ji that is found on the soles of your feet and allow you to keep marching on bravely and confidently.

As I mentioned, you need persistence, patience, and willingness to begin, but there is another condition that is required to expand the energy of Ji: the power to stop when you need to stop. This power is a must-have condition to grow your Ji power. While you work hard on something, there are times you need to stop for the next stage, and there are times you realize the road you have taken is not the road for you. When you realize the road is not for you, you have to be brave and stop without any regret, and when you realize it is something that you have to devote yourself to, you need to learn how to let go of your greed and stop to ensure continuity.

In fact, those who have a strong Ji power don't hesitate to start something, and they don't hesitate to stop when necessary. Those with a strong will power know how to stop the work that they are doing to eat when it's time to eat, and when climbing a mountain, they choose to descend with the peak just in front of them the moment they realize continuous ascending is too much strain for them. But in general, people often skip meals because they cannot stop the work that they are doing until it is finished and continue to ascend to reach the peak even if it is too straining. We put ourselves in difficult situations because we don't know how to pause and stop. We overwork until we get sick or have a nervous breakdown before being able to finish the job we've been doing or make the mistake of focusing only on one thing at the cost of others and eventually become negligent of our other roles. This is the result of our inability to use the power of Ji that lets us stop when necessary. You are destined to run into trouble in life if you are not able to sense the time to stop and fail to stop when you need to. Running into trouble in life signifies that your Ji energy is in an unbalanced condition.

The writer Bernard Werber is the best example of people who know the beauty of pause. Werber gets out of bed at dawn each morning, writes for four hours, and spends the afternoon hours doing other activities including walking and exercising.

I sit on my desk in early morning, and quickly jot down the thoughts that pour down like the water on the faucet. We all know overeating is not good for us. Writing is the same. I stop when it's time to stop even if I wish to continue the writing.

That's what he said in an interview. It takes a tremendously strong will power to stop writing when ideas keep flashing in your head and you want to keep going. The will power that lets you stop at an appropriate time is the power of Ji that is as admirable as the will power of sports players who put themselves through extreme training. The effort of trying to stop when you need to is another way to expand the energy of Ji. Therefore, the beautiful coexistence of work and the rest you take by pausing even when you wish to continue writing or continue to play can provide you with a broad and level road without any bumps for you to achieve what you wish to accomplish.

The figure skater Kim Yuna was able to enjoy a stable life as a champion because she had the balance between training and rest. In the early days of her career, she was always suffering from various injuries. Each season, she competed in games while enduring pain resulting from various injuries beginning from the mid-to-late-season. In those early days, she refused to take enough rest because she wanted to spend more time training, and she participated in training even if she was in pain. Then she changed her schedule to include days that were exclusively dedicated to rest and faithfully followed it, and she lived by that schedule even when she had games just around the corner. By faithfully following the schedule and maintaining the balance between training and rest, she was able to make the most of her skills in all games without suffering from injuries, until she was able to record game performances that made her a legend in figure skating history. Letting go of your greed and pausing your work to take rest when necessary and returning back to work as a refreshed new self after a good rest is the right way to prevent and solve various problems life presents to you.

The life-creating energy of Ji enfolds within will powers such as courage and perseverance as well as soft powers such as complacency and tolerance. That's the reason the healthy urge of Ji includes the desire to take rest such as the urge to sleep and the urge to seek pleasure. Therefore, you just become full of the desire to take rest, which is the healthy urge of Ji, so that you don't necessarily have to sustain setbacks from overstraining yourself while doing your best. And it is important to rest and play well when it is time to rest. Playing well is another way to expand the energy of Ji, while being the manifestation of healthy Ji. When you choose play activities, it is important to choose the ones that will give you joy and pleasure, but you also have to make sure the play activities are separated from your work.

If your job requires sitting in front of a monitor all day, watching TV, or playing online games is just a continuation of work instead of a rest. Looking into a monitor just as you would do while at work cannot relax your muscles or refresh your mood. On the contrary, if your job requires the use of physical muscle, working out in a health club during your break cannot serve you as a rest either. For those whose job requires serenity work, dynamic activities can qualify as a good rest, and for those whose job requires dynamic activities, meditating in a peaceful environment will be a good choice of taking a break. Only then can you ensure a trouble-free life because your work and rest create a virtuous cycle. Therefore, you have to make a good choice on what to do during your break. Only the play activities that suit your situation and give pleasure to you can recharge you and grow your energy of Ji.

It is also very important to work and rest alternately and regularly by reasonably adjusting the ratio between work and rest to ensure your personal growth. Most Korean workers might think Werber is not working hard enough since he said he was writing only four hours a day, but in terms of the stage of life Werber has achieved as a writer, working for four hours might be indicating that he is loving his life in the most ideal way. You have to find the ideal ratio between work and rest in accordance to the growth stage of your life. If you are in the stage of growing and achieving something, you might need to ensure there is more work than rest in the ratio, and nevertheless, you have to ensure you can set the time where you can take a break and rest away from your work. If you are at the stage of stable career growth, you might have more time for rest and increase the routine rest so that you can put yourself up for a new challenge. Having the reasonable balance between work and rest and regularly enjoying the rest that is most applicable to you is the way to love your life correctly.

Therefore, I advise you not to try and work excessively for the sake of your healthy energy of Ji. Just put as much effort as you love your life and play just as much as you love your life, while at the same time continuously growing your love for your life. When you continuously grow your love for life, it will let your love for life replete your Ji with energy that will make you a diligent person who can accomplish anything you set your mind to while finding more pleasure and joy as you live.

In order to work hard for our dreams and to love our lives, we have to do the best we can while at the same time keeping a cool attitude and tell ourselves that it's okay if the dreams don't come true. Only then can we love both the success and the failure of our dreams and eventually everything about our life. Once you learn to love your life, Ji can achieve a balanced growth, but if you insist only on making success, Ji becomes twisted and rebellious. When Ji is twisted, any success you make is followed more by the sense of void instead of happiness, and failure is followed by regret over your life.

Our Ji wishes to love everything about our life. That's the reason I am sitting in front of my monitor today with a firm belief that this book will be loved by many people and make them happy. And I also enjoy this job, because I believe that even if things don't pan out as I wish, I will find a different way to love again. Whatever your dream is, it is sure to come true. And it doesn't matter even if it doesn't come true. Most of the time, we dream of things that don't necessarily have to come true. All that matters is for you to love the dream and the day that is given to you today, while moving forward toward your dream, whether you succeed or fail to make it come true. Then your Ji will take care of everything else and fill you up on its own accord.

We can create a peaceful and happy life with the help of the energy of Ji that loves the entire process of building a life including success and failure, by loving our lives; taking up challenges bravely and remaining persistent about them; and allowing ourselves to pause with our will power whenever necessary to recharge ourselves through healthy leisure and play activities. When we learn how to love life, it becomes fun to live. The obstacles that we come across once in a while during our challenges add vitality to our lives so that they don't become dull; the excitement you feel when you overcome those obstacles adds pleasure to your life; taking rest and making yourself feel comfortable helps your well-being; and fun play activities revive your pleasant vitality. When the energy of Ji grows stronger, a virtuous cycle is created wherein you find it fun to live and this fun fills up the energy of Ji.

However, there are too many people who complain that it is not fun to live these days. Too many people have lost the joy of life even though there are more than enough books and lectures that celebrate the energy of Ji, and the world is offering more convenience and diversity than ever. One evidence of this situation is the rapid growth of the game industry.

The development of the smartphone industry gave rise to the game industry. When you get on the subway, you can see almost all passengers looking at their smartphones, and most of them are playing games. Games with simple rules, in particular, are enjoying the long-run popularity. Playing games indicates the players are not finding fun in their present lives, and it also causes players to lose interest in their lives. They most likely have started playing games when they were a little bored, but the more they play games, the more moments they find that are boring and dull. This principle of games is the reason that explains the growth of the smartphone-utilizing game industry.

When you have a weak Ji energy, the desire to enjoy healthy leisure and play activities degenerates into an addiction. Some of the examples include addiction to games and gambling, and also addiction to hedonistic entertainments. The more you become addicted to these unhealthy activities, the weaker your energy of Ji grows and your will power to put a stop to the addiction. Therefore, you need to carefully examine yourself to find out if you are not addicted to something to the degree that it disrupts your daily routines and gives negative influence on your interpersonal relationships. When your urge to play degenerates into obsessive desire, you have to be able to notice it in the beginning stage and put a stop to it immediately, because when it becomes a full-blown addiction, it becomes too difficult to stop. Addiction to hedonistic lifestyles deprives you of opportunities to interact with others, thereby making your life feel more and more empty. It even affects the lives of the people around you and destroys them.

Another greed that weakens the energy of Ji is the get-rich-quick mentality. Therefore, you should not be attracted to the things that are offered for free, because it is the short-cut to ruining your Ji energy. We have seen numerous people in the media, people who won jackpots only to have their lives ruined because of the windfall of money. There are numerous examples of people who became rich overnight but ended up ruining their lives because the sudden riches made them lose their love for life. Those who became rich overnight but still enjoy a happy life are the ones who were able to continue to love and protect their lives with a tremendously strong Ji energy. It is not something you can do unless you have an extraordinary will power. If you want to become rich by winning a jackpot or windfall return from stock investments, the first thing you need to do is grow your Ji energy to an extraordinary level. Only then can you keep your life when your wish comes true.

The most fundamental consciousness that weakens the Ji energy with desire is indifference. When you become indifferent to your life, it becomes really difficult to take the first step to loving your life. You cannot love your life, and worse, you become vulnerable to various addictions, a get-rich-quick mentality, and even a lethargic attitude. And the most common path that leads you to the indifference to your life and makes you become overwhelmed with the weight of life begins when you compare your life to the life of others.

For us humans, life is a series of one after another mountains to pass. However, when the mountain you are climbing seems rugged and tall while the mountain others are climbing seems easy and low, you lose interest in trying to find love for your life. In general, those who think they have a better life after comparing their life with the lives of others don't compare their lives with those of others that often in the first place. But those who frequently compare their life with those of others have a much higher possibility to believe others have a better life than theirs than the possibility to believe they have a better life than others. Therefore, what you get when you compare your life with those of others are despondency and depressing lethargy, and you become more indifferent about your life in order to shake off that despondent feeling.

Sometimes you come across people who are indifferent to life describing themselves as if they have the mastery of life, but that is just an avoidant indifference and it is completely different from the mastery of life. The mastery of life can be achieved only when you fully love your life and treasure everything there is in life, knowing so much so that you learn the truth about nothing in life being more important than others since everything in life is equally important. The time I simply write this book is just as important as the time I eat, and it doesn't matter what you do because they are both equally important. When you are indifferent toward life, however, you don't have the eagerness to write this book because you are not sure if it is going to be published or not, and you don't care about eating because it is something you do every day. Those who are indifferent toward life have few things that they want to do because most of their times are not really significant to them. On the contrary, those who have the mastery of life treasure every moment of their lives, and no moment is less precious than others. That's the reason they don't insist on applying themselves only on specific things that they want to do, and they want to do everything because everything is what they want to do. The awakened sages who sought happiness and obtained peace are teaching us that "there is nothing that we must do and accomplish." I understand this proposition as to mean "we only have things that we wish to do and accomplish."

It is unnecessary to compare with others in order to love your life. In fact, when you think about it, it is impossible to objectively compare your life with the life of others in the first place. We can never fully understand the lives that other people have, and we can only guess about them, but we know everything about our own life intimately. Therefore, if the grass in your neighbor's yard looks greener than yours, it is only a misunderstanding caused by the quantitative difference of information. If a third party makes the judgment on the lives of yours and others based on the same information, the third party would never be able to tell who is living a more comfortable life, because the truth is, we are all equally struggling as we lead our lives.

In particular, we often make the mistake of believing that money and power make life more comfortable. But the shameful and disgraceful behaviors that those who have money and power demonstrate once in a while are the proof that they are suffering from depravity and pressures in their lives. And the admirable choices and accomplishments that they demonstrate once in a while are the proof that they obtained wisdoms by overcoming numerous trials and challenges. Living while shouldering the weight of money and power is not easy, and in fact, it must be a life that wears out beyond our imagination. Our lives unfold in a wide variety of shapes, but the mountain you climb is different from the mountains that others are climbing only in terms of their shapes and courses. Ultimately, they are the same difficult mountains to climb. You can answer your calling with happiness only when you shake off that delusion that makes your mountain look more difficult to climb than others, so that you can break free from your indifference and lethargy and give a rise to the passion to truly love your life.

The growth of Ji is dependent on your will to believe in and love your life. When you truly love your life, you naturally want to fulfill your life with care. You are willing to do anything to fulfill your life with love, overcome any obstacles, while waiting and resting peacefully, having fun playing, and gladly taking responsibilities for your daily activities. Since you believe in your life, you can also put out efforts to make your dreams and hopes come true. You can expand the energy of Ji just by believing in and loving your life at all times, even if you don't fully understand the physiological power of Ji and the negative power of unhealthy urges. Let's love all moments of our lives, gently and passionately embracing them with firm courage. Let's trust all moments of our lives with firm patience, warmly and intimately. Strong will power alone can cause trouble in life, and carefree rest alone cannot help you get anything done. Therefore, we have to do the best we can in everything we do, while making sure to take a good break and rest whenever it is necessary.

Therefore, let's pay more affectionate attention to ourselves to see what we have more – the strong will or the relaxed will. By doing so, when you run into trouble while leading your life passionately, I want you to realize that what you needed at those troubled moments was a little relaxed attitude, instead of blaming your passion and telling yourself that it was useless to do your best. Your passion was great enough. You just needed a little soft, relaxed will. On the contrary, if you lose important opportunities and run into trouble while embracing and respecting your life, let's not blame yourself for having been relaxed and for having waited and respected those situations. I want you to realize that your courage and passion were just one step behind. Your relaxed catholicity was beautiful enough. You were just a little short on courage and agility.

All the efforts you had put out in every moment of your life were beautiful and great. It is not fair to disapprove of those efforts just because you are left with a little regret. All you need is to realize that regret is just what it is. You can use the regret as an opportunity to integrate two extreme sides of Ji so that you can build a stronger Ji energy and enrich your life with pleasure. Therefore, whatever efforts you had put out, you must love and believe that your efforts were not in vain, and trust and love the regret that makes you realize the importance of the balanced will to live. Once you can fully believe and love your life, every moment of your life is precious, and none of the moment is more or less important than others, you will be able to enjoy a life that is filled with everything you wish to do freely.

You have to make sure to fill the both sides of the life-creating Ji – the committed mind and the relaxed mind – because it means the process of life is our duty that we must fulfill while at the same time a fun play. Life may look like a mission that we have to accomplish, but it is just something we do because we want to as an existence with immortal soul. Let's fulfill our responsibility to be happy by living a joyful life.

Endnotes

5 *The Secret* by Rhonda Byrn.

6 *Watching*: Korean self-development book by Kim Sang-woon.

7 Yang Hak-seon: Korean mechanical gymnast player who won in London Olympics.

8 Jang Mi-ran: She is a Korean weight-lifter who is the Beijing Olympic gold medalist.

9 Kim Yuna: Korean national figure skater who won a gold medal in the Vancouver Winter Olympics and the silver medal at the Sochi Winter Olympics.

10 Sohn Yeon-jae: The Korean national rhythmic gymnast who won a gold medal at the Incheon Asian Games.

11 Park Tae-hwan: He is a Korean competitive swimmer who is the Beijing Olympic gold medalist and world champion.

2. Hon (魂): I Love God the Creator

Hon is the mind that is connected to the Creator who is also the absolute God, the entirety of the world. Do you believe in the existence of the absolute God? Since there are people who believe in God and people who don't believe in any god, I will talk about God first to facilitate the understanding of Hon.

I believe in God. I started going to a Catholic church since I was a first grader and learned the Christian doctrines, and I liked learning about the doctrine of creation which was about God having created the world. I liked learning about the doctrine of creation because the fact that I was an existence created by God made me feel happy and secure. There was no reason to reject the doctrine, and I simply loved it, because instead of being an existence that came to be by pure chance, I was an existence created by some great presence with special objectives and values, according to the doctrine. I think I was able to grow up happy and carefree all thanks to my knowledge of the doctrine. After learning the doctrine, I had never doubted the existence of God, because my being here and now seemed to be the proof that God existed.

It is difficult to confirm the existence of God with our senses because we cannot see, hear, touch, taste, or smell the existence of God. When you are hurt by somebody or witness destructive disasters that happen in the world, you might doubt the existence of God because you think that cannot happen if God is real, or simply because you want to vent your anger to the world. But can we truly question the existence of God just because we cannot confirm it with our five senses or because we – or the world as a whole – are exposed to various disasters and crises?

When my daughter was a low elementary grade student, she borrowed William Steig's book *Yellow and Pink* from the school library and asked me to read it to her. In this story, Yellow and Pink were two tree dolls, and the story was mostly about their conversation over the question of "How did we come about?" Yellow claimed that they happened to fall to the ground and split to grow two legs, and they grew into what they were today after they were exposed to hail, woodpeckers, and lightening by pure chance. But Pink claimed it could not have happened purely by chance, because they were too elaborate to be the outcome of pure chance. Pink claims that they had to become what they were now by somebody who carefully and devotedly created them. I hope we think about it the same way too.

Could anything in this world have been created by pure chance? We humans are a species with highly advanced intelligence, and can we really say the human species came about by chance without any sense of purpose? Mankind must have come about through a certain process of revolution, considering how mankind did not exist at a time when dinosaurs were roaming on the ground, and I find it hard to believe that the birth of humanity could have been possible just by chance without the power and purpose that led the evolution process. Even if that was really possible by chance alone, wouldn't the power that created the chance have been the will of God? All living creatures on Earth including humanity are born with the will to live and overcome sufferings while continuously evolving with the will. I think the energy that has been leading the evolution is the same energy that is responsible for the origin of the power to overcome sufferings in order to survive. That energy must be the will of the Creator.

We don't sense God through our five senses, but the great creation of those five senses are testifying to the existence of God. All living creatures are wondrous existences, and the evolution of mankind who share almost identical genes with chimpanzees is nothing short of a miracle. Such casual wonder of our existence is the manifestation of the mind and will of

God. More than anything, I hope that many people will become secure from the deepest subconscious level by acknowledging the fact that we were created with our unique purpose and values. I hope that people will find relief in times of pain by believing that we are all born with the will of the absolute God within us and the will of the absolute God is always in touch with our existence. I hope that people believe the existence of God the Creator in this way.

Hon, which is directly connected with God, enfolds the energy that guards the dignity of existence. To me, the doctrine of creation has been always the root of my dignity and the source that made me rise up again and find peace in heart. The dignity of "being the creation of the almighty God" was what made me bolt up and have fun playing like any child would do even after I was picked on by being so short in my childhood and cried my eyes out. And it was also thanks to that belief that I was able to recover from any pain and remain strong and upstanding in my wholesome self. Dignity is the fundamental power for humans to protect themselves in this world. The healthy urge that protects human dignity is found in Hon, the energy that is directly connected to the Creator. You can unfold brilliant honor with the dignity that keeps you standing firm and strong when you understand the energy that connects you and the Creator.

Since we are all divine existences, we have to live without having our dignity violated. All humans are equally born with dignity to be respected and treasured within their Hon regardless of our social status, age, and wealth. When you have a healthy energy of Hon, you can remain uninhibited by the words and behaviors of strangers who harass you, and it brings out solemn anger that serves you as the shield against such transgression so that they cannot continue to harass you. When you are harassed or provoked by others, there is nothing wrong with your mind and behavior intending to stop it. Rather, it is the fundamental right of life that everybody is entitled to, and it is a healthy, natural urge of all humans.

However, the fuller your energy of Hon grows, the less you become angry to the people who look down and harass you. Rather, you are left only with a peaceful smile for them. That smile is the manifestation of your belief that your dignity cannot be undermined by any misunderstanding and disrespectful attitude, and it originates from the strong energy of Hon. Therefore, you must love the healthy urge of Hon to protect your dignity. As long as you love your dignity, you can always respond with calm and a beautiful smile to others with a firm belief that no intentions of others can degrade your existential value. The misunderstanding of the others will become lost, and the other people will eventually become capable of their own dignities through your dignity.

When you shine your dignity, you are providing opportunities to others to discover their own dignity as well. Therefore, you must wholeheartedly love the urge of your Hon to make yourself shine. Since we all share the same urge to discover and shine the light that is bestowed upon us by God, we have to awaken the light of others with our dignity. If you can truly love your urge to shine, it can be the starting point for the dignity of all to shine. We should arm ourselves with beautiful smiles, dream of becoming brilliantly shining existences, while fulfilling the healthy urge of Hon toward honor.

But when your Hon becomes ill and weak, the urge to protect your dignity degenerates into the sense of inferiority, and the urge to shine yourself degenerates into the desire for fame which makes you want to be admired by others. The urge for dignity that makes you wish to shine is completely different from the greed for honor that makes you wish to become higher than others. The distinction between these two minds depends on whether or not you are conscious of the judgments of others.

If you keep wondering about what others would think about your shining when you try to express your divinity, that is the sign that greed is growing in you. If your desire to look good to others is bigger than the satisfaction you get when choosing a dress, and when you find yourself being concerned about how others would judge your plans and work performance, that is the sign of the growing desire for fame and the sense of inferiority that makes you forget about your dignity. In general, people think the desire for fame is restricted to those who belong to the higher social classes, but regardless of social status, you are suffering from a degenerated desire for fame when you let yourself be under the control of the mind that is hungry for the compliment and acknowledgment of others.

Since you and God are the only two beings you should be concerned about, you have to build your dignity with your own hands. You are grateful and happy when you are complimented by others, but it is valid only on the moment you are being complimented. But the dignity that you build on your own is valid in every moment of your existence. Therefore, the fame achieved through the compliment and acknowledgment of others is only a delusion, and it cannot become a sustainable dignity. But that doesn't mean you should avoid the compliment and acknowledgment of others. All you need to do when somebody compliments and acknowledges you is be happy and appreciative at the moment. And you should not forget that it is the joy of that very moment. Let the emotion of the moment pass happily without feeling the need to keep relishing and chewing on it, so that the compliment disappears from the world as a delusion and also perishes within you as well.

We experience anxiety when we don't have our existential value confirmed repeatedly by others, and we experience the sense of inferiority when we delude ourselves into thinking that we are not being acknowledged by others. The sense of inferiority grows when you lose the sense of value and purpose that are bestowed upon you by God, and it manifests itself mostly in the form of anger. In psychoanalysis, majority forms of anger are the narcissistic anger that boils up from the delusion that you are ignored or rejected by others. For example, when you become angry at the other driver who cuts you off, it is only an emotion that comes from your delusion about having been ignored by the other driver. When you become angry to the carelessness and unintended behaviors of others, that anger is the manifestation of your unconscious sense of inferiority. When you let that inferiority complex grow, you become the kind of person who is jealous and envious of others for the things that you don't have, and worse, you suffer from the pain of hating others. And sometimes when you let your deeply wounded anger continue to boil up, it generates the emotion of hatred on the side as well. Hatred is the desire for the other person to be painful or wrong. Hatred can make your Hon sick more than any other consciousness.

Therefore, when you find yourself suffering from hatred against somebody around you and you find it difficult to drop the hatred, I suggest you just try to dislike the person. We have the freedom to dislike something. The emotion of dislike does not harm us. For example, when you say, "I like the color yellow but dislike the color blue," it keeps your emotion about the color blue at the "dislike" level. You can enjoy the freedom to dislike something as much as you want, as long as you can discipline yourself to avoid looking at the color blue, consider the color unfavorable, or the cause of bad luck. While keeping the things you dislike at an arm's length, you have to remember your own dignity again.

The sense of inferiority and hatred grows when we forget about our dignity. When your sense of inferiority grows bigger, you tend to try to find your existential value from the outer world instead of your inner world and God. In principle, everything in the world circulates. All things of the world leave you instead of remaining with you, until they return to you. If you seek dignity from the world and other people, you feel extremely sorry for the things that leave you and hesitant to accept them back. The sense of inferiority feeds on the nervous and unstable emotional gap between the things that leave you and return to you.

But we are the existences that don't need to feel nervous about anybody. We have been given the value that will last forever from the beginning of time, and since our existential purpose is one with the purpose of the almighty Creator, we have to remember that we are naturally dignified toward anybody. Therefore, we have to realize that it is the sense of inferiority that you have within that harms your dignity, not the outside world. The jealousy and hatred we have within us will melt away as long as we release the sense of inferiority and fulfill the urge for dignity that our Hon wants. You can forgive those who hate, and you can understand and embrace them instead.

In order to understand our Hon correctly, we have to know the Creator, the existence who created us and makes us stand as dignified beings in the world. Of all explanations about the absolute God that I'd come across, the book *Conversations with God* offered the most articulate and clear explanation. As far as I understand, the relationship between God and us is explained in *Conversations with God* as follows:

In the beginning, God was a single perfect existence. However, being the only existence, it could not confirm or experience itself through anything else. Therefore, it split itself into multiple existences, and created the space where the existences spread out into an illusion that was not itself, so that multiple existences could confirm and experience itself to each other within the illusion. And that experience is expanding that single perfect existence.

The single perfect existence from the beginning of time is what we call God the Creator. He is almighty and is full of love because He is the perfect existence. Since He needed things other than love in order to experience Him, who is full of love, He split himself and created all things of the universe. He created an illusion that was not love with the space that was created during the splitting process, and so came about the relative world that contrasted with the absolute world. Beings experience how they are perfect love through each other in the illusion within the relative world. And experiencing and confirming one's self as being love becomes the power that expands God's almighty power. We are a small part of the absolute God, and God is all of us. Therefore, our souls are perfect love and always connected to God. The purpose of our creation was given by the Creator, and the will of our soul and God's purpose of creation make one same existence.

When you understand the relationship between God and yourself, the easiest idea to think about is the relationship between you and your cell nucleus. You are a creature consisted of an infinite number of cells. And within the cell nucleus, there is all your genetic information. Be it a skin cell, heart cell, or any other cell, their nuclei equally contain all your genetic information. These cell nuclei perform various activities in their own fields with that information. The cytoplasm and the space between cells are relative illusion that manifests its shape differently depending on their location and roles. The life activities of your cell nuclei pan out depending on the purpose of your existence, because the purpose of your existence and your cell nuclei's goal of activities are one being that cannot be different.

Our soul is God's cell nucleus, and it contains information of God's perfect love and truth. Therefore, whatever you are and whatever you do in life, the truth of creation is alive within you, and the purpose of your existence cannot be different from the purpose of God's creation, because we exist as a whole at the same time a part of the whole. Just like we are the existences more intelligent and sacred than the sum of all our cell nuclei, the sacredness of God as the sum of us is perfect, and, therefore, His love is wholesome.

Hon is the body of energy that rests in the mind that wishes the communication between God the whole and us the parts, and to seek the purpose of our existences. Communication with God makes us realize what we are seeking in life and guides us to continue that journey. Therefore, those with strong Hon experience less confusion in life, and they live in the glory that you feel when your life is headed toward the purpose of life. In order to communicate with God, Hon is situated in pineal, which is dubbed as the third eye. Found in the center of our brain, pineal is understood as the channel for our conscious to communicate with the universe in yoga practice in India, even though its specific role in the human body is not clearly and medically explained.

The pineal gland is found in the center of our brain in the shape similar to our eyes, and it is from this gland that melatonin and serotonin — two hormones that are responsible for our physiological reaction to the day and the night — are discharged. While we are awake, Hon guides us to let our mind move toward the purpose of our existence as the master that commands our consciousness and unconsciousness, and while we sleep, it goes out to the universe and directly communicates with God, helping us to get the energy for our mind to become one with God. Sleep is necessary not just for our body to recover from exhaustion, but also for the Hon of our mind commander to regularly reach out and directly connect with God. Therefore, if we don't sleep, Hon cannot have the direct communication with God, and the result is, we lose control over our mind and therefore it becomes difficult to control our emotions.

The stronger the energy of Hon grows, the stronger our capability to communicate with God, the absolute being in the vast universe, grows. The results manifest themselves as the outstanding intuition, inspiration, creative thoughts, and wise insight. In order to fulfill the purpose of our beings in life, we need the insight to tell truth from lies and the intuition to identify the path we have to take in the jumble of confusions and lies. While your daily life is in peace, you can judge and make right decisions through logical reasoning, but while your daily life is in the jumble of confusions and lies, it is not easy to make logical decisions at all. We come across such situations numerous times while we lead our lives. If you have the wise insights, you can keep mistakes and errors to a minimum, and you can make yourself grow smoothly because you can gain big wisdoms even from small mistakes.

We all understand the helplessness we feel when we encounter one after another piece of bad luck and trouble. If we cannot find the wisdom that we have to awaken while experiencing bad luck, we become stranded helplessly instead of continuing to keep moving forward. If we have intuition in the same situation, we can bring an end to the suffering earlier than later by awakening to the wisdom that we have to find in the middle of bad luck and misfortunes. Therefore, you desperately need the power of Hon when you are wounded and down, because it is the power that makes you realize that injuries and despair are not the final results but are just parts of the process of moving forward toward the purpose of life. Intuitions and insights – which are the healthy manifestations of Hon – allow you to find light in the middle of misfortunes and despair and fill you with hope and courage within. Hon makes you heal from wounds and grow to become a more brilliant existence with the light found in the process.

These days, I often notice strong energy of Hon in entertainers. The privacy of entertainers is helplessly open to the public and exposed to public sentiments, making them easy targets of unfair misunderstanding and criticism. And the entertainers' lives are more clearly laden with ups and downs than any others in other industries. The entertainers who continue to thrive while maintaining their existential value nevertheless are the model of outstanding energy of Hon. We can see their Hon that has grown beautifully while conversing with God when we hear them talking about how they healed wounds and found wisdom, and how they rise from despair like a roly-poly and continuously move forward on their paths. People say we all grow through pain. But having pain does not necessarily mean you grow from it. Pain can give you an opportunity to grow and provide you with the fertile soil for your existence only when you move forward toward the purpose of existence with all the energy you can get from Hon.

Other outcomes of the strong Hon include brilliant inspiration and outstanding creativity. Our lives are the complicated mixture of repeated routines and numerous variables. We have to prove our existential value in this wide world and establish our own territories. In my case, I practice medicine based on the same medical knowledge every day, but I often encounter situations where unexpected medical reactions throw me off balance. But it is when I come across such variables that I make a creative challenge to discover new treatment. Those in the service industries will come across variables resulting from having to serve a wide variety of people, and those in the technical industries will come across variables resulting from errors in calculation, and in administrative industries, complicated relationships. Creative thinking skill is a must in order to respond to the numerous such variables. Life can change brilliantly when the variables of life are met with creativity.

In addition, you need inspiration to express the existence you call "I" in order to expand your territory in this world. While treating patients as a Korean medicine doctor, I rarely have patients who come to see me with textbook symptoms. With every patient I meet, I have to make my assumption on the pathology of the patient and think about how to treat their symptoms in my imagination. Therefore, each of my treatment processes is determined by adding inspiration to my medical knowledge. It applies the same to the cooks, who complete their dishes with their inspiration, and the artists, who describe their artworks with their inspiration. Salesmen and saleswomen make successful sales with their inspiration; businessmen plan their business with their inspiration; and teachers guide students with their inspiration. As such, we all express our inspiration in our own way, establish our territory, and prove our existential values.

The origin of all truths is in the universe, and we express those truths in the world though the filters we call "I." Therefore, the inner power that lets us express our existential value in our own ways and continuously expand it comes from Hon that communicated with God. Therefore, while Ji creates life in the human territory with best efforts, Hon creates life in God's territory with the inspiration and creativity bestowed upon us by God.

Therefore, we have to express our inspiration and creativity in the fields where we stand while growing the energy of Hon. Only then can our life be created in God's territory and the world with the truths. Those who expanded their creativity to God's territory with the support of outstanding energy of Hon can establish their own unique and exclusive position in any fields they stand. For example, the figure skater Kim Yuna was able to be reborn as a sports player who added a beautiful artistic touch to her performance after she made the sign of the cross before games and acknowledged how she was connected to God, thereby touching the hearts of audiences more than any other players. I can say confidently that the rich and endless imagination of the writer Bernard Werber comes from his devoted quest to seek and enjoy divinity, which is manifested in his writings. And all others who have established their own domains with their unique individuality and essence in their respective fields are the ones with strong energy of Hon.

When someone's creativity and inspiration are maximized by Hon, new truths unfold in the world. A few examples include Albert Einstein and his theory of relativity; Yi Je-ma[12] and his Sasang constitutional medicine; Carl Gustav Jung and his analytical psychology; Sigmund Freud and his psychoanalysis; Neale Donald Walsh and his book *Conversations with God*; and Dr David Roman Hawkins and his consciousness research and spirituality. All these truths were discoveries that stood apart from any previously existing theories and became the gateway to a completely new world. These are historic figures who had contemplated on their relationships with God. The opening line of Yi Je-ma's book, *Longevity and Life Preservation in Korean Medicine* (東醫壽世保元), is describing how he sought truth from heaven based on the standards of heaven, and Einstein declared the divinity that he was seeking by stating, "I believe in Spinoza's God, who reveals Himself in the lawful harmony of the world, not in a God who concerns Himself with the fate and the doings of mankind." Carl Jung evolved his theories on human psychology into a new religious discovery on this quest to find the divinity of humans, while Neale Donald Walsh attempted conversations with God every day through his diary on his quest to grow Hon and wrote a groundbreaking book on divinity.

They were able to become the founders of new worlds because their strong energy of Hon served them as the medium to open the gateway to the truth. But new discoveries can never happen by the power of one individual alone. It happens when the truths gathered by the group of numerous energies of Hon are exploded by someone who serves as their fuse. Therefore, we must have the pride of being the individuals who bring about changes in the world by putting all our energies of Hon together and building the frames of lives in the fields where we stand. The world will evolve more brilliantly if numerous people become the fuse for the collective consciousnesses of humanity with the wish of opening a new world.

Then the question is: How can we grow our Hon so that we can always rise and stand firm and dignified and bring the creation of life to the domain of God? First off, it helps if you believe in the Absolute like I do. In my case, of all the five energies of Hon, Baek, Shin, Ui, and Ji, the energy of Hon is relatively stronger than others. I've never doubted the existence of God since I learned and liked the doctrine about God having created me in my childhood. As I grew up, I learned scientific knowledge and was awed at the scientific facts about evolution instead of completely believing in the creation and the stories about Adam and Eve that I'd learned at Bible school in church. But still, I had no doubt about the preposition that all living things and materials of the world including myself were created by God. While I was learning about captivating facts about evolution, I even amazed and cried out, "God is truly creating life in a truly great way!"

But that doesn't mean I was particularly religious. I started skipping church after a friend of mine who always went to church with me emigrated to a foreign country, and I left my family and hometown after I started college. Therefore, many of the people who knew me in my college days were not even aware that I was a Catholic. Even though I was not going to church, I always had the subconscious conviction that God was always watching over me. And I never doubted that God would be mad at me for not going to church because He was the Almighty. Even during the days when I was not faithfully reflecting on myself, I always thought of God when I went through and came out from major events in life – I used to tell myself, "God made that happen to me so that I would be awakened to this truth."

After reflecting on myself became a routine, I used to tell myself whenever I was shaken inside, "I am not alone. I am with God. So, I will move on from this troubled time holding the hand of God." I internalized the belief that my existential value was bestowed upon me by God, and everything that happened to me was the will of God since childhood through repeated Bible studies and mass.

The heart that believes in the existence of God and follows His words like I do can expand the energy of Hon. To believe in and follow God is to believe in His almighty power. The almighty power means perfection and wholesome love. Since God is a wholesome love, God does not harbor narcissistic anger or hatred, or punish those who don't believe in Him or go against His will. The ideas about us being sinners and God being there to punish us are just a convenient imagination to control ourselves, and it is even blasphemy to suspect the perfectness of God. Think about it! Even in our human world, we consider it a matter of course to disrespect and even ostracize those who harass others just because they are different. Even more, God is the Creator. How can a being that grows angry against those who go against their will create such a massive and wondrous world? How can we even imagine the scale of the love that is sacred enough to create this world?

In the book *Conversations with God*, the author explains that God the Creator answers to us only in three signs: joy, truth, and love. He decisively claims that all signs other than these three are not from God the Creator. That means this wondrous and marvelous world was able to be created only through the perfect love, joy, and truth. God is the Creator and the Absolute, and He is never angry at us or punishes us. It is impossible from the very beginning because for God to punish us is the same as punishing and disapproving His self. In other words, to believe in God is to believe in His perfect love. The belief that God is always there with us to love and bless us, and watches over us instead of interfering with our affairs because He respects us is what grows our Hon bigger and healthier. God the Creator is always with us in every moment and watches over us with love, blessing, and respecting, because we are His creations, parts of Him, and His life. If you fully accept and believe in the love of God, and therefore your Hon becomes capable of freely communicating with God, your Hon will grow into a brilliant light.

Then the question is: Is it impossible for atheists who don't believe in God the Creator to grow their Hon? Indeed, there are numerous great people who fulfill the purpose of life even though they don't have any religion; they don't believe in the existence of God; and they don't even think much about God. These are the people who prove that they can have strong energy of Hon even if they don't think too much about God. That is correct. Hon does not feed only on the belief in God and His love. Hon being a spiritual being, it feeds on your awareness to the free will of soul. In other words, your master makes the same growth as you when you awaken to the subjectivity of yourself. Awakening to the subjectivity of your self is the beginning of exercising the free will of your soul, and it is a domain that establishes with the energy of Hon. Therefore, philosophical contemplation to seek and explore your subjective value and purpose is the same as awakening to the free will of soul, and the efforts to practice philosophical contemplation are the same as practicing the will of soul. Hon can freely communicate with God and grow its energy through any methods that are meant to fulfill the purpose of existence.

In fact, nowadays, the method of raising the energy of Hon with free will rather than religion is growing more popular among many people. Psychoanalysis, for example, helps you realize the purpose of existence as a wholesome self by understanding the unconscious features that are the source of one's feelings and thoughts, and eliminating the unconscious causes that set limits on one's self. The psychoanalysis process of identifying the unconscious causes of one's emotions and actions is possible only when one is awakened with a strong sense of goal. Recently popular brain science identifies the errors that occur due to the human neurological characteristics and proves that a significant number of our thoughts and emotions are the consequences of errors, thereby awakening us to break free from the limits of error. Contemplation supported by brain science that helps us find out whether our feelings and thoughts are neurological errors or not is also possible only when you have a clearly awakened sense of goal. The theory of relativity, quantum mechanics, parallel theory, and other theories of physics all explain in scientific and rational logics that there are infinite values and possibilities for all beings, thus leading us to the awareness of the divinity of being.

As we can see, there has been dynamic and proactive progress in exploring truth about existence and overcoming limitations to ensure the manifestation of our spiritual free will since the modern era. This is a brilliant outcome of the collective consciousness that mankind has raised with the power of Hon. And these results are completing the opposite light of Hon that the existing religion could not fulfill.

Whatever the methodology is, there must be a subjectivity wherein you become the master of yourself supported by the belief that you have sufficient values and purpose to exist forever within you. And you can grow the energy of Hon by deeply embedding in your consciousness and unconsciousness your desire to fulfill your existential purpose in that eternity so that the free will of Hon can manifest in your heart and in your actions. God has split himself and planted all truths, love, and joy in our soul as well as in cell nuclei so that we can fully experience Himself when we want to experience love in the delusional relative world. And God also gave us wholesome free wills to choose and experience it as well. Experience by force or coercion is not the way to reveal the whole self. Since only the choice and experience that we have achieved with our free will can fully confirm ourselves, God gave us free will by fully respecting us, who are part of His self. We are choosing to experience with our free will as we move forward on our quest to find the purpose of life.

After all, realizing the subjectivity and purpose of oneself is like realizing the will of God. Realizing our spiritual free will and experiencing a choice for that purpose is like fulfilling the purpose of being that God has given us. Even if we do not recognize that the free will is from God, it is not different from praising God's divinity to experience the truth, love, and joy that we have and to attain the purpose of being. God, the Absolute, is a perfect being. Therefore, He does not feel sorry even if we fail to recognize Him, and He equally reaches out and communicates with those who don't believe in God and empowers them as well. Realizing one's own spiritual free will is another way of raising the energy of Hon.

Even if you cannot believe God's presence right now, I hope you will begin by believing that you are the eternal master of yourself. You are not a finite being with only a limited significance that will perish after one lifetime. You are the master while at the same time a being with an infinite significance that goes beyond this lifetime. Remember what makes you happy and touches your heart when you choose and experience what. Use those memories to find and experience the purpose of you being here. As you move toward the purpose of being with the free will of the soul, the opportunity to experience the existential purpose and the truth about that vast universe will unfold before you, and your Hon will grow brilliant in the glory of freely communicating with God.

Believing in God's omnipotent love and following him, and living a life faithful to one's spiritual free will are both good ways to grow Hon. These two paths may seem like entirely different from each other, but the Creator and us being one existence, they are essentially manifestations of the same divinity. So, it does not matter what you choose first. It is a blessing if you raise your Hon brightly by following the path of your choice.

But whichever path you choose to start first to grow your Hon, the two paths must eventually come together. If you start with a heart that believes in God the Creator and follows Him like I did, now is the time for you to become aware of the free will that God has given us. It is another form of blasphemy to ignore the free will or entrust it to others. God never wants us to praise and follow Him without exercising our free will. If He did, He would not have given us free will in the first place. God, who is our whole, is pleased when we experience the process of making our judgment and choice with our own free will to shine our existential value. Since the result of His pleasure unfolds in the form of the glory of our joy, truth, and love, fulfilling our free will is the supreme praise and loyalty we can give to God.

If, unlike me, you have been proving your brilliant existential value by awakening to your own free will so far, now is the time for you to think about where that great free will has originated from. You must feel in your heart to see if the brilliant glory you have experienced had really originated from and ended with you. If your free will was indeed restricted only to yourself, you should realize that it cannot be that glorious and brilliant, and you should feel God, the whole of the universe, who has given you the free will. It will surely make you happier and bring you bigger joy, and your free will shall lead you to the glory of fulfilling your purpose with greater power.

That's the reason I feel really sad when I see the praise of God overpowering one's free will. God, the Absolute, does not need anybody's praise because He is a being who has everything and wants for nothing. If your religious activity is filled only with praise of God without the support of your own subjective judgment and actions, and when you deny your free will believing that the only way to cleanse your sin is faith in and praise of God, God will certainly feel sorry that we are failing to let our existential value shine brilliantly, because to make us shine is to make God shine. He or she does not need anything, but they are the beings that grow with the experience of love just as we all do. Therefore, God wants us to experience love through our free will and shine our existential value. God will only rejoice or feel sorry while holding hopes for us without anticipating or getting disappointed.

On the one hand, I feel sad when I see those who deny God after some passionate religious activities. When you believe in and praise God while doing your religious activities, you experience glory for some time with the growth of your Hon, but sometimes the growth reaches a stagnating point and you experience the pain and despair for being a sinner. I feel pain in my heart when I see those who blame God in pain, because they fail to realize the fact that the growth of Hon continues and expands glory, if only they open their eyes to the divinity of free will when they reach that point.

Even the people who have continued to grow with their free will come across that point of limit. I know someone who was exploring the truth of the universe and experiencing his divinity through the chakra training but turned to the extreme opposition direction when he came across a limit, at which point he started denying the human divinity and believed praising God as a sinner was the only way to live. It is a pity to deny all past experiences in the face of limit after having experienced the bliss that was brought about by one's free will so distinctively.

Kim Hyung-kyung, the author who stripped illusions with her free will through a long psychoanalysis and wrote *Human Landscape* and *Ten Thousand Behaviors*, stated that the world of truth that one meets beyond psychoanalysis is the domain of religion and it is a world of selflessness where there is no expectation of redemption. I sincerely hope that many people will fully remember the experience of growing their Hon for the first time and avoid the pain of denying the past upon coming across the pain of limit. I sincerely hope that readers will have their divinity meet the divinity of God so that they can enjoy the glory of continuous growth without exposing the energy of Hon to pain and suffering, like the writer Kim Hyung-kyung did.

When I was in my early 20s, there was something that my father – who loved to drink – used to tell me whenever he was drunk. He would tell me, "You may be born gifted, but you cannot beat those who work hard, and you may work hard but you cannot beat those who have luck. Nobody can beat those who have the help of God." Since I was not fully mature back then, I always felt uncomfortable whenever he lamented like that. I thought it was not fair that those who work hard cannot beat those who have luck, and I wanted to believe that it was not really what's going on in the world. But now, I see that his words had truth in them, and the meaning of the truth makes perfect sense instead of being unfair.

Creating a life by doing the best and using the energy of Ji to the fullest is valid only in the domain of man. But we are a spiritual divine being beyond the flesh and a limited time, and we are one with God the Creator. He who remembers and acknowledges his divinity can have his Hon to freely communicate with God in the vast universe and lifts the work of creation into the domain of God. The lucky ones were the people who understood their joy, truth, and love, and remembered and practiced the divinity of free will that is respected by God. It was absolutely natural for them to have the help of God because they don't hesitate to move forward toward the purpose of existence. Now I understand nothing, not even the best efforts, can beat their creation because it belongs to the domain of God.

Therefore, now I wish to become, to be in the process of becoming, and will become the one who has the help of God. I wish everyone to become the one who has the help of God.

Please remember that your divinity is one with God, and widely open your Hon so that you can freely communicate with God. Extend your creation to go beyond the human domain with brilliant insight and great inspirations so that it can unfold in the domain of God. If you remember your divinity, God will surely help you to fulfill the purpose of being. There is nothing in this world that can stop your march to your glory. I sincerely ask you to live brilliantly and gloriously as a small God.

Endnotes

[12] Yi Je-ma: He suggested a new paradigm that divides the world into four elements in Confucianism, and based on this philosophy he founded a new medicine that divides the human constitution into four.

3. Baek (魄): The World Exists Only for the Purpose of Experiencing Love

Baek is a body of energy that determines how to accept and pioneer the logic of the world and the universe that is realized in our lives. We cannot fully understand the cause and effect of everything that happens to us. With so many misfortunes and fortunes scattered in our lives, and with fortunes being so hard to notice and misfortunes being so distinctively noticeable, it is hard to tell if there is any fairness in all of them, or to figure out if there are any causal relationships between them at all. But one thing is certain: If this world were made to run by random forces, we would not have been able to live in civilization for such a long time together. There is a fair power of the world that allows us to be together. Wouldn't we be able to feel less frustrated about the world if we could have even just a little understanding of the power? Wouldn't we be able to be a little happier in our lives?

Human beings have long wanted to know why we were born to live and why we should suffer the hardships of life. Religions offer us various doctrines that suit their characteristics in an attempt to give answers to that primal question. First off, Catholicism and Christianity answer the question with the theory of the original sin. According to these religions, we are all descendants of Adam and Eve, and we are born with the sin of having picked the forbidden fruit because Adam and Eve have sinned against the word of God when they picked and ate it. We are all born in this land, not in the Garden of Eden, because we are born with the original sin, and we have to cleanse our sin by living the life of suffering, according to these two religions. Buddhism explains that all the sufferings and defilement that we experience in our lives are the consequences of the past lives we have lived through reincarnations. Buddhism justifies our sufferings by stressing that everything that happens to us is the consequence of what we did, even though we don't remember what we did in our past life today. I don't know how other religions explain this with what doctrine, but perhaps religions that have had much influence on mankind will have their own doctrines on this matter. Existing religions guide us to humbly accept the uncertainty and misfortune of life in one way or another.

To be honest, I could not bring myself to agree with the notion of the original sin as explained in the Catholic doctrine. When I was young, I could not understand why I had to become a sinner because of the wrongdoing committed by Adam and Eve. But I didn't rack my brain too much over the question of the original sin because I simply thought about it without trying to reach a clear yes-or-no conclusion. Fortunately, I did not even need to be bothered by that question because the catechism and the priests' preachings that I had in childhood were more about our close relationship with God than about the original sin. Then, when I grew up and life became complicated and I was burdened with exhausting responsibilities, I recalled the question of the original sin again. I really wondered if life had to be so hard on me because I was a sinner, and while treating patients, I was able to notice how nobody in the world was living without suffering. The concept of the original sin that explained how we were all born to live the life of suffering encouraged me to expand my compassion toward all.

But even then, I didn't think we were born with the original sin because of what Adam and Eve did. That was such an absurd symbolic story to me that it didn't have any convincing effect on me. Rather, the Buddhist doctrine about karma(causality), which explained that everything was of my own making through the process of repeated reincarnations, was a more rational and convincing doctrine to me. So, when I acknowledged the original sin, I understood and accepted my original sin in terms of my suffering being the consequences of my past lives and I being responsible for everything happening to me.

The theory about each of us being an existence that lives through numerous lives and accepting the consequences of past lives that we cannot even remember sounds very intriguing. For all I know, if all the misfortunes that happen to me were caused by myself, and all the fortunes that I had enjoyed were also my own making, that clearly shows how each of us is the most important subject in our lives. It is also a rational explanation about our free will being the gift from God. To accept this notion about karma, however, we must first be able to believe that we have lived through many lives.

In fact, the past life is a truth that is deeply rooted in our collective subconscious. We routinely say, "It's all my karma from previous lives," "You must have saved your country in your past life," "I will surely accomplish this in my next life," or "We will meet again in our next lives." We talk about past and next lives as if it is a matter of fact. That proves how deeply the logic of reincarnation is embedded in our subconscious. Then a new era opened where this reincarnation is explained not in terms of a religion, but in terms of science called the theory of the parallel universe. "Parallel Universe" is a theory of physics that originated from quantum mechanics. I will briefly explain it with a reference I found in the book *Genius Learning Encyclopedia*.

The theoretical background of a parallel universe originates from quantum mechanics. Electrons, like protons, can exist in different places at the same time and can have conflicting properties at the same time. According to "worlds interpretation," which is one of the hypotheses in quantum mechanics, protons always have two choices no matter where they are in the space, and the universe splits into parallel universes in accordance to the choices given to particles. Thus, whenever one choice is made, the universe is divided into two universes with one on this side, and the other on the other side.

However, according to the "multiverse interpretation" that is slightly different from this theory, the universe is not divided into several universes in accordance to our choice. Instead, there are already an infinite number of universes, and we choose one of them as if a train chooses and follows only one of the many points of intersection. If you supposed our universe is an infinite plane, we can imagine that other parallel universes are stacked up and down of our universe. However, since our universe is a three-dimensional space (four-dimensional space-time), we have to assume the existence of four or higher-dimensional space (more than five-dimensional space-time) in order for parallel universes to exist, and if that space actually exists, there can be numerous parallel universes.

A proton refers to the smallest unit of a physical substance (physical quantity), so small that it cannot be divided any more. Ultimately, we are made into this physical being by the collection of protons. Since the nature of a proton is equally applicable to us, we can simultaneously exist in different places and in different properties. When we understand the flow of time in terms of a one-dimensional segment, our life will be perceived either as the past life or the next life depending on the posterior of time, but when we consider it in terms of a fourth dimension of time and space, we reach a conclusion that time is ultimately part of the space, and an infinite number of "I" can exist in parallel universes that exist infinitely. Our past lives and next lives have unfolded at the same time in other spaces, and even though our numerous past lives, present life, and the next lives exist in all different spaces, they are connected through one channel. And that one channel that passes through them all is none other than our own karma (result of a cause).

Since every karma comes down to the present time, we as of today are the center of the cluster of karmas accumulated from numerous previous lives as well as our next lives. Therefore, everything that makes up today's "I" and everything that happens to me now is attributed to a karma that comes from all my times and spaces. The idea of reincarnation was intriguing because of its rational persuasiveness, and now, it is supported by the validity that can be scientifically explained. The reincarnation paired with the parallel universe theory supports the fact that we are more than just beings carrying our own karma; we are the beings of infinite possibilities coexisting in all parallel universes and we are also carrying divine value with us.

And the most important is the fact that one karma is cutting through all our beings that exist in multiple parallel universes. Since this is a rational hypothesis that we all live on the same principle, it supports the truth that the world in which we live and the laws of the universe where we exist are fair and rational, even if our individual lives unfold in different forms. Our lives might be inexplicable and unfair, but the fact that one karma is cutting through all our lives that exist in parallel universes qualifies as the rational truth since the fact applies equally to all of us.

So, the energy of Baek that connects you with the world grows with the belief that everything that happens to you is fair and just, even though you don't understand the causality of complicated and disorderly affairs of the world. The present you cannot recognize the you that exists in different time and space. So, it is natural that you cannot understand the causality that exists in your life, and it is also natural for you to feel unfair in the face of suffering. The power to overcome all the things that are unfair and fully accept them as your fair share comes from Baek. Baek grows when you believe in the fairness and justice of the universe and you love the world you belong to. In fact, believing in the world is the same as believing in the fair and impartial integrity of God the Creator who presides over everything. After all, beliefs on both the world and God are like two sides of a coin. In other words, Hon and Baek are like twins that look similar but different from each other.

Indeed, Hon and Baek are the bodies of energies that work together. During the day, Back stays with Hon in the pineal gland and guides you to love the world and believe in the universe so that you can move forward toward the purpose of life, and it returns to the cochlea of your ears at night. Our auditory organ is a channel through which we receive the world. Helen Keller, who lost both visual and audio senses, said, "Losing vision means being separated from things, and losing your sense of hearing means being separated from people." The fact that people in a coma can remember the sounds from surroundings in the unconscious state is speaking volumes about the fact that auditory sense is the last connecting link to the world. We keep the auditory sense that receives the world till the last moment of our lives. Therefore, the original location of Baek – the energy that determines how you should deal with the world – is the cochlea of ears.

Just as Hon and Baek are like a twin, I sometimes feel that Catholicism and Buddhism are like twin religions. While Catholicism focuses on our relationship with God and leads us to the purpose of existence by the power of Hon, Buddhism leads us to achieve the purpose of life by the power of Baek by explaining that all things in the universe are perfect within the fair and just cycle. Ultimately, these two religions are addressing stories that are different but sound the same. Just like it is the law of nature that Hon and Baek work together, I think that two religions might come closer to perfection through the law of nature when they become one in doctrines.

However, when the power of Baek that believes in and loves the world grows weaker, you become vulnerable to such emotions as anxiety and fear. You feel afraid because, when you don't believe in the world you belong to, you will always feel like you are the light before the wind. Being anxious about the uncertainty of life is the sign that your Baek has grown weak. In fact, fear is a great barrier to life for all humans. In the book *Life Lessons*[13], the authors explain that if you trace the origin of all emotions that keep you from doing what you want to do, you can find there is the fear of death. We can change many things in life if only we can overcome the fear of all emotions because it means you have eliminated a big barrier. The anger, which is an emotion that we easily expose to others, is an emotion that is like two sides of fear. In psychoanalysis and psychology, anger and fear are perceived as the same emotions, because in the deep subconscious level, we get angry because we are afraid of our existence being rejected.

If you are entrapped by fear and anxiety about life, you cannot change anything because you cannot do anything as if you are frozen like ice. There will be no prison as brutal as the life that has stopped. Therefore, you have to choose the physiological energy of Baek and overcome fear and anxiety. The world cannot be either favorable or unfavorable only to you. Therefore, I hope you will think about the principle about your own karma being of your own making, and firmly believe that God is always on your side. This universe being so equitable, believing it to be on your side can awaken courage to overcome fear and anxiety.

The biggest tragedy that makes Baek become ill more than fear is the grudge. The mind that put blame on others or other objects for the things that happened to you is the most opposing mind to the physiological power of Baek because it is denying and refusing your karma. If you refuse to acknowledge that you are responsible for what happened to you, you cannot change anything. We can influence others, but we cannot have the control or make decisions for others. If other people or things are to blame for what happened to you, you cannot change anything and passively deal with them because you don't have the power to change them. Ultimately, choosing to hold a grudge against others is a declaration that you will live a passive life without changing anything. That declaration becomes the reality because it is valid to yourself and the world.

If you are holding a grudge on something, you have to drop it as soon as possible. Holding grudges on things means you haven't found the meaning of what has happened to you. When you let go of the grudges, you can find the true meaning of what has happened to you and change the current situation that made you resentful. You have to be aware of the moment when you start building resentment and grudges while feeling the emotions of fear and anxiety. And when you notice that moment, you have to let go of fear, anxiety, and grudge, believing that God is on your side. Tell yourself, "It's okay; It could happen; It is a meaningful process in my life; and I am going to love the meaning of the thing that happened to me..." When you do this, your heart will calm down the anxiety and bring peace to you. Once you make the energy of Baek grow healthy, the peace – which is the opposite of fear, anxiety, and grudge – will be with you.

It is money that you seek instinctively when you are trapped in anxiety about life and resentment of the world. The resentment toward the world fuels desire for money, which represents financial wealth, because when you cannot trust the world, you want to believe that it is money that moves the world, and you can forget the anxiety, if only temporarily, when you have money with you. But the truth is, making money is a healthy urge of Baek. Making money is an essential condition to solving basic needs, such as food, clothes, and shelter, and it is mankind's universal way of loving the world. We make money by presenting something to the world. You give our wisdom through books and take money in return, or you get money in exchange of treatment to relieve pain. You can also make money in exchange for delicious food, make money by developing convenient products, and make money by providing physical labor. We are making money by giving what we have to the world. Therefore, making money is rewarding and fun, and it is also a universal way of loving the world.

I still remember how proud I felt of myself when I received my first paycheck. It was more than just the joy of making money; it was rewarding to have my work being acknowledged by the world. We love the world by delivering what is necessary for the world to turn, or present something that will enrich the world, or unfold something that will make the world a little more convenient. In return for the love, we are given the money, or financial payback, with which we can solve our basic needs to live. That's the reason we have to work hard to make money, and love and be proud of the work we do to make money, because the more money we make, the better we love the world.

However, if you miss the point and put focus on money instead of loving the world, a healthy urge degenerates into an unhealthy desire. In fact, people who are steadily making good money are more interested in how they earn than how much they earn. If you are a food merchant, you are more focused on what food to make, and if you are a financial planner, you are more interested in which company you should invest in, and if you are an artist, you are concerned about what kinds of beauty and sensibility to describe. You can ensure to steadily making good money when the process of making money and the value it gives to the world are more important than the final outcome of how much money you made. On the other hand, if you start to get more interested in the results, the continuous success of making money becomes nothing but a pipe dream. As soon as the amount of money earned becomes more important, a healthy urge degenerates into a greedy urge, and as the result, making money becomes a heavier burden than necessary, and worse, you might even lose everything at once.

Therefore, if you want to make money well, you have to love the process of making money in the right way by thinking more about how you can love the world more with the job of your choice and gladly practice your conclusion. Since the money you earn is a reward for your love that enriched the world and made the world more convenient, you should proudly enjoy it as much as you can. If you complete the cycle of loving back the world with the wealth you enjoy, peaceful financial stability will be with you and enrich your life.

It is not good for you to let your emotions control you with regards to the things that happen to you if you want to make money with the healthy energy of Baek, keep yourself free from anxiety and resentment, and believe that the universe is fair and just. Take one step back and put everything in perspective, and you will sense your energy of Baek growing. Ven. Seongcheol Sunim[14] showed us the epitome of this relaxed attitude when he taught us about the enriching energy of Baek by saying, "A mountain is a mountain. A water is a water." Ven. Seongcheol Sunim gave a lesson for us to take a step back to appreciate and acknowledge everything that happens to us as karma, because everything is just what it is, just like a mountain is just a mountain and a water is just a water. As long as you acknowledge that everything that happens to you is the karma of your soul, it is a matter of fact that you must accept it, and being angry, resenting, and feeling sad about a plain fact is the same as being angry at the mountains and waters that are just there as they are supposed to be.

It is impossible, however, to have no emotions in the face of pain, frustration, sadness, and despair, because we are living humans. That's the reason we must remember that karma is moving without stopping and that all beings are in a cycle. Even if you are in a dark and difficult situation now, or in a joyous and exciting situation, it is just a moment that will pass instead of staying forever. The karma that comes to you now is passing through the time and space where you belong, and even yourself is constantly moving within the circling cycle of the universe instead of remaining where you are now. Since no pain or joy can last forever, we should always remember this phrase: "This too will pass."

Since the fateful karma that you will encounter is just a natural process, try to take a step back and measure it up instead of being overwhelmed by it or getting emotional about it. Imagine what signal this karma means and represents, as you would observe mountains and waters to figure out what feelings the mountains render and what color the waters demonstrate. And remember that every karma is in the process of going through you at the moment, and that there is nothing that remains unchanged. I cheer you to stand tall and strong with the full support of the energy of Baek even as you are surrounded by the whirlpool of emotions whipped up by karma.

If so, you might wonder if we can just passively accept karma that has been building up as the result of our fate. Of course, the answer is no. We have certainly been given from God the free will to choose and create. We have been building up our karmas with our own free will, and even at this moment, we are recreating our karmas. Depending on how we interpret and accept the karma that comes to us, and what actions we take to deal with it, existing karma is transformed, and a new karma is formed. And the signal that we make at this moment becomes a karma and manifests itself as the reality to our multiple other selves that exist in the parallel universe.

Therefore, it is all decided by Baek – whether you should accept everything that happens to you as justified; how you want to change yourself as the result of karma; and what you wish to accomplish as the result of the karma. Since there is nothing that remains the same without any change, we have to decide how to change our lives every moment. So, choosing to build up a new karma with the power of Baek is the power to change my life while at the same time a power to change the world and expand the energy of Baek.

How do you want to change your life? At this moment, what signals do you want to send to your many other selves that exist in the numerous parallel universes? If the karma you want to create is a way to peace and happiness, you should love the karma of this world that has come to you and send a sign of love to your multiple other selves. The love you have given to your multiple other selves that exist in numerous parallel universes will allow you to enjoy the karma of happiness and peace. So, you must interpret and accept with all your sensibilities all the conditions that form you and everything that happens around you. And you have to choose the way of loving the world, with all of your humanity.

To believe in the justice of the universe, we must be free from emotion, but we can never give up the sensitivity of human. Our sensitivities are the only channels through which we sense our karma with love. Our sensitivities are the key to the secret that will transform karma into happiness and peace, and they are an indispensable medium to bring about the evolution of the world. Therefore, we have to enrich the humanity that originates from our sensitivities. We have to sincerely sympathize, share pain and anger, regret deeply, dearly wish, have our hearts deeply touched, and smile and laugh as much as we can. Baek is the source of the power to make the choice to create a new karma that changes our lives and the world with the humanistic beauty originating from our sensitivity. The sensitivity that comes from Baek can beautifully sublimate tragedies of life into brilliant happiness.

Therefore, our Baek grows sometimes as the impartial observer that is free from life emotions, and sometimes as the Creator of a new karma that changes our life with our sensibilities. The forces of these two directions become one loop. You can change life by rising your humanism only when you can grow as the observer that is free from emotions. Probably you know by experience that emotionally-charged choices you make always end in regret. You can also remain free from emotions only when you interpret and handle your karma with sensibilities. You might have experienced how you could get over the pain of breakup when you accepted the significance of the breakup with your sensitivity. If you know the sensible meaning of what happened to you, you can free yourself from the burden of emotion. When your observation is not burdened by emotion, you can empower your choice of sensitivity.

It is not possible to extend Baek just in one direction alone, and if you extend it in one direction only, you will develop a lopsided world view. If you start thinking that all things in the world are karmas that need to be resolved one by one, thereby trivializing everything that happens in the world and it becomes impossible to recover the humanism, you are going to break yourself from the world and develop a world view that makes you look at the world in a twisted way based on your twisted sense of superiority. Alternatively, if you reach the point where you, as an observer, cannot accept karma as your fair share, cannot realize its significance, and try to change everything in life only based on your sensitivities, you will become a person like Don Quixote who lunges at a windmill.

However, be it an observer or sensitivities, the problem is not about being excessive. Ven. Seongcheol showed us the epitome of Baek as an observer free from emotions by observing life as if he was observing mountains and waters, but he was truly beautiful. Cardinal Stephen Kim Sou-hwan[15] who had shown us his humanism dedicated to the peaceful changes of our society and the shared love of the world was the epitome of the unshaken greatness. As we can see in these two religious leaders, excessiveness of one direction is not a problem. The problem of developing a lopsided world view with the wrong energy of Baek is not about one side being excessive but about one side being absent. In order to grow wholesome Baek, it is necessary to have both directions: undaunted appreciations of life and rich sensitivities to change life. When we really love something, we observe it as it is and embrace and protect it wholeheartedly. Observing and acknowledging the meaning of karma within the context of the world and embracing it with humanism is ultimately the same as loving the world in which your karma belongs. The energy of Baek expands brilliantly when you have the trust and love for the world in your heart.

Those who grew the energy of Baek by loving the world in both directions have something in common: They show their wisdom in action. Cardinal Kim Su-hwan and Ven. Seongcheol Sunim both shared their wisdoms with others as religious leaders, and their wisdoms became the power that earned them respect from so many people across religions. So, when the two religious leaders died, they were mourned by people from all different religions. Wisdom is the most typical manifestation of the healthy Baek.

The former United States president Barack Obama opened many people's hearts by showing the down-to-earth, humanistic side of him better than any other political leaders. From his playful and humorous personality to the heart-warming side of him that was revealed when he sat down to be at the same eye level as children, earnest tears he'd shed in the face of tragedy, and agony he felt as he waited for an important bill to pass in Congress – all these humanistic sides of him were the manifestation of his sensible energy of Baek that attracted and moved the hearts of many people. He said he had been filling up his sensible beauty with the help of books.

Reading gives me the ability to slow down, build view, and think in the perspectives from others at a time when complex information flows quickly.

He said he was able to take the heavy-looking present lightly and put it in perspective by reading great epic stories, and he came to love the world by reading books about understanding humans. And with the strong energy of Baek, the former US President Obama was able to find the wisdom that allowed him to deliver powerful speeches that opened the hearts of the people.

Another example I would like to introduce is the travel writer Oh Soh-hee[16], who communicates with readers through her blog. Sometimes she provides her advice on life problems for her readers. Oh Soh-hee's advice covers a wide variety of topics including marriage and relationships, and her answers help readers to drop unnecessary pride and ego and love others more, even those husbands who are responsible for marriage problems. Her wise answers and advice always draw out inspiration and awe from me. The wisdom of life that she shares on complicated love and relationship issues inspires readers including myself and makes us feel our brains are expanded. Her followers – inspired by her answers and advice – often make commends and ask her, "How can you be so wise? Where does your wisdom come from?"

She travels many places in the world as a professional travel writer, but mostly she travels to third world countries and shares her travel experiences in her books. In her books, she introduces the untouched beauty found in the third world countries and the livelihoods of people who live there. Oh Soh-hee loves the world by writing books and sharing her experiences with the beautiful and wondrous nature and people who live in harmony with nature. That serves as the source that lights up her Baek brilliantly and manifests as her wisdom.

Lastly, I want to introduce the anchor Sohn Suk-hee[17] as someone with a strong energy of Baek. As a veteran journalist, he has been analyzing and delivering current affairs and news of the world to the people through news programs and interviews. When he broke the scandal about Park Geun-hye and her close aide Choi Sun-sil, he delivered in-depth reports about the tablet PC that he had secured by way of presenting evidence that rebutted the responses from the Park administration. Instead of trying to follow emotions and break the news all at once, he chose to report carefully in phases, thereby making numerous people angry at the corruption of the administration and cry out for changes. The following is the text message he sent to fellow reporters at a time when he was cheered by people around the country immediately after he broke the news about the Park Geun-hye and Choi Sun-sil scandal[18]:

Since yesterday, JTBC has become one of the most popular broadcasting channels again. Interest in our channel immediately translates into the interest in the members of the channel. Let us remember to be humble and cautious, again and again.... (sic).... In fact, this is what I wanted to say since our channel was voted as the most reliable news channel. I do not know how well I am with it, but that's what you must do as long as you are a member of JTBC team...(sic)...Besides, our recent exclusive scoops are acclaimed by many of our viewers but at the same time, they also can make many others feel despondent. Intended or not, we have been making some people suffer from deep wounds that are hard to heal. Therefore, our attitude is extremely important."

Even though he is a successful journalist, he is cool-headed and humanistic enough to care about the wounds of others. In addition to the exclusion of emotions in news program development, he expresses in his anchor briefing and closing music that all news should be treated as sensible humanism that evolves the world. The wisdom he shows in the news program was acknowledged when his program was voted by viewers as the most trusted news program.

Now, as an ordinary person instead of a celebrity, I want to introduce my energy of Baek. When reading books, I mostly enjoy reading nonfictions, but when I watch movies and dramas, I enjoy watching fictions. And those are where I find inspiration and also the greatness and wonders of the world and the people. I keep myself updated on current affairs by following news on the internet, while sincerely hoping for the world to evolve without getting too emotional about news reports that make people sad and angry. I am grateful for the music that caresses my soul, and sometimes I laugh out loud while watching variety shows on TV. I don't travel very often but I admire the beauty of our planet by watching various videos on the computer that I use every day, and I always try to remain cool about the fact that I am an existence that belongs to that brilliantly beautiful world. And as a professional Korean medicine practitioner, I try to provide patients with my sensibility and cool-headed medical knowledge. Ultimately, I try to love the world no matter in what ways I come into contact and deal with the world.

Anything will do: religion, reading, traveling, appreciation of art, news of the world, or occupation. It will be all the better if you can grow your Baek with all of the above. I sincerely hope you will love the world through religion, reading, appreciation of art, news, and occupation. Then, your Baek will become the energy that shines as brilliantly as the energy found in Ven. Seongcheol Sunim, the anchor Sohn Suk-hee, Cardinal Kim Su-hwan, President Obama, and the writer Oh Soh-hee. Then you will be able to bring about changes with the full support of your humanism and sensibilities while observing the world and life composedly, and you will find peace in you with the most supreme wisdom.

Before closing the chapter about Baek, there is something I really want to say. In order for us to fully develop the energy of Baek, we must break away from the ideas about the original sin as taught by the existing religions. Existing religions preached that life is the process of cleansing mankind's original sin and the sin of previous lives in order for us to humbly accept the life of suffering. But be it the original sin or sin from past lives, we are not sinners who live on this planet as the punishment for our sins. Now the time has come for mankind to break free from the delusion of us being sinners and confront the truth about existence instead.

We are by no means sinners, and we are only living as humans to experience love. Life is all about experiencing love among the things that are not love in order that our soul – which is purely love – can confirm itself through experience. This was clearly accomplished with a sincere wish by the soul that chose and agreed to do it. The life we live among the things that are not love is a series of pains and sufferings as the result of numerous karmas, but for our soul, these karmas are simply similar to the natural gravity. Just like we are living standing on the ground thanks to the gravity, and just like we accept the gravity as a matter of fact instead of complaining about it being heavy and burdensome, karma to our soul is just a gravity that makes it stay in the relative world to experience love, and it is only a natural opportunity to experience love.

The relative world where love can be experienced is a space created by the splitting of God, the perfect love, and therefore, the things that are not love are only delusional, non-existential spaces. To our soul, the relative world in which we live is like the space in virtual reality. The wind that blows in this space is here one moment and it will be gone without trace soon after. In this universe, existing and eternal entities are all love, and the opposite of love is the illusion of space that is meaningless and vanishes without trace. The wind that blows in the space vanishes when we realize that anything in life that is not love is just an illusion and refuse to give any meaning to it. But the love that we choose exists forever in our soul and the universe. The fact that only love is a substantial entity and the rest is the illusion of space means the universe and the world were designed and structured solely for the purpose of experiencing love.

Our soul is a vast and expansive being that encompasses all of our selves that exist in the parallel universes, and it is also an infinite and divine being. Our souls desperately want to experience love through our karmas, while fully acknowledging and accepting karmas that our numerous selves have created in all universes like we accept the gravity. Life is all about the process of recognizing fakes as illusions and making them disappear from our lives and confirming itself by acknowledging and experiencing love that is the eternal reality instead.

Therefore, nothing happens to us unless our soul agrees and wants. Every karma that happens to us is an opportunity to which our soul agreed and wanted. All we need to do is to be the leverage for our soul, and search and experience love while avoiding fakes that exist in the world, because that is the only reason why we live this life, even though it is laden with sufferings. The book *Conversations with God* provides us with an answer to our question about the reason we – the manifestation of perfect love – choose to experience suffering in the relative world: "Because that's the only thing we need to do." In other words, all that we can do is just sit and do nothing if we do not choose this path of experiencing love. We try to experience love as an instinct of all beings to expand and be on a cycle, because experiencing love expands our soul.

Now, let's break ourselves free from the bridle that says we are sinners. I sincerely wish that, in this universe that is built only for the purpose of experiencing love, we will run the full course of the path of karma peacefully and with the full energy of Baek.

Endnotes

13 *Life Lessons* by Elisabeth Kübler-Ross and David Kessler.

14 Ven. Seongcheol Sunim: One of Korea's most eminent Buddhists whose teachings have touched many Korean followers.

15 Stephen Kim Sou-hwan: The first Korean Cardinal of the Roman Catholic Church and the former Archbishop of Seoul, he was a social activist, widely respected across all sections in Korean society.

16 Oh Soh-hee: A Korean travel writer, she is famous for her essays about traveling third world countries with her young son.

17 Sohn Suk-hee: The president of JTBC's news reporting division, he is considered one of the most influential figures in the Korean media.

18 Park Geun-hye and Choi Sun-sil Gate: The eighteenth President of the Republic of Korea, Park Geun-hye, was found to have collaborated with a close civilian aide, Choi Sun-sil, and committed massive corruptions with their economic community-like friendship. This political scandal resulted in the impeachment of the former president in accordance with the law.

4. Shin (神): I Treasure and Love My Self

The hottest topic in today's psychology is self-esteem. Self-esteem is all about viewing yourself as an important person and believing that you are an able person and deserve to be loved by others. Psychology emphasizes the importance of healthy self-esteem because you can establish your identity, enjoy happiness and peace in your heart, and can recover from pain quickly only when you have healthy self-esteem. In the past, however, how you view yourself wasn't considered important. Rather, human civilizations had been developed by the people who were taught how to make choices and decisions based on their ethical and religious ideas. It was after the introduction of psychology that pursued individual happiness that people were able to identify the common grounds shared by those who were healthier and happier than others. One of their common grounds was their positive self-image, and it led to highlighting the importance of self-esteem. The development of psychology became a blessing that opened up new ways for mankind.

Among Hon-Baek-Shin-Ui-Ji, the body of energy that makes you believe in and love yourself, is the energy of Shin. In other words, in psychology, Shin is the energy largely responsible for you determining your self-esteem that makes you healthy and happy and even love yourself. If Shin grows into a bigger healthier body of energy, you can view yourself positively, heal faster, and grow stronger. Shin is located in the heart, the organ with which you feel yourself. Of all internal organs, the heart is the only one whose activities you can fully feel. Perhaps there is nobody who feels how gas is exchanged in the lungs or toxic substances are filtered in the kidneys. The heart is the only organ we can touch and feel in the form of the pulsation caused by its function of pumping and circulating the blood. The beats of the heart, the home of your Shin, clearly demonstrate our feelings and emotions.

The Shin of the heart is the mind that governs our identity, and it makes us experience joy each time we overcome and break ourselves free from our limits. Therefore, the energy of Shin is fully involved in overcoming our pathological forces found in the energies of Hon-Baek-Shin-Ui-Ji. And whenever we overcome an obstacle, it sends us a gift of joy that fills our hearts. If there were moments of joy when reading this book, you can rest assured that those moments testify to the signs of affirmation sent by your Shin that you have expanded yourself by breaking free from your limits. A person who feels full of joy in his heart more often than others is a person with a strong power of Shin and higher self-esteem and self-love.

Among the energies of Hon-Baek-Shin-Ui-Ji, Hon is the master that guides you to the purpose of your being, while Shin is the loyal vassal who controls your identity. Therefore, the two work together as one team to supplement each other. When the energy of Hon makes you recognize your dignity, it lays the groundwork for the Shin of the heart to love and believe in yourself. And when the energy of Shin makes you love yourself, it awakens your mind to recognize the dignity of Hon. Therefore, these two bodies of energies grow together while supplementing each other to a certain degree. One cannot love oneself without being aware of one's dignity and cannot keep one's dignity without treasuring oneself. When the gap between the two energies grows, the growth of the preceding mind is suspended until the lagging mind catches up.

So, if you have a healthy self-esteem and consider yourself to be a good person, I want you to extend your love to God as well. But if you have a weak self-esteem that falls easily even with small failures, I want you to remember that you are created with love and blessings of God the Creator and therefore are always respected. Awareness and love of the heavenly God will brighten up your Shin.

In order to love and believe in yourself, you first have to be able to appreciate and value the existence that is you. Self-esteem that values yourself is the basic foundation of Shin. Psychology emphasizes that the framework of self-esteem is greatly influenced by your relationships with your family members, especially with parents. When the expressions of love that parents send to their children are accumulated, the children can grow their awareness that they are worthy of love. Since the framework of infant self-esteem is formed from the unconsciousness level, it must be the wholesome affection and trust that comes from the self-esteem of the parents themselves, because pretentious praise or action has little effect on the unconsciousness level. So, when parents send their sincere, trusting eyes to their children and share their affectionate love, self-esteem can be rooted in the child's unconsciousness mind.

If you are a parent, you should express your wholehearted love and trust to your child for your child's self-esteem. When you play with your child, you should sincerely enjoy the time you spend with your child, and even when you discipline your child, you have to do so while sincerely believing that your child will grow without any sense of self-pity or lamenting about your child being a disappointment to you. I feel pain in my heart as I write this part, because I am not able to fully believe in my daughter when I discipline her, and I am sorry and regretful for the times when I was not able to play joyfully with her, looking at her eyes.

However, you cannot put the blame on parents alone for the low self-esteem of their children. There is a big individual difference in the degree of absorbing parents' love depending on the natural born tendency. There are cases where a good self-esteem is established with a little love, and cases where a low self-esteem is established with abundance of love as well.

Lack of parental love in childhood does not necessary mean you can never have the foundation of self-esteem either. Self-awareness about you being a precious and valuable being can help you establish the roots of self-esteem just like the parental love you receive in childhood. So, if you think you have a low self-esteem, you have to ask yourself if you are not acknowledging yourself.

In terms of psychoanalysis or psychology, when your self-analysis tells you that "I have that mind now because of such and such influence from my parents in childhood," it is only a measure to understand you. Therefore, it is not a conclusion that tells you "Therefore, I can never change." Psychoanalysis through childhood experience is a therapy intended to give an opportunity for the Shin of your heart by telling yourself, "The uncomfortable mind I have now is a misunderstanding arising from the pain of a child. Now console my pain, let go of the misunderstanding, and live with the consciousness that is appropriate for my age." When analyzing yourself with psychoanalysis and psychology, it should never lead to the grudge against your parents in a conclusive view. It is not a way of understanding and loving yourself: rather, it is a means of abusing yourself. That also goes against what psychoanalysis and psychology pursue.

If you have been able to build a healthy self-esteem thanks to your parents who showered you with love from your childhood, thank your parents with all your heart. I hope that you will keep that basic frame strong and healthy throughout your life so that your parents' devoted love for you will never go wasted. If you have a low weak self-esteem because of your parents, please wholeheartedly sympathize with your parents, because your parents were not able to develop a good self-esteem and loving heart for the lack of love from their own parents, and therefore it was difficult for them to express love to you. In this case, just feel proud of yourself and love yourself for having grown up to be what you are today despite the lack or absence of love from your parents.

We are all previous beings capable of loving, regardless of whether we have received much or little love from our parents, because we are all a part of the Almighty, God. Nothing can deny our nobility. If anything, there are only people who fail to remember their own nobility. You have to remember that you would not even exist now if you were not a noble being blessed by God. Just the fact that you exist today is the proof that you are a noble, precious being.

A while ago, the singer Lee Hyo-ri[19] talked about her experience of a counseling treatment at a talk show called *Healing Camp*. She said the counseling made her realize how much she cared about what others thought about her and how little about what she needed for herself, and how negligent she had been to her own needs. She did not buy soft towels to dry herself after taking a shower or feed herself with good food. She left her fridge almost empty while treating herself carelessly and feeding herself with unhealthy alcohol. She apologized and told herself that she was sorry for having been so negligent, and she confessed she found happiness by reconciling with herself. After the reconciliation, she said she had found a way to love herself with her constant efforts to turn the meaningless gold she had accumulated into the rice she needed. Her confession showed reviewers the natural beauty of Lee Hyo-ri who restored healthy self-esteem.

I want you to do the same and check and look around yourself. Do you provide yourself with what you should provide to the one who is dear and precious to you? If you truly love yourself, shouldn't you watch comforting and inspiring dramas instead of immoral dramas, and positively funny variety shows instead of dehumanizing sadistic ones? Shouldn't you prefer a wide variety of healthy foods over packaged or fast ones, and when you do something that is rewarding and makes you happy, shouldn't you be able to be patient and endure pain and obstacles? The one who loves and cares about one's self is the one who knows how to reflect and contemplate to find out what is ultimately good or bad for one's self. The efforts of taking actions on the results of your contemplation is the heart that treasures your self, while at the same time a process of making yourself precious.

If I may borrow Lee Hyo-ri's expression about how to make yourself a valuable being, it is to follow what your mind tells you instead of reacting to whatever life throws at you. Following what the mind tells one is the attitude of those who have a high self-esteem. Following your mind and putting out efforts to turn gold into rice is an arduous process, but you can build self-esteem only when you try hard and find joy in your efforts. Lee Hyo-ri seems to have found the way to love herself through the counseling. The food she cooked herself and shared on her social media looks delicious and healthy. She is living with honesty and pride, following her beliefs and practicing love for animals that bring her happiness and the sense of a rewarding life. She is now unfolding the Shin of her heart after expanding herself from a sexy female singer to a woman with beautiful humanism and sexiness. Let us be committed to reflecting on what is good for us and make ourselves worthy by trying willingly to live according to our own thoughts. The only existence that can make you a precious being is you, yourself.

Those who care for themselves and treasure themselves are physically healthy as well. When you cherish yourself, you are destined to become healthy because you fill yourself with the things that are good for you, while providing yourself with healthy and nutritious food and working out to keep yourself in a good shape. Even when you are sick, you believe in the recovery of your physical health by focusing on your recovery process instead of sickness. You don't easily get disappointed with a sickness, and you don't become despondent and complain about getting sick so frequently whenever you get sick, all of which help fast recovery as well. We must be careful about our health because we have physical limits of physical body. The desire to look after and maintain our body is a healthy desire of Shin.

Also, there is another healthy desire of Shin: sexual desire. Sexual desire is what makes people reproduce and enables mankind to last. It is an indispensable desire for life. The pleasure of sexual intercourse that happens as the manifestation of love is also a function of giving vitality to our bodies and minds. Therefore, the purpose of sexual intercourse is not just the proliferation of offspring; it is a means of loving the bodies and minds of two involved parties. Sexual intercourse between two loving people – who care and love their bodies and celebrate their senses – is a fulfillment of desire of the healthy Shin that loves themselves. Self-esteem guarantees not only our mental health, but also physical health and pleasure.

To live a joyful life both mentally and physically, you should be able to protect yourself and treasure yourself. You can see how healthy your self-esteem is from the way you protect yourself in an unexpected situation. A few days ago, I went to a public bathhouse and came across a lovely old woman who volunteered to scrub my back. I usually don't like my skin being scrubbed hard, but I accepted her offer gratefully. But she scrubbed my back harder than I had expected. It was painful and I wanted to stop it, but I could not ask her to stop more aggressively. I just cried out, "You can stop now because it must be tiring you." She was exercising her compassion for others, and she scrubbed my back harder. She didn't stop until she put soap on my skin and scrubbed more as the last step. As a result, the back was seriously scratched. After the bath was finished and I dried myself, the skin became thinner and started to itch, and when I put lotion on it, my skin was so sore and painful that the pain made me jumpy. For the following two full days, I suffered from discomfort and pain whenever my cloth touched my skin, during which time I reflected on not having been able to protect myself.

I should have been honest, expressed myself more clearly and protected myself by telling her, "You are scrubbing too hard. It's painful. Please stop." But my dishonest and timid expression did not stop the old woman, and eventually it did not protect me, and it did not do anything good to the old lady either. Whenever I felt pain, my gratefulness for her favor was diminished, and the old lady did not have the opportunity to realize how her favor can hurt somebody unintentionally. I was able to realize that my self-esteem needed to be improved thanks to this absurd episode that happened at a time when I believed I was loving myself adequately.

The power to honestly express our own thoughts and feelings comes from our belief in ourselves and love that protects ourselves. We cause wounds to ourselves when we fail to be honest to our feelings and therefore fail to protect ourselves. When we are misunderstood and hurt because we failed to express ourselves honestly, it shows in the form of self-pity. In our society, there are many people who are hurt and suffer from self-pity all because they could not be honest to themselves. Perhaps that's the reason the book *Courage to be Hated*[20] could become one of the longest steady bestsellers.

Self-pitying people get easily annoyed. Annoyance is a general expression of disappointment over trivial situations. They snap easily when the bottle does not open easily; when there are a lot of typos in their writings; and when they don't like the food that they order in a restaurant. The annoyance that happens frequently in everyday life is the deep subconscious self-pity expressed on the face in the form of disappointment. The disappointment grows into despair when this self-pity spreads not only to the subconscious level but also to the conscious level. When we cannot find the light in the darkness of despair, we deny our existential value and the existence of true love in this world, and this denial draws us into a deeper despair.

The most reliable prescription to heal self-pity that draws us deeper into the pit of darkness is honesty. Taking actions while believing that it is okay to be honest will heal and even prevent the self-pity. Even if others refuse to acknowledge your honesty, you will be unhappy about it, but you will not self-pity yourself. But if you do not reveal your thoughts and feelings to others when you are refused by them, it will lead to self-pity. Honesty is the only shield that protects you.

Honest expression of yourself protects and defends you while at the same time giving you an opportunity to correct yourself when you take a wrong direction. It's because when you reveal your true self to the world, you encounter barriers resulting from your shortcomings, and it inspires you to reflect on and think twice about yourself. Ultimately, the frankness coming from healthy self-esteem is an opportunity for self-protection, as well as an opportunity to free yourself and rediscover yourself. If you do not honestly reveal yourself, you cannot find a chance to find yourself. Let's be frank and transparent for self-emancipation and a new self-discovery to protect ourselves from self-pity. There is no reason for us not to be honest, because we are precious and beautiful enough to be loved. Honesty is the beginning and the completion of healthy self-esteem.

We develop self-pity when we are hurt because we have not been honest, but we also develop self-pity when the values we believed in crumble down. When you lose faith in the people you trusted, the things you believed in, and the values you stood by, and you become overwhelmed by the resulting disappointment, you are likely to pity yourself, and this self-pity can also change you drastically. When the Park Geun-hye and Choi Sun-sil scandal broke, the approval rating for Park took a plunge to 4%. The rating indicated that even those who had fully supported the former President Park acknowledged her wrongdoing and stood accusing her. But her approval rating made a slight improvement when the investigation revealed further details about the scandal. Some politicians, such as former governor Kim Moon-soo[21], had a quick change of heart and objected to her impeachment even though they had called for it in the beginning.

They must have endured more serious self-pity than they had felt in the beginning after they found out more about the wrongdoings committed by somebody they had trusted and supported. The pressure of self-pity that they felt is not even comparable to the sense of loss suffered by those who did not support her. When the pressure became overwhelming, they would justify their actions by saying, "what is a big deal about it," or "you are worse than her."

If disappointment and despair are the apparent manifestation of self-pity, the blatant refusal to acknowledge one's own wrongdoing is the fallout of the distorted self-pity. We frequently experience people who seem to acknowledge their wrongdoing and are remorseful about it when the wrongdoing is only partially exposed, but drastically change their attitudes and refuse to have done anything wrong when their wrongdoing is fully exposed. When you are accused by somebody for having done something wrong and feel your wrongdoing is not a big deal, you have to calm yourself by telling yourself that your hidden self-pity is manifesting itself in the form of refusing to accept your wrongdoings. You have to acknowledge your wrongdoing by raising your self-esteem that went down by your self-pity, while comforting yourself by telling yourself that it is okay to acknowledge your wrongdoing because it doesn't collapse your existence as the result. The courage to acknowledge your own faults honestly expands your Shin. Therefore, honest acknowledgment of your own faults is the manifestation of excellent self-esteem.

The process of comforting oneself and comforting each other restores self-esteem by healing self-pity. Those who changed their stance from supporting impeachment to objecting to it need solace to recover their self-esteem. Just because the former President Park committed many wrongdoings doesn't mean the many values you tried to abide by are collapsing, and it also doesn't mean the time and efforts you had put forth will be wasted. Therefore, they desperately need to be comforted by telling them that it is okay.

Three Steps to Raise Your Self-Esteem as a Precious Being
Step 1: Recognize that you are a precious and lovable existence.
Step 2: Try to follow your heart as you live.
Step 3: Protect and extend yourself with honesty.

Now, we have to protect ourselves we call "I" so that we will not get hurt by anything and love ourselves properly so that we can accomplish what we desire, because what we call "I" is a precious and lovable being. If you have established the frame called self-esteem, now is the time to put flesh called "self-love" over that frame.

First of all, in order to love yourself properly, you have to be able to love the negativity in your heart. We always and routinely grow negativity in a corner of our heart. It grows in the form of anxiety, inferiority, disappointment, lethargy, and doubt. Moreover, stressful and tiring situations give rise to all kinds of dark emotions and thoughts. It is natural because pathological energies can flourish in the cracks between the energies of Hon-Baek-Shin-Ui-Ji.

You do not have to feel guilty about those negative emotions. It is natural for us to be troubled at the moment. Whatever thoughts we have in our mind, they are justified, even if those are negative thoughts. So even ourselves should not be allowed to criticize our own thoughts. We may be full of immature emotions, or cowardly, nonsense imaginations, but they are all justified and natural. Therefore, we must love those justified thoughts, because they are parts of our heart and ourselves, and those are the areas that are known only to ourselves and we are the only beings that can love them.

We have to accept our negative thoughts as being natural, sympathize with them, and comfort ourselves, telling ourselves that it is all okay, as if we are observing the thoughts of others. We have to love them until we really come to terms with them. Only then can we see our true heart that lies beyond the negative thoughts and feelings. And we can see the innermost true heart – the heart that is completely the opposite of what you feel at the moment – that has been waiting to be discovered. Resting behind the doubt that others do not understand your heart is your desire to give your sincere love to the others. Resting behind the anger against the world for not recognizing yourself is the love that makes you wish to give all of yourself to the world. We can feel joy when we come into contact with our true self in that way.

Since humans are the beings comprised of complex mentality, one thought is always accompanied by numerous other different thoughts. And contradictory as it is, most thoughts are accompanied by opposite thoughts. For example, when old people say that they wish to be dead, they always have the wish to live longer in their mind as well. Just because they say they wish to be dead when they wish to live longer in heart doesn't make them liars. Both thoughts are honest thoughts. And when we are angry at somebody, the anger is always accompanied by the wish to understand the person. Just because you are angry at somebody does not mean you have no desire to understand that somebody. Rather, you wish to understand the person as much as you are angry at the person. You simply don't recognize the opposite feeling because the opposite feeling can reveal itself only when the anger is relieved and comforted.

However, we condemn and avoid our feelings, or neglect and leave them to keep begging us instead of confronting them. Our anger that has not been comforted and loved by ourselves faces our subconscious instead of being relieved, and it ultimately blocks the true heart that is in the opposite side so that it cannot reveal itself. In this way, we lose the chance to meet the true self that is deeply embedded in our hearts.

The true heart of the true self is always within every one of us without exception. It is because it is human nature. We did not know that it was always with us because we did not love our heart. We can find another true heart beyond the darkness when we accept, embrace, and love our feelings and thoughts. Only those who love their own darkness and discover another sincere heart can find peace in self-satisfaction. The combination of inner light and darkness does not mean a gloomy gray area. Light and darkness integrated by love brings out a brilliant rainbow of colors and serves as the starting point of the expansion of genuine self-love.[22]

The crucial point in the good nature theory, the evil nature theory, and the Confucian Four Beginnings Seven Emotions theory[23] is the preposition that we all have to love our thoughts that pop up in our heart, be they evil or good. Everyone has two contrasting thoughts in one heart, and both thoughts are authentic. It is not the case where one is authentic, and the other is fake. Rather, we have to understand that one authentic thought is always accompanied by another opposing authentic thought. When you love your evil thought and childish emotions, the light is revealed. On the contrary, when one's light is revealed first, it requires you to acknowledge the opposite dark heart and comfort it. We have to love all our thoughts, always remembering that our heart is ambivalent by nature, until we become a perfect trinity. We can feel it, when the contradicting thoughts become gradually integrated through love, that in our nature, Four Beginnings[24] control Seven Emotions.[25]

We can also look at our own strengths and weaknesses correctly in life when we love all our hearts. We usually forget our strengths and blame ourselves in situations where we are disappointed with failures, or we forget our weaknesses and fall into remorse. However, the important thing is that we are mostly disappointed at the results only because we have tried so hard to reveal our own light. If you don't work hard to reveal your light, you don't really get upset too much even if things go south. You can just brush off the disappointing outcome. You get upset only when you have tried hard to reveal your light.

The greater your disappointment and anger is, the more it indicates how hard you worked to reveal your light. Therefore, when we acknowledge the emotions of failure and love it and comfort ourselves, we are reminded of how wonderfully we have revealed our light. Although the work may not have worked out well and others may not know about it, the frustration that only you can feel can make you think deeply about all your great strengths. "I am so upset right now because I have endured so much with my great strengths." The emotion resulting from failure is justified by your greatness, how ironic it may sound. The stronger your emotion is following a failure, the more you have to acknowledge the fact that the emotion is justified by recalling how proud you feel about yourself, and how brightly you shined your strengths. And you have to compliment on your strengths that you'd revealed during the process. This process of complimenting can calm down the storm of emotions.

Once you find peace after identifying your strengths, now is the time to quietly and peacefully think about your shortcomings, because you can look into your shortcomings with an affectionate outlook only when your emotion is calm. If you look into them hastily out of frustration, you are more likely to blame yourself and become more disappointed. You can love your shortcomings only when you look into your shortcomings when your mind is at peace. However, when your mind is at peace, you don't want to think more about what happened. If you acknowledge only your own strengths and move on from your failures, you will gain fewer internal assets from failures. In order for failure to become a mother of success, you must be able to view your weaknesses from an affectionate point of view. If you love your weaknesses from an affectionate point of view, it will expand your power to understand others and the world. "It had to happen that way because of my shortcomings." Therefore, I hope you will look at your weaknesses from an affectionate point of view and give comfort to your weaknesses. You can understand the world better when you love your shortcomings.

If you cannot identify your strengths and weaknesses in your life in a timely manner, you will not understand yourself objectively. If you do not know your own weaknesses, you are subjecting yourself to danger and hardship that you cannot deal with because you become easily aggressive to criticism or become arrogant when others compliment you. In the end, it results in putting yourself in harm's way. On the other hand, if you do not know your own strengths, you will not allow yourself any opportunity because you become easily intimidated in the face of your weaknesses, and you refuse to accept compliments and turn to distorted humility instead. Ultimately, you become the meanest person to yourself. Objectifying yourself is all about being satisfied at what you are now by loving all your hearts and acknowledging your weaknesses and strengths. You can protect yourself from danger with objective self-satisfaction and realize self-love that generously provides you with opportunities.

It is the dramas written by the scriptwriter Kim Eun-sook[26] where you can find numerous characters who are full of healthy self-satisfaction. Her drama characters are all confident and full of self-satisfaction, be they main characters or supporting ones. The male and female protagonists who are looking for love in her dramas candidly show off themselves and reveal their attraction to others. The female character is from a poor family but is never intimidated by the wealth of the man, and the protagonist who was raised and abused by a relative since she was little confidently demonstrates her attractiveness while remembering the love she received from her mother in childhood. Even the supporting characters who play the roles of the main protagonist's secretaries are the kind who speak up their minds bravely instead of being intimidated in the face of their boss. Kim Eun-sook's dramas are the feasts of characters who demonstrate charm with self-satisfaction probably because they reflect the writer's own healthy self-loving satisfaction.

In the interview, Kim Eun-sook showed how she clearly understands her strengths and weaknesses. She clearly recognizes and embraces the parts of her unpopular scripts that describe professional stories, and how she is more talented than any others in writing romantic dramas. So, she focuses on writing romance drama, which is her strength, and in the case of dramas that deal with professional stories such as *Descendants of the Sun*, she supplements her weaknesses by collaborating with other scriptwriters. And she achieved a success in a new genre drama such as *Guardian: The Lonely and Great God* by expanding her specialty to the fantasy genre where she was able to describe humanistic romantic stories with a more dramatic touch. I believe that the charming characters in the dramas written by Kim Eun-sook were possible because her brightly shining energy of Shin was reflected on her dramas.

Her dramas are widely popular because all her viewers are charmed by the characters who are full of self-love. When you incorporate your light and darkness and become unashamed of yourself, the bright energy emanating from Shin in the heart turns into charm that envelops your entire body. On the other hand, since those with a weak energy of Shin cannot emanate charm, they see the growth of physical desire instead. They constantly need to undergo skin procedures to make themselves feel better by looking prettier; they are always on a diet because they are always unhappy with their shapes; and they always worry about their health because they are excessively sensitive to all signs coming from their bodies. They often become addicted to sex or workout which requires constant confirmation of physical senses. These are the examples where the weak and sick energy of Shin has degenerated physical urge into desire.

If you look at them closely, you can notice they are abusing and tormenting themselves. They peel their skins off with chemicals or lasers for skin procedure, and they insert needles or threads under their skins in beauty regimen that is similar to a torture. Besides, if they receive such beauty procedures more than necessary, they ruin their beauty because their skins become thin and get damaged in deep layers. Repeated diets also damage health because it is a form of abusing one's self with starvation. The abused body gradually changes into a condition where you become fat even if you cut down eating and you become more and more overweight. If you become addicted to health supplementing food out of excessive concern about your health, you only damage your health more because your body is abused by pills and herbs. Working out even when you are sick is similar to the labor torture where you constantly whip your body, and not being able to find joy of life other than sex is the metaphor of self-pity.

As such, sick physical desires torment and abuse one's self, and eventually destroy it. Therefore, physical desire has to be restored into healthy urge, and you can restore healthy urge only when you acknowledge your own charm with self-satisfaction of Shin. Charm is your own unique individuality, and everybody has their own charm. Charm is not a relative evaluation that shines when compared to others but is an absolute personality that shines as it is. There are people who are pretty or handsome but not popular among people, and then there are people who are loved by many people even though they are not good looking. It is because there is only a difference between those who acknowledge their own charm through healthy self-satisfaction and those who don't, and also because charm is something that spreads out naturally when you recognize and acknowledge your charm properly.

Being satisfied at ourselves doesn't mean being satisfied at what we are now as the results. It is about being satisfied at ourselves because we know and love both our light and darkness and also because we know we are changing beings. We are always in the process of changing, and we always strive to move forward toward expansion. That is the reason we can be satisfied at ourselves despite our shortcomings, because we believe we can grow. What we are today is not the result; it is the process. We must be proud of our present greatness and dream the greatness to shine more brilliantly, and root for ourselves with love to overcome our shortcomings while feeling sorry for the present shortcomings.

We usually think that we grow through dissatisfaction with ourselves, but we are growing because our sole purpose is love experience, not because we are dissatisfied with ourselves. There is no stopping in the purpose of love experience, and there is no stopping in our expansion either. We are, as always, growing and expanding beings now and forever. Our soul does not stop even when our mind feels it's enough and wants to stop, because continuous expansion is the rule and law of the universe.

It is impossible to continue this unstoppable process by being motivated by such dissatisfied emotions such as complex and the sense of inferiority. If the growth is motivated by dissatisfaction, it is inevitable for you to fall into despair while asking yourself, "How long should I have to keep doing this?" and, "When will this suffering ever end?" It must start with self-gratification to continue the process joyfully and with a sense of accomplishment instead of any problem.

You don't need to blame or criticize yourself even if you sense your shortcomings because the present is always the growing process. All you need is an affectionate cheering. And there is no reason to become arrogant about yourself even when you feel proud of yourself because the present is always the growing process. We always have the natural right to dream of a new self. We need to celebrate our greatness, cheer and console ourselves for our shortcomings, and this process has to continue tomorrow and even the day after tomorrow. And knowing that the continuous expansion will last forever is awakening to the truth about our greatness having no limit. Growing while enjoying the process of rediscovering ourselves as beings with no limits is the second step for our Shin of the heart to accomplish self-loving expansion.

The charm and the unlimited greatness nurtured by self-gratification becomes the light that shines the world. In fact, it has to become the light that shines the world. We feel happiness when we appeal our charm to people and feel joy when our greatness is used for the good of the world. Hiding our light within us and keeping it from others' view is self-betrayal. Therefore, we must find and create opportunity to reveal the light of our identity that we have grown for the sake of our happiness and joy.

It does not have to be a significant opportunity. Any situation or position where we can reveal and express ourselves will do. For example, we can express our compassion and wisdom to console and council our friend who is in pain. It is also good to express our pain in whatever way so that those who are in similar pain don't have to feel they are alone. Posting messages or uploading photos on social media to express ourselves is also a good idea. Communicating with the world through your blog is also a wonderful idea. Showing your talent through interest groups or clubs is charming and enjoying hobby activities is also beautiful. Whatever method you choose, all moments in which you reveal yourself as a being with objective self-gratification become the light that shines the world and the joy for yourself.

I am revealing myself to the world by practicing medicine professionally. I appeal my humanistic charm by counseling and conversing with patients, and I deliver my greatness through my examining and treating activities. I reveal my faith by making comments to news articles, and I live by the principle of sharing my treatment methods with my peer Korean medicine doctors through writing and making resources available. I haven't made significant progress in revealing myself and making myself useful as a neighbor and friend yet, but I hope that my fatal charm and unconventional greatness can shine the world more brilliantly by discovering more situations where I can be used. And that wish is the motivation behind my writing this book. Writing this book for me is a big challenge while at the same time the joy of revealing myself. Therefore, I am writing this book for the sake of my happiness, and I am always happy even though it is difficult to write this book because it is the process of loving myself. I am hoping that my joy and happiness will be shared by all through this book, and the dream of expanding myself is the completion of self-love that makes me happy and joyous.

Be it big or small, your light is essential to the world. You are in this world because it is absolutely necessary. The world needs your little light, and sometimes, the world needs your big light. The world is in need of you every moment as a member of your family, your society, our planet Earth, and even our universe. Therefore, I hope you will always express yourself with the power of the objective self-satisfaction. It is okay if it is not perfect. Revealing yourself will be another beginning of expansion because you are currently in the process of expanding. Expressing yourself to the world just as the way you are now will make you happy and pleased, and make your heart beat more dynamically, eventually perfecting you so that your energy of Shin shines brightly.

Three Stages of Self-Love through Loving and Expanding Your Self
Stage 1: Love your light and darkness and integrate them
Stage 2: Always see your self as a being in the growing process
Stage 3: Present your self out to the world

Let's all cherish and treasure ourselves, so that we can generously love, protect, and liberate ourselves and be confidently proud of ourselves. You are a very precious, beloved being to all of us. Now, let us love all our hearts and gratefully accept them as they are, while presenting to the world our selves that we discover anew every moment as an expanding being. You are a great existence that is in need for us all. Your brilliantly shining Shin carries joy to every part of your body by flowing along your veins at the beat of your heart, revealing how precious and lovable you are from head to toe, and becoming the greatness in all your deeds.

Don't you ever worry about your greatness and preciousness going the wrong way. You just need to practice with confidence that you can always put yourself in the world, so that the mind that treasures you more than anything else will not turn into selfishness. And you just also need to keep the mind that cherishes and treasures you so that the confidence that you can always put yourself in the world doesn't turn into arrogance. Your self-esteem and self-love will be combined as one and will safely and joyously grow your Shin, and therefore, all you have to do is to firmly believe in yourself. The beauty and greatness of being that flows from your heart and emanates are becoming the lights of the world every moment. Ultimately, the brilliance and greatness of our existence that sputters out from all our hearts are dominating this world.

Endnotes

19 Lee Hyo-ri: a former member of a Korean girl band, she was a singer and entertainer famous for being voluble and for her candid expressions and opinions.

20 *Courage to be Hated* by Kishimi Ichiro and Koga Fumitake.

21 Kim Moon-soo: a Korean conservative politician, he is the former Governor of Gyeonggi Province in South Korea.

22 *Owning Your Own Shadow* by Robert A. Johnson.

23 The Theory of Four Beginnings Seven Emotions: a Confucian theory about four beginnings about the good nature of humans, and seven emotions that refer to raw human emotions. The claim that the four beginnings are the original nature of human beings and the claim that the seven emotions are the true nature of humans have been the main theme of Confucian arguments.

24 Four beginnings: good nature of human.

25 Seven emotions: raw human emotions.

26 Kim Eun-sook: a famous Korean drama writer who wrote numerous popular hit dramas.

5. Ui (意): I Love Others

You love your life, you love God, you love the world, and you love your own self. Now all that is left to love is the others. In fact, the first subject that comes to our mind when we say we love something is not yourself or God; it is somebody other than ourselves. Since the love you share with another is the ultimate destination of love, Ji-Hon-Baek-Shin, that I've addressed previously, is the cornerstone you need to love somebody properly. And Ui, the last energy that I introduce in this book, is the body of energy to trust and love others. So, when we believe, sympathize with, and love each other, the energy of Ui will expand, but the energy will shrink when we doubt and deceive each other. And as the energy of Ui grows, we love our family and friends more deeply and have stronger power to love more people.

Ui is located in the ovaries and testicles where reproductive cells are produced. The ovaries and testicles produce the only incomplete cells that contain only half the genetic information. And these cells enable the miracle of giving birth to perfect life by combining with the reproductive cells of others. That is the reason Ui – the energy that guides us, the imperfect beings, to the way of becoming perfect beings through relationships with others – is situated within our reproductive cells.

And the relationship that is most intimate and affectionate to us is the relationship we have with family, which is established through the combination of reproductive cells. Families eat together, live in one space together, and share everything in life together. Ui creates a healthy desire to pursue the convenience of life and provide basic necessities for families, such as food, clothes, and shelter. When we eat delicious food, we think of people we love and want to share it with them, and when we find some convenient and good products, we also want to share it with people we care about, or give them to our loved ones as presents. Therefore, the more we love one another, the more abundance and convenience of food, clothes, and shelter we create. The material growth that human civilization has achieved so far is credited to our healthy urge of Ui to share everything good with our family and other loved ones.

But when you are hurt by love and cannot trust people, the healthy desire of Ui gets sick and degenerates into obsession about food and materials. Obsession over popular restaurants, luxury products, automobiles, and house is our struggle to fill the void left in your heart when you cannot trust anybody. The fact that modern society is becoming more and more materialistic is a proof of many people who are lonely because they have issues with their relationships with others.

Most life problems are caused by inability to love others properly. Materialistic problems such as financial problems become only a passing process when you share them with people you love and you have smooth loving relationships, but when you don't have smooth loving relationships, they become the black hole in your life. How good would it be if we could all share love with others? What should we do to love others properly? Love is so important, but why is it so difficult for us to understand, accept, and forgive others? If this problem is resolved, we will be able to resolve most of the conflicts and pains we experience in our lives. Perhaps, if you live in love with someone completely, you can easily guess that you will appreciate life and enjoy happiness. But it is too hard to love. You tried to love, but it is hard to give it with love, and it is hard to accept it with love. We have to start with thinking about "why is love so difficult?"

The reason why we find loving so difficult is because of the problems of others that are unacceptable and unforgivable. Those problems and limitations that we really cannot accept and forgive take away our opportunities to experience more love.

In particular, in relationships with people close to you, these problems cause big conflicts and pain over trivial things. If we can tolerate and understand their problems and limitations, we will be able to love them more broadly, share more, and live more fulfilling lives together.

In fact, the fundamental resolution to this problem was found a long time ago through psychoanalysis. It was found that the unbearable and unacceptable problems of others are the result of the reflection of your inner self. We can be angry with injustice; deny the things that go against our preferences; and dislike something or someone according to what we think are right and wrong. It is natural for us to be angry with injustice, and, therefore, anger itself is not a bad feeling. And everyone has the freedom and right to dislike someone or something. Just like we would like the yellow and dislike the blue, we can like the person A and dislike the person B. Just because experiencing love is our existential purpose doesn't mean we should love everybody.

Natural anger and dislike feelings do not interfere with love. Natural anger boils up at the respective moment and disappears with the passage of time, and all that you need to do with somebody you don't like is to turn your eyes away from them. Therefore, it doesn't stop you from loving something. You are free to dislike something or somebody and tell yourself, "That person is really distasteful. So annoying." This much antipathy does not disturb love.

The problems that are serious enough to interfere with our love arise when the problems of others or your difference are more than just dislike, and you cannot tolerate them each time you are faced with them and you become compelled to do something in your mind, such as cursing, if you cannot blatantly display your emotion. Such strong emotions interfere with your ability to love the specific person you hate, as well as all other objects. And those kind of strong emotions and feelings, without exception, are the internal reflection of your mind that is similar to the other person. When we notice the sign of problem that is not deeply embedded appearing in the other person, we simply dislike it. But when the problem that is deeply embedded in our subconsciousness appears in the other person, we cannot tolerate it at all. Therefore, the disadvantage of somebody that we hate is our own problem as well. If an intolerable problem keeps appearing in the other person, and if you cannot put up with it unless you vent your strong feelings outwardly, you have to look into your inner self instead of turning your attention to the other person.

Usually, the heart that projects your inner self to the other person is a heart that is settled as your own unconscious shadow. The unconscious shadow refers to the mind that rejects and negates itself and refuses to accept it as it is. So, you often don't even realize that mind is your own mind. The human mind is complex and stereoscopic by nature. You can love at the same time, you can dislike something; you can desire something and you can reject it at the same time; you can also like to work and you can like to play at the same time. Just because you love something doesn't make your dislike a lie; just because you strongly refuse something doesn't mean your sincere desire for it is gone; and just because you like to play doesn't mean you dislike working. All those conflicting minds are genuine. That's the nature of human beings.

However, we find it really hard to acknowledge these conflicting minds. We tend to consciously accept only the light as our true mind. We aggressively reject something claiming that it is not right and ignore and brush off the desire to have it – the desire that is found in another corner of our mind. All these ignored and neglected unconscious shadows build up into a power. When it grows too big to bear, it is projected on to others and is expressed in violent reproach and unacceptable anger.

If you are harboring too-sensitive anger toward and criticism of your spouse's minor mistakes, you must realize that you also wish others to be more tolerant to you and make you feel comfortable when you make mistakes. And you also have to acknowledge that, unlike your desires, you are struggling not to make mistakes in reality, and comfort and care for yourself. When you are angry at the disadvantages of the child that resembles you, you can love the child only when you realize that you are dissatisfied with your own shortcomings, forgive yourself, and comfort yourself. Whenever you are angry at others beyond your control, you have to recognize that the same problem is in your inner self, and that it is part of your genuine mind, and heal it with love. Only then can you have the obstacles that interfere with love removed. It was not the others that made it hard for us to love others; it was the shadows that we have within us.

The area where we can most often observe the people who cannot love others because of their own pain reflected on others is the internet and the malicious comments people make on websites. The malicious comments are the clear trail left by those who cannot tolerate, cannot resist, and cannot control the urge to vent their anger. Within the hearts of those who make malicious comments is a large shadow that interferes with the loving heart, and when it finds someone who has a common element with the wound, they express their anger and hatred in a persistent manner. Those who project the wound to others keep their focus only on the others, so they do not notice that their reaction is strange. That's the reason the same pattern is repeated.

It is natural for most of us to get angry when we read articles about the Park Geun-hye and Choi, Soon-sil scandal and all the corruption that had been committed. But within the hearts of the readers who leave all those vicious and malicious comments on those articles is their desire to build wealth even through corrupted ways just like they did. And you become compelled to make vicious and malicious comments because your desire is reflected on the other when you see somebody who is living by the desire that you have while you are trying to live as a righteous person while working hard to suppress that desire. And you also have to realize that life is so hard and exhausting for you that you let such desire grow so big within you. Therefore, you have to be proud of yourself for trying to be a righteous person; comfort yourself for enduring hardships of life; and root for you, telling yourself that it is natural to develop such desire and that everything will work out just fine for you. When you care for and heal your wound that is being reflected on others, you will be left only with natural anger and dislike and keep your commitment to love from cooling down.

Whenever I read those vicious comments, I pray for those who made those comments to recognize their own wounds. And the malicious comments that always break my heart are the ones made to articles about the rhythmic gymnast Son Yeon-jae. Son Yeon-jae has truly a lot of haters who leave numerous malicious comments to articles about her. Son was the best gymnast in the history of Korean rhythmic gymnastics, and she was a top-notch gymnast who ranked number five in the world. Although her objective performance deserves praise, she is attacked largely because she became such a popular gymnast.

Her celebrity-level popularity is credited to her excellent skills and beauty. Her beautiful appearance attracted media attention, and she was given privileges that result from the nature of capitalism. And it was her popularity that drew just as many haters who criticize her as the supporters who cheer for her. Her haters criticize her, claiming that it is unfair for her to receive special treatments from gymnastic associations, appear in TV commercials and enjoy more popularity than the top players in other sports genres when her performance records are less than them. However, finding more opportunities resulting from her popularity is the structural consequence of capitalism, and it is not her fault. Nevertheless, all those criticizing arrows are flying to the popular sports players like Son.

When I read all those irrational criticisms on news articles about Son Yeon-jae, I am amazed at all those numerous people who had worked and tried hard but were never given opportunities in our competitive society, and who were hurt during the process of working so hard to find opportunities at the present moment. Their raw criticism and hateful comments clearly show the pain of those who are upset to see a player who never won a gold medal getting more attention and popularity than those who won gold medals in international tournaments, while they struggle and work so hard to get the results they have now. I wish there was someone who would apologize to them for the hardships that they had to endure to be what they are now. I wish our society was no longer a society where only the records and performances are accepted as the criteria for opportunities. I wish they could confront their wounds and desires hidden in their shadows and heal them instead of targeting Son Yeon-jae.

Son Yeon-jae fulfilled her role as a player gracefully despite so many hateful comments, and recently she announced her retirement. I am so proud of this young lady and admire her for the way she moves forward courageously despite those attacks by her haters. I want to share her message about her retirement she'd left on Instagram, because it could bring healing to her haters if they apply the message for themselves. She wrote:

I am so grateful and happy because I know how significant the last 17 years have been to me, and how much I've learned and grown during those years. What I did during the time was more than playing sports. I became hardened. I learned how to accept outcomes that do not compensate for the efforts I put out while enduring hard and difficult routines, and I came to believe that my efforts bring me results someday in whichever way, if not immediately. I sometimes pushed myself to the limits, and I learned how to believe in myself more than any others. I believe that what I've learned through rhythmic gymnastics will be more valuable and strong power than anything else to me, to whom everything will be new from now on. I wish to be a gentle yet solid person, and a person who might not be gorgeous but integral. Now, I believe that I can be happier than ever doing all the things that I wanted to do, and I wanted to do for myself. And I really want to extend my appreciation to all the people who have been there for me.

I sincerely hope that her haters will become happy by getting enlightened like Son Yeon-jae did. I hope they will warmly embrace their shadows that they have been projecting on others.

Another reason we find it hard to love others is because we all have different desires. Humans are destined to be social animals because we cannot live as an individual away from groups, and we are beings with shortcomings. And we all live with different appearances and thoughts because those who are identical to us do not exist in the same time and space. Therefore, we all have different ideas about what we want to do. It is not easy to reach an agreement even among family members about what we like to eat, play, buy, and where we like to travel. Worse, each individual has different ideas about what they need to do and what they should not do. Therefore, when our suggestion or pressure on what to do is rejected by others, it makes us angry, and the restrictions on something result in clashes among us and end up hurting us.

Our feelings are hurt when our suggestion is rejected by others, because we naturally suggest what we think is good to others. And because we always want to be a free man, we find proposals made by others burdensome and unreasonable. For example, it is a form of love that parents force their children

119

to study so that they get more opportunities. However, when their children are not interested in studying or don't think it is necessary to study, they perceive it not as a form of love, but as a form of betrayal that prevents them from making their own free choices. So, the children respond to the parents with rebellion or indifference, the parents feel frustrated and upset about their children's response, and then the children – particularly those who trust and love their parents – become more rebellious and repulsive to the parents.

As such, we play a ping pong game with our thoughts and emotions about the things that we should and should not do. Too often, we fail to grab the ball and look into it to notice the love that is found within the ball of thoughts and emotions and return the love in the shape of love.

At this time, when someone yields, the problem is easily solved, and we treasure yield and sacrifice as our virtues. So, for all those years, we believed that in order for us to love, we have to hold our urge to do what we want to do, yield to others so that they can do what they want to do, and sacrifice ourselves. And we tried to endure the dissatisfaction and regret that are destined to follow sacrifice, even though tragically, the enduring efforts turn into the heart that desires for reward and cannot complete in the form of love. We think, "Is that all you can do for me after all that I have done for you?" and this complaint turns into a chuck of dissatisfaction that weighs heavy in our hearts. Even if you control your desire for reward and keep it from exploding, the heavy weight of dissatisfaction in your heart is destined to leak and seep out and try to find relief by venting at others. You try really hard not to do it, but ultimately your patience runs out and the condensed energy of the complaint explodes. You repeatedly fail to convince yourself that true love is all about enduring and sacrificing yourself till the end, and not showing it off. Therefore, you could not help mistakenly thinking that love was difficult.

But the idea that love is all about concessions and sacrifices is an illusion. The essence of love is not concessions and sacrifices, but the question of "what do I want to be?" Love cannot be a sacrifice because it is the result of the choices and processes to be what I want to be. It is only to become a being I want to be, and it is only a choice for my purpose. It is not a sacrifice but an opportunity. But we are making the mistake of focusing on what to do rather than thinking about what we want to be. We are in conflict with each other because what we want to do is different, but in fact, it does not matter what we do.

The space created by the division of the perfect and wholesome being is the world we live in – the relative world that is consisted of materials. The situations that develop in the relative world are the spatial delusions, and the question of "what to do" is only an illusion that will stay here for a short time before perishing. So, there is nothing that must be done, and there is nothing that should never be done. What we do is just what we seem to do by force depending on situations and it is only what we want to do.

This may sound weird but in fact everything in the relative world is consisted of such "Divine Dichotomies." The things that you must do are ultimately the things that you just want to do; you believe in the almighty power of the Creator but ultimately you live your life on your free will; everything is just an accurately calculated karma, but it is a matter of sensibility that will bring about such emotions as tears, pain, joy, and anger; we are precious beings but we have to be willing to offer ourselves to the world; and we all have different thoughts in our mind but we share the same mind that wishes to love and be loved. These kind of "Divine Dichotomies" are the basic principle of the relative world in which we live. Even though the world in which we live in is a delusion compared to the absolute world, everything is destined to be "this" while at the same time "that" because we are eternal and absolute beings. We can accomplish what we want with freedom and move forward toward a being as colorful as a rainbow when we understand and act upon this idea of dichotomies.

So, what you do while holding on to illusion is not important at all. The only thing that matters is the existence itself, and therefore, what is important is what we shall become as an existence and what kind of an existence we shall become. When holding on to something that is not important at all, it is difficult to love because it causes conflicts as the result of clashes between illusions, and you feel it's unfair when you have to yield. But when we dream of the being that we want to be, and when we make choices to be what we want to be, the beings become one even amidst clashes. Think about it! Think about what kind of a being you wish to be. Do you want to be a being who deprives others of their hopes and dreams? Do you want to be a being who hurts and wounds others? Do you want to be a being who goes against love? Perhaps there will be no one who lives with these wishes. Therefore, even if people have different beings that they wish to become, you don't need to be intimidated by the collision of existence. The collusion of actions invites destruction, but the collusion of beings creates a new world and invites new forms of love.

The reason we cannot love amidst conflict and collusion is because we dreamed of doing illusions, and also because we did not dream of being that we wish to be. Dream about and decide what kind of a being you wish to be as a parent, a spouse, a coworker, a neighbor, or as a friend. If the dream of being who you want to be is always kept in your heart, the opportunity to fulfill that dream becomes a joy, not a sacrifice. True love has the appearance of joy. Only when you concentrate on "being who I want to be," does the love for others naturally blossom with joy. Let us not forget that we became separated from one being to form relationships with one another, because we need people other than ourselves in order to experience our self. Because we cannot fully experience ourselves, we are experiencing ourselves through others and becoming the being that we wish to be.

It was by reading the book *Conversations with God* that I came to realize that the important topics of love are the "Divine Dichotomy" and "what kind of a being do we really wish to be?" At that moment, I felt my heart pumping hard, brain expanding, and the cells of my entire body vibrating. I had tried to love hard, and therefore had my inside full of the heavy and tiring baggage, but they all melted away like snow the moment I witnessed the essence of love. Ultimately, it was all for my own sake. It was the process of realizing my wishes and achieving what I wanted to accomplish. I cheerfully recalled what I'd done, and I accepted with overwhelming happiness what I became and what I was in the process of becoming. After all, loving others should be the same point as loving myself, not different from it. Only then it is the true love.

We have talked about sacrifice and concessions in the name of love so far and have justified psychological and selective violence against each other. If you are not really pleased when you make concessions, it can never be love. Love is the choice you make to be what you want to be. If we expect someone to give us concessions and sacrifices in the name of love, it is like violence against that someone. On the contrary, if we choose to sacrifice ourselves for someone, it is nothing more than violence against ourselves. We should no longer justify the violence of sacrifice in the noble name of love. The violence we call sacrifice eventually keeps accumulating with time and brings tragedy to all.

There are numerous righteous heroes who have demonstrated supreme sense of sacrifice and love for others. However, they would not have thought that all that mattered at the ultimate moment was saving the others and that it didn't matter if they died during the process. Perhaps they considered all lives as precious as their own, and I think they were able to become heroes because the mind that wished for their own survival and the mind that wished for the survival of others became one. So, I think they would have willingly chosen to risk their lives to be a being who loves others.

For us, love is an eternal spiritual instinct, and perhaps you have endeavored to wholeheartedly love just like I did. In the process, you must have been hurt and suffered, and it would have been exhausting and tiring. Let us now reconsider the endeavors and processes of love in terms of the essence of love. At the difficult moment you chose to make concessions to others, you became a person who could lay down your wishes. At the moment when you tried to share your values with others, you became a person who shared your life with others, even if the others did not accept it. At the moment when you rebelled against the oppression by others, you became a person who provided them with an opportunity to reflect on themselves. At the difficult moment you loved, you became a being who you have dreamed of. Since it was harder on you because you couldn't realize all that, now you can let go of that hard feeling by realizing what kind of a person you became at those moments. In the future, I hope you will always dream and take actions on "what kind of a person you want to be," instead of "what you want to do or should do."

Because our purpose is only a love experience, we are destined to always dream of love in the being we want to be. If your children insist that they hate to study and want to stop studying, you can dream of being a mother who loves her children while inducing your children to study based on understanding of the world. Or you can also respect your children's opinion and let them stop or take a break from studying and accept it as it is. What matters is not whether you can make your children study; what matters is what choice you make to become the mother who loves your children. Therefore, all you need to do is make the right judgment and decision so that the way you practice love is reflecting how much you love your children. A child who has grown up in the love of her mother will have the power to make her life happy no matter how much she studied or not.

If you want to become a person you want to be, you are free to make any choices for that direction. In fact, when we dream what we want to be, we have bigger freedom to choose, and our love flourishes in free choices.

Now, let's get rid of the misunderstanding that love is hard. There is no need to sacrifice unfairly for love. Never sacrifice for the sake of love. There is nobody and nothing in this cosmos that desires your sacrifice. The important thing is your being itself, and you can only go toward something that you want to be as much as you can love with joy. I ask you to recognize your wound that is interfering with your desire to love. You are the best person to find and heal your wound. We cannot give up love because there is no way to be happy without loving the ones we are together with. So, acknowledge that love is the realization of your being, remember that the barrier to love is within you, and take your first step toward true love.

Loving somebody other than yourself begins with trusting that person. It is important to believe that the behavior of the person that makes it difficult for you is not caused by the person's evil thoughts against you, and that the person is doing his or her best in their own way. But when we do not fully understand the other person's behavior, we doubt if the person is behaving that way out of some questionable intention. We worry if that person is not going to do as told, or we suspect if that person will misunderstand us and criticize us. Consequently, if you let yourself be overwhelmed with worries and doubts, you grow more dissatisfied and unhappier with the person, and the dissatisfaction and complaints form a vicious cycle in which they make it more difficult for you to acknowledge the other person's efforts. And, in doubt and dissatisfaction grow lies that break the trust among one another.

The energy that started from doubt and concern about others makes it impossible even to start loving, because they prevent the way to communicate with each other based on trust. Since worrying and doubting others can become the pathological source of Ui, we should believe that others are doing their best without ill intent. In fact, we do not act with any malicious intention of hurting and harassing others. When we fight someone, there is nobody who fights with the desire to make the opponent suffer and be tormented. The reason we fight is because it is difficult for us to make others understand us, and we are overwhelmed with our own pain. Think hard about it. Have you ever acted solely for the purpose of harassing and tormenting someone? Has anyone acted purely for the purpose of harassing you? Even for the hardened felons, the main purpose is to satisfy their desires. There is no malicious intent in the way we hurt each other.

Nevertheless, when people try less than our expectations – less, based on our own standard – we suspect them to have hidden intentions, thinking that they are not doing their best. But the best effort is a very subjective matter, and there is individual difference. We hurt each other not because we are not doing the best we can, but because we have limits. We are doing our best within our current limits. Here is an interview with Dr David Hawkins, who made me believe that.

Peace of mind comes from the way you look at the world. If you look at the world with compassion, you take into account the limits of human evolution. People are doing their best only within their capacity. If they are better and brighter, they will do better. Compassion is about accepting that someone's particular behavior is the limit of the person within the context of that time.

When I think about it again, the way I lived was my best. What made me struggle so hard was the best I could do. Of course, there were many regretful moments when I wished I could do better, but at that time, I was doing the best I could. Just because you have regret doesn't mean you did not do your best. There is no one who does not do their best like I do. The patients who suffer from depression are doing their best when they barely hang on helplessly, and the pleasure-seekers who neglect their families are also doing their best to fulfill their responsibilities in their own ways. Their best efforts might not satisfy our standard, but it is their best efforts nonetheless within the limit of the pain, wound, and misunderstanding that they have. So even if someone hurts you now, you have to trust them that they don't have any malevolent intention, and that they are doing the best within their limits. Even if their best efforts are far below our standards of best efforts. And being sincerely compassionate about their limits is the beginning of love.

I was very happy when I first read Dr David Hawkins' definition of compassion. Even though I became an adult when I did not understand other people or when other people made it difficult for me, I was so frustrated that I had to vent my frustration outwardly. In short, I would become overloaded within if I did not say anything nasty about the people I hated. So, I always found somebody to spill my frustration immediately when I started getting frustrated. Then my energy of compassion started growing stronger when I accepted the fact that those who made it so difficult for me did not really have evil intention, and rather, they were struggling in their own ways due to their limits, just like I was. Now, I can live without having to make hateful comments about others and increasing my peaceful happiness while expanding my compassion to a broader range of people.

The ROK President is being impeached[27] as I write this book, and I see many people who find it hard to believe in the common goodwill of all. He claimed that he acknowledged that she was motivated by good intentions, but it backfired because her methods were wrong, and he stressed the importance of legal procedure and methods. But for those who suffer from anger, it is so difficult to acknowledge her good intention that they can hardly hear the elaborating explanation that follows the statement. It was so difficult and painful for us to admit good intention in someone's wrongdoing because we have mistakenly believed that everything is all right as long as it is motivated by good intentions and it is your best efforts. People wrongly believe that tragedy can never start from a good will, but it is only a myth that is suspending the human evolution.

Human good intentions can also create horrific tragedies. It is much easier to think that a wicked man is responsible for the tragedy. That's what we believed so far. But good will is exercised by anybody without exception. But the outcome is decided by the framework within which the good will is exercised. Therefore, when we are stuck in the wrong frame, we create unimaginable tragedies even if it was our best efforts and good intention. Just because the outcome is a tragedy doesn't mean we can deny the good intention and best efforts. It is very important to acknowledge each other's good intentions and best efforts regardless of the outcomes. It is because when we believe in each other's good intentions and best efforts, we can correct the wrong result of the present, and we can heal our wrong frame with righteous logic.

Think about it. When my fault is revealed to someone, our reaction is to give excuse to justify our action and intention. And if the other people acknowledge our good intention and best efforts, we find it easier to acknowledge our fault and apologize and take responsibility for it. When our best efforts and good intention are not acknowledged, we cannot break the frame that keeps us in, and fall into the error of emphasizing our own good intention. Therefore, when we acknowledge and accept each other's good intention and best efforts, we can acknowledge faults faster and easier; heal the cause of tragedy and overcome the faulty frame with righteous logic. And the healing and growth made possible by righteous logic can more clearly liquidate the past.

I want you to sincerely express to the people who make it hard for you to let them know that you are aware that they are doing their best out of good intentions. When you let them know how you believe in them, they will realize the fact that they are hurting you. I believe that former President Park Geun-hye was doing her best out of her patriotism as she claimed in her speech. And I sympathize with her for having been a being that had been stuck within such big limits of her own. And I hope that many people will believe her good intention. I hope they express that they believe that she did her best out of good intention; that we are not criticizing her true intention; and that all we want from her is to acknowledge the results that came out of her best efforts. Only then can the former President Park stop emphasizing her good intention and her best efforts and objectively see how many people were victimized, deprived of opportunities, and witnessed the foundation of our society crumbling down. That trust can be an opportunity for a human being who is trapped within her own limits to overcome the limits and take the path toward forgiveness. That path to forgiveness can heal our society fast and thoroughly.

Humankind still has a lot of resistance in accepting that those who think we are evil have lived with good intentions while doing their best. So, it is very cautious to apply this story to real life. It is difficult to communicate the true intention correctly, and it could cause misunderstanding and hurt others. We still mistakenly believe that acknowledging good intention means forgiving all. That's the reason we do not acknowledge each other's good intentions with regards to personal or social problems while we dissect and criticize other people's frames and try to achieve integration only after correcting the wrongs. But this method slows down the development of society and human relationships too much. We have to change this order. First, we have to achieve the integration of trust and acknowledgment of each other's good intentions and best efforts, and then analyze and dissect each other's frames while being compassionate about each other's limits.

By changing the order, we can broaden our perspectives and identify the root of the problem without becoming obsessed with the superficial phenomenon of the problem we face. If you first analyze the problem of children's rude behaviors, criticizing and modifying the behaviors themselves becomes important, but if you believe in the children's good intentions first and then analyze their behaviors, you can see what was bothering the children when they demonstrated such problematic behaviors. And then we can see how to heal the mental discomfort of the children and what kind of beings they can be. We tend to become superficially obsessed with what other's did, but what matters is what kind of beings they can be.

This broad perspective obtained by trust-first analysis-later allows us to see the fact that the others are in the process of changing as well. Nobody knows how others will change. I once was the kind of person who could have exploded with anger unless I cursed at others at least, and at that time, I did not know that I would change this much to be what I am now. Nobody knows how far you, the reader of this book, will expand, and how much those who frustrate you will change. We are all beings with infinite possibilities. When you believe and analyze the good intentions and the best efforts of others, you can see the changes of their very beings, and you can also see the role you have to play to support those changes. And through that role, we get the opportunity to become the being that we want to be, and we can love even those we dislike for the realization of our beings. It is very natural that we like and dislike somebody, and we can love even those whom we dislike when we see their beings themselves instead of their behaviors. Now, you don't have to force yourself to try to like everything.

It may sound awkward to say that you love someone you dislike, but in fact, most of us love the objects of dislike already. For example, we have love-and-hate relationships with our closest family members, where we dislike each other while at the same time love each other. When your child refuses to listen to you, you don't even want to see your child, and when your parents don't understand you, you feel resentful and dislike them too. Even between husband and wife, there are numerous moments when you do not like your spouse. But we love them just as much as we dislike them. You can dislike and love others just like you love your family members, even though you sometimes dislike their flaws, as long as you realize that they are in the process of changing through the trust-first, analysis-later approach.

Just as our beings are the outcomes of processes rather than results, other people are also beings in the process of growing and expanding, and just as it doesn't matter what we do now, it doesn't matter what others did. Just as it matters what kind of beings we are becoming, it matters what kind of beings others could become. That's the analysis of compassion based on the trust-first, analysis-later analysis.

The analysis of compassion is not the same as unconditional tolerance; it is about interpretation that celebrates the growth of others based on the belief that being is love in itself. When we analyze based on our beliefs about good intention, we can love each other more easily and facilitate the evolution of human civilizations because we can smoothly improve many things with regards to our relationships — marital relations, parental relationships, relationships with coworkers, relationships with friends, relationships with boyfriend or girlfriend, political relations, economic relations and international relations. The change brought about by changing the order will broaden the range of your love like a miracle. So, I really wish that we can all witness how this small change of changing order can bring about miraculous changes in our lives and society.

Since we are divided from one being into several beings in order to experience ourselves, other people are ultimately our other selves. When I see people who have not expanded more than I did, I see my past in them. I think of my past when I was immature and could not move toward the essence of life in this life, identify with them, and cheer for them. I cheer for them, telling them that since they are the same beings as mine, they would become more free and happier if they can see the essence like I did. When I see people who have not been more evolved than what I was during the immature days in this life, I think that they could be what I was in my past lives that I cannot remember. I wonder if the ways how I've lived through the cruel histories of mankind are still remaining in them. I sincerely pray that they will achieve the expansion, in which they overcome the cruelty in this life. When I see people who are greater and more beautiful than I am, I see my future in them. I think to myself that such greatness and beauty must be found within my eternal expansion, and perhaps I can realize the same greatness and beauty by being an existence that is most true to myself. And I pray for their greatness to shine more brilliantly. I become humble in the face of the truth about "me being them, and them being me," and I feel exhilarating happiness. Therefore, we are the same single being, we try to love each other, and we become happy when we love each other.

Yet we are also a wholly independent being. We are one but divided beings and so we can only be different. Our appearances, characteristics, given fortunes are different and individual souls experience different stages. We have to respect these differences. And therefore, we should not force our own styles on others who have characteristics that are different from mine. We should not judge, with our own common senses, other souls who are on a different stage. In addition, we shouldn't allow others to intrude on our independence. Instead, we have to keep the healthy borders that do not intrude on others' free will and love each other. We should acknowledge others' styles, advise based on our experiences but not make any decisions. We should take it step by step so that others can accept it. We should protect our own independence. If we fail to keep the borders, not only us ourselves but others will become miserable. We often witness parents identifying themselves with their children or each other and becoming miserable because of it. We can only be happy when everyone's independence is ensured.

However, such differences and independence provide the motivation to love each other. If we only have people that are similar to us, we cannot encounter ourselves. We are able to experience who we are as there are those who are different from us. And love is the strongest experience that lets us encounter ourselves. When we meet someone who is different, acknowledge and accept the differences, we get to complement each other and become united. Just as putting together a puzzle by assembling the pieces with knobs and holes, we can become united as we can be assembled through our differences. That is how we become united, while loving each other as an independent being.

So present yourself to us just as what you are. There are a lot of people in this world who can complement your shortcomings. There are people who will find out what you have not thought of, possibilities to correct your mistakes, and courage and hope for you. Also, there are a lot of people in this world who need your strengths. There are people who need your comfort and encouragement, people who need to model after you, and people who need what you think and pursue. So when we admit each other's differences together, we become perfect beings like a finished work of a puzzle. That's the reason we try to love each other for the perfection of ourselves as individuals each with their own shortcomings.

We can be together because there are many beings that are different from us in this world. Our differences make the world beautiful and brilliant with various colors. I am glad that there are people out there who have thoughts, personality, and emotions that are different from mine, and there are people out there who have desires, hopes, and plans that are different from mine. In addition, we are all the same being because we want to love and be loved since we are originally one being. We are all the same because we share the same spiritual instinct to expand ourselves through our given lives, and we live our lives while doing our best with good intentions. We are all different because we are different individuals, and we are all the same divine dichotomous beings because we are one. Therefore, the way of love must also be done in divine dichotomy.

Because they are me and I am them, we can sympathize with each other, and we can share generously, and we can accept fearlessly. So, what I did to others is what I did to myself, and what I did to myself is what I did to others. By sharing generously and accepting fearlessly, we realize love that is integrated into one. If you really want something, you can provide it to others. The more you provide others, the more you will have it piled up in you. Because we are one, the heart that wishes true happiness for others and communal efforts to make it happen eventually become your own happiness.

Also, since we all live doing our best and with good intentions, there is nothing that we cannot forgive and be forgiven, and there is no reason why we cannot bless and be blessed. I just hope that the best efforts of others will expand beyond their limits, and that my best efforts will love beyond my limits, and we all go toward love that is united with apologies, gratitude, forgiveness, and blessings. Love is all about generously sharing and fearlessly accepting, while becoming one as we feel apologetic, grateful, forgiving, and blessed, and rejection is the opposite of love.

But we must love each other as a single, individualized being that admits and respects each other's differences. Intervening without respect for those who are not yet prepared is only a way to undermine and hurt their values. Also, no one should become subordinate to us for the sake of love, nor should I be subordinate to anyone for the same reason. Dependence that makes a life dependent on someone is the opposite of love, and respect for the way of oneself is love. The sober attitude of the mother bird when the cubs leave the nest is a great love that does not subordinate the young to herself. Therefore, it is a true practice of love to honor others who have made a choice different from mine and let them be and wait for them.

We must understand each other's differences, try to communicate that others can accept, and respect the choices others make in situations where communication is difficult. It is also the love to wait and believe that the way they take is eventually the process of love. We should not subordinate others in the name of protection, nor should we reject others for having taken a wrong way. We just need to be the mirror for each other, while repealing the results of our choices to each other. Our differences serve as the mirrors that can reflect ourselves to each other. The love of respect is all about us taking our own paths, while waiting for us to become one with love.

So let us honor and respect for the sake of wholesome love, while at the same time integrating and embracing and loving each other as one as well as different individuals. We can love while letting them be, and we can love while being together as well. Since love is composed of divine dichotomy, we can love one another in any case. Therefore, for us loving each other is simply natural.

Endnotes

27   Impeachment of the president: the 18th President of the Republic of Korea, Park Geun-hye, was impeached by the unanimous vote of the constitutional court in 2017. It was triggered by Park Geun-hye and Choi Sun-sil Gate.

6. Hon-Baek-Shin-Ui-Ji (魂魄神意志) and Our Daily Routines

1) Theorem of Hon-Baek-Shin-Ui-Ji

We are creators. Hon-Baek-Shin-Ui-Ji is a group of energies that determine how we should live, and what kind of creators we should be. We created our own life with the power of Ji; we create the expansion of God by the power of Hon; we create the world and the universe with the power of Baek; we recreate ourselves with the power of Shin; and we create opportunities for the lives of others with the power of Ui. Ultimately, what we create is everything, and therefore we are the great creators and as a group we are God the Creator. Now, when I call God, I call "God who is all of us." If the process of creation unfolded in the darkness before we understood Hon-Baek-Shin-Ui-Ji, understanding Hon-Baek-Shin-Ui-Ji opens the way to freely utilize our creativity.

In order to unfold Hon-Baek-Shin-Ui-Ji in accordance to our will and wish as creators, we must follow through the three steps of "Awakening-Understanding-Practice." Books are the means that usually guide us only up to the awakening and understanding steps. When I think about it, I have come across a lot of grateful truths that have filled my heart with excitement, but I have always felt a constant sense of despair when I tried to apply them in my life. It was because I was missing the third step, which is practice, that I felt the despair even though I became awakened and understanding by numerous books and the truths that were found in them. Perhaps readers of this book might experience the same sense of despair as well.

So, from here, I am giving you tips on applying the energies of Hon-Baek-Shin-Ui-Ji to daily routines. The tips introduced in this book are part of the laws of the universe we belong to. And when applied and practiced, you can easily tell how your understanding of Hon-Baek-Shin-Ui-Ji brings about changes in real life. I hope that readers will personally experience the power of Hon-Baek-Shin-Ui-Ji through these tips. I am sharing these tips here with readers because it is my wish for you to become inspired to practice what you've learned from this book in daily routines. And that process will solidify the three steps of awareness, understanding and practice by making you remember more laws of the universe on your own.

Theorem of Hon, Baek, Shin,

	Hon (魂)	Baek(魄)	Shin(神)	Ui(意)	Ji(志)
Definition	The power connected with the Creator	The power connected with the world	The power connected with oneself	The power connected with others	Power connected to life
Location	Pineal body	Cochlea	Heart	Ovary	Sole
Emotions	Glory	Peace	Pleasure	Satisfaction	Joy
	Anger	Fear	Sadness	Dissatisfaction	Depression
Consciousness	Dignity	Justification	Self-esteem, self-love	Selflessness, trust	Passion, relaxation
	Inferiority	Anxiety	Self-pity(loathing), disappointment	Suspicion, concerns	Indifference, obsession
Desires	Urge for respect and honor	Urge for goods	Sexual and physical urge	Appetite, urge for convenience	Urge to sleep, play, rest
	Greed for honor and fame	Greed for wealth	Sexual and physical greed	Greed for materials	Greed for pleasure and quick fortune
Myungsu	Faith and love for God	Faith and love for the world	Faith and love for oneself	Faith and love for others	Faith and love for life
Anti-Myungsu	Hatred	Resentment	Denial	Falsity (truth)	Irresponsibility (coercion)

2) Mind-Sacred Boundary through Hon-Baek-Shin-Ui-Ji

The first practical tip is the self-fulfilling prophecy that Hon-Baek-Shin-Ui-Ji can accomplish. Self-fulfilling prophecy is a psychological term referring to the phenomenon where what you think about yourself materializes in reality. For example, the more you think that you are attractive to the opposite sex, the more you actually become attractive to the opposite sex. On the contrary, if you think you are the type not attractive to the opposite sex, you actually become unattractive to the opposite sex. The self-fulfilling prophecy is all about what you think about yourself becoming what you really are in reality. Before the development of psychology, we thought that what we see in ourselves was what we thought about ourselves, but psychology proved in diverse ways that what we are is determined by what we think we are.

It is easy to believe in self-fulfilling prophecy, but it is difficult to change ourselves by our understanding of self-fulfilling prophecy. It is because we feel resistance about specifying and continuously believing in what we wish to become. So, it is not easy to reach the stage of changing ourselves in accordance to self-fulfilling prophecy. When you complain about the difficulty, you will be advised to believe until you become what you wish to become, to be more specific about what you wish to become, or to think more about your prophesy. The advice is correct, and not wrong, but it is not specific enough to give you momentum. That's the reason we could not change ourselves even though we believe in self-fulfilling prophecy. But if we understand that the main pillars of our consciousness are Hon-Baek-Shin-Ui-Ji, self-fulfilling prophecy to become what you desire to become gets easier. The self-fulfilling prophecy becomes a reality easily if you configure all of the existential forms you want within the context of Hon-Baek-Shin-Ui-Ji.

Hon-Baek-Shin-Ui-Ji are the five pillars of our mind. Be it positive or negative, self-fulfilling prophecy takes place in reality depending on which desired self-image is filled in which main pillars of the mind. It is the law of the universe in which self-fulfilling prophecy materializes in reality. In reality, our pessimistic thought does not easily turn into reality even though we sometimes hold pessimistic thought about ourselves, and we cannot easily change ourselves even though we try hard to be positive about ourselves. It is all because we can experience the materialization of our prophesy only when we have the full five energies of Hon-Baek-Shin-Ui-Ji.

If you want your prophesy about becoming someone who is attractive to the opposite sex, you have to ensure the following: determination and practice of Ji about continuously trying to become an attractive person; dignity of Hon about you being destined to be attractive; the energy of Baek about believing in everybody being equally attractive; the self-esteem of Shin about accepting yourself being attractive; and the warm compassion of Ui about recognizing the attractiveness of others. The same applies to negative prophesy. This is the law of self-fulfilling prophecy. Now, in order to be what you want to be, I urge you to forsake the absurd advice about being "constantly trying harder" and take advantage of the meaning of Hon-Baek-Shin-Ui-Ji instead.

Elements of Hon-Baek-Shin-Ui-Ji in Self-Fulfilling Prophecy

① Ji: Commitment

It is the consciousness of creating with the will of oneself. It is an awareness that I create my life according to my will and putting out effort through this awareness. The will includes harmonious efforts such as "sincerity, persistence, passion, commitment, courage, warmness and tolerance." In addition, it includes acknowledgment of the efforts you made in your life and confidence over future happiness.

② Hon-Baek: Destined Justification and Perfection

It is a consciousness about the justness and perfection by the law of the universe. The relationships formed in life or the opportunity given to us are all explained in terms of destiny instead of pure chance, and our perfectness is explained in terms of us being one with God. It also includes beliefs and values toward the purpose of life. It is a recognition of the spiritual purpose of accepting everything as it is, growing and evolving through the process, and enjoying freedom in glory and peace. Hon and Baek are separate energy bodies but act together as a team. They can be applied separately or bundled together into one.

③ Shin: Self-esteem and Self-love

It means faith and confidence in oneself. The faith in oneself is about believing in your goodness, beauty, and greatness, and it is the positive consciousness of believing that you can do it. Further, it is about realizing there is no limit to the growth of oneself and being born with greatness and divinity by nature. It is also a consciousness to love, care, and reveal oneself to the world.

④ Ui: Love

It means that the meaning of compassion, love, and consideration for others, such as other people and nature, should be included in the purpose you are after. Your self-image should be the being established through your relationships with others instead of the being that exists only in your head. And of course, that has to be love.

⑤ Integration= Appreciation, Forgiveness, or Blessing

It is appreciation, forgiveness, and blessing that binds the meanings of Hon-Baek-Shin-Ui-Ji together tightly. What integrates the energies of Hon-Baek-Ji-Shin-Ui are the forgiveness or appreciation for the reality that is given to you at the moment, and appreciation or blessing for the conviction that your wish will turn into reality.

Things become reality when you fulfill all meanings of Hon-Baek-Shin-Ui-Ji because when we think with all power of the main pillars of the mind, the universe resonates with our desires. Even if one or two meanings of Hon-Baek-Shin-Ui-Ji are missing, self-fulfilling prophecy can materialize if only by a small degree. It materializes only a little bit at a speed so slow that one can hardly notice. But when all five pillars are erected, it resonates with the energy of the universe and materializes into reality at a speed so fast that we can clearly recognize the change.

Since this change is a change that happens by becoming one with the universe, instead of on your own, I think self-fulfilling prophecy by Hon-Baek-Shin-Ui-Ji is a sacred boundary. It is a sacred boundary because we protect ourselves from all obstacles that are in the way as we become what we want to become, and the universe is there to protect us. It is also an inevitable prophecy because it is communication we make wholeheartedly with the universe. You can declare this sacred boundary and prophesy either to yourself or God. Whichever is fine. It doesn't matter to whom you declare them, but the best bet is to declare them twice to both, because it is like engraving them on both sides of a coin to complete a single coin. And if you completely break down the boundary between yourself and God and declare to both yourself and God at once, it will be the icing on the cake.

When explaining the inevitable prophecy and the mind-sacred boundary of Hon-Baek-Shin-Ui-Ji, there is a reason to list them in the order of Ji-Hon-Back-Shin-Ui-Integration. It is because that's the order of consciousnesses that is common to all humans. When faced with a difficult situation, everyone tends to try to endure and persevere with their own efforts

(Ji), turn to God when it is difficult (Hon), try to find answers in the world (Baek), and if it is still not enough, they turn to themselves and contemplate finding the reason for themselves (Shin), and finally try to overcome with selfless attitude for others (Ui). When we assess and think of something, we all go through a process of Ji→Hon→Back→Shin→Ui→Integration. Immediate effect will surface when following this order of sequence. Of course, it is not necessary to follow the order just as it is because you will get the same results anyway even if you follow a different order, but if you have the urgency and have to make it happen immediately, it helps to know the rule of following this order.

I found a way to build a strength to move toward the self-image that I want by disciplining myself with Hon-Baek-Shin-Ui-Ji and strengthening it by repeating the process myself, and that is the three-level composition. I was able to establish this three-level composition thanks to the book *Conversations with God*. *Conversations with God* explains that dichotomous classification such as good vs. evil and good vs. bad is not a process of truth, and that all divine truths are divided into three. The human being is a triad being consisted of soul-mind-body, time is consisted of past-present-future, space is consisted of here-between-there, and the process of realization of everything is consisted of beginning-process-result or awakening-understanding-realization. A divine completion is achieved when three becomes one.

Thus, it was composed by having self-fulfilling prophecy filled by the time elements of the past-present-future. For example, the meaning of Ji is filed with the reflection on the past, the determination for the present and the confidence about the future, and the same for other energies. Then I realized that the inevitable prophecy and the power of the protective sacred boundary are becoming stronger. Our present consciousness is determined by the past results and the thoughts of the future.

Since now is the time when the past and the future are united, the idea of fulfilling the past, present, and future of Hon-Baek-Shin-Ui-Ji completes the present consciousness.

In addition to this, I applied the three-layer composition to the time elements as well. Since everything happens at each moment as the combination of beginning-process-ending and the three layers of awakening-understanding-realization, I thought of overlaying the three-layer composition on all time elements. As a result, I completed the nine-step composition – 3x3=9 – by overlaying three time elements and three realization steps on Hon-Baek-Shin-Ui-Ji. The effect was truly amazing. At the time, I was practicing the sacred boundary through Hon-Baek-Shin-Ui-Ji for a painful situation. Then I experienced the relief of my suffering, and was grateful for it, when the completion of the nine-steps effectively eliminated all my longstanding sufferings all at once.

In Korean studies, number nine (9) is the number of completion. In the West, numbers begin with one and complete with 10, but in the East, it starts with zero and completes with nine. Therefore, number nine signifies the completion of everything, and that is the reason number nine is considered very important in Korean culture. Nine is the number you get when the number three where all sacred truths are completed and overlapped with each other (3x3). The sacred boundary and prophecy of Hon-Baek-Shin-Ui-Ji – created by that number of completion – makes you experience a realization so powerful that you cannot miss even if you tried.

When you think about it, the people who realized their self-fulfilling prophecy in the past must have been the people who'd filled in time by all means with regards to the being that they wanted to be and became awakened to its significance. Even if they did not know the meaning of Hon-Baek-Shin-Ui-Ji, or the Trinidad of times and steps, they were able to make their dreams come true by filling in the significances through their awakening to life and had their dreams to align with those significances. The universe has always resonated with those who dream of themselves with the meaning of Hon-Baek-Shin-Ui-Ji from the beginning of time. The more they filled it completely, the bigger it resonated and amplified. This is the law of the universe that has always been and will always be. And mankind has repeatedly evolved and reached the stage of unfolding this law into knowledge.

The inevitable prophecy by Hon-Baek-Shin-Ui-Ji is not limited to the enlightened ones. It has become a knowledge that everyone can understand, so here I introduce some self-fulfilling prophecies to make good use of this knowledge. As an example of the dream realization, I will show the composite meaning of Hon-Baek-Shin-Ui-Ji that applies to the popular dream of quitting smoking and my daughter's dream of rhythmic gymnastics training. And I also introduce examples of self-fulfilling prophecy through the rules given in our lives and the mind-sacred boundary that heals the mental wounds. These are some kinds of personalized prayers as well. I would like you to look at these prayers and take them for yourself as examples of your own self-fulfilling prophecy.

Prophecy on Parental Roles

There is a role given to each one of us in our lives. We accomplish self-realization by faithfully fulfilling our roles as a family member and as a member of society. So, firstly, I introduce the self-fulfilling prophecy about the role given to us. The role of a parent is a process of making a child grow to realize their limits on their own, and it accounts for more than half of the entire life to the respective individual. It is also the role of creating a driving engine for the child to run their lives, and therefore is the most noble and universal role for our humanity. It makes me happy just to imagine how brilliantly mankind can evolve if only we all fulfill our role as a parent properly.

① Ji: Commitment and the Creation of Life

* I am sorry that I have been tired and exhausted myself,
Because I could not exercise my will harmoniously in appropriate matter
In different situations in a proactive, broad, and gentle attitude that is required of a parent.

* Now, I stand by my child wholeheartedly, wait patiently, and fulfill my role
As a parent with harmonious and diversified commitments.
By doing so, I create the sense of reward and joy of a parent without tiring myself.

* I realize happiness in playing the role of a parent with harmonious and diversified commitments,
And fill my child's growth with happiness,
And bless the road that unfolds and leads to the happiness and prosperity of my family.

② Hon-Baek: Perfection and Justification

* I am sorry that I could not accept the process of becoming a parent with joy and truth,
Sometimes complaining it being difficult,
And failing to move forward toward the given opportunity of growth in glory.

* Since the fateful combination of my child and myself is the natural law and my soul's wish,
I am truly grateful for being a parent to my child,
And I am committed to fulfilling the role of filling my child with love in glory and peace.

* I will become a free being who overcame the limits of fate

Through the truth about realizing the limits I must overcome as a part of the role of a parent,
And growing while overcoming the limits one by one.

③ Shin: Self-Love and Conviction
* I am remorseful that I did not believe in my qualification as a parent,
While blaming myself for not being a good parent
All because I failed to discover my great and beautiful qualifications of a parent.

* Now I am a loving and caring parent who tries the best
Because I have a beautiful mind that truly loves my child
And I am in the process of acquiring great wisdom to guide my child with that loving heart.

* I will fully shine my sacred and great light on my child,
While loving my child with a bigger beauty in the future
And perfecting my wisdom greatly with my ever-growing love.

④ Ui: Love and Compassion
* I am remorseful that I have been treating my child in accordance to my greed
While subjugating such a precious being to myself,
Because I did not respect my child as a dignified human being.

* Now I am committed to respecting, embracing and loving my child,
Acknowledging that my child is different from me while trusting and blessing that my child's efforts and good intention are aligned as mine,
Because my child is a being just as precious as my being.

* In the future, I will sympathize and comfort the pain of my child,

Pray for my child to grow in accordance to her dream with that power,

And identify her happiness as my own.

⑤ Integration: Gratitude-Forgiveness-Blessing

* I am grateful for meeting my child,

Being her parent,

And establishing a family with her.

* I am sincerely thankful for the moments I had with my child,

I seek forgiveness for my shortcomings as a parent,

And I bless this moment when I am about to be born as a new parent.

* As a parent, I sincerely wish my child to be blessed with my happiness, growth and love,

And her happiness, growth and love to be passed down to my grandchildren,

And my blessings will last forever.

Prophecy on Rhythmic Gymnastics

This prayer is a prayer that I prayed with my child when my child was about to upgrade rhythmic gymnastics from the level of a hobby to a professional training. This is a prayer for a dream, but this was a dream marked by uncertainty, because we could tell if it was going to come true or not only by trying, and environmental and social conditions could affect its outcome. We don't dream only on dreams with certainty. In fact, most of our dreams are marked by uncertainty. For dreams with uncertainty, such as wanting to pass to the desired college or workplace and hoping to make some progress, we should focus on the process of moving toward the dreams and our beings, instead of aiming at the consequences. Only then the dream can come true as a natural law of the universe in a destiny where the dream is supposed to come true and avoid getting wounded by errors and mistakes when the dream is not appropriate, and the natural law will guide us on our journey toward the dream.

① Ji: Commitment and Creation of Life
* God, please remember my past commitment to rhythmic gymnastics
And remember the moment when I felt good and the sense of rewarding in rhythmic gymnastics.
Please support my hard work and commitment as I take the challenge in rhythm gymnastics.

* Please let me believe that there is a reward that will improve my ability
If I endure physical pain and horrible criticism with my commitment and love for rhythmic gymnastics,
And give me strength to hold on as I take up this new terrifying and difficult training.

* Whether I continue or stop being a rhythmic gymnast,
Let this difficult training be an opportunity to cherish and love my life.
Let me create a happy life with my hard efforts and my power.

② Hon-Baek: Perfection and Justification
* God, the fate that started rhythmic gymnastics was great,
And it was good to heal and grow the pain of my heart with rhythmic gymnastics.
It was God's love that I encountered rhythmic gymnastics.

*I believe that God is always with me in my new training.

I know that training is hard and difficult, but it is a destiny to become a good player.
I believe this difficult training is meaningful because I am with God.

* I believe that God always loves me when I become a rhythmic gymnast.
I know that God will always be with me even if I find another dream
And that He will always love and be with me whatever I do.

③ Shin: Self-love and Conviction
* God, I found my greatness while learning rhythmic gymnastics,
Which made me healthier and happier.
Please praise and commend what I am now that is created by rhythmic gymnastics.

*I know this is hard to see my strengths because I am just starting this training now.
But I can find my greatness in new training in the future too.
Please be proud of the new me that will be created through a new training.

* Let me become a great player when I become a rhythmic gymnast.
Even if I do other things, let me be a beautiful and wonderful person.
Let me express myself proudly no matter what I become.

④ Ui: Love and Compassion
* God, I loved my friends and teachers I met in rhythmic gymnastics.
I am thankful that I was able to be loved by rhythmic gymnasts and teachers.

I am happy that I met many people I care about through rhythmic gymnastics.

*I know now that the coach who is tough on me is not a bad person.
I also know that other players feel the same.
Therefore, please let me love my coach and other players.

*I want to share love with everyone I meet on my path of an athlete.
Let me share the love with people I met even if I take a different path.
Let me become somebody who shares love with others no matter what I become.

⑤ Integration: Gratitude-Forgiveness-Blessing

* God, I am thankful for everything I had enjoyed while learning rhythmic gymnastics
And I ask you to forgive me for all the wrong things I did with rhythmic gymnastics as an excuse.
And please bless my past days when I played rhythmic gymnastics.

* Thank you for the opportunity of new training now.
Thank you for your new friendship
And please congratulate me for the changes new training will bring to me.

* Thank you for letting me have a dream,
And I am grateful for all the process of moving toward the dream.
Please bless all my dreams in the future whatever my dream will be.

Prophecy on Stopping Smoking

Quitting smoking is a sure dream without uncertainty. When we dream of jobs and college, its realization depends not on the person but on the social circumstances, but the dream of quitting smoking is a matter that is dependent only on the person's commitment and devotion. Quitting smoking is a difficult but sure dream. The essence of a sure dream is to reflect what you want to be through the process in your conviction of achieving the goal.

① Ji: Commitment and Creation of Life

* I am remorseful that I made my life tiring and difficult
By forgetting the convenience of life that I can have by quitting smoking,
And I am going to quit smoking to fully love my life.

* Now I will not look for a place to smoke.
Everywhere is restricted for smoking, and therefore,
I eliminate unnecessary waste from my life.

* I forgive my hesitance to stop smoking,
Celebrate the courage to stop smoking,
And congratulate my life for having succeeded in quitting smoking.

② Hon-Baek: Perfection and Justification

* I am remorseful for having become a smoker who goes against the natural law at some point
After I forgot that I was originally a non-smoker,
And I forgot the day when I lived by non-smoking as the matter of fact in daily routines.

* I was born a non-smoker.

I walked the road of non-smoking since the day I was brought into this world.
I live by that natural law I was born with.

* The peace of mind comes to life that follows the principle of non-smoking.
Glory is with the life that follows the natural law.
Bless me, God, who have returned to the original form given by God.

③ Shin: Self-love and Conviction

* I am sorry to my body that must have been suffering for my failure to quit smoking.
I am really sorry for having been dependent on smoking and not being able to fill the void in my heart.
I am remorseful about the past when I lost the opportunity to love myself because I did not quit smoking.

* I stop smoking because I love my body.
I stop smoking because I love my heart.
I stop smoking for myself.

* I want to share with everybody my joy of having my body recover its full vitality thanks to quitting smoking,
For having my heart shine brilliantly thanks to quitting smoking
And for myself having recovered my original shape.

④ Ui: Love and Compassion

* I am sorry that I made people who care about me be concerned about me because I could not stop smoking.
I am thankful to them and I am sorry to them,
Because I fully remember the love that I saw in their concerns and worries.

* I strongly believe that their love will always be with me,
And I want to return the love of my loved ones by loving them back,
While always remembering that I am not alone on my journey to stopping smoking.

* I am thankful for having succeeded in stopping smoking thanks to many people who care about me.
I will not forget that my success is credited to them,
And I am happy that I made them happy by stopping smoking.

⑤ Integration: Gratitude-Forgiveness-Blessing
* I celebrate myself for having started to stop smoking,
 I am thankful I could stop smoking,
And I forgive all the troubles that came to me on my journey to stop smoking.

* I am thankful for the wisdom I've discovered while I stopped smoking,
I am thankful for the new me I'd discovered while trying to quit smoking,
And I am thankful for the people and the world that I've discovered while trying to quit smoking.

* I am thankful for the happiness I enjoy by stopping smoking,
I celebrate the future where I will have growing happiness,
And I congratulate the happiness of closing my life as a non-smoker.

Sacred Boundary on Healing Wounds
Life often throws curbed balls to hurt us. We are hurt by human relationships, failed dreams, and unexpected accidents. Since life is about bumping into the things that are not love in order to experience love, getting hurt might be the natural law of the

world. However, when we heal and overcome the wound, we can enjoy greater freedom and greater happiness than we do when we were never hurt before. In the end, we can move on as a free existence that is not hurt by anything. These prayers are not specifically made for specific wounds. I want you to refer to these prayers to protect yourself by substituting them for the difficult situations you are faced with, be they caused by cheating spouse, betraying business partner, depressing financial loss, breakup, broken dream, or dysfunctional family members or anything else.

① Ji: Commitment and Creation of Life

* I am sorry for having been helpless with regards to the creation of life

After having pain and suffering hurt my will to live, and the time I have been irresponsible.

But all those efforts I put out to resist and accept them.

* I fill this time with my will by raising it within me in this troubled time,

Be it a strong will or a gentle will, no matter what kind of a will I can raise,

While strongly resisting or gently embracing it.

* I am filled with a colorful and balanced will through pain and suffering

And growing into a being who raises harmonious will in all situations.

Therefore, I will become somebody who refuses to get hurt in any situations in life.

② Hon-Baek: Perfection and Justification

* I was angry and found it unfair about the relationship and situation that caused me pain,

And therefore, I was lonely and hurt.
I desperately need the love and solace of God.

* I acknowledge that this situation and relationship are my inevitable destiny,
And in this troubled time, I believe that I am with the Creator instead of being alone.
As with everything, this pain and suffering will surely pass.

* Having moved on from this pain and suffering,
I am paving a road to glory and peace with the blessings I receive from God.
Therefore, I will be a free existence in any situations in life.

③ Shin: Self-love and Conviction

* I regret for having been negligent about caring for and loving myself,
While being intimidated by the unbearable pain.
But in this painful time, I am committed to treasuring and protecting myself more than anything else.

* This relationship and circumstances are testing my limitations now.
The pain and suffering that I have now is a process necessary for me to break down the limitations that restrict me.
Now, I am in the process of discovering a new me.

* It is a joy bloomed in pain that I was able to discover the side of me that I'd never knew before.
Since this joy is filling me and completing my new me,
I will become a being that creates joy in any situations in life.

④ Ui: Love and Compassion

* I keep wishing others feel the same pain

Because the wounds caused by the unforgivable others hurt me so much.
I've found a way to become peaceful by letting go of the hatred, blaming, and pain.

* I believe that their faults are caused by their limits and shortcomings,
And I acknowledge that their best efforts are not much different from my best efforts.
I pray for them not to be hurt just as I pray for myself to break free from the pain.

* I hope I can see the limits of others when I am hurt and in pain,
And I hope I can truly understand their limits and forgive them.
I want to be a being who gives only love even to those who make me suffer.

⑤ Integration: Gratitude-Forgiveness-Blessing

* I pray I could forgive all the process of pain
And be forgiven about all the process of pain.
I pray no wounds to be left.

* I am thankful for everything of mine that endures this pain,
I am thankful to everybody who encourages me,
And I am thankful for God for always being there with me.

* In the end, I will bless my entire process,
And be blessed in all my process.
I pray only love will remain in my blessing.

The inevitable prophecy and sacred boundary of Baek-Shin-Ui-Ji can be applied to everything you want to be. I myself am writing this book now under the protection and the self-fulfilling prophecy of Hon-Baek-Shin-Ui-Ji. So far, the prophecy is going well. As such, I encourage you to broadly apply to everything, such as addiction to alcohol or smoking, your studying or working or any habit you want to change, as well as your roles and responsibilities.

You don't have to completely follow through the nine levels from the beginning. You can just start by recognizing the five pillars of Hon-Baek-Shin-Ui-Ji, and when you become familiar with it through repeated practice, you can move on to the past-present-future plans, and when you become familiar with it after repeated practice, you can try to make your own nine-level prayers. Probably, it will be the winning move to change you as you please, become a reliable protection for you to fulfill your responsibilities, and create the blessing of opening fortune, inspiration, and commitment with the prophecy for the realization of your dream. I bless your own sacred boundary and inevitable prophecy that reflect the image of the being you wish to become.

3) Applying Hon-Baek-Shin-Ui-Ji in Human Relationships

The second tip of real-life application is human relations. We are always exchanging energy from each other's minds through each other's unconscious minds. Even if we do not express ourselves in words or actions, the heart with which we like or dislike others becomes one energy and is delivered to the others' unconscious minds, and our own unconscious mind is also always affected by the minds of others who think of us. Our consciousness being a closed door, we can open it only by banging, but our unconsciousness is always an open door so all hearts can communicate freely with each other. Our inner heart is always directly conveyed to the unconsciousness of the others. And the emotions and thoughts that are held for each other are determined by the unconsciousness and are expressed in consciousness.

The source of the feelings we have for each other is unconsciousness. The fact that this unconsciousness makes unrestricted communications is established as the theory of psychology by psychologist Carl Gustav Jung. According to Jung, since there is no restriction on the transmission of our unconscious energy, the unconscious energy is formed within me and almost simultaneously arrives at someone at the opposite side of the planet. He also discovered that the unconsciousness communicated by people becomes a big power and establishes a collective unconsciousness. Just as our unconsciousness is the basis for our relationship, our collective unconscious is the fundamental force that builds this world.

The main pillar of our consciousness and unconsciousness is Hon-Baek-Shin-Ui-Ji. Hon-Baek-Shin-Ui-Ji determines the state of energy that we unconsciously exchange with each other. Therefore, if we can consciously control the energy that we understand and exchange by analyzing Hon-Baek-Shin-Ui-Ji as the source of emotions we have in each other, we can make a reformative change in our relationships. And if we can consciously control the energy we give and grow it in the desired direction, we can bring about the reform of the world.

(1) The Rosenthal Effect

The Rosenthal effect is a phenomenon of us giving and taking unconscious energy with each other. The Rosenthal effect refers to a psychological mechanism in which the involved parties are changed in response to external expectations and love. For example, if A maintains a relationship with B as a passionate and warm person, B becomes more passionate and warmer in response to that belief and love. In 1968, this phenomenon was named after Dr Robert Rosenthal, a Doctor of Psychology, who discovered the effect. In the experiment that confirmed the Rosenthal effect, students of a school were to take an intelligence test and their teachers were told beforehand that some of the randomly selected students had outstanding levels of intelligence and the possibility of improving school performance. For the following eight months, the teachers believed those students had outstanding potential. When the intelligence test was carried out 8 months later, those students actually showed intelligence that was higher than average, and they also made a big improvement in their school performance.

The essence of the Rosenthal effect is that teachers were not encouraged to influence the students by controlling their words and actions. Although there may have been some actual changes in the teachers' attitudes, the changes might have been minimal considering the characteristics of the teaching job that requires treating all students equally. This means that in order for the Rosenthal effect to appear, the inner mind is more important than words or actions. The Rosenthal effect does not appear if you commend students on the outside but hate them on the inside. This means that the Rosenthal effect is the result of unconscious communication. The Rosenthal effect is in line with the self-fulfilling prophecy that proves what you sincerely wish for becomes a reality, but it is significant that the implication happens not on yourself but on the other people. Since the range of change is determined by the others, the scale of its power is less than the case where the motivation is aroused within yourself. Therefore, the Rosenthal effect requires longer time and repetition than self-fulfilling prophecy.

The Rosenthal effect is widely known, and many people try to see this effect. The target is often a child. The Rosenthal effect played an important role in emphasizing the importance of believing and supporting children in parenting. Unfortunately, when we explain the Rosenthal effect, we have interpreted it as a result of behavior rather than the mind that comes from our inner side. So many mothers who believed in the Rosenthal effect tried hard to praise and cheer on the outside, while holding down their disappointment on their children inside.

I was one such case. I tried really hard, but honestly, it was not easy to realize the Rosenthal effect on my child. It was expected because on many occasions, I didn't really mean it when I praised or commended my child, and sometimes I was so frustrated that I exploded. It was only after I realized that what mattered was my true intention, not the action, that I was able to experience the Rosenthal effect on my child. I stopped making fake praises, and I commended my child only when I tried hard and I honestly wanted to commend my child. And I was able to experience the Rosenthal effect by conveying the physiological power to my child's Hon-Baek-Shin-Ui-Ji through my prayer.

The Rosenthal effect is a phenomenon that empowers the mind of the others. In fact, the Rosenthal effect causes the other people's Hon-Baek-Shin-Ui-Ji energy to increase. The Rosenthal effect is a phenomenon in which the Hon-Baek-Shin-Ui-Ji of a person who is supported by love and faith grows into a larger energy body. Our Hon-Baek-Shin-Ui-Ji grows as we awaken and practice our love, and it can also grow its energy when we receive the love and trust of others, because the unconsciousness is all open space. The proof is the Rosenthal effect.

So if you want to empower your loved ones with the Rosenthal effect, it is more effective to give strength to their Hon-Baek-Shin-Ui-Ji – the main pillars of unconsciousness – instead of random cheering from the heart, under the assumption that you can empower them only when you are sincere in heart. When we nag our children to put the laundry in the basket, we are nagging to blow energy of Ji into them while believing that the efforts of putting laundry in the basket will become the will of life and grow into the power to make them happier. When we nag at our children to wash, we are blessing their Shin with the heart that wishes for them to love their body and to be more beautiful. Therefore, it would be better to deliver your intention in the following way instead of randomly hoping they grow into good people.

You will always make happiness with a harmonious will. God's blessing is always with you, and it's all right. Believe that the world is fair and is on the side of all, and in the end, it is on your side. Always remember that you are a great and divine being. I am very thankful for all the love I received from you. Please know that everyone who is loved by you is happy thanks to you.

Love for Hon-Baek-Shin-Ui-Ji does not have to be expressed in words. The Rosenthal effect is formed by looking at the face of a sleeping child, or caring and thinking about others whenever you can and want to during the break at work or at any time of your convenience. And, of course, you can do it to anyone you want, not just your children. The Rosenthal effect not only allows others to grow, but it also exerts the power to solve the misunderstanding when you are misunderstood by others. Therefore, the Rosenthal effect is especially useful in a top-down relationship. In the top-down relationships such as between parents and children, teachers and students, and bosses and subordinates, the person in the top position is mostly engaged in instructing and ordering the other in the down position. The one who instructs others might say something that he is entitled to, but his intention can be misunderstood when the instruction is made at a wrong time at a wrong place. As a result, those who are instructed can easily develop dissatisfaction, resistance, and misunderstanding. Consequently, the higher you move up the corporate ladder, the lonelier and more troublesome you become. Naturally you grow unhappy at work because it is difficult to become friendly with those in the position of commanding you; you are also required to instruct others, and you cannot talk about the situation freely with others. The Rosenthal effect can be a solution to solving the hostility caused by this misunderstanding. Even if you are misunderstood and hated by others, you can disarm the hostility by believing in the love enfolding in the other people's Hon-Baek-Shin-Ui-Ji and raising the cheering spirit and delivering it to the other people's unconsciousness. In the opposite situation, the Rosenthal effect can guide you into the right direction when you misunderstand others.

Yet, we have mainly been doing the opposite. With regards to those who misunderstood our intention and sincerity, we only grumbled about them being mean to us and their lack of understanding. We used to imagine the intention of the others maliciously without knowing the whole story about them. In that way, we let our imagination associated with the pathological power of the other people's Hon-Baek-Shin-Ui-Ji amplify the sense of rejection in the unconsciousness of each other. Now, when others misunderstand you, I want you to trust their dignity, individuality, efforts and love, and cheer for them. This repetition of this attitude exerts the power to dissolve the other people's hostility. To the child who has been nagged and upset, to the subordinates who are sick and tired of the instructions by the boss, and to us who misunderstand others, the Rosenthal effect is the key of magic which opens communication of smooth feelings and thoughts.

Moreover, conveying the love of Hon-Baek-Shin-Ui-Ji to someone for the Rosenthal effect will eventually fill your own Hon-Baek-Shin-Ui-Ji with love. So, what we did to others is just the same as what we did to ourselves. When you give love, your Hon-Baek-Shin-Ui-Ji is filled with love. When you send hatred, your Hon-Baek-Shin-Ui-Ji is filled with hatred.

However, when you try to raise love in the other person's Hon-Baek-Shin-Ui-Ji with the Rosenthal effect, the effect is destined to be smaller compared to what you raise for yourself, because there is a distance between your heart and the other person's heart. In general, the love you give to others forms 1/29th of the energy you created in your mind. Therefore, it means that you need at least 29 deliveries of love to the other person's heart if you want to realize the same effect as happens in your heart. Repeat patience is a must in order to change others with love.

However, even though we can grow each other's Hon-Baek-Shin-Ui-Ji, we cannot grow it indefinitely. We can change others with love to the point where we do not have the right to decide for them with regards to their lives. No matter how hard you pray and put out your efforts, you cannot make somebody who is looking in this direction look in the other direction. You can empower their Hon-Baek-Shin-Ui-Ji only to the point where you cannot give critical influence over their decision to look in that direction. You cannot make a child who hates to study to apply themselves to studying, and you cannot make somebody who doesn't love you, love you. It is the law of the universe that, even though we are constantly exchanging energy with each other at the unconsciousness level, we can never invade each other's free will. Unconsciousness-level communication among individuals cannot exercise control over the other people. The only unconsciousness that controls us is the collective unconsciousness that we form together.

Although the Rosenthal effect is not a controlling force, it can be powerful enough to clear misunderstandings. Also, if the others and you are headed in the same direction, the power of the change can lead to a positive change of life that can never be ignored – the same as the change sufficient to improve children's intelligence and school performance in the previously mentioned experiment. And a significant change happens to you, the party that delivered the love, and then it can also change in the other parties, about 1/29 of your change. And the collective unconsciousness, which many people form by conveying love to Hon-Baek-Shin-Ui-Ji, has the power to exert control over everything. Therefore, the resonance of the heart that delivers love and trust to others' Hon-Baek-Shin-Ui-Ji is always right.

(2) Hostility and Guilty Conscious in Individual Relationships

If you look into our human relationships, you can observe many phenomena that cannot be explained logically. Our unconsciousness is at play in the foundation of those phenomena. In psychoanalysis, actions and thoughts we display in human relations without clear reasons are explained in terms of the relationship trauma from the infant and toddler stages. That explanation is pretty reasonable. However, there is a limit to explaining both the behavior and the thoughts people display in human relationships solely by the psychoanalytic method. For example, if you are strangely susceptible to having your pride hurt by a person named A, but not by the persons named B and C and D who are in a similar relationship with you, psychoanalysis cannot fully explain it, because it is the unconscious reaction of the individual relationship that is formed only between you and A.

In many human relationships there is such an individual characteristic that applies to specific relationships. So even though you try not to cause the inconvenience, you repeatedly experience the same problem with that specific person. But the cause is not created in this life alone; it is the result of causes created in numerous lives in the universe (past lives). For example, in any life, if you hurt the Hon-Baek-Shin-Ui-Ji of a specific person in any of your past lives, the person will have unconscious hostility against you, while I build an unconscious sense of guilt against the person. In this case, the other person keeps hurting you out of the wounded unconscious feelings, and you keep experiencing the situation where you cannot face that person undauntedly due to your sense of guilt. Of course, the hostility and the sense of guilt can be experienced the opposite way depending on the person you are dealing with. The energy that is connected to the unconsciousness of others is called individual relationship karma, and the unconscious sense of guilt and hostility belong to the category of negative karma.

We cannot understand this unconscious hostility and the sense of guilt because we do not remember our past lives at all. Therefore, we find it difficult to resolve discomfort we feel towards each other in this life. Now, if you have any relationship problem that you cannot understand, let's think about it in this way: "What could I have done to that person in my past life to make me so vulnerable and easily hurt by that person?" or, "What kind of a wound could that person have caused me to make me so hateful of him?" You will be able to resolve many problems you experience in your personal relationships and communicate more easily and earnestly with them if you find answers to these questions.

There is a method you can use to interpret those unexplained relationship unconscious problems: Hon-Baek-Shin-Ui-Ji. Even though we cannot remember the wounds that we gave and received in other lives, the meanings of those wounds are left on our Hon-Baek-Shin-Ui-Ji and manifest themselves in the form of current emotions. Therefore, you can figure out which part of your Hon-Baek-Shin-Ui-Ji is wounded by carefully observing the emotions you have now. If you convey your feelings to the unconsciousness of the others in accordance to the meanings of those wounds, you can resolve the negative karmas you have with each other and resolve the problems. The relationships weaved by the karmas of hostility and the sense of guilt can be classified by Hon-Baek-Shin-Ui-Ji and explained as follows.

① Hon-Baek (魂魄)

The wrongs that interfere with the purpose and the right direction of the other's life, or the wounds that hurt the identity of the other bind negative energies to each other's Hon and Baek.

Those whose Hon and Baek were hurt in the past lives tend to provoke the others who had hurt them, insist that they are always right, change their minds constantly and confuse them.

They also give trouble to others by putting others in difficult or frustrating situations. Even if they sometimes realize that they are being unreasonable and annoying and tell themselves, "I should stop this," they cannot help but repeat the same behaviors unconsciously. Those who had hurt other's Hon and Baek in the past lives tend to become gullible to the people that they had wounded, experience particular confusion even if they are not being particularly capricious, and easily become frustrated even over trivial matters. They feel overwhelmed by the emotions that keep repeating in their minds, even if they cannot outwardly express the two directional emotions.

If you are struggling because you are constantly confused and frustrated by somebody, you have to realize you have wounded that person's Hon and Baek, and all you need to do is to express how sorry you are for having disturbed the person's glory and peace. The negative energy that is connected to Hon and Baek disappears just by letting the other person know how sorry you are even only at the unconscious level. On the contrary, if you keep provoking, annoying, and crossing somebody even though you keep telling yourself to stop doing it, you have to realize your Hon and Baek were hurt by that person. In this case, you can eliminate the karma of Hon and Baek by offering your forgiveness, because that person is now no longer able to disrupt you when you move forward toward the purpose of your life.

The hostility that is linked to Hon and Baek can manifest in the form of belittlement of the dignity of the other person. When you belittle others, it is usually the manifestation of wounded Shin, but if somebody insults your parents or ancestors, it is the manifestation of wounded identity and the karma of Hon and Baek. In this case, you can also acknowledge the dignity of the other and apologize accordingly or acknowledge your own dignity and forgive the other to eliminate the negative energy that is linked to Hon and Baek.

② Shin (神)

The wrongdoings that hurt the other's self-esteem link negative energy to each other's Shin.

Those whose Shin was wounded in past lives tend to ridicule and hurt the pride of the one who'd hurt them, and sometimes they insult the other person, too. Some of the good examples include laughing about the other's appearance or metaphorically ridiculing the other's behaviors. Most of those times, they don't even realize what they are doing, but even if they realize it, they keep behaving in ways to hurt the other's pride. Those who had wounded the Shin of others in previous lives tend to become vulnerable and easily feel pain and wounded pride even at the slightest cause. Even if they cannot outwardly express two directional feelings, they repeatedly insult, hurt the pride, and pity themselves in their minds.

If you keep hurting your pride and feel insulted by somebody, you may acknowledge the fact that you have wounded the other's Shin and let the other know how sorry you are for having underrated their greatness, preciousness, and beauty even in the unconscious level. If in the opposite situation where you are compelled to disrespect and despise the other for no good reason, you have to recognize the pain of Shin caused by the other. And then you can offer your forgiveness because now you can show your greatness to the person. Be it apology or forgiveness, any resonance coming from your heart from whichever direction can make the negative energy that is linked to each other's Shin disappear.

Sometimes it is difficult to distinguish between wounds inflicted on the subjectivity of Hon and Baek and the wounds inflicted on the pride of Shin. We can usually put up with insults to ourselves but not insults to our parents; the wounds connected to Hon and Baek are directly linked to parents, and the wounds linked to Shin are linked to self-pity. Therefore, you can distinguish the anger that makes you snap and the self-pity that manifests in tears and annoyance can be distinguished by the emotional difference.

③ Ui (意)

When you wrong somebody by betraying their love and trust, or hurt somebody with complaint, dissatisfaction, and loneliness, these wrongdoings link negative energy to each other's Ui.

Those whose Ui was hurt in past lives reveal distrust to the ones who are responsible for the wound, and easily distort their sincere intention. They easily snap and feel betrayed even at the smallest mistake of the other, and worse, they don't have conversation with the other and enjoy badmouthing them behind their backs. It is all because the wounded Ui builds a cluster of irritated emotions inside. Those who hurt others' Ui also feel unpleasant because they feel they are suspected by those they'd hurt or feel anxious because they are afraid that they will hear their complaints. Even if they cannot outwardly express two directional feelings, they repeatedly feel suspicious and anxious in their minds.

If you keep feeling annoyed to hear the other repeatedly complaining and grumbling, and anxious for not having been trusted, you may acknowledge the fact that you have wounded the other's Ui and let the others know in prayer how sorry you are for having ignored their love and trust and paid them back with betrayal and loneliness instead. If in the opposite situation where you constantly complain and badmouth others, you have to recognize the pain of Ui caused by the other. And then you can offer your forgiveness because now you are satisfied at the fact that you had loved even if the other did not accept your love. Be it apology or forgiveness, any resonance coming from your heart from whichever direction can make the negative energy that is linked to each other's Ui disappear.

④ Ji (志)

When you wrong others by destroying or disturbing their dreams and hopes, or discouraging or depriving them of their daily rewarding, these wrongdoings link negative energy to each other's Ji.

Those whose Ji was wounded in past lives tend to underrate the efforts and possibilities of others that they'd wounded when they try to do something, and repeatedly hinder them from realizing their dreams, and finding joy in life and peace. They may tell themselves to stop it, but they cannot help but think, "Whatever you do, it's no good," "I doubt you can do it," "Stop it. It's not fun," or "You are making me uncomfortable and difficult." Those who wounded Ji tend to be sensitive to others who ignore their efforts, and they easily give up and become dispirited, because the wound on Ji is linked to the emotion of depression that weighs down to the bottom. Even though the two directional feelings cannot be outwardly revealed, they feel burdened by the feelings that repeat constantly within their minds.

If you are constantly depreciated and dispirited, you may recognize the wound you've inflicted on the other's Ji and let the other know you are sorry for having frustrated the other person's dreams and efforts. On the contrary, if you try to ignore the efforts of the other and frustrate the other's will to live, you may recognize the wounds the other had inflicted on you, and offer your forgiveness to the person because now you can move forward toward dream and rewarding life. No matter which direction you choose, the karma that is connected to each person's Ji will disappear.

The relationship in which a negative relationship karma is formed creates a vicious circle that is uncomfortable but rather obsessive. Because the negative energies connected to each other's Hon-Baek-Shin-Ui-Ji constrain each other. Therefore, when the unconscious relational sense of guilt and hostility are resolved, the emotions of each other come to a new starting point that is suitable for the present, and both parties feel unbounded freedom. If your karma with your child is relieved, you will become less inclined to become nervous about the child's behavior and more inclined to observe the child with relaxed mind. If your friend had been being a difficult and uncomfortable friend, you will become less inclined to keep your friend away. If your boss had been a difficult person, you will begin to have the courage to speak up to the boss. It becomes much easier to create a relationship in the direction you want from a new starting point.

In a relationship of high intimacy with each other, the karma described above is clearly visible. But in a relationship where you cannot speak your mind easily, such as between customers and employees and between a boss and a subordinate, it is possible to recognize the karma with the thought that each person has inside. Observation shows that intimate relationships such as family, friends, and lovers are intertwined with individual karma.

If you try to make an unconscious apology that solves the relationship karma, there are relationships that may be improved by a short prayer, and relationships that may be improved by a longer prayer or repetition. Sometimes a relationship is a combination of two or three emotions. This is because of the diversity of the volume of karma formed between the two. In addition, observations show that there is karma exchanged with each other in one relationship so entangled that when you are wounded, the other party is wounded at the same time. So, I hope you will try to make unconscious conversations and talk about how uncomfortable your mind is, how uncomfortable your other party's mind is, while taking account of the changes that prayers would bring to you and your partner.

Because children candidly express their feelings, hostility and guilt between children can be observed clearly by bystanders.

It is really easy to figure out their karma by observing their actions: bullying, picking on others (Shin); bothering others when they play (Ji); getting angry when other children don't pay much attention to them (Ui); being self-centered and picking a fight; and confusing others (Hon and Baek). And when the karma is dissolved, suddenly changed behaviors are clearly observed. When I look at the change, I am very amazed and proud. However, adults are not easy to judge by action only because they control the uncomfortable feelings about others. You can identify which karma is involved only when the involved parties disclose their inner feelings. However, when karma is resolved, adults also feel the same relaxed emotions as the children. If you experience an apology and forgiveness that resolves the karma of hatred and guilty conscience, anyone can easily feel the change of mind that makes it easy to deal with the other party.

However, when conveying an unconscious apology and forgiveness with the karma of a previous life, you need the consent of the opponent's soul. Apologizing in my heart is not the end. Unconscious apologies and forgiveness are only effective when You have to be sincere enough to be accepted by the souls of the opponents.

This relationship karma can be created in the present life as well as the past life. The wounds given and taken in the past life will be completely resolved by the delivery of the heart without direct apology. But in the wounded heart of this life, the clear memories of it remains in consciousness, and therefore it is often necessary to apologize directly about the situation. When one with a little pain or wound tries to overcome it, one can heal only by conveying apology or forgiveness unconsciously. However, in the case of a great deal of pain or lack of conscious effort by the involved parties, you must directly apologize. Because our consciousness is a closed door, the memory of consciousness can be cured when you knock the door and the other party permits the opening of the door.

Even so, if the negative energy linked to the unconscious mind is resolved before the apology, the apology for consciousness is more likely to be accepted. Our consciousness is under the control of unconsciousness. And even at this time, you have to ask for the consent of the opponent's soul for the fact that you can only apologize from your heart. That way, the apology you made with your heart can effectively reach the other opponent's heart.

On the other hand, you are hurt in the present life, the forgiveness that releases my opponent so that you will not be bound by that relationship frees you. Forgiveness can release you if the pain is small, but in the case of big pains, all aspects of Hon-Baek-Shin-Ui-Ji have to be forgiven to clearly heal the wounds and find power to find peace.

The new starting point of releasing relationship karma in the form of hatred and guilty consciousness refers to the condition where the energy that generated all the uncomfortable emotions is resolved at the unconscious level. And this leads to an actual change of thinking, emotion, and behavior. We are thinking, acting, and feeling by the unconsciousness. However, even after eliminating karma, old thoughts and emotions may remain. For example, a child may have been ridiculing the other child's dream and interfered with his/her play, but the intensity went down significantly by releasing the negative karma, but it didn't completely stop. If the other party has low self-awareness about themselves, the past thought and behavior may remain in accordance to the law of inertia.

If this is the case, there are two options. One is to tell the other party honestly to make him aware of their actions and the other is to give the power to the light to the unconsciousness of the other party. Of course, it is better to do both. Therefore, for a person whose past emotions remain out of inertia even after the elimination of karma, it is possible to convey the gratitude and blessings to the unconsciousness of the other party and make the negative inertia lose strength by the newly connected karma. Thankfulness and blessings form karma of love that connects us with affirmation. The thicker the karma of love is, the better we can have positive influence on each other and grow together.

The negative karma that is intertwined within us is a system that is once again given the opportunity to experience what we have not experienced in our past lives with love. You can think and experience the meaning of love with this given opportunity. The one who is connected with you through negative karma – and gives you pain and discomfort – is a being that brings you a new chance again. The other party is covering his light and giving you a chance. What you need to do is to recognize the opportunity, convey apology and forgiveness and experience love, bless it with gratitude and start the path to love. It is difficult to be thankful to the party who makes it hard for you from the beginning, but after the negative karma, which connects him and you, has been resolved, you can appreciate with a little lighter heart. You can be thankful and feel blessed that you have enjoyed the experience of love and been given a chance again.

I think of the feelings I had when I was hurt to convey my sincere heart when I relieved the relational karma, and I think of apologies and forgiveness, imagining the past wounds inflicted by humans. Especially when the opponent poured out insults and accusations against me, I send my apology while thinking in my mind, "You would have been hurt by my insults and accusations just as much as I am hurt now." I feel fortunate to be able to understand the pain that I had caused, even now, and I am willing to apologize. When I read the meaning of relational karma enfolded in Hon-Baek-Shin-Ui-Ji and the emotions it shows, I can see that my other party is returning the same to me as I have given him. So, you do not have to distinguish the karma of Hon-Baek-Shin-Ui-Ji. You can conceive that the imagination and predictions that come to your mind about the other party is what you have done to the party in the past life when the situation was the opposite. Since our unconsciousness is connected to the memories of previous lives, it is exposed as the opposite position when it is expressed as consciousness.

All karmas of the life that are realized to us as well as the relational karma have retribution significance and are realized in the form of the realization of the retribution justice. This verse of the Koran that defines retribution justice as "life for a life, eye for an eye, nose for a nose and a tooth for a tooth" is about the retribution law of karma. In other words, it means the pain and suffering that happen to us now is the karma that you have done in the past life that you cannot remember. Unfortunately, it is misinterpreted as to mean that we may retaliate against each other in this life. This verse is not a command of Allah to allow revenge. It is the consideration of Allah who guides us kindly who cannot remember all our lived lives. It teaches us that if you find out what karma means to you, you can easily get rid of that karma, so please follow the truth that I am guided to be forgiven and free. Now, let us recognize the karma that is intertwined with each other and sincerely apologize and forgive, and bless each other as a free being as we move forward.

But not all relational karma is resolved by apology and forgiveness. Hostility and guilt are solved by the resonance of unconsciousness because it is a matter of the mind, but when karma is piled up as real-life problems – such as hurting someone's health and taking their money – apology is useless because it is not a matter of heart. If this physical karma was formed in a previous life, then there is no memory of it and therefore it is not a matter of mind. So, it does not easily inflict emotional wounds. Instead, it is a karma that makes life difficult and hard, so it is resolved by helping the other party's life become a little easier. So, if you look around you have a friend you wish to do more without feeling discomfort in mind. On the other hand, there are people who are generous to you, giving you presents and caring about you in many different ways. In this case, it is mainly a way to solve physical karma while giving and receiving physical things to each other.

On the contrary, if you are in the position to receive a real karma, the more you appreciate the materials and efforts that somebody gives you, the sooner you can resolve the physical karma. It is a process of filling your inner world with love to receive them with gratitude rather than taking them for granted. Subsequently, the other person's efforts amplify the positive impact on your life. In addition, there are cases where a person who owes you something is not able to pay it back, and just circles you around. In this case, the person is constantly subjected to something that the person is required to do for you, but nothing to your satisfaction. In cases like this, where somebody owes you something but has trouble paying you back, you can solve the physical karma with love that understands the person's scarcity and limitation, and root for the person, because in the end, you can gain positive results in which your life becomes happier by acquiring love through the person's existence. So, when you create and amplify the positive influence in your life through the efforts and presence of the other person, the physical karma that you should receive is dissolved and the peacefulness is unfolded.

Physical karma is energy linked to each other's lives, and hostility and the sense of guilt is energy connected to each other's Hon-Baek-Shin-Ui-Ji. So, the space in which the relationship karma exists is neither the other person nor you; but it is between the other person and you. This karma does not belong to one person but belongs to the space between the two of you. Here we have the room for miracles.

All divine truths are separated into three: in the case of time, it is past-present-future; in the case of human beings, it is soul-mind-body; and in the case of space, it is here-between-there. And the middle parts – present, mind, between – are the spaces marked by no limit. Present is always the time for all things to happen, and our minds can always change. When we influence each other's Hon-Baek-Shin-Ui-Ji, there is a limit that cannot infringe on the free will of the others. The space called "between" where the relational karma exists is neither here nor there; therefore, anybody can get involved in that space without restriction. The space "between" the two is neither yours nor the others'; it is a space for all. Therefore, anybody who can recognize the karma between the two can resolve that karma. It can be resolved by you, by the other, or any other third party. Of course, a third party can resolve it only if the souls of both parties agree. So, before dissolving karma, you need to mentally organize a purpose they will agree on.

You relieve the karma associated with yourself through the difficulties of your experience in your relationships; you relieve the karma of your family when you see them in troubled relationships by conveying apology and forgiveness for them; and you relieve your friends' relationship karma by listening to your friends' laments. There is no limit to the amount of karma you can resolve as long as you are capable of recognizing relational karma. You can also resolve karma of many people simultaneously in proportion to the size of mind you can arise at once. It can be resolved only when you apologize, sympathizing with the pain, and with a heart that sympathizes with how burdensome it is to forgive. Apologies and forgiveness with empathy are the only necessary and sufficient conditions. Thanks to the blessing of the space called "between" being shared by all of us, we can experience that we are one. World peace is never impossible if we solve the negative karma that is entangled in this space we are in and connect each other with the light of gratitude and blessing.

4) Myungsu (命數)[28]: The Field of Energy Formed by Hon-Baek-Shin-Ui-Ji

Each of Hon-Baek-Shin-Ui-Ji is a body of energy. As our consciousness expands, each body of energy in Hon-Baek-Shin-Ui-Ji grows into a larger body of energy. For example, if you believe in the omnipotence of God and commit yourself to living by your free will, it makes the energy of Hon grow, and if you are determined to sincerely sympathize with others and be compassionate toward them, it makes the energy of Ui grow. In addition, each part of Hon-Baek-Shin-Ui-Ji is a separate body of energy while at the same time organically working together. Therefore, there is one field of energy of an individual that is formed by the entire energies of Hon-Baek-Shin-Ui-Ji. The most important point here is that we can measure the energy field of mind we form. The size of the heart, measured from the numbers between 0 and 100, is called "myungsu," or the degree of inherent vitality in English. Originated from the term of Myeongmaeksilsu(命脈實數), myungsu is a system created by Yi Je-ma, the founder of the Sasang Constitutional Medicines, in which the degree of health is classified into 24 indexes. The mental energy field is another expression of health, and the degree of mental vitality is called myungsu.

Perhaps the first person to express numerical measurements in relation to the human mind was Dr David Roman Hawkins. Those who are familiar with Dr Hawkins' book *Power vs. Force* will not find the numerical measurement of mind strange, but in general, people might find it absurd that the size of our mind can be measured in numbers. I was not an exception in the beginning. But once you acknowledge that our mind is a body of energy, measuring it in numbers is only so logical in modern medicine. As I mentioned in the "On Human Beings" part earlier in this book, our mind is an energy created by all cells. Hon-Baek-Shin-Ui-Ji are the five pillars that support all those minds. All minds are raised and run by Hon-Baek-Shin-Ui-Ji.

The places where Hon-Baek-Shin-Ui-Ji resides all form a space. The pineal gland where Hon is found is structured like an eyeball, and there is a space at the center of it. The cochlea where Baek is found is in the form of a duck, and therefore it has space inside. The heart where Shin is found is an organ that consists of spaces called two atria and two ventricles, while the ovary and testicular, the home of Ui, are shaped like pouches, and the sole, the home of Ji, is where a space is formed due to the arch shape of the bottom of our feet. Hon-Baek-Shin-Ui-Ji are the energy bodies that fill those spaces. Their high spinning speed creates a magnetic force.

Speedy momentum of a body of high energy forms a magnetic force. When the hot matter (iron) of the deep outer core rapidly rotates, it forms a magnetic field which makes Earth into one large magnet. The Earth's magnetic field acts as a protective barrier by changing the direction of the solar wind, which contains radioactive particles, so that it does not enter the Earth. Thanks to the Earth's magnetic field, the Earth's air cannot be shaken by the solar wind and living things can be protected from radiation and not exposed to genetic mutilation.

The energy of Hon-Baek-Shin-Ui-Ji also rotates in its own space, creating a magnetic field, just like the high energy in the outer core of the Earth rotates to create a magnetic field. Just as the Earth protects the Earth's air and life with its magnetic field, the magnetic field created by Hon-Baek-Shin-Ui-Ji protects our cells and mind. Therefore, when Hon-Baek-Shin-Ui-Ji grows into bigger and stronger energies, our magnetic field becomes stronger, cells become healthier, and minds become closer to the truth.

The magnetic field of Hon-Baek-Shin-Ui-Ji increases the efficiency of the cell's power. Our cells are like capacitors that store charge as a dielectric. On the other hand, it is the same as a coil that stores current in a resistor and can produce power. You will remember experimenting with the current through a magnet through a coil in your school days. Since the magnetic force forms electromagnetic induction, the magnetic force of Hon-Baek-Shin-Ui-Ji regulates our cells to produce active power, and the larger the magnetic force, the higher the power production efficiency of the cell. Therefore, the power efficiency of our cells improves as Hon-Baek-Shin-Ui-Ji's energy capacity increases.

Hon-Baek-Shin-Ui-Ji uses cell power to form an electrical signal to oneself. Hon-Baek-Shin-Ui-Ji stimulates the current by inducing electromagnetic induction in the cell to produce active power when the thought we make is a positive match to our unconsciousness. The magnetic field of Hon-Baek-Shin-Ui-Ji does not generate active power when the thought we make is a negative match to our unconsciousness. This is also the essence of muscle testing and O-ring testing. This technique has become a field of medicine called applied kinesiology. Dr David Hawkins used muscle testing techniques to explore the world's truths. If he asks himself curious questions and his or someone else's muscle with him sustains when he puts resistance to it, it is judged as positive, and if the muscles fail to sustain, it is judged as negative. These methods are developed by the phenomenon that the electric energy of the human body forms the active power by the unconscious "yes" and the muscles work, and the active power is not formed by the unconscious "no."

In our minds, the cell forms a power and reacts to make us physically strong with valid energy with affirmation that corresponds to our unconsciousness. It was from this principle of thought that we make the choice that intuitively empowers us when we want to do something. The more effective the generated power is, the easier the intuitive choice becomes. The number of myungsu, the size of our mind, can be confirmed by measuring how effective the biomagnetism is in the idea of unconscious affirmation. Thus, myungsu is confirmed by measuring the power factor of the bioelectric power.

The power factor is a measure of how effectively the applied voltage and current actually work. It is a measure of how efficiently the electricity supplied is used for its intended purpose. The formula of the power factor is "power factor = active power / apparent power." When 100 percent of electricity supplied and consumed for the intended purpose is counted as 1, the more distant the number is from 1, the more it is considered to be inefficient, with a significant portion of the supplied electricity being wasted.

The electric current of the human body is the depolarization process of the cells, which is an alternating current (AC) circuit in which the direction and amount of the electric current are periodically changed. In the AC circuit, the larger the phase difference (θ) in the change of current and voltage, the more reactive power is generated. That is, there is a phase difference between the current and the voltage, and the power factor is smaller than one. However, when there is no phase difference in the conversion of voltage and current, only the pure resistance component remains in the AC circuit, so that there exists only the active power that all the power works. In other words, when the phase difference becomes zero, the power factor becomes one, in which the entire supplied apparent power becomes active power (the power factor is calculated by calculating the phase difference θ as a trigonometric function and $\cos\theta$).

Hon-Baek-Shin-Ui-Ji not only determines the magnitude of the magnetic force but also controls the magnetic force formed in each cell. Thus, the process of transmitting the electric power generated by the unconscious mind is controlled by the magnetic force, and the phase difference between the current and the voltage is adjusted to be closer to zero as the number of myungsu increases. Eventually, as Hon-Baek-Shin-Ui-Ji grows and myungsu increases, the positive thought forms electricity whose power factor is closer to one in the unconsciousness level. The fact that the power factor is one also means that Hon-Baek-Shin-Ui-Ji exercises complete control over all cells.

The most important point, however, is that the power factor of the human body associated with myungsu corresponds to the AC power generated appropriate thoughts in unconscious mind. It is not the power factor measured at random frequency. It has to be the power factor measured at the frequency of thought affirmed by the unconsciousness.

The idea that happens as we speak is expressed in the middle frequency (audible range: 250-2,000 Hz), but our thoughts that happen in our mind consist of very high frequency and very low frequency. Inner thoughts that are inconsistent with the unconsciousness have a linear effect on a narrow range with a very high frequency, and the inner thoughts that are appropriate for the unconsciousness affect the wide range of diffraction at very low frequencies. When the power factor of the human body is measured, the power factor becomes lower as the frequency becomes higher, and the power factor becomes higher as the frequency becomes lower. The frequency at which a human mind thinks is either very high or low, so it is clearly distinguished without a middle level. Therefore, there is a dramatic difference in the active power formed by the inner thinking depending on whether or not it is a match to the unconsciousness. In other words, active power is formed only in thinking that is appropriate to the unconsciousness and generates power intuitively. Ultimately, the power factor that identifies myungsu has to be the power factor identified at the frequency appropriate for the unconsciousness.

In addition, depending on the thoughts a person has, different power factor is formed. Simple and ordinary thoughts do not need strong intuition and thus, a low power factor is formed. However, issues that are of great significance to the person demand strong intuitive power and thus, leads to the highest power factor possible. Therefore, myungsu is reflected not in the power factor formed during ordinary situations but in the highest possible power factor manifested at significant moments.

The frequency at which an inner thought of a person is formed is estimated to be 857EHz (= 857×10^{18} Hz) for a high frequency and 0.857aHz (= 0.857×10^{-18} Hz) for a low frequency. It is impossible to directly measure the power factor at that frequency, since there is not yet a technology to generate and receive as high and low frequencies as human thought. Nevertheless, measurement of myungsu is possible because the power factor forms a consistent function as the frequency changes. Therefore, it is possible to calculate the power factor at 0.857aHz which is appropriate for the unconsciousness.

Among commercially available portable LCR meters, there are meters capable of measuring at 3 to 5 frequencies and calculating the value of θ which is the phase difference of voltage potential. When the value of $\cos \theta$ is obtained from this θ value, it becomes the power factor of the AC. If you measure the power factor of the human body directly with the LCR meter, you can observe that the measured value changes as the measurement range continues to fluctuate. The reason for this is that the measured value changes as the pressure at which the contact terminal presses the skin continuously changes.

You might have experienced how the skin, when pressed, would turn red and leave marks. Behind this phenomenon is the process of depolarization of the skin and dermal cells. Because the pressure determines the intensity of this depolarization, the measured value will continue to change and errors will form. Therefore, in order to properly measure the power factor of the human body, a weak pressure (about 1.7 to 1.8 Pa), in which depolarization due to pressure is not formed, should be maintained constantly while the terminal is in close contact with the skin. More precisely, it is more certain when the terminals are inserted under the skin without pressure, because skin has wrinkles that are invisible to our eyes, and it is impossible to make perfect contact with simple contact. Therefore, the error due to the mismatch of these contact surfaces occurs, and it is estimated to be about 0.02 lower than the actual power factor in the simple contact measurement. This error can be confirmed by filling the terminal and skin with water.

Unfortunately, the LCR meter, which can adjust the contact pressure of the current terminal, is not available. I also did not have the infrastructure to develop and manufacture such a machine, so I could not confirm it through a real experiment. However, as a result of casual experiment with a portable LCR meter, I was able to confirm the possibility of a constant function in which the power factor is high at low frequency and the power factor is low at high frequency. Hoping that some day mechanical equipment capable of measuring myungsu will be developed, I disclose the logic behind myungsu and the power factor.

Hon-Baek-Shin-Ui-Ji expands every time you have a love experience that overcomes your limitations, and your myungsu improved by one. If the myungsu number is increased by one, the power factor of 0.0025 goes up. In other words, the power factor of the human body increases by 0.01 when you have four limit-overcoming love experiences and improves the number of myungsu by four, and when the myungsu number reaches 100, the power factor of the human body reaches 0.25. And the number 100 of myungsu is a completion of a stage, and it allows the rebirth as a new being.

Human rebirth can be accomplished up to five times. In other words, the process of having myungsu reach the number 100 and complete can be repeated up to five times. And the fourth rebirth signifies the perfection of a human. In the perfection of a human, the power generated by the positive unconsciousness results in perfect efficiency of power factor one ($0.25 \times 4 = 1$). The fact that the body has a power factor of one means that Hon-Baek-Shin-Ui-Ji controls all cells completely. It means the mind and the body form a perfect unity. Completion of the final fifth of the number 100 is an extension where the power factor remains unchanged at number one.

However, no one has zero power factor. Most human beings start at zero, the first stage of myungsu population, at birth, but not the power factor of zero. Everyone has the power factor of 0.05 until the first myungsu number of 20. The power factor starts to rise to 0.0525 when the first myungsu number becomes 21 and changes according to the described rule. We are all born with the minimum power factor that can intuitively recognize the affirmations of unconsciousness.

In the course of confirming my myungsu, I always had the number value that explained my growth and changes. If a machine that could measure the power factor was invented, you would have been able to observe the improvement of power rate that corresponded to how you overcame and expanded your Hon-Baek-Shin-Ui-Ji. And you would also have been able to discover the expansion and change yourself when your power factor improved. Numerical measurement of the size of our mind can be a friendly indicator of our lives. If your myungsu is on a gradual improvement, that means you are moving forward toward the direction that corresponds to the purpose of your life. If the growth progress of your myungsu has been stalled for a while, it means the path you have is not taking you to the purpose of life, or it is stalled to overcome your limits.

Once accumulated, the improved myungsu never disappears until the present life is over. That is, myungsu being the number that indicates the size of mind, it can only grow and can never decline, and the power factor also does not decline. However, the amount of love you fill in the bowl the size of your improved myungsu is a variable that can change at any time. The amount of light contained within myungsu is always changing due to the thought, emotions, and choices of the moments. Even if your myungsu index is 50, you might live with the light only of

30 if your will to love cools down. But if you recover the will to love again, you can easily fill the light up to 50 because the size of bowl was always 50. When we make the choice to fill the bowl of heart, which is our myungsu, and put more light of love into it, we can improve our myungsu, increase the bowl of heart, and improve the power factor.

This is the difference between myungsu and the consciousness energy explained by Dr Hawkins. In his book *Power Vs. Force*, Dr Hawkins described the energy system in which the human consciousness can be measured in numbers as it advances to a higher level. Dr Hawkins' consciousness energy can be measured by the numbers between zero and 1,000, which refers to the amount of light contained in the bowl we call myungsu, and this is a variable that is constantly changing. It can increase or decrease depending on our choices and situations. However, myungsu is the conclusive outcome of a person's expansion of being. It doesn't become smaller once it is expanded, and it only has the possibility of growing through expansion.

Myungsu is the size of mind that repeats the process of growing to become 100 five times. Each time myungsu finishes a process of growing to 100, a bowl that is filled with 200 of Dr Hawkins' consciousness energy is completed. In this way, the consciousness energy can become 200 at the maximum when the first myungsu completes the number 100, and the consciousness energy keeps growing to 400 maximum when the second myungsu completes; 600 maximum of consciousness energy when the third myungsu completes; 800 maximum of consciousness energy when the forth myungsu completes; and up to 1,000 conscious energy when the final fifth myungsu completes. We can contain the light of love as much as the size of our heart. Therefore, we must expand our myungsu to seek Dr Hawkins' consciousness energy and reach enlightenment.

When the active power of the human body increases as the result of improved myungsu, you can control the movement of an object such as a small metal pendulum that is available in stores with your active power. When you hold a pendulum with your finger and concentrate on a thought, the electron moves toward the active power if the answer is affirmative in unconsciousness, and the electron that moves to the pendulum flows along the inverted triangular cone and generates active power that makes it spin. Conversely, if the answer to the thought is negative in the unconscious, the pendulum will be fixed because the electron does not flow.

Picture of a pendulum

The experiment of the pendulum and Dr Hawkins' muscle testing are two different tests intended to do the same: the confirmation of the active power of human body that is generated by the unconscious affirmations. The spinning pendulum and the strong reaction of muscle are two different forms of the same fact: the thoughts are affirmative in the unconsciousness of the test taker. In my personal experience, it was not easy to exclude consciousness from the muscle resistance, but when observing the movement of the pendulum, I could exclude consciousness more clearly. I personally think that the use of a pendulum is a more convenient way to determine the effective power of the human body than muscle testing.

In the experiment of a pendulum, the metal material is more advantageous in the movement of the electron, and a shorter cord is better to demonstrate the spinning. Conversely, the longer the cord is, the easier to fix the pendulum, and the bigger the upper surface diameter of the pendulum, the greater the movement force of the electrons to rotate. Therefore, when confirming the effective power, it is advantageous to use a cord that is not too short to spin, and a pendulum with an adequately wide upper diameter to make the spinning more visible.

In general, when the first-stage myungsu is over 75, or the active power is more than 0.20, you can generate enough active power that can clearly distinguish fixation or spinning of the light metal pendulum that is available in stores. Anything less will generate effective power that is not strong enough to move the pendulum, and the power of consciousness is too weak compared to your unconsciousness. In muscle testing, it is more accurate and easier to confirm the weakness and strength of muscle with more improved power factor of human body.

The fixation and rotation of the pendulum to the question is the result of the full reflection of the person's unconsciousness. We want to get closer to the truth by visiting fortune tellers, reading horoscopes or astrology, taking muscle testing, or observing the movement of objects such as a pendulum. However, since our unconsciousness is housing both the physiological force and pathological force of Hon-Baek-Shin-Ui-Ji, we cannot reach the truth of the universe when the pathological force blocks us. However, the state of our unconsciousness can be identified through the answers of the pendulum test. Our general self-reflection takes place at the level of consciousness, but when we look at my unconscious through a pendulum, we can see how the pathological forces that we have not been able to identify are hidden. Therefore, if you held a pendulum and asked your consciousness and received affirmative or non-affirmative answers, you have to carefully reflect on the significance of the answers created by your unconscious and check the state of your unconscious. The same applies to muscle testing. If you look into your unconscious mind at random without careful reflection, your unconscious may attack your own irresponsible consciousness. The way to hold a pendulum and seek answers from your unconsciousness is a blessed opportunity to look at yourself that you do not know, while at the same time a risk you have to take if your big unconsciousness attacks yourself.

But because our unconscious reaches the truth of the vast universe, we can reach the truth of the universe through the pendulum test or muscle testing. However, in order for our unconscious to reach the truth of the universe, we need to understand the chakra as well as the physiological power of Hon-Baek-Shin-Ui-Ji. Later, I will explain how our unconsciousness can reach the truth of the universe at the end of the chakra part.

5) Mechanism to Grow Hon-Baek-Shin-Ui-Ji

I introduce Hon-Baek-Shin-Ui-Ji in this book because ultimately, I want to explain how to expand and make our Hon-Baek-Shin-Ui-Ji stronger. So, the last real-life tips are the methodology to grow Hon-Baek-Shin-Ui-Ji. In other words, I introduce the mechanism by which myungsu – the energy field of Hon-Baek-Shin-Ui-Ji – expands one by one.

The reason we live as beings of free souls and at the same time as humans with restrictions is to experience ourselves and create everything. The experience and creation consist of a process through which we define ourselves on our own while at the same time confirming ourselves through our relationship with others. In this sense, there are two main ways to improve myungsu. One is to expand while reflecting on oneself, and the other is to expand through the relationship with others.

(1) Expansion Through Self-Reflection

The first step to expanding Hon-Baek-Shin-Ui-Ji is to make the reflection on oneself a daily routine. Myungsu improves as you strengthen the physiological power of Hon-Baek-Shin-Ui-Ji while weakening its pathological power through self-reflection. We constantly recreate ourselves through the perception of ourselves, and in that sense, self-reflection becomes the positive work of creation.

① Prayer to Build Physiological Power of Hon-Baek-Shin-Ui-Ji

You can improve myungsu through prayers and determination to strengthen the physiological power of Hon-Baek-Shin-Ui-Ji. You can expand the energy of Hon-Baek-Shin-Ui-Ji by: having the harmonious commitment to creating your life in mind (Ji); remembering the omnipotence of God and your free will (Hon); raising a heart that firmly believes in the fairness and perfection of God (Baek); and having time of prayer and reflection to grow the self-love to love yourself (Shin) and selflessness to love others (Ui). You can increase the number of myungsu by one when you expand the energies of Hon-Baek-Shin-Ui-Ji's five minds. Of course, you can improve it by more than one if one reflection is overflowing with meanings that expand yourself, and it might not improve at all if you reflected once but failed to find the meaning that expands yourself.

It is more effective to pray in the order of Ji→Hon→Baek→Shin→Ui. This order being the stream of consciousness that is common to all human beings, it is advantageous to let the energy that reflects on us flow to the heart. Of course, Hon-Baek-Shin-Ui-Ji grows even if the order is different, but it is more effective when it is the same as the circulation order.

The prayer that strengthens the physiological power of Hon-Baek-Shin-Ui-Ji forms a defense wall in our minds. Hon-

Baek-Shin-Ui-Ji's sacred boundary can heal the pain that is caused when the external walls of our minds break down due to breakup or fraud. In other words, the previously mentioned sacred boundary and prophecy are ways to expand myungsu while at the same time ways to heal and protect. Therefore, when you are shaken and in pain due to external circumstances, you can protect yourself and expand your myungsu by committing yourself to the love of Hon-Baek-Shin-Ui-Ji.

As the number of myungsu increases, the circulating condition for the next expansion of Ji→Hon→Baek→Shin→Ui will grow. In other words, you can ensure continuous growth only when the circle drawn by the entire prayers continues to grow. You can make the circle drawn by prayers grow larger by adding enlightenment you achieved in today's life. If it is difficult to grow the circle of prayer, it is a good idea to actively utilize the material that gives resonance to the mind including this book. There are many materials and arts in this world that convey love to us. The process of firmly carving them in your heart is another effective way.

② Repent to Overcome One's Limitations (Pathological Force)

Hon-Baek-Shin-Ui-Ji contains negative energy (pathological consciousness, desire, guilty conscious). Among them, pathological consciousness is the starting point of everything else. Therefore, you can strengthen the physiological power of Hon-Baek-Shin-Ui-Ji by bringing down its pathological power through the reflection intended to overcome the pathological consciousness. You can think about the things that you have been indifferent about in life (Ji); think twice about your inferiority complex that made you forget about your dignity (Hon); think again about the anxiety that forgot about fairness (Baek); think again about the moment when you were disappointed at yourself for no apparent reason (Shin); and think again about the concerns you had because you could not trust others (Ui).

This process of discovering and overturning the pathological consciousness contained in Hon-Baek-Shin-Ui-Ji in our daily life can also extend myungsu. Of course, myungsu can expand when you overcome your limits in the same way as strengthening the physiological power.

It is more effective to keep the physiological order of prayer of repenting the pathological consciousness in the order of: Ji: indifference → Hon: inferiority → Baek: anxiety → Shin: self-pity (disappointment) → Ui: suspicion (concern). In addition, as the Hon-Baek-Shin-Ui-Ji grows, the circles drawn by the whole prayer must be enlarged as well, just the same as in the case of strengthening physiological functions. At first, it grows by discovering the pathological consciousness that is apparently growing, but as myungsu grows, it expands while finding smaller details such as routine daily indifference, inferiority, anxiety, disappointment, and worries.

Repentance for overcoming limitations does not have the power of protection unlike strengthening physiological function. However, when myungsu remains in status quo despite of various efforts, you can open a path for the continuous expansion by eliminating limitations that are blocking your expansion. Also, repenting of apology for yourself (Shin) and the Creator (Hon) has the effect of healing inner pain. In the case of pain that always remains deep in heart regardless of external situation, you can recover mental health through the repentance that delivers your regret and apology to yourself and God.

(2) Growth Through Relationships with Others

Humans cannot live alone and constantly create the world through the process of communication. The love that blossoms from relationships with others becomes the work of creation that brings light to the world and expands the respective individual's Hon-Baek-Shin-Ui-Ji.

① Practicing True Love and Compassion for Others

When you show your love and compassion selflessly without expecting anything in return other than the compensation mentality, you can expand all five energies of Hon-Baek-Shin-Ui-Ji and improve myungsu by one point. It is a natural logic to expand myungsu because the practice of love is the purpose of life. Myungsu increases whenever you overcome the limitations of love, and there is a difference by age and myungsu in this mechanism.

The first half of life that ends around middle-age is the time when you overcome the uncertainty of life, and a time when you overcome the fear of life where you never know what could happen at what time. In this period, Hon-Baek-Shin-Ui-Ji expands when you give love to others based on Shin's trust on yourself. In other words, you have to provide earnest love to others just as much as you love yourself while you are young. Consideration without self-confidence includes a defense mechanism through compensation and dependency on others. From middle-age onward, it is the second half of life when you accept the results of life and overcome anger over life. In this period, Hon-Baek-Shin-Ui-Ji grows when you give love to others based on Ui's trust of others. In other words, expansion can be achieved when you offer trust and love to objects where foolish mistakes and failures are sure to happen.

There are individual differences in the standard of age. The important thing is that regardless of age, two mechanisms are formed depending on myungsu. Up until the early 75, which accounts for three-quarters of the 100 myungsu, you expand myungsu while practicing love under the guide of Shin, and after 75, which is the latter part that accounts for one-quarter, you expand myungsu by practicing love under the guide of Ui.

② The Result of Letting Go of the Greed for Recognition and Love of Others

The result of abandoning the desire to get love and approval from others expands myungsu just as much as the result of giving your love to others. You can improve all five energies of Hon-Baek-Shin-Ui-Ji at once when you are working with somebody or become the victim of psychological attack and respond to the situation by letting go of your desire to have your heart and efforts acknowledged and embrace the other person instead. Because, in human relationships, our desires and wishes clash with each other and our individual differences cause misunderstandings, but when you accept and embrace the negative energy that generates in such situations, it helps the positive creation of the world. Such practice of embracing love also helps improve myungsu by one point while renewing the limitations that we can love.

This method also involves different momentum between the first half and the second half of life. In the first half of life when you overcome fear of life, you can grow when you overcome the urge for love and approval with the Baek's power of believing in the fairness of the law of the universe. In other words, when you are young, you can grow when you embrace others while believing that God is on your side and will acknowledge your efforts. In the second half of life when you overcome your anger over life, you can strengthen Hon-Baek-Shin-Ui-Ji by overcoming your urge for love and recognition with the Ji's power that bears the weight of life. In other words, growth can be achieved when you mature enough to embrace and take the responsibilities on all processes and results of human relationships.

In this case, the difference between two mechanisms is formed depending on the degree of the expansion of myungsu. Up to point 75 out of 100 of the entire myungsu, myungsu expands while embracing love under the guide of Baek, and after the point 75, myungsu expands while embracing love under the guide of Ji.

Myungsu is the average value of the entire energies of Hon-Baek-Shin-Ui-Ji combined. Hon-Baek-Shin-Ui-Ji can individually grow as separate bodies of energy. That is, myungsu increases by one point each time the sum of the increased energies of Hon-Baek-Shin-Ui-Ji becomes five. Therefore, myungsu expands by one point if only the energy of Hon increases by five points. In the case of the expansion of myungsu as the result of reflection, the energies of Hon-Baek-Shin-Ui-Ji do not grow equally depending on individuals. Therefore, Hon can grow stronger while Ji grows weaker. On the other hand, the energies of Hon-Baek-Shin-Ui-Ji grow all together at once and increase myungsu by one point when you give your love or accept others in love in human relationships with others.

You don't expand myungsu with knowledge. You do it with the heart that wishes to love. Myungsu is about building up with a single yearning for love with a heart that wishes to love under any circumstances for any reason. Our energy expands and we can move forward toward happiness when we love each other just for the sake of love; forsake anything that is not love; give love and embrace others with love; and define everything about our power of creation as love, since we are the beings whose purpose of love is love itself.

However, it is very useful to know myungsu – which builds up as the result of love – as a form of knowledge, because then, we can start practicing the reflection of Ji-Hon-Baek-Shin-Ui once every day and improve myungsu, instead of just making up our minds, telling ourselves, "All right! I will love for the sake of love!" Even though we don't expand myungsu with knowledge, it is the knowledge that makes us act on our realization and understanding.

The number of myungsu starts with zero upon our birth. When myungsu reaches 100, it means one stage is completed. Completing myungsu to become 100 means all five energies of Hon-Baek-Shin-Ui-Ji become 100. When myungsu completes by reaching 100, we experience a major change in our Hon-Baek-Shin-Ui-Ji, and we are reborn as a new human being even within the same life. The process of completing myungsu by reaching 100 does not occur only once; the process repeats five times in which myungsu expands from 0 to 100. This is what the first, second, third, fourth, and fifth expansion of myungsu is all about, and it is the law of nature that the expansion of myungsu follows the predetermined sequence of beginning with the first stage and ending with the fifth stage.

The first-stage expansion of myungsu is a process where we experience how love is the only purpose of our living. In the end, through the first-stage expansion of myungsu, we realize the truth that all that actually exists is love; anything that is not love is just realistic-looking illusion; and only love is forever. The majority of humanity is experiencing this first stage. Therefore, we tell stories of miracles to children, in which love heals all pains and sufferings. *Beauty and the Beast* is a story about love breaking a curse and the movie *Frozen* is about love making a curse turn into a blessing. As such, the animation movies that became world-wide blockbusters are all about love conquering all. And this theme is sure to make world-wide success because humanity is in the process of the first-stage expansion in which we realize experiencing love is the most important purpose of life.

There are still many people who fail to realize how love is a priority because they are buried in the fakes that life present them. They think they need money or good looks to love, and they think they have a lot of things to do before they could love. But the law of the universe is that money comes to you when

197

you earnestly love the world, and you become pretty when you sincerely love yourself. Nothing is more important than love because we are the happiest when we experience love. When we put love as our priority and think and fill myungsu with love, our myungsu improves by one point, and when you reach 100, the first-stage expansion of myungsu completes.

At this time, Hon becomes united with Baek and becomes one wholesome body of energy, and the two never separate again. When Baek is integrated into Hon, the fear and anxiety that originated from Baek can be under the control of Hon. Even though you cannot eliminate fear completely, you can find yourself having overcome fears according to your mind. The fear you feel cannot easily stop you. The completion of the first-stage myungsu is the completion of experiencing the true nature of everything as being love. It signifies that resistance is gone when you think about the truth about things that are not love as false, and you can move forward with freedom that is not restricted by fear on your quest to realize the being that you wish to be. In this way, you can fill Dr Hawkins' consciousness energy to 200, making the positive attitude and courage of overcoming fear to take the center stage in your consciousness.

Dr Hawkins emphasizes that a consciousness energy of over 200 is a crucial turning point. From this point on, the voluntary power to fill life with positivity begins to be generated in full swing. It is because when we fully realize that our purpose is experiencing love and take actions to make that happen, we are no longer stopped by fear. After the completion of the first-stage myungsu, we will no longer hesitate in the face of love, and we can grow love itself bigger and more brilliantly.

The completion of the first-stage myungsu is the same as reaching zero myungsu, because it is the beginning of a new life in which a new person is born as the result of the union of Hon and Baek and starts to take a new path in new conditions. From this point on, myungsu starts to accumulate again, and this is called the second stage expansion of myungsu. The second stage expansion of myungsu is a stage where you experience the truth about you being one existence with others and you are they, and they are you. Even though we live by different ideas, we all want to love and be loved. Myungsu begins to increase by one point when you realize a love in which you are not separated with others and you fill your inner self with the truth of love in which we are all one. When myungsu reaches 100 again, you complete the second stage expansion of myungsu.

At this time, the heart's Shin becomes united with Ui and becomes one wholesome body of energy, and the two never separate again. When Ui is integrated into Shin, the suspicion and dissatisfaction that originated from Ui can be under the control of Shin. You can find yourself having less suspicion and dissatisfaction in everyday activities, and even if you are dissatisfied in the face of some situations once in a while, you can willingly overcome those negative emotions according to your mind. In other words, you can overcome complaints and suspicions because it is understood as the true reason where Dr Hawkins' conscious energy reaches 400.

The completion of the second stage of myungsu and completing the experience of us being one is the same as loving others equals loving yourself and loving yourself means loving others at the same time. Now the frustrated and fearful resistance can disappear from communication. Thus, it is natural that the two-way love of self-love and selflessness can be completed in one circle with true love.

In the third stage expansion of myungsu that begins after the completion of the second stage, myungsu becomes zero and starts to increase from there. It means you start living a new life as a new human being whose Ui is integrated with Shin. The third stage expansion of myungsu is the process where you become one with God, realize God's truths are all within you, and bring those truths out and experience them. When these experiences accumulate and myungsu reaches 100, the third stage is completed. At this stage, the integrated Hon absorbs the integrated Shin of the heart and becomes one body of energy and they never separate from each other again.

Hon integrating Shin means that the disappointments you have been feeling in daily routines can be under the control of Hon because you can always bring out God's truths at any time and also because you can always find God's truths in everything that comes into your view. Of course, your disappointments remain still but you can willingly overcome disappointing situations you come to face according to your mind. Once you can overcome disappointments, you no longer need to look for God from outside of you. In other words, you can fill Dr Hawkins's conscious energy to 600 and find peace by becoming one with the universe.

When we complete the third stage of myungsu and experience the truth of us being the Creator, we cannot only see ourselves as the bearers of all truth but realize how resistance disappears when trying to regard all other beings as divine. To see all beings as divine is to regard all of us as being of infinite possibility. Thus, you can love everything that you like and dislike, and you can put out efforts without resistance to view existences just as they are. And we can freely recognize the process through which existences become themselves. As a result, we can expect to be liberated from "what we should do" and see the process of becoming existence within infinite possibilities.

In the fourth stage expansion of myungsu that follows the completion of the third stage, only the Hon of the pineal gland that integrates everything and Ji, the will of life found in distance at the soles of feet, remain. The fourth expansion that is headed toward the integration of Hon and Ji indicates the experience in which everything we do becomes one with the will of God. That is, everything that is given to you is everything that you want to do, and you reflect the wish of the Absolute in everything that you want to do. When these experiences accumulate, your myungsu becomes 100 and you complete the fourth stage expansion. At this time, the last remaining Ji is integrated into Hon, and Hon-Baek-Shin-Ui-Ji becomes a perfectly wholesome body of energy and never becomes separated again. This is the perfection of human beings where body and mind become one unity.

The integration of Hon and Ji indicates that it is possible to have indifference and meaninglessness eliminated in life. So, you can recognize the intention of God in the work that is given to you, and you have no difficulty in starting and stopping without hesitation. We might still hesitate because it is hard to do but if we decide to do it, they can no longer stop us even when we are faced with difficult situations. Because indifference originated from Ji can be under the control of Hon. Realizing the completion of a human being was the result of Hon-Baek-Shin-Ui-Ji being integrated into one body of energy means we become the master of our lives. Therefore, you can remain at enlightenment because you filled the conscious energy to 800. There is nothing meaningless in anything in life, you can treat everything with affectionate interest, and you can do everything willingly and gratefully because everything is what you want to do, and you have no resistance to anything.

The expansion of each stage is explained previously in the part about myungsu's mechanism. In the early stage of growth that accounts for three-quarters of the process (up to 75), Baek and Shin take the lead, while in the later stage that accounts for one-quarter (75 and over), Ji and Ui take the lead. In the first expansion that chooses love first, you believe that God is on your side and you grow up with the power to love yourself. In the latter half, you accept everything as your responsibility and trust others. In the second expansion, in which the distinction between you and the other disappears, you believe the rationality of the universe means that the self-love that loves yourself is the same as your devotion to others. Then in the latter stage, you grow with the conviction that self-love is all about loving others and giving all of yourself to them. In the third stage expansion that we all experience ourselves as divine beings, we believe rationally that the truth within us is the same as that of God as we grow to realize our existence. In the latter half of the stage, we expand while fulfilling our roles that are appropriate for the realization of existence of the others while recognizing others as divine beings. In the fourth stage expansion for the perfection of human being, we grow as we understand what we do is made wholesome with the truth of God, and it completes as we love everything around us and makes everything wholesome in the later stage.

Finally, the fifth stage expansion of myungsu is the stage where Hon-Baek-Shin-Ui-Ji that has integrated into one body of energy becomes one with the soul. This process takes place as you review and repeat the previous four stages. There is no order in the review process. All you have to do is to recall all the love you have experienced in the previous stages. Myungsu increases by 25 points as you experience all beings as love, anything other than love is false, and love is the only eternal truth like the first stage. Like the second stage, myungsu increases by 25 points as you recall the process where love becomes perfect in the truth of us all being one, without a barrier between self-love and love for others. Myungsu increases by 25 points like the third stage as we discover divinity in all beings and celebrate all growing into divine beings. Like the fourth stage, myungsu increases by 25 points as we review and reflect the will of the Absolute in everything we want to do and fulfill our work with willingness and gratitude.

In the fifth stage expansion where you review all the previous stages, you review the expansion method of the second half of the process that accounts for one-quarter of the entire process. In other words, it is a way of experiencing love with a mind where Ji and Ui take the central part. Therefore, the more accurate representation of the review is as follows. In the first review, you vouch everything on yourself, embrace others, and experience love. In the second review, you believe that loving others is the same as loving yourself as you exercise your love. In the third review, you find divinity in others and fulfill your role in revealing their divinity, and in the fourth review, you fill love with your actions that make all things complete. You confirm it one more time because it is the way of life we need to live by to the end.

When we repeat all these four steps and complete the fifth stage expansion, we can completely overcome the last subtle inferiority of Hon. As to the changes that take place in us in this way, I introduce an excerpt about God found in the book *Conversations with God*.

> *You would never experience your Self as being in what you call "trouble." You would not understand any life situation to be a problem. You would not encounter any circumstance with trepidation. You would put an end to all worry, doubt, and fear. You would live as you fantasize Adam and Eve lived— not as disembodied spirits in the realm of the absolute, but as embodied spirits in the realm of the relative. Yet you would have all the freedom, all the joy, all the peace, and all the wisdom, understanding and power of the Spirit you are. You would be a fully realized being.*
>
> *This is the goal of your soul. This is its purpose—to fully realize itself while in the body; to become the embodiment of all that it really is.*
>
> *This is My plan for you. This is My ideal: that I should become realized through you. That thus, concept is turned into experience, that I might know my Self experientially.*

Every time Hon-Baek-Shin-Ui-Ji is combined until the completion of the fourth stage, a significant number of emotions created by anxiety, dissatisfaction, disappointment, and helplessness will disappear, but they do not disappear completely. However, you have the power to be in control so you do not get swayed. It is because the inferiority complex, which is the negative part of Hon that integrates everything, is affecting Hon-Baek-Shin-Ui-Ji externally. Inferiority is consciousness associated with all negative consciousness. Thus, whenever Hon integrates the rest of the energy bodies one by one, the inferiority sense gradually decreases, and a small remaining number of others touch outside not inside of the integrated Hon-Baek-Shin-Ui-Ji after the perfection of human being.

When even the remaining sense of inferiority is finally gone, we can accept the truth that everything is right. I am right, you are right, and everyone is right in one's experience process. Everything had to be so, so everything is right. There will be things you like or dislike out of your spiritual instinct, but there is nothing wrong. Thus, we can embrace forgiveness and blessings only in all the processes of clashes between what we like and dislike.

And even when the fifth phase is completed, all human emotions remain intact instead of disappearing. But all those feelings are no longer from inferiority, anxiety, dissatisfaction, disappointment, and lethargy. It comes from forgiveness and blessings. Thus, there is no emotion that is no longer subject to control, and the moment all emotions occur, you can make choices that become one with sensitivity with a natural will simultaneously. You can laugh as hard as you want at funny jokes, you can melt completely into sweet romance, and you grow yearning when faced with difficulties and failure. You are sincerely thankful and enjoy success, you root for yourself when you feel tension in the face of new challenges, and you grow yourself with heartbreaking regrets. You will be wholeheartedly angry and sad in the face of human tragedy, and you become deeply touched and shed tears in the face of human nobility.

Now all the emotions become one with sensitivity and you naturally make choices to start with blessing and forgiveness – which are the constant heart of the Absolute – emotions, your life unfolds more gloriously.

Human emotion is not a flat plane. It is always formed in three dimensions. If I may explain the shape of the human mind in three dimensions, it may be a small tetrahedron in the beginning of the first-stage expansion. So, one thought exists along with four sides of a mind. Of those four sides, we choose one to illuminate the light of consciousness, and push away others that are the opposite of the side unconsciously. For example, when you sincerely try to yield to others, it is always in the company of the opposite urge to do the things as you please, the thought that you don't really need to do it, and the thought that it will be good to yield. In this situation, we suppress the contrasting thoughts with a strong consciousness, define them as being selfish, and lock them up in our unconsciousness. Of course, there are people who push away the thought about yielding and satisfying their urge. Anyway, everyone has these four sides of a mind, but it is hard to recognize or acknowledge the other sides of a mind because of the sharp angle of the tetrahedron. Thus, we continue the errors of trying to erase the sides of a mind hidden from consciousness in the tetrahedron.

However, as we experience love and expand myungsu, the mind not only expands its size, but also transforms into more sophisticated polyhedrons. Initially, it starts from a small tetrahedron, but it gradually transforms into a larger cube and creates a sense of stability. And then it becomes a more imposing octahedron and it holds a more diversified mind, until it continues to expand into a rather large dodecahedron with gentler obtuse angles which makes it easier to notice a diversified mind; next it becomes a big icosahedron to bring a sense of freedom by connecting the mind, and then to a magnificent sphere shape in the end.

When our hearts become spheres like the stars of the universe, all emotions can become one with sensibility through love. Although the opposite mind still exists in one side of the mind, the mind of all sides naturally leads to love. You can give love while willingly yielding to give love or while willingly not yielding to help the other grow in love. The concern over whether you are doing well is only a different form of a strong love that wishes to convey wholesome love. Any doubt about others will be a process of preparing for forgiveness in an unknown situation, so all suspicion and anxiety will only amplify love. Now you can have a colorful mind in every way, any heart can do it all in love, and you can love it as the happiest choice for all hearts because it is round. This is the mandala of Carl Jung who preached about finding happiness by uniting the shadows of the mind, and it is the perfection of myungsu.

Dimensional Structure of the Mind – Regular Polyhedrons

Hon-Baek-Shin-Ui-Ji, united with the soul in the form of a huge sphere, is completely wrapped in the light of the Creator. That means it becomes a star. God the Creator is a colorful existence who laughs with us when we laugh, rejoices when we rejoice, curses when we are angry and curse, and sheds tears with us when we cry in sadness. All of God's feelings He shares with us come from His forgiveness and blessings. By the completion of the fifth stage, our Hon-Baek-Shin-Ui-Ji becomes wrapped with the light of the Creator, which means we become one with God. According to the book *Conversations with God,* we are a part of God, and of his Soul, Mind, and Body, we are the Body that is His life. Becoming a being that realizes the ideal of God means that we become one being with the Absolute's mind as a part of His life and we form the Trinity as our body and mind merge into our soul. Therefore, we can always share the same hearts with Him, and we become the beings who always live wholesome lives here and now by freely applying the absolute values of the universe. It is the only reason we exist and live, and the final conclusion of the expansion of myungsu.

There is something we need to know additionally. First, there is always a chance to resolve our karma while we move on toward the competition of the fifth expansion of myungsu. Sometimes the negative emotions that you overcame by the completion of each stage might appear distinctly. This is mostly due to individual karma. Both the karma you have to pay and the karma you have to receive come to you before the completion of the fifth stage. You can continue to expand myungsu only when you resolve all the karmas according to natural law. In that way, you will be left with no karma to resolve by the time you are about to complete the fifth stage.

Another thing to know is that the difficulty level of each stage is the same. The order of expansion is the same to everybody because it is the law of nature. It might feel difficult if you think of the fourth expansion during the first-stage expansion, but the difficulty level is ultimately the same, whether you start from zero to complete the first stage or you complete the first stage and try to complete the second stage, because you are born into a new being and start from the beginning all over again in each stage. I want you to remember that you do not have to be scared, wondering, "Will I really be able to form a trinity?" because the difficulty level is the same at all stages. Besides, the last stage is the easiest reviewing part! It is an open road that anyone can tread.

And the power factor of the human body continuously improves in each dimension's expansion. That is, the completion of the first expansion results in the power factor of 0.25, the completion of the second expansion is improved to the power factor of 0.5, the completion of the third expansion reaches the power factor of 0.75, and the active power of the human body reaches the perfect level when the power factor becomes one at the fourth stage. That means the mind and the body become one unity. There is no change in power factor in the last fifth expansion. The power factor continues to improve along with expansion, but myungsu does not recognize the number that comes after 100 as 101. Since the integration of Hon-Baek-Shin-Ui-Ji signifies the rebirth as a new being, the 100 of myungsu is the same as a new beginning of zero myungsu.

I don't know what we will be headed for after Trinity. That is an area beyond my imagination. But one thing I am sure of is that becoming one with God's mind doesn't mean the end, because we are eternal, constantly evolving beings, and because everything in the universe is in a circle. I am really curious about the time that will follow after I became the incarnation of everything that is true. Perhaps the time that follows will be a path for another being to take toward new evolution.

In general, when Hon-Baek-Shin-Ui-Ji is completed at each stage of integration, it naturally dissolves its meaning into life. As the experience of love being the most important accumulates in the first expansion, it becomes natural that all things that are not love are perceived as unimportant and meaningless. Thus, when the first expansion is complete, you find yourself finding it easier to find and see love in everything, and no longer have resistance to the awareness that things that are not love are just false.

However, not everyone who has accomplished each step spontaneously makes sense in reality. If the first expansion process is completed by building love with the concept of war between good and evil, it is important that the view of evil, which is the object of war, and the reality of everything may not accept love. In other words, the first reality is that the reality of everything is love and the rest is fiction, but the meaning is not realized in life unless you try to see the truth yourself. There is nothing that can be done on our own without our own choice because we are granted the full free will. If you stay in that wrong frame, you will not be able to expand any further.

So, it is very beneficial to know the meaning of each step that we expand. In this way, you can avoid getting lost because you don't lock yourself in a wrong frame, and you know the direction you are headed to. Since it is like living with a navigation of life, arriving at the destination of Trinity requires practice and time only. If you are now doing the first expansion, you just need to make up your mind to choose and put love as the priority. If you are expanding the second stage, you can try to accept what the other person wants and generously provide to the other person, believing that your mind is one with the other even though you and the other person have different ideas. If you are on the third expansion, try to regard yourself and everything as a God the Almighty, and if you are on the fourth expansion, you only need to live and fulfill every moment by practicing only the absolute values in life. In this way, you are aware of the meanings of the stages you have to follow through, and therefore can avoid the error of not choosing those directions.

It is very important that errors can be avoided, because when we lose the direction we have to go, we can realize the path we need to follow again after going through troubles and suffering from the pain that comes along the way. That's the way the universe is guiding us to the right direction. Therefore, the majority of the troubles we face are a sign that we are lost, even though it doesn't apply to all of the troubles. But if we have the exact knowledge of the significance of the road we should take and try our best to practice in life, many reasons for suffering are eliminated. We can keep the pain to a minimal level while achieving the goal of our lives.

However, it is all the better if you can think of all these stages at once instead of thinking about them one stage at a time. Even though the order of the integration of Hon-Baek-Shin-Ui-Ji is predetermined by the law of nature, it doesn't mean you have to think one at a time in accordance to the growth you make at each stage. If you understand all the stages of integration and acknowledge it right now, you can get traction in the process. Even if you are in the stage of the first expansion at the moment but you are already embracing the significance of the second, third, and fourth stages and try to practice the truth of the paths, you will be able to experience how the expansion of myungsu gets accelerated.

Let's pay as much attention as possible to see which is love no matter under what situation you are in, and remember that in the end, all the eternal beings and existences are love. Know that within us is the same heart as everyone has, and that within everybody is the same heart as your heart. By doing that, acknowledge that everyone is your own self and your self is them. You must firmly believe that all the truths of God are within you, and that you are the light, truth, and life. By doing that, seek God's truth from your self, and find and discover God's truth in everything that you see. Always choose only the absolute value, which is the desire of the soul. Since we don't need anything other than that, we should fill our lives while freely crossing between absolute values that are enfolded in chakra. By doing that, acknowledge that all hearts are becoming the beings that bring out blessings and forgiveness. When we acknowledge and reveal all these at once, the path we take opens wider and bigger. We can move forward at an accelerated speed while experiencing only the minimal amount of confusion.

In the history of mankind, we can sometimes find those who were headed toward human perfection. Suh Hee[29], who defended the country through diplomatic rhetoric, and Admiral Yi Sun-shin[30], who led the Great Battle of Myeongnyang to victory even though his military force was weaker than the enemies, are the examples of people who had completed the first expansion and put fears under control. King Sejong[31] did not put himself above his court slaves even though he was living in a class society. He made numerous achievements including the creation of the Korean writing system, Hunminjeongeum, by pursuing truth for the people with a compassionate heart that cared for his people just as he would himself. Perhaps he was the one who spread his divinity outside, passing the stage of completing the second expansion and moving on to the competition of the third expansion.

Jesus Christ taught us, "Truly I tell you, whatever you did for one of the least of these brothers and sisters of mine, you did for me," and showed the competition of the second expansion where all is one. He also declared, "I am the way and the truth and the life. No one comes to the Father except through me," and taught us how He is a divine being and we can all become the same divine existences by showing what it is like when you complete the third expansion. I think that with the miracle of resurrection, He became the guide of souls for the human beings till today and showed us more than just human perfection.

Others who have achieved the ideal of human perfection or unity with the Creator include Dr David Hawkins and Charlie Chaplin. When you read Charlie Chaplin's poem *As I Began to Love Myself,* you can see the self-love through which he expresses broad and clear truth has no selfishness or boundaries. He is also expressing how he sees himself and everything in the world as perfection and accepts it as the truth. And he claims that it is not the perfection of his loving his self, but the beginning of it. It makes me guess that perhaps he was feeling the rebirth in which he becomes one with God. When you read books by Dr Hawkins, you can see how he is expressing that all beings are love and becoming all beings by focusing on the beings themselves. This is what it is like when you complete the third expansion. The perfection of all moments that he was looking at is originated from the peace by taking an implicit attitude that is proactive while at the same time acknowledging everything, and at this level of peace, the thoughts you have in your mind become reality powerfully and swiftly, according to him. That is expressing how he is a being of trinity who is capable of accepting everything because he completely let go of the inferiority complex.

There might be people who read about my guess and ask, "So, do you mean Charlie Chaplin is greater than Jesus?" My answer, of course, is no. Myungsu is never a criterion for determining who is better. How can anybody dare to compare the greatness of Jesus to anybody, considering how He has been a guide for countless human beings on Earth for two thousand years with love that He had practiced and proved by being calcified? However, I can feel His sorrowful love for humanity in his statement, "No one comes to the Father except through me," and it is heartbreaking to think of the painful crucifixion created in the collective consciousness of the time. I cannot help but express my infinite respect at the miracle of His resurrection and the love He kept for humanity despite the pain.

Occasionally, I hear people saying that only those who believe in Jesus can be saved when they preach in Christianity. Each time I hear that, I think that it is Jesus who is most heartbroken and sad to hear anybody saying that. Jesus has been a guide to us for over two thousand years with love so great as to achieve the miracle of resurrection. Now, I think we should let Him go free, while following His words and practicing them in return for His love. I think that we've truly arrived at the point where we can let go of Jesus Christ with our true love. I hope you will put down your separate anxiety that you can't do without him, and continue to honor and think about Him, and follow His words. I sincerely pray that Jesus Christ will be free from mankind.

Myungsu is not a measure of excellence, but a measure of how well you create happiness. Happiness is the goal of our soul. On the road to the purpose of the soul, some people move forward while leaving behind great things that would be remembered by mankind, while others move forward leaving only silent traces. Each one of us moves on in our own unique way. Our goal is not about becoming great: It is about realizing our true self and becoming happy.

Most people are in the process of making the first expansion, but sometimes I come across people around me who have moved beyond the first expansion. There is one mischievous four-year old boy who approaches anybody without fear, shows himself, and accepts them. He accepts most of the information given to him with love and smartness. Besides, he has such an empathy for others that I cannot help but be amazed. Whenever I see the boy, I think to myself, "This boy must have completed the first and the second expansion in his previous life for sure." And I also wonder, "Is his smartness originating from the completion of the third expansion?" Then there is an old lady who frequently visits my clinic with her husband. She always demonstrates a brilliant beauty and always impresses me, and I keep wondering, "How can she care for her sick husband with such elegance for such a long time?" She empowers her family, friends and many neighbors with love. And she has no fear of giving love to anyone. Every time I see her, I'm sure that she moved beyond the first round of expansion, and her choices that show no distinction between her love for herself and others means she moved beyond the second expansion, and perhaps she is in the process of completing the third and the fourth expansion with her love for her family. Also, whenever I see the writings of my favorite columnist and radio script writer, I have a happy imagination in my mind, thinking "They must be in the process of the second and the third expansion at the least."

In addition, I frequently meet people who show the completion of a stage in my neighborhood. The majority of the people are in the process of the first stage of expansion, but there are a growing number of people who have moved beyond the first stage of expansion since modern times. If you carefully look around, you will also be able to find people who have been completing each stage. They are all uniformly beautiful, have warm personalities, and they are living happy lives regardless of the circumstances.

I don't know how many people have realized the union with the Creator, but the road to reach trinity is not restricted only to the great people. It is also not a road you can take only through great achievements that will awaken mankind. This is a road to the universal happiness, and it is open to everyone. It is only a road taken by those who wish to be happy, and it is the only road that we cannot refuse to take. There is no road we wish to take other than this road. Since there is only one road, the only difference is how long it will take and in which method you will take it. In the book *Conversations with God,* the author said, "We can't help being saved. Except if you don't know the way..." Now, having read this book, you come to realize what it means to become one with the Creator, and the law of nature about the process through which you can get there. It's up to each of you to make the choice and decide whether to take this road or not. Whatever you choose, all is fine and good because you're bound to end up taking the road to happiness. All I can do is to congratulate and bless you on any choices you've made, and I truly congratulate you on your happiness and your trinity that will unfold someday.

As I Began to Love Myself
By Charlie Chaplin

As I began to love myself I found that anguish and emotional suffering
are only warning signs that I was living against my own truth.
Today, I know, this is "AUTHENTICITY".

As I began to love myself I understood how much it can offend somebody
As I try to force my desires on this person, even though I knew the time
was not right and the person was not ready for it, and even though this
person was me. Today I call it "RESPECT".

As I began to love myself I stopped craving for a different life,
and I could see that everything that surrounded me was inviting me to grow.
Today I call it "MATURITY".

As I began to love myself I understood that at any circumstance,
I am in the right place at the right time, and everything happens
at the exactly right moment. So I could be calm.
Today I call it "SELF-CONFIDENCE".

As I began to love myself I quit stealing my own time,
and I stopped designing huge projects for the future.
Today, I only do what brings me joy and happiness, things I love to do
and that make my heart cheer, and I do them in my own way and in
my own rhythm. Today I call it "SIMPLICITY".

As I began to love myself I freed myself of anything that is no good for
my health – food, people, things, situations, and everything that drew

me down and away from myself. At first I called this attitude
a healthy egoism. Today I know it is "LOVE OF ONESELF".

As I began to love myself I quit trying to always be right, and ever since
I was wrong less of the time. Today I discovered that is "MODESTY".

As I began to love myself I refused to go on living in the past and worry
about the future. Now, I only live for the moment, where EVERYTHING
is happening. Today I live each day, day by day, and I call it "FULFILLMENT".

As I began to love myself I recognized that my mind can disturb me
and it can make me sick. But As I connected it to my heart, my mind became a valuable ally. Today I call this
connection "WISDOM OF THE HEART".

We no longer need to fear arguments, confrontations or any kind of problems
with ourselves or others. Even stars collide, and out of their crashing
new worlds are born. Today I know THAT IS "LIFE"!

Endnotes

28   Myungsu(命數): The destiny number.

29   Suh Hee: the diplomat in the Goryeo Dynasty.

30   Admiral Yi Sun-shin: the marine general of the Joseon Dynasty.

31   King Sejong: the fourth king of the Joseon Dynasty. In the sense of respect, he is called the Great King.

32   The book *Power Vs. Force* introduces a summarized table that shows the characteristics of consciousness and emotions beginning from the conscious energy level of 0 to 1,000. The integration process of Hon-Baek-Shin-Ui-Ji is in parallel with the contents of the table.

Completion of Myungsu and Dr David Roman Hawkins' Conscious Energy[32]

Myungsu	Status of Existence			Conscious Energy
Completion of the 1st Myungsu	Hon,Baek+Shin+Ui+Ji = Cube	Overcome fear	Courage, positivity	200
Completion of the 2nd Myungsu	Hon,Baek+ Shin,Ui+Ji = Octahedron	Overcome dissatisfaction	Reason, understanding	400
Completion of the 3rd Myungsu	Hon,Baek,Shin,Ui+Ji = Dodecahedron	Overcome disappointment	Peace, whole	600
Completion of the 4th Myungsu	Hon,Baek,Shin,Ui,Ji = Icosahedron	Overcome indifference	Awakening, language transition	800
Completion of the 5th Myungsu	Unity with the Soul = Magnificent Sphere	Overcome inferiority	Awakening, language transition	1,000

6) Myungsu of the Intellectually-challenged People

Every human being comes to Earth with the goal of achieving trinity through the expansion of his or her myungsu. Therefore, they raise their own thoughts and minds to experience love. However, there are people who have difficulty in realizing the general-sense love: intellectually-challenged people. It is particularly true for those who are suffering from severe autism who cannot make common communication specifically. But they also came to Earth with the goal of experiencing love to expand myungsu and move forward to find happiness. Then, in what form do they feel love and love others to expand their myungsu? Their expansion of myungsu happens in ways slightly different from others, and also has a different meaning.

First of all, there are various causes for intellectual disability, but here, it refers to the intellectual disability at birth without trait or functional abnormalities in brains. In addition, there are differences in degree in birth intellectual disabilities, but I will explain here on the basis of those whose severe intellectual disorders prevent them from recognizing the circumstances surrounding them and therefore cannot react to situations properly. They are in a condition where their Hon-Baek-Shin-Ui-Ji energies are turned off one by one and are in a dormant state. And every time their number of myungsu increases by 25, their energies are turned on one through four stages in the order of Hon, Shin, Ui, and Baek.

When their myungsu reaches 25, their Hon awakens, and the energy is turned on. As a result, they become capable of realizing the dignity and divinity of existence and understand the objective of being. When their myungsu reaches 50, the Shin of their heart awakens and becomes turned on. As a result, they acknowledge the joy of life, embrace themselves as precious beings, and become capable of loving themselves. When their myungsu reaches 75, their Ui awakens, making them capable of

219

looking at others and communicating with them, building trust, and keeping love for them. Lastly, when their myungsu reaches 100, Baek in their ears awakens and gets turned on, making them capable of understanding and accepting the world and realizing their existence as a member of the world.

When Hon, Baek, Shin, Ui, and Ji are all turned off, that is the most serious case of disorder. When Hon is the only thing that is turned on, the person's disorder is at the level of having a certain degree of perception; when Hon and Shin are turned on, the person's disorder is at the level of having a certain degree of ability to observe himself or herself; when Hon, Shin, and Ui are turned on, the person's disorder is at the level of communicating with others; and when Hon, Shin, Ui and Baek are turned on but Ji is turned off, the person's disorder is at the level of understanding the world because the perception and communication abilities are integrated, but is not capable of leading a life with his or her own will.

In the case of people with such intellectual disabilities, the expansion of myungsu takes place through communication with others. Their myungsu increases by one each time they form the sense of identity with others through communion. The myungsu expands when the people with intellectual disabilities look at us, the common people, and feel the sense of identity, telling themselves, "I see how I am the same as them." In addition, their myungsu expands when we find a sense of identity from the intellectually-challenged people as well. It doesn't matter in what direction the communication takes place. The myungsu of the intellectually-challenged people expands as long as one of the two parties feel the sense of identity during the two-directional communication. If they feel the sense of identity with us, that becomes the process of gradual awakening, and if we feel the sense of identity with them, that means they helped us to become awakened, thereby expanding the myungsu in both directions.

Therefore, the key point to the education and learning for the intellectually-challenged individuals is not in repeating our ways until they learn them: Rather, we have to be aware of their ways and relate to how they feel, and during the process, discover that we share the same essence with them in the fundamental level and encourage them to have the same sense of identity with us. The mutually felt sense of identity is the key to connecting them and us with love.

For the sake of love between us and the intelligently challenged individuals, I suggest you put aside the way you feel you are normal and they are not, and share the same behaviors and interests with them, however peculiar they might be. We accept them while experiencing how they feel and sharing what they like with them. Their raw expressions are in fact not much different from what we have deep in our hearts. They act on the things that we only imagine in our heads; they perceive the things larger than how we perceive; and they feel the things less significantly than how we feel. Since the only difference is how they perceive and feel things smaller or larger than we do, we can discover that we have what they have, and they have what we have as well. And while feeling yourself sharing the same ways as they do, you can feel how the intellectually-challenged individuals are the same beings as us. A subconscious sense of identity that makes you realize "they are the same as us" is enough. With that sense of identity and love you share with them, the myungsu can grow both in us and in them. That is the principle of awakening the "Hon-Shin-Ui-Baek" of the intellectually-challenged individuals with the power of love.

After all the energies of Hon-Shin-Ui-Baek are turned on, the last Ji energy can be awakened not through the communion with us, but through the love that the individual has raised. The key to awakening Ji is found in the intellectually-challenged individual when he or she builds gratitude on top of the love for the people who had raised the sense of identity with them.

This gratitude is what turns on the energy to create their own life with their own will. The energy of Ji is turned on when they build the gratitude for the love of all life that had turned on their Hon-Shin-Ui-Baek and when that gratitude reaches the same number of 100 as the hearts that had turned on their Hon-Shin-Ui-Baek. When the stages of myungsu expansion complete by reaching the number of 100, all their energies of Hon-Shin-Ui-Baek-Ji are turned on.

It doesn't matter what they are grateful for. Any thought will do as long as it is about how they became awakened by love from others, and how grateful they are for the love. They only need to fill their minds with gratitude as much as with the love they have received. Therefore, it is important to encourage the people with mild levels of intellectual disabilities to express their joy, praise, and gratitude sincerely and frequently so that the virtue of gratitude becomes a part of their everyday life. A person who has been at the receiving end of grateful action understands what gratitude is about and can naturally internalize it. When the Ji energy is turned on in the end, they can complete in the original form of being who can create life with their own will. Perhaps, after this stage of completion, they will take the same path of myungsu expansion as we ordinary people do.

Epilogue: The Wounds Left by the Inquiry To Open the Unconscious

I have something to sincerely ask readers who read this book this far. As mentioned in the prologue, I was able to reach the truth of happiness by starting the process called the "AGD." When the accumulation of deeds crumbled down due to a frame of a war between the good and the evil, they hurt so many people in the process and the process is still continuing. I wanted to heal the wounds they'd left, and I wanted to stop them making more wounds, but I could not do it by myself alone. What I need to open a path of healing those wounds is a collective consciousness with the support of many people. And I ask readers to open their hearts and read my prayers together with me. I sincerely ask you to read these prayers out of your compassion for me, the writer of this book, and for those who are trapped within their limitations, and out of love for those who have wounds in their hearts with the mind of reaching out and speaking to us and to God.

To My Dear Pendulum Colleagues Who Are Holding a Pendulum

* The anticipation of directly coming in contact with the truth by holding a pendulum became an unfamiliar anxiety while at the same time a greed for life to us. Let's think again about the suffering we've experienced as our lives became dependent on the pendulum with that anxiety and greed.

We failed to notice the pure reason of love and lost the purpose we called love when we distorted the significance of holding a pendulum into a war between the good and the evil. We have to think again about how we dishonored this path.

While holding a pendulum and communicating with the vast unconsciousness, we ended up shrinking ourselves instead. We have to think again about how the light of chakra kept growing dimmer while we were holding onto the pendulum, until eventually we failed to present a light that would bring us the true answers.

We became oblivious of the true essence of love that is fulfilled through communication because we trapped ourselves in delusion and arrogance in which we believed we are superior to others. Let's think again about how we turned the pendulum into a tool of judgment and caused the tragedy of exclusion and hurt those who had been with us.

Let's forgive ourselves for having distorted the essence of the pendulum. This path being an unknown path, it was dark and made us feel lost. And now, let's ask for forgiveness for all our wrongdoings. I sincerely pray that we take the responsibility for the pains we've caused and be forgiven in the face of all laws of nature.

* It is time for us to put down the pendulum, because the pendulum we have distorted is causing so much pain and is creating a storm of collective consciousness. Please raise the will to acknowledge our wrongs and have the faith that we can live an integral life without the need of the pendulum.

The expression of opinions of non-communication and the answers that are against humanity that the pendulum is giving us now are the messages from God that tell us that we are on a wrong path. Now we need to heal the pain, bring order to the chaos, and recover the honor of this path.

We were able to hold the pendulum while expanding our beauty and greatness. We have to realize that we can achieve the self-realization by finding true answers when we discover our own lights anew courageously in front of the answers of the pendulum.

The pendulum is a tool that completes love with unrestricted communication, and we are the same existences with all others. I hope that you will put down the pendulum and feel and fulfill the love as it is supposed to be until we return to the love in its integral shape.

We grew brilliantly through the pendulum; savored the bliss of contacting the truth; and experienced the full extent of the involved risks. Let's be grateful for all those processes. And let's be grateful for the freedom of our choice, because once we recover our natural shape, any choice we make with regards to the pendulum will correspond to the will of the soul.

* Let us love all the opportunities that life gives us, regardless of whether we pick up the pendulum again or put it down again on our quest of awakening in life. Let us create happiness while loving our lives colorfully and harmoniously.

Please don't forget that God will be with us and loves us no matter what we choose with the pendulum. I pray that you will enjoy truth and freedom while expanding glory and peace in God's love with the experience of love which is the only purpose.

I hope you will remember everything – our greatness and divinity – whether there is a pendulum or not. I pray that you will fill and fully bloom all nine chakras with that remembrance and become the beings that manifest the greatness and divinity of God.

Let's give without sparing anything and take without fearing for anything, while always remembering that we are all one being, whether we are picking up or putting down the pendulum. Let's make the choice of picking up or putting down the pendulum in order to love and bless each other.

I sincerely bless the moments of choice you will make with the pendulum in the future. Whatever your choice will be, I cheer for you and congratulate you for the glorious journey that you will be taking, and I wholeheartedly congratulate you on the magnificent results your choice will bring to you.

To Those Who Were Hurt Because of the Pendulum

* I sincerely apologize for having devastated and destroyed your life and for having inflicted wounds on your hope and devotion due to their distorted path of pendulum. I sincerely pray and root for you to be allowed to take a break when you need a break, to find solace when you need to be consoled, and to find the energy when you need it for your efforts to heal your lives that are wounded by them. And I hope that you will find the wellness in your lives again and find new hope and dreams in that wellness. I will wait for the future with faith, a future when your new dreams will raise you up and fill your lives with happiness.

* I sincerely apologize for having damaged your faith and the sense of values and for having caused chaos due to their distorted path of pendulum. I am aware that it is an unforgivable wrong to have disturbed your noble faith with their words that justified the distorted answer of the pendulum. I cheer for you to remember for what you are moving forward by recalling the moments of bliss and glory that you had in the past, and to raise the values that kept you not to lose yourself in the middle of the sufferings. I have no doubt that the faith and values you recover will shine more brilliantly and imposingly. I earnestly hope that the glory and the peace will bring you a greater freedom so that you can unfold your vitality infinitely.

* I am sorry and apologize for having denied your nobility and divinity and inflicted wounds by undermining your beauty and greatness due to their distorted path of pendulum. They denied your brightness only because they were reflecting the darkness of themselves who were holding up a pendulum, and it was not meant to be your darkness. Please remember that you are noble and great beings who guarded yourselves in the storm caused by the pendulum that was on its distorted path. And remember how you were brilliantly growing and expanding before the days of the distorted path of pendulum. I cheer for you to continue on the road to rediscover your beauty and greatness with those memories. In your own method and in your true self.

* I am truly sorry for having inflicted scathing pain while betraying the love and trust you've given them due to their distorted path of pendulum. I cheer for you with the belief that all your wounds will be healed by loving those around you and recognizing more love around you since love is the best medicine to heal the wounds left by love. And I humbly wait for you to forgive those who have wounded you with the pendulum and be compassionate about them in someday in the future when your wounds are healed, and your love grows bigger. Please have a sympathy for those who have lost touch with the true essence of love. Please pray for them to remember what love is all about, and how to find love again.

* Please don't blame yourself for having been on the distorted path of pendulum. Even though I am not sure if I can ask you this, please forgive those who have wronged you so that the pain and wounds caused by them will not remain with you at all. Lastly, please pray that nobody will be wounded like you were and everybody will take the path to forgiveness. I am thankful because I have some idea about how difficult it is to forgive, and I am thankful for the miracle your forgiveness will bring. I hope that a path will open brightly for your future, and I congratulate you for the glorious results of your expansion in advance.

I deeply and wholeheartedly thank my readers who read this book this far. I received more than my fair share of blessings from you. I sincerely hope that you will find happiness in life and live a life full of love as a joyous existence, enjoying peace and unfolding glory.

How and What to Pursue in Life
Part 2

9 Absolute Values of Chakras
WHAT We Should Live For

Contents

Prologue

In his book *Power vs. Force*, Dr David R. Hawkins introduced muscle testing as a way to find truth through unconscious reactions. I introduced how to use a pendulum as a way to look into the unconscious mind in the first part of this book. I explained that these two methods are based on the phenomenon in which the active power of the human body is generated differently depending on everyone's thoughts. A small number of people were actually able to look into their unconscious minds using these methods. However, some people who sought to find truth through their unconscious minds experienced destructive phenomenon, unlike what Dr David Hawkins experienced. Suspicion and disruption resulted because the answers they found in their unconscious minds differed so greatly, and the weight of the consequential sense of responsibility kept piling up in their minds and lives until they lost their true selves. I am one of those people who have gone through that process. I was able to see the real nature of the reactions that gave me a look into my unconscious mind through "yes-or-no" answers while finding the path that would lead me to recover my true self, and I started writing this book to talk about it.

The unconscious reaction clearly needed to know how humans should live. I also had to know what human beings should live for. When I understood these two questions, I was able to understand the principle behind our unconscious reactions of "yes or no" and the reason different people have different answers. Ultimately, this book goes beyond the initial purpose of guiding readers to the study of truth on an unconscious level to presenting answers to the questions of how we should live, and what we should pursue. In the first part of this book, I explained the question of "how we should live" in terms of the mental analysis practiced in Eastern medicine, and in this part, I am going to explain "what we should pursue in life" in terms of chakras.

For humans, chakras are the channels through which we communicate with the universe, a scaled down solar system in the human body. In chakras, absolute values that are always right for us to choose are communicating with the solar system. And the key of this book is to specifically identify what the "Absolute Values" are. These absolute values have not been clearly explained in any religion or philosophy. They were presented only vaguely by Aristotle as a conceptual philosophy of the Golden Mean. Instead of explaining the ambiguous image of the Golden Mean that embraces two extremes, I will present ten specific values, and explain in detail why they guarantee us happiness with examples. This will be a new leap forward in the history of philosophy, because it is about disclosing the concept of optimization of the Golden Mean as discussed by Aristotle in ten specific themes.

The main content of this book presents prayers that remind us of the significance of the absolute values and lets us know their consequences. These prayers are the driving force behind my recovery, healing, and growth. It is my hope that you will be able to find what you need and fuel yourself with it when you are in pain and confused in life, or when you are fully motivated to grow. If you ever experience a moment when you feel you are in need, you will be able to find and read the prayer that you need for the moment and easily use it to help you heal and grow.

Presenting answers to the two questions regarding How and What in life will guide you to happiness. I sincerely hope that you will be able to draw a good blueprint of your life for "how to live and for what" by reading this book.

November 2019
Kim Yoon-jeong

What is Chakra?

[Hon-Baek-Shin-Ui-Ji] [魂魄神意志]is the truth about our mind, which is one of the three elements that make us what we are: soul, mind, and body. Understanding [Hon-Baek-Shin-Ui-Ji] helps us think wisely about how we should live and how we should exercise our creativity. Chakras that I will explain now in this book are the truth about the soul. The soul is the greatest part of our trinity because it encompasses the "I" that exists now in this universe as well as all other "I's" that exist in other parallel universes. The soul is our eternal domain that exists forever and never disappears. It can be described as the *de facto* ruler who unleashes significant influence over our bodies and minds. The soul is part of Shin; it contains all truths; it is all love; and it is the *de facto* ruler. We can understand this through chakras.

The word "Chakra" came from the Hindu culture and therefore is unfamiliar to our culture. But lately, it has become widely known to us thanks to yoga. Chakra, which means "wheel" or "circle" in Sanskrit, is the pivotal energy that swirls in the shape of a disk where the spiritual energy, mind energy, and physical energies of a human come together. There are seven chakras in our body, and they run through the center of the body beginning with the perineal area and extending to the top of the head. They begin with the first chakra found in the perineal area in the lower part of the body and end with the seventh chakra that is found at the top of the head. Their locations are shown in the following figure.

These seven chakras are considered to have been officially confirmed by theory. Chakras are the most spiritual parts in the human body, and they control everything. Therefore, the practice of yoga aims to open these chakras and let our energies flow through us and control our mind and body. I am not

235

introducing chakras in this book with the intention of having this training improve our spiritual power. Instead, I am going to talk about how the values of life that our souls seek can be found in chakras.

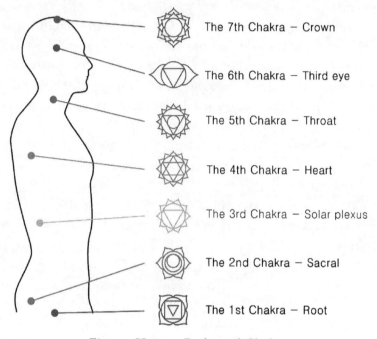

Figure: Human Body and Chakras

Chakras contain the values that our souls pursue in life. To be more specific, they contain the absolute values that make up this universe. And chakras are the human channels through which the energies of these absolute values communicate with the universe. The universe is continuously supplying energy to us by communicating with us through chakras. The energy of the universe we receive while seeking absolute values in this way creates a vortex in each of our chakras to control our body and mind.

The universe is designed solely for the purpose of experiencing love, and it also runs solely for the purpose of experiencing love. And when God the Creator created this world, he had the perfect idea about how to let us experience love through What. In the proposition of "what should we experience of love through what," the "what" part is referring to the absolute values we should always choose and seek to experience in love. The Creator created this universe and us humans with these absolute values as standards. Therefore, these absolute values of the universe are cutting through the center of our physical body. To understand chakras where absolute values are swirling like whirlpools is to understand our nature and the purpose of our creation.

Since the universe is made up of absolute values, the world is created only for the purpose of experiencing love, and because we hold absolute values in chakras, our only purpose is to experience love. The creation of the universe allowed us to experience love through absolute values. Absolute value always means the right value for love. Absolute values are the ones we must always choose and pursue under any circumstances at any time.

We can experience love while minimizing the pain and suffering we must endure if we design life based on the meanings of chakras and choose the meanings of chakras in any circumstances. Therefore, "what should we live for" is a proposition that we must know along with "how should we live," and in fact, the former is the higher-level concept, because the choice we make with regard to the proposition of "what should we live for" determines the outcome of life. But we haven't understood what we should live for while leading our lives. All mankind have lived in good faith while doing their best, but we humans have been designing our lives with the wrong frames, consequently causing numerous tragedies by entrapping ourselves in them.

Human history has evolved while going through and overcoming those tragedies. We have experienced the Holocaust because of the wrong frame known as nationalism, and then we recovered the value of life while overcoming the tragedy. In addition, nationalism made us suffer from the tragedy of sex slavery (comfort women), which violated Asian women's human rights in the age of imperialism. Mankind has also suffered a divided international community due to the limited value of system ideology, and our society is still in the process of breaking away from it.

Now, the younger generation of South Korea does not accept and criticize the claims of the established generation, which emphasizes the system ideology of the past. But when today's younger generations grow older, some of the currently valid ideologies could turn out to be the frames that entrap them and become a target of criticism in the future. Throughout human history, non-absolute values have changed over time and become values that are no longer worth pursuing. Confirmation that shows us that a certain value is no longer worth pursuing can be found by answering a question: "Is the value I pursue valid for a new design? Or is it valid to oppose something?" If the value is valid to design a new life and society, it is worth pursuing. But if the value is valid only to oppose something and protect something else instead of a new idea, you have to realize that it has changed into a value that we must let go.

System ideology is no longer used in designing a new society. It simply has lost its utilization value. As of today, there is no country in the international community that approaches the North Korea issue in terms of system ideology. All countries perceive it in terms of human rights and peace. Now, nowhere in the international community can you find a country that uses system ideology as a solution to the polarization problem and economic growth. System ideology remains a value to oppose communism in the Republic of Korea, which is the only divided country on Earth.

But letting go of the value you have been pursuing is painful and difficult. The value of system ideology was a very useful tool for the wartime generation to rebuild and grow their society. They have experienced the efficiency of the value with their entire beings, and it is frightening for them to let it go because it is to deny their past, and also because it is painful. That's the reason mankind has been repeating the history of tragedy. A society that is not capable of breaking free from an existing frame that has lost its utilitarian value can no longer grow, and the bigger tragedy is that when new values clash with existing values, society can no longer maintain peace. In the case of our society, the value of system ideology that we could not let go has become a cause of social conflict and hinders national development and peace.

The same is true in individual lives. What we choose and pursue besides the absolute values of the universe changes its utilitarian value over time. Therefore, even if a choice was made because it was useful to you, you have to look closely to see if the choice is used for a new design depending on the situation. There's little problem when you recognize the change right away and let it go, but it is painful to let go of something you've been seeking. There are not many who can bear the pain because we are all governed by the law of inertia. So, if you can't let go of something that was useful to you in the past due to the law of inertia, you become a being entrapped in a wrong frame. You cannot become a being that experiences love and expands, no matter how hard you work with good intentions.

If we design our individual lives and society with the absolute values of the universe, we can put an end to the repetition of this tragedy. Since choosing absolute values is always the right thing to do regardless of the changing course of time, you don't have to endure the pain of letting go of the values you have been pursuing. Since pursuing and choosing absolute values can bring about growth under any circumstances, you can achieve evolution while minimizing chaos. Therefore, we need to know what the absolute values of chakras are. We need to know how to expand our existence and peacefully evolve our society.

Now mankind has reached a stage where it can stop the evolution that entails tragedy and open up an evolution of joy with the absolute values of chakras instead. When some new truth unfolds in the world, it is something that cannot be handled with the power of a person alone. When the evolution of collective consciousness – which we have all created together – has progressed enough to unfold the truth, it unfolds in the world through a medium that is best suited for that purpose. That was the case with Albert Einstein's theory of relativity, Yi Je-ma's Sasang philosophy[1], and Karl Gustav Jung's analytic psychology. These were the truths that we were able to unlock with the power of collective consciousness that humanity has grown together. Einstein, Yi Je-ma, and Karl Jung were the mediums. Therefore, no truth can be the truth of a single person. The truth about chakras is also a truth that we all have opened through me, the writer of this book, as the medium. It unfolds with the collective consciousness by the readers of this book. The truth of chakras that will reveal the absolute values are the truth of you.

Endnote

[1] Yi Je-ma: he suggested a new paradigm that divides the world into four elements in Confucianism, and based on this philosophy, he founded a new medicine that divides the human constitution into four.

1. Chakra and the Solar System

Then the question is: What are the absolute values that are right to pursue at any time? To understand this question, we must look at the solar system first. I mentioned previously that, when the Creator created this vast universe and us, he designed everything only for the purpose of experiencing love. He designed us and the universe based on the perfect idea about how we would experience love and through what. Therefore, a look into the universe can provide us with a clue to understanding absolute values.

In Eastern medicine, humans are defined as "microcosms." It indicates that, since the logic behind the composition of human life is a miniature of the principles of the universe, man is the miniature version of the universe. And since we are microcosms that live in the solar system where the Earth belongs, we are the miniature version of a solar system that we belong to in this galaxy. Therefore, within us the microcosms are all the planets such as the sun, Mercury, Venus, Earth (the moon), Mars, Jupiter, Saturn, Uranus, and Neptune. Our chakras are the stars in the solar system that we are embracing.

Our solar system, which is part of the universe, consists of nine stars including the sun and eight planets. And the souls pursuing evolution are living together on Earth, which is one of the planets in our solar system. The solar system is designed with the highest values in the universe. The sun and eight planets are stars that enfold absolute values. The universe is made up of the nine absolute values, just like the stars (sun and planets) in our solar system. The composition of the absolute values designed for us to experience love is nine, which is the maturity number.

The sun, Mercury, Venus, the moon, Mars, Jupiter, and Saturn – which we can see in the sky with our eyes – are the seven chakras that run through our body, while Uranus and Neptune, which we cannot see in the sky with our eyes and can be confirmed only by telescope, are two chakras that are above our heads. The power created by our soul while communicating absolute values with the planets of the solar system is swirling in our chakras. That spiritual power is ruling us together with the energies of our mind and body. We are the microcosms that were formed when the universe that was perfect at the beginning of time split, and our chakras are the nine stars of the solar system.

Nine chakras in the human

Then the question is: What are the absolute values that are swirling in these nine chakras, and based on what standards can we confirm that those absolute values are the perfect values? The absolute values that we should always pursue and always choose are the values that make circles and meet as one when we pursue opposing meanings. For example, suppose you chose the value of individualism and moved on with it in life. The path where individual opinions matter and individuals' existential value shines ultimately leads to self-realization. And in order to achieve self-realization, one is sure to look for work where one can demonstrate one's own existential value within society. There is no self-realization in which an individual's value shines in isolation, because in isolation, nobody will be able to see the light. Therefore, one is destined to choose a path that one can take with all others instead of oneself alone in order to achieve one's personal self-realization. Consequently, individualism becomes one with the value of solidarity in which one searches for and connects with like-minded individuals with self-realization at its center. If one pursues a collective solidarity that brings everybody together, all the individuals who belong to the alliance are precious. Therefore, everybody respects each other's opinions, fulfills their wishes, and opens the path where each of their values will shine. The collective solidarity that brings everybody together becomes one with individualism in which every member of the group is treasured. Even though individualism and solidarism are two contrasting values, they become the absolute values in which they circulate as a single circle with self-realization – which makes existential value shine – at its center. The values where two contrasting directions come into one circle with something at its center are the absolute values of the universe. God has given us kindly the channel where the spiritual energy of the absolute values is given the name "chakra," which means a wheel.

Thus, if there are two contrasting values that you are pursuing but don't circulate to make one circle, those are not absolute values. Some examples of these contrasting values are truth and falsehood, and peace and chaos. We believe that we should pursue the truth. This is valid at many moments.

But even if you continue to pursue the truth, it does not come into contact with falsehood. These two values run in opposite directions from each other till the end because there is no center that could bring these two values into one. So, truth is not always the right choice. Sometimes you have to cover up the truth and sometimes you need to lie. We make our children believe in Santa Claus, and with this falsehood, we are able to bring the joy of Christmas to our children. The value of truth is a value that changes from time to time depending on the situation. The same is true with peace. You may pursue peace as hard as you can, but peace never comes into contact with chaos. So, peace is not a value that is always right. We want peace but there are times when chaos is necessary, because as Charlie Chaplin said in his poem, stars create new worlds by clashing with each other constantly. There are times when we need chaos to create a new world. Peace and chaos are also the values that must be chosen depending on the situation.

Absolute values are the ones that are always right to pursue under any circumstances. Those are the values that don't stand by themselves; they are the values whose ideologies are contrasting but ultimately come into contact with each other and create a circle with one ideology at its center. Pursuing just one out of these three ideologies can never culminate into an absolute value. Absolute value is possible only when these three ideologies come together and create one circle. If we design our lives with this idea of a circle, the path to experiencing love opens. Of the nine chakras, the first to the fifth chakras that we have in our body enfold the absolute values that circulate to become one circle and communicate with the universe.

In the first chakra that is found at the bottom, birth and death communicate with the universe while circulating around the value of life at the center. Every person moves forward toward death once they are born. Being given that life at birth is a blessed opportunity to experience love. Therefore, it is always right to preserve and nurture life and make it prosper. But on the other hand, since life is trapped by physical restrictions, death, which is the end of life, allows us to move toward infinite freedom beyond the weight of a finite life. Also, we can appreciate the value of life only because there is death. For that reason, death is a blessing for us, just like we celebrate birth and try to save lives. The cycle of birth and death is an absolute value that makes the infinite life that is given to us more glorious.

In the second chakra, the individualism and solidarism I've mentioned previously communicate with the universe while circulating around self-realization at the center. We as individuals are precious beings, and we pursue love as a form of self-realization, and we experience love through the solidarity that we form together. The cycle of personal self-realization and collective solidarity is an absolute value that makes the value of all beings shine.

In the third chakra, the value of analysis and synthesis circulates through communication and interacts with the universe. If you analyze many stories in the world, you can see that there are all the special differences. We need to make a detailed analysis of another area to others, as we can properly understand the difference that should be clearly known. However, we are fully aware of their differences and find something in common with them when they are communicating. We live different lives but feel similar to each other, and the world works with the same logic while opening the way to integrate with different fields. Through the process of such discretion-communication-integration, we open up a new place of understanding, and we get a little closer to the truth. Analysis-Communication-Synthesis is the absolute value that opens the truth.

In the fourth chakra, the values of love and faith make a circle with hope at the center as it communicates with the universe. They might seem to be one value because they have been a pair for so long. But faith is contrasting to love in that it is directed at something that is not love. It is the value of faith that makes us believe the world to be fair even though it doesn't look fair; believe some people to have no bad intentions even though they may look evil; and believe that there is God even though God is not visible. It is with such wishful faith that we ultimately love the world that seems unfair, love those who seem evil, and love God who is not visible to us. On the other hand, since we wish to love everything as absolute values, the more we love, the more we become convinced that all that is not love are falsehoods. In this way, we love substantive beings by sending wishful faith to the things that are not love, and that very love makes us believe that all that is not love are falsehoods. Therefore, even though love and faith are looking in opposite directions, they become the absolute values that circulate with hope at the center.

In the fifth chakra, the values of freedom and responsibility circulate around the calling and communicate with the universe. We must pursue a path that sets us free from all things. To enjoy such freedom, we must fulfill the responsibilities assigned to us. We cannot be free when we have not fulfilled our responsibilities. So, to be free, we have to be beings who always fulfill our responsibilities. Also, those who fulfill their responsibilities at every moment ultimately become beings that are free at every moment. It is the calling from heaven that makes heavy responsibilities lighter and keeps freedom from flying away from us like feathers. Heavy responsibilities are the callings that will eventually save us, and therefore, they become our path to freedom. Since we are born as free beings originally, we gladly answer callings from heaven and fulfill our responsibilities. The responsibilities that bid us and the freedom that is as light as a feather are the absolute values that circulate with the calling at the center.

We must envision a life that seeks absolute values from the first to the fifth chakras, because these absolute values are the ingredients for the perfect experience of love.

The sixth to the ninth chakras, all of which are found by our head and above, enfold the values that we have to give and take with each other to experience love. We need nothing more than feeling sorry, gratitude, forgiveness, and blessings in order to give and take love. These are the absolute values about the things that you give to others and are then returned to you, and the things you receive from others and then return to them. These higher-level absolute values connect all of us into one and open the path to expand the lower-level absolute values. Therefore, they are always the right choices to make.

The sixth chakra communicates with the universe through apologies you give to or receive from others. The seventh chakra communicates with the universe through the gratitude you exchange with others. The eighth chakra communicates with the universe through the forgiveness you give to and receive from others. The ninth chakra communicates with the universe through the blessings you give and receive from others. And these notions you give and receive from others for love circulate as a circle with the "us," you and others, as the center.

It is always right to pursue values in which two opposite meanings circulate into one circle. Also, it is right to choose the ideas we give and receive for love under any circumstances. Absolute values are the right values for us to always seek and choose to experience love. In a life designed with the values of the lower chakras from the first to the fifth, we can exchange the values of the upper chakras from the sixth to the ninth and complete everything through unification. Therefore, the higher our chakras are – beginning from the lowest first chakra – the more metaphysical their values are.

When we design life from the bottom, we cherish life more through the values of birth and death that mark the beginning and the end of life. We design the foundation of life with the precious life as we build society together and pursue self-realization. As such, while living as a member of society, we realize that we are individual beings but essentially one, and we explore the path to live in faith and love because all people are ultimately "I." Through the path of believing in love completely, we can fulfill our calling and responsibility and achieve freedom of existence. Now, as a being free as a feather, we apologize to each other, heal each other's pains, and relieve suffering. We give and take gratitude, empower each other, and guide each other so that we don't get lost. We give and receive forgiveness as we eliminate all the darkness that covered our light, and we give and receive blessings to fully reveal the light of beings. This is the composition of humans and the universe designed to experience love with the absolute values of chakras and to experience the light of our beings.

This composition is valid either in the top-down direction, or bottom-up direction. As being to bless each other so that we can fully reveal the light of our beings, we can forgive the darkness that blocks us. And we become thankful to each other with the power of forgiveness, we become empowered, and we heal pains while giving and taking apologies. Because we have our pains and sufferings healed through apologies, we become free to fulfill our responsibilities and callings. We can dream more with stronger faith in love because we are beings that fulfill our callings with free minds. Through strong faith in love, we know we are essentially one even though we are all separate individuals. So, we can move forward to perfection only when we are together in the society we build together, and we pursue self-realization and let our existence shine in society. In that way, while living together as brightening beings, we become thankful for the life that is given to us, and we become beings that are not intimidated before death.

A perfect path to experience love opens to us when we move from bottom to top, or from top to bottom. We are beings that were created with these absolute values as the frames. That is the essence of our nature. Therefore, all we need to do is to fill love with the full physiological forces of Hon-Baek-Shin-Ui-Ji in our lives that are designed with absolute values. As a result, we will be able to overcome all obstacles that stand before us, and we will become aware of the essential light of our souls through experience.

However, there is one more absolute value other than the nine absolute values we must seek and choose: greatness and humility. Greatness and humility are contrasting virtues, but they make an absolute value because they come around and become one circle. We are all dignified creatures born with the will and objective of the Creator, and nobody is a non-dignified being. Therefore, no one can claim to be greater than others, as we are all great beings with infinite possibilities. The awareness that all are great beings with infinite possibilities allows us not to be too conscious about being superior or inferior to others, and it also makes us remain humble to others because we know the great possibilities they have. The desire to be humble before others leads us to discover that others are great in different ways from us, and it ultimately leads us to the realization that we are all great beings. Therefore, greatness and humility are the absolute values that come around to become one circle.

But this greatness and humility do not exist in us as a chakra. The absolute values swirling in the nine chakras are the values that enable us to experience love, like making us treasure life, accept death sacredly, and love them through self-realization in solidarity. Greatness and humility are the absolute values that we obtain as the result of experiencing love instead of experiencing love through them. When you try hard to love, you can discover your greatness as well as the greatness of others. When you try hard to love, you will find a humble place for others to shine and come to the truth that you are not the only one who is special and that everyone is special. In other words, greatness and humility are the absolute values that result from love.

Therefore, if we love properly, we will have the dignity to recognize our greatness and the humility to humble ourselves before others. If you are doing your best in life yet you have a poor self-image, or on the contrary you feel you are more special than others, it is a sign that you are headed in the wrong direction. Greatness and humility are absolute values by which we can check ourselves to see if we are headed in the right direction in accordance with the purpose of existence.

So, the centripetal point that causes greatness and humility to circulate into one circle is the centripetal value of all chakras. We can find greatness in life, become humble before great life, and lower ourselves to the members of our society who stand together with others for our greater self-realization. We are great because we communicate together, have great wishes, and receive a calling from heaven. Also, we can lower ourselves to communicate, to fulfill our wishes, and to fulfill our calling. We are great beings who give apologies, gratitude, forgiveness, and blessing to others, and we are also humble beings because we accept those from others. Therefore, greatness and humility are the forces that connect all chakras as a result of love. In yoga, the force that runs through all chakras from bottom to top or from top to bottom is called Kundalini, and the absolute values of Kundalini are greatness and humility.

Therefore, greatness and humility do not exist even as planets in the solar system. Instead, they communicate with the energy of the asteroid belt, which exists in the middle of all the solar planets, because it is the force that connects all chakras. The asteroid belt is located right in the middle of the solar system's orbit around the sun. The planets orbit in the order of Mercury, Venus, Earth, Mars, asteroid belt, Jupiter, Saturn, Neptune, Uranus,, and the asteroid belt is found right in the middle of them.

There is a rule in the spacing of planets orbiting around the sun. The rule is called Titius-Bode's rule. It is through this rule that we were able to estimate the positions of Uranus and Neptune, which we did not observe with the naked eye, and find those two planets. It was with this rule that we were able to find that there is too much space between Mars and Jupiter and found that, according to the rule, there is space enough for another planet to exist between Mars and Jupiter. And when we investigated and looked for that location, we found that millions of asteroids were orbiting. The absolute value of the result that connects all nine chakras is interacting with millions of asteroids in the middle of the solar system. The asteroids are scattered all over the orbit, giving directions to all the stars in the solar system so that love experienced through nine chakras can find greatness and humility everywhere.

We humans are small universes. More specifically, we are a small solar system that holds all the absolute values. The sun and moon rise and fall within us, and so do other planets such as Mercury, Venus, Mars, asteroids, Jupiter, Saturn, Uranus, and Neptune. Our chakras interact with the solar system's giant planets in space and lead us to cycle as one with space. Our vast and perfect souls rule our everything through the chakras and let us remember that our essence is an absolute value. We were created by the will and purpose of the Creator. And we hold chakras, which is the perfect map for us to fulfill that purpose, and we were given Hon-Baek-Shin-Ui-Ji energy, which is the power with which we can perfectly fulfill that purpose. There is nothing we need more than that to fulfill our existential purpose. Therefore, we are destined to fulfill it. The reason is because we are all entire universes...

Solar System

Chakras, absolute values and the solar system

Chakras	Location	Absolute Values	Solar System
9th Chakra	Above the eighth chakra	Exchange of Blessing	Neptune
8th Chakra	Above the head	Exchange of Forgiveness	Uranus
7th Chakra	Top of the head	Exchange of Gratitude	Sun
6th Chakra	Between eyebrows	Exchange of Apology	Moon
5th Chakra	Neck	Freedom-Calling-Responsibility	Venus
4th Chakra	Chest	Faith-Hope-Love	Mercury
3rd Chakra	Solar plexus	Analysis-Communication-Synthesis	Jupiter
2nd Chakra	Stomach	Individual-Self-realization-Solidarity	Mars
1st Chakra	Perineal	Birth-Life-Death	Saturn

2. Chakras' Ruling Power

Within our chakras, the mental energy of Hon-Baek-Shin-Ui-Ji – whose principal axis is the spiritual energy of absolute values – and the organic energy that integrates our physical body are swirling and circulating together. This circulation of chakras' energy unleashes significant ruling power over our minds and bodies. As a result, the lack of spiritual energy that communicates with the universe in each chakra will inevitably weaken our minds and bodies.

This is a signaling system that tells us that we are on a wrong path when we do not pursue absolute values in our lives. It is because of this signal that we experience physical and mental difficulties. And it is the law of the universe that allows us to find the path we were supposed to take through those difficulties. Therefore, we can tell which power of chakra is weak through the chronic health problems and mental difficulties that we experience. And those physical and mental difficulties can be healed fundamentally by building up the power of the chakra in question.

When the first chakra cannot communicate well with the universe with the value of life, its physical result is an unbalanced immune system. Our immune system plays a role in protecting itself from life-threatening external elements. Therefore, the immune system is an organic system of the body whose duty is to protect life. Immunological diseases – including minor diseases such as colds and infection as well as hypersensitive immune responses and allergies – are affected by the first chakra. The first chakra restores its energy and boosts our immune system when we value life and bless our birth and death. The result is a strong resistance to infection, and well-maintained immune balance, all of which ensures hypersensitivity-free stability.

In addition, the first chakra being the chakra responsible for the birth of life, it is linked to sexual consciousness in the realm of emotion. Therefore, sexual sensibility issues – such as sex addiction, and anorgasmia – are affected by the first chakra. In the rational realm, it is directly related to the power to act. In order to protect and maintain life, physically moving activities are necessary. Therefore, a person who has a healthy first chakra is very active. On the other hand, those with weak first chakras tend to be slow movers, and they can easily suffer from "Tonic Immobility (TI)" symptom which is responsible for immobilizing your body when faced with crisis.

If the second chakra fails to gain the power of self-realization, there will be an imbalance in the autonomic nervous system. The autonomic nervous system controls functions of the human body on its own without being directly affected by the brain. The sympathetic nerves that induce excitement and the parasympathetic nerves that induce stability affect a single organ and create different metabolic functions depending on the situation. The autonomic nervous system phenomenon – expressed individually or in a group – is the organic system of the human body that best suits self-realization. Thus, autonomic neuropathy is governed by the second chakra. Autonomous neuropathy entails symptoms such as over-excitability and hyper-anxiety, and it can cause significant ups and downs in metabolic functions.

In the emotional realm, it is also a chakra that controls mood swings. Therefore, when there is a problem with the second chakra, people tend to suffer from bipolar disorder due to aggravated mood swings. In the rational realm, it is directly involved in memory. In order to achieve self-realization in a group setting, it is advantageous to have a good memory about what to do, what to change, changes in situation, and the characteristics of other people. If the second chakra is weak, however, you often suffer from forgetfulness and easily forget about them.

However, if you make your existential value shine through self-realization – either by yourself or with others – and restore the second chakra, this autonomic nerve system is stabilized, the metabolic functions become balanced, the emotional ups and downs are stabilized, and your memory is improved. Thus, the balance of metabolic functions along with emotional stability and improved memory can make your self-realization process easier and brighter.

If the third chakra does receive energy from space with the value of communication, you suffer from physical problems in the lymphatic system. The lymphatic system being the body's drainage system, it functions to help excess fluid from the blood that has been supplied to all tissue to return to the heart. When this drainage system is functioning well, tissues are subject to more or less pressure, and cause such symptoms as swelling, bloating, chronic inflammation, and pain. Therefore, chronic inflammation, muscle aches, and disorders such as swelling are governed by the third chakra.

Meanwhile, it is also responsible for the emotional cycle. While the second chakra contributes to changing the range of emotional ups and downs, the third chakra contributes to the general flow and expression of emotions. It prevents emotions from building up, and helps emotions to flow naturally and be expressed externally so that they do not keep piling up. Therefore, if the third chakra is weakened, you are likely to suffer from depression as the result of emotional congestion. In the rational realm, it controls concentration. Concentration is essential in order to understand a story and find the truth. Healthy third chakra gives you persistent concentration. On the other hand, when it is not healthy, you might suffer from "attention deficiency disorder."

When you are able to discern situations instead of being overwhelmed by them and realize that all is the same with the support of the power of the third chakra, your body's drainage system works smoothly, and you will feel physically light and refreshed. The pleasant feeling from this circulation can make you feel physical pleasure and joy more easily, thereby empowering your communication. It also strengthens the smooth expression of emotions, so that you can accept the pains of life as a part of the growth process and overcome them without suffering from psychological trauma. It also enhances concentration and helps you to become empowered to seek truth in what you do. If you recover the third chakra through communication, you can realize the truth in pleasant life because you have a virtuous cycle both physically and mentally.

If the fourth chakra fails to communicate with the universe with the value of faith, hope, and love, the balance of the cardiovascular system will be broken. The recently increasing disorders such as arrhythmia, high blood pressure, low blood pressure, cerebral vascular paralysis, and dementia are associated with the condition of the fourth chakra. On the emotional realm, it causes anxiety disorder. The most common symptom we experience when we are nervous and anxious is heart attack. If the fourth chakra is weak, you tend to suffer from unexplained anxiety. In the rational realm, it is in charge of your agility. If you can spontaneously recognize love in chaotic and confusing situations, it is credited to the power of the fourth chakra. Therefore, if the fourth chakra is weak, you are likely to regret the thoughts and words you haven't been able to think and speak in the past.

When you restore the fourth chakra by the power of love and faith, our hearts can beat with joy and all our blood vessels carry the beat with joy. The healthy cardiovascular system is the foundation for activating the function of all cells because it improves the circulation of blood in every corner of the body. Therefore, the recovery of the cardiovascular system eventually improves the functioning of all cells. In addition, it gives you stronger belief to shake off anxiety on the mental level, and the emotion of joy grows more powerfully. The powerful emotion of joy will give a boost to the pursuit of happiness and love, because it infuses your life with vital energy. In addition, your improved agility gives you the advantage of choosing to love under any circumstances.

When the fifth chakra is not empowered by the value of calling, you experience metabolic dysfunction as the result of an abnormality in the hormone system. Hormones are substances that organically control the functions of our organs. Disorders caused by the weak power of the fifth chakra include hypothyroidism, diabetes due to an insulin problem, stress hormone abnormalities in the adrenal glands, menstrual irregularity, and premature menopause.

Hormones are also substances that integrate emotions organically. Therefore, hormones are also called emotional molecules. Thus, when the fifth chakra loses power, emotional ambivalence may not be integrated, resulting in compulsive traits. Ambivalence refers to a situation where opposing feelings over an object or situation occur simultaneously and confuse you. For example, assuming that you are shopping for merchandise, you have a situation where your wish to buy it and your urge not to buy it clash in your mind, creating a situation where you cannot make the decision whether you should buy it or not. When you are caught in these ambivalent feelings, you cannot fulfill your responsibilities because you are not free to make a choice; you become obsessed with minor issues and develop a delusion that you might get into big trouble if you don't take a certain action; and you are also caught up in the constraining emotion of fear due to the delusion that you might get into big trouble if you go ahead with a certain action.

The fifth chakra is directly involved in creativity and imagination in the rational realm. It is in charge of creativity so that we can fulfill our calling and create a new world. Therefore, when the fifth chakra is weakened, our poor imagination results in less creative thoughts; we become more obsessed with worldly trends; and we become less adaptable to new situations.

But if we seek to fulfill our calling with freedom and the sense of responsibility, the fifth chakra starts recovering while communicating with the universe. This process not only restores the organic functions of our hormones, but it also improves its metabolic function by improving its efficiency. In other words, we develop a more efficient body and become free beings who can fulfill our calling with less energy. Even on the emotional realm, it helps us avoid getting caught in ambivalence, and it empowers us with the courage to escape fear and freely make our choices. In terms of rationality, we become more creative and pleasantly pursue new challenges. Eventually, we can find our callings through free choices and fulfill our responsibilities with an innovative mind.

If the sixth chakra – whose realm is apology – loses its power, we experience impaired functions of the pineal gland and the pituitary gland. The pituitary gland is the main player in controlling all hormones, and it affects our entire body. Therefore, a restored sixth chakra is essential for the comprehensive recovery of any physical problems. In addition, the pineal gland is where Hon is found, and a malfunctioning pineal gland results in the lethargy of the king that rules our mind. In other words, disorder in the pineal and pituitary glands mean disorder in the function that comprehensively controls our entire physical and mental domains. Therefore, basically, many physical and mental problems are likely to indicate that you have a problem in your sixth chakra.

The problem in the pineal gland is linked to all emotional problems, especially sleep disorders and anger control. In the early days of trouble in the sixth chakra, you experience an increased demand for sleep, and when it develops into a chronic problem, you experience insomnia. In addition, anger being a destructive emotion, it directly harms one's self and those around you. That's how serious the ripple effect is with the sixth chakra. Additionally, since it is involved in making rational decisions in human relationships, it governs your ability to grasp the causal context of a situation and understand the consequences of your actions. Therefore, when the sixth chakra is weakened, people tend to snap and get angry first before trying to figure out the context.

Offering and accepting an apology makes the sixth chakra healthy and helps comprehensive recovery from mental and physical problems – not just a simple recovery, but a development of the pineal gland where the spirit, the lord of our mind, resides. As a result, your emotional leadership becomes stronger; you make fewer mistakes because you make rational decisions; and your physical functions improve overall because the hormone system in the pituitary gland is comprehensively developed.

When the seventh chakra that handles gratitude is weakened, the nervous system fails to perform all its functions. Neurological disorders such as dystonia, Parkinson's, Alzheimer's, Huntington's chorea, and schizophrenia are all governed by the seventh chakra. In addition, the organic linkage of the nervous system determines overall judgment. If the seventh chakra is not activated, it is easy to become a person of poor choices because of the degenerated judgment, understanding, and learning skills. More than anything, your ability to empathize with others is weakened because the mirror neuron system that helps you identify with others emotionally is not activated.

The development of the seventh chakra, which deals with gratitude and accomplishment, stimulates brain activities. In other words, it increases the range of the brain by increasing the organic connection of neural circuits. As a result, it helps you develop your senses, judge comprehensively, and work well with accurate understanding. More than anything else, it stimulates the development of the mirror neuron system, consequently enhancing your ability to empathize with others and the world. When you use your brain extensively and expand your empathy and understanding, you have a head start in achieving what you want to achieve. This can be done through the power of gratitude.

If the eighth chakra that deals with the value of forgiveness fails to communicate smoothly with the universe, your Hon-Baek-Shin-Ui-Ji will have trouble communicating with the soul. In particular, within Hon-Baek-Shin-Ui-Ji, there is anti-myungsu (反命數) that directly interferes with expansion, and it is the eighth chakra that determines this anti-myungsu. When the anti-myungsu grows within, our hearts and souls become estranged from each other, and we suffer both emotionally and rationally. I will explain more about the anti-myungsu later in this book.

The power of forgiveness opens a path for us to overcome the anti-myungsu. The overcoming of the anti-myungsu results in the restoration of the distanced soul and mind and makes the continuous growth of Hon-Baek-Shin-Ui-Ji possible. More than anything, it helps us develop insights into the truth, thereby making our minds able to focus with the support of the will of the soul.

If the ninth chakra fails to communicate smoothly with the universe with the value of blessing, the power to expand Hon-Baek-Shin-Ui-Ji grows weak. As a result, it is difficult to expand myungsu. If we live in blessings, our Hon-Baek-Shin-Ui-Ji dances, keeping steps with the soul. The expansion of myungsu is a natural consequence. Additionally, just like the eighth chakra, it helps you develop insight into truth so that a path opens for the will of your soul to unfold gloriously.

Our chakras dominate our body through all its organic systems and have the balance of power to resolve all emotional and rational problems. Therefore, we can see which chakras are weak now by identifying our problems, and we can also realize what we should pursue more diligently in life. Understanding chakra is a whole blueprint for designing our present lives.

But sometimes, our problems are the results of a combination of more than one chakra. For example, if you analyze the recently increasing cases of panic disorder in terms of chakra, you will find the following. Panic disorder is a mental problem caused by fear and those who experience this problem suffer from severe panic attacks. This disorder is affected by the first chakra that is associated with the value of life. Also, panic disorder is not a real threat to life, but a dreadful fear created by the reaction of our nervous system. Therefore, it's influenced by the seventh chakra. And a panic attack is also affected by the fourth chakra that creates anxiety with the fear of sudden death. In other words, panic attacks can be interpreted as a disorder caused by the first, fourth, and seventh chakras. In the case of erotomania, it is likely that this disorder of sexual urges is the direct result of the dysfunctional first chakra that is associated with the value of life, as well as the dysfunctional fifth chakra that is associated with the value of calling if the abnormal sexual desire is accompanied by problems in sex hormones. In addition, most of the chakras might need to be mobilized in the case of incurable diseases. Therefore, in order to solve our problems fundamentally, we need to consider the controlling power of all the chakras that are applicable to the individual problem.

The problems we currently have with each chakra are not just the consequences of this present life. The consequences of all the lives we have lived previously are reflected in our current chakras. Therefore, just because you are suffering from an immune system disorder now doesn't mean you can conclude that you have been reckless about the value of life in this current life. Instead, you will have to realize that in the many lives you have lived through – including this current life – you failed to understand the value of life for a long time. And you have to recognize that you are living this life in order to learn the value of life itself. With that recognition, you can make the choice to expand your chakras.

Expansion of chakras should be carried out in three dimensions. The extension of chakras happens in the order of the expansion of the external size; expansion of the depth which is the volume; and finally, the extension of the color, which is the brightness. Chakras' external expansion is something that happens in the form of physical reactions. When we make a sound, we can do it by vibrating the bottom of our abdomen, or we can make vocal sounds by vibrating our chest. We can also make a sound that vibrates our throat, or the head voice that vibrates our head. Just as we can make a sound in various ways, we can expand individual chakras externally by keeping our breathing on specific chakras.

As a matter of fact, this is a natural phenomenon. The reason we experience our hearts getting warm when we witness a touching love is because our breath is concentrating on the fourth chakra in our chest. When we try to fulfill our calling, we have tension in our throat and it causes our breath to concentrate on the fifth chakra, and when we feel the greatness of life and sexual desire, our breath concentrates in our perineal region. Yoga practice is a training that is developed in order to externally expand our chakras by taking intentional breaths in accordance with this principle. When our chakras are expanded externally, you can feel chakras sensually and experience a euphoric feeling caused by the chakra energy. We were able to build knowledge about chakras and spread that knowledge all thanks to this euphoric feeling you can get by practicing yoga.

The expansion of depth is the expansion that happens with our minds. The depth of chakras expands when we understand the significance of absolute values and make determinations. Our process of understanding the absolute values in our lives becomes the energy that protects chakras. And if we fully utilize the energy of Hon-Baek-Shin-Ui-Ji during this process of understanding, we achieve stronger power to protect our chakras and we can increase expansion of the depth. Therefore, we need to understand the absolute values by making the most of our concepts of Hon-Baek-Shin-Ui-Ji. By doing this, we can maximize the expansion of depth and form a sacred boundary that protects our chakras. Now, I am going to specifically explain each chakra and open a path to protect our chakras with the Hon-Baek-Shin-Ui-Ji Sacred boundary.

Lastly, chakras' color extension is an area that expands through the realization of specific methods and practice. The moments of realizing ways to realize the absolute value with love and practicing it with love shed bright light on the unique lights of the chakras. If, in some circumstances, we have discovered methods to realize love by the values of forgiveness and blessing and practiced them, the colors of our eighth and ninth chakras glow brightly while the colors become thicker to become the colors of Uranus and Neptune. If we have treasured life and practiced love, the color of the first chakra will become as thick as the colors of Saturn and shine more brightly. The result of choosing and pursuing absolute values of life allows our chakras to shine as brightly as the stars in the night sky.

The expansion of chakras has to be done through the balance of these three factors. If the exterior is small or distorted in the balance between exterior-depth-color, it mostly shows in the form of physical problems. If the depth is clearly insufficient, it mostly shows in the form of mental issues. If the color is not up to a satisfactory level, it shows both physically and mentally in the form of spiritual issues. Occasionally, you encounter problems when the euphoric feeling strikes you stronger through the chakra and yoga training, consequently upsetting the balance of life. This happens when the depth and the color fail to catch up with the expansion of the exterior. And when the depth and the color expand, it requires the process of expanding the exterior to accommodate their expansions. This book will introduce the absolute values of chakra to expand the depth through the changes in consciousness and expand the color with changes in life. Since training that expands the outer boundary of the chakras is risky, I will introduce it if a method to ensure safety is prepared in the future.

Chakras are a system through which our souls govern our lives and existence. Their power of dominance leads us to fulfill the purpose of our existence. The problems we have must be solved fundamentally at the level of chakra. Only then can we heal and grow without having to repeatedly experience the same problems. I dream of a day when the numerous solar systems on Earth shine brightly with great, deep, strong light.

Domains of Each Chakra

Chakras	Absolute Values		Domains in Charge	
9th Chakra	Exchange of Blessings	Hon-Baek-Shin-Ui-Ji	Myungsu	Insight into truth
8th Chakra	Exchange of Forgiveness	Hon-Baek-Shin-Ui-Ji	Anti-myungsu	Insight into truth
7th Chakra	Exchange of Gratitude	Nerve tract	Sympathy	Comprehensive judgment
6th Chakra	Exchange of Apologies	Pineal gland, pituitary gland	Sleep disorder, anger disorder	Cause-effect judgment
5th Chakra	Freedom, Calling, Responsibility	Hormonal system	Ambivalence	Creativity
4th Chakra	Faith, Hope, Love	Cardiovascular system	Anxiety disorder	Agility
3rd Chakra	Anaysis, Communication, Synthesis	Lymphatic circulation system	Depression	Concentration
2nd Chakra	Individual, Self-realization, Solidarity	Autonomic nervous system	Bipolar disorder	Memory
1st Chakra	Birth, Life, Death	Immune system	Sexual disorder	Acting power

3. The 1st Chakra: Birth – Life – Death

Respecting life is so obvious that I don't need to emphasize it. However, it has not been long since mankind valued and respected life. In the past when treatment for disease was not widely available, the lives of family members were easily lost, and consequently people grew rather indifferent to the loss of life. Also, as recently as 100 years ago, many lives were lost tragically and cruelly as the result of war, social class system, and persecution. Even today, we are experiencing terrorism, war, and massacre because life is not respected and treasured.

The first chakra that contains the value of life determines the body's immune system. Therefore, it is perhaps a natural consequence that we frequently suffer from immune system disorders. In the past, numerous lives were lost all at once as the result of plague, but fortunately, that history is no longer repeating today. There are only individuals who are suffering from various diseases including autoimmune disease or allergic disorders. This evolution itself was also possible only because people started to value life.

What we need to think about in today's world in terms of the value of life is not just caring about human life, but caring about the lives of other species as well. As our institutions, technologies, and medical science make progress, it has become a matter of fact that human life is precious, but the lives of other species that share Earth with us are still ignored. Livestock animals that provide us with food are constrained in confined spaces and barely manage to remain alive while being exposed to unsanitary environments and toxic antibiotics. How can we say we acknowledge the value of the life of a chicken when we force it to live confined in a space smaller than a sheet of letter-size paper? What about the life of a pig that is exposed to an environment that can make it get sick and die with other pigs unless it gets antibiotic shots? Are the lives of the crops and fruits that are exposed to pesticides and chemical fertilizers for higher harvest yields being properly treated? Many animals and plants are facing extinction because of the natural environment that is damaged for the sake of the convenience of humans. They are in danger of disappearing from the Earth due to reduced space and food supply.

We have made a significant advancement after realizing that human life is precious. But we still haven't treated the creatures that provide us with food with dignity. Also, the preciousness of plants and animals living on Earth with us has not been reflected in our lives. The lives that provide us with food are suffering and desperately appealing to us. Avian Influenza, foot-and-mouth disease, and insecticide-contaminated eggs are the results that show their pain. Similar problems will inevitably continue until we respond to their suffering and treat them properly. Fortunately, however, efforts are under way to recognize their preciousness and take actions to respect their lives. The human race is now producing food more than enough to feed us all. So, now the days when we have to strive to produce more food are over. Now is the time we should start thinking about how to equally share the food, and how to properly treat the value of lives associated with food.

Man is the highest-level predator and the occupier of Earth. Man determines the ecosystem of this planet. And we humans have a responsibility to shine the value of the lives of all the creatures that have been pushed aside as the result of our occupation of Earth. Life is cyclical, so the food chain is a natural law. I accept this natural law, and I feel no guilt for eating animals and plants. But that doesn't mean we can forget about the preciousness of their lives. We are responsible to make sure not to take the value of the lives of what we eat for granted. We have a responsibility to live in ways that do not disrespect the value of the lives of other creatures that grow in the space we occupy. This is the fate of human beings who are the top predators in the food chain and the occupier of Earth. And when we fulfill this destiny of fate, only then can we become the beings that truly respect lives and become filled with the light of the first chakra.

Therefore, our decision to fill our first chakra with light begins at our meal table. We shall give thanks for the numerous lives of the animals, vegetables, and grains that we eat, realize that we are beings that embrace all these lives, and live in ways that make their value of life shine. I don't object to meat eating because I believe that eating meat is part of the law of nature. However, it is necessary for us humans to reduce the consumption of meat. We are alarmed by the popularization of various "adult diseases" that are on the rise because we are consuming meat more than necessary. Livestock animals live in deplorable environments to supply the excessive amount of meat that humans consume. The pain of those living creatures creates a vicious circle in which their sufferings become our own suffering.

To solve this dilemma, we must implement an animal welfare system so that livestock animals can grow in healthy environments. Farms that practice animal welfare measures will inevitably experience reduced production. But that reduced production is just the right amount of meat that is necessary for us. Perhaps, if we move forward with a food policy that reduces meat consumption, we might be able to solve many of the chronic diseases that we're experiencing today, while at the same time reducing the pain of livestock and ensuring their happiness, because that is the natural law of the food chain.

Meanwhile, we must make life our priority in other industries as well. Regretfully, however, we humans have been unable to protect life due to economic logic. Even in Korea alone, dozens of dams that interrupt the natural flow of major rivers have been installed based on economic logic. As a result, we can't even estimate how many lives have been lost in rivers that developed the phenomenon called "green latte," the spreading green algae blooms. Besides, we don't know how much economic loss we will suffer from those lost lives and for how long. Perhaps we will learn a hard lesson about the preciousness of life when the current economic gains turn into economic loss someday.

It is not just Korea that fails to respect the value of life in the face of economic gains. Humanity managed to sign the Paris Agreement in 2015. Aimed at keeping the rate of global average temperature rise under 2 °C compared to the pre-industrialization era, it was an encouraging achievement with 195 countries participating. But the fact that the agreement aimed to keep the temperature rate under a 2 °C increase shows that we still place economic logic before our lives. Besides, unfortunately, the US – an industrial giant that has a major responsibility for global warming – has withdrawn from this agreement.

The economy is not the value we should pursue. None of our chakras contains the value of the economy. The economy is only a result that we get as we live in pursuit of chakra values. When we elect a president, we must elect a life president, not an economic president. The major powers that have achieved industrialization ahead of others should acknowledge their responsibility for having caused so much pain on Earth and not spare any investment in helping it to recover. The institutional performance for life will bring about a change in mankind's immune system. An important choice we can make to eradicate such troubling symptoms as allergy and autoimmune disorders is to exercise our citizens' rights to install a system that prioritizes the value of life. What you can do is vote for a politician who prioritizes the value of life, and exercise citizens' rights in issuing a system for life. It is directly linked to the person's immune system through the first chakra.

To make this happen, we must bless every birth, and cherish every death. Investing in flourishing life and revealing the truth of death is always the right choice for us, because it is about investing in the absolute values. No matter how much it costs to salvage the doomed Sewol ferry[2], the money we spent to find out the truth about the countless lives that were lost in the tragic accident will eventually bring us more than what we spent. The truth of their deaths will be a great force in keeping more lives safe in the future. Our society does not need to worry about maternity leave and wages, because those are systems that help to make life prosper. Since this is all about life and self-realization – which are absolute values – its return will be double the investment. We should no longer hesitate or be reluctant to invest in saving lives and expanding such systems.

We welcome the birth of life with joy and are extremely generous to young life. For mankind, birth has become a value of blessing. Perhaps soon, institutional changes and investments intended to celebrate birth will be carried out as they are supposed to be. However, mankind has not established any positive conception of death. Death is a value that should be celebrated as much as birth. We must open a path to reveal the truth of death, pursue peaceful death, bless those who have ended a life, and live as beings unfazed in the face of death. Considering the current trend of declining populations, it is a time when the blessings of birth and death should be emphasized more than ever. At a time when population continues to decline, the birth of each and every life should be celebrated, and the death of the increasing number of elderly people should also be blessed so that their death can be peaceful.

The most common way to bless one's death is to perceive one's body that is changing as a result of aging cells as beautiful. We can't die naturally if our cells don't age and remain young and dynamic forever. There are many movies and novels that show us what a terrible tragedy it is to live forever as a person who cannot die. Life is made more glorious because it terminates by death, and the fact that death is a blessing in the long run is perceived to be somewhat self-evident to us. Therefore, in order for us to die naturally and peacefully, cells must grow old. The only way to die with cells that never age is to die by accident. But I don't want to die suddenly in an accident. If possible, I wish that I will be able to tell that I will die soon before it happens, so that I can take care of the remaining days of my life, express my gratitude and love to family and friends, and die with joy, thinking that I had a good life. Perhaps everyone has the same wish as I do.

Everyone wants a peaceful death, yet, they all refuse to accept the aging of cells. They refuse to accept saggy skin, wrinkles, and declining mobility, and they resent the changes of blessing that would lead them to a peaceful death. Life is another side of the slow dying process. There is no way to face a peaceful death, as long as we deny and resent the natural changes leading us to death. The weight you gain in your middle-age is a change that comes as cells begin to lose vitality. It is also a way to protect your body so that you don't lose energy even as your cells lose their vitality. Therefore, the statistics show that heavy people live a healthy life for a period of time longer than thin people, and such results make perfect sense. If you are a middle-aged person who is worried about gaining weight due to your age, you should now accept that you are not young enough to eat a lot and burn your energy any more, and humbly adjust your diet and maintain your proper weight, while celebrating the change. If you try to stay thin in your middle-age, you are more likely to have an angular outline rather than the smooth curves you used to have when you were young, and you become a person with weak energy. You can have a happier life by remaining dynamic and showing your beauty in the natural round body lines that come with the aging process.

In addition, the deteriorating mobility and wrinkles you experience in your old age reveal the greatness of you having been a being who has lived life fiercely. When I hold the hands of elderly patients to check their pulse, I somehow feel an unexplained sense of awe and my heartstring is tugged at the sight of their wrinkled hands and skin that sags as the result of losing weight in their old age. It is a feeling different from what I have at the sight of chubby babies. And when I see elderly patients over 90 years of age visit my clinic in great shape unaccompanied by others, I feel happy and excited just to look at them. The changes that happen in old age when the vital energy is slowly withdrawing inside are natural changes for the soul to extinguish the fire of life and leave. At the same time, they are measures by which the infinite possibilities of beings are exposed. The sight of older people who are losing their hold on life and enduring their physical limitations shows that we eventually master life at some point. A natural and peaceful death is completed in accordance with this mastery.

We were given life and born in this world, and therefore we all wish to experience the energy of life brilliantly before we age and die peacefully. In order to make it happen, we must be thankful for our birth, find joy in our lives, and bless our aging process. Celebrating our own death is a way to celebrate your aging process. That celebration replies to you with a peaceful death. Therefore, I sincerely suggest – be thankful for being able to die after going through the cell-aging process, and be thankful for the vitality your extra weight is giving you. Humbly organize your daily activities in accordance to the level of your vitality and be proud of your beauty that is manifested in the form of wrinkles and dark spots. I hope that you will complete a life where death is celebrated just as much as birth.

There is something that has to be pointed out with regard to the proposition that both life and death are values to be blessed: suicide. The beginning and end of life is naturally determined by the agreement between our souls and God. However, suicide is when we determine the end of life based on our conscious judgement. In hypnotherapist Michael Newton's *Journey of Souls*, there is a story about hypnotizing a soul that had committed suicide in its past life. The first spiritual thought the soul that ended its own life had when it was let out of the body was "I couldn't do it this time. I should do it again." Just because one gave up in this life doesn't mean that the karma will disappear. The same opportunity is given until the karma is experienced with love. If there is no more karma we need to overcome with love, then our soul selects a peaceful death. That is why those who earned a peaceful death are those who were able to end their karma well. This is the reason why we should not choose death consciously.

The heaven blesses, with honor and glory, death that completed one's karma with love. I firmly believe that the afterlife of the righteous who cherished others' lives as if their own will be filled with glorious fortune. Jesus Christ may be the greatest figure who ever sacrificed his own life to love us, mankind. Apparently, he could have fled from those who tried to kill him, but he chose to take the path of death after bidding farewell to his disciples at the last supper. We can never imagine how much pain he had to endure as he was killed slowly on the cross. But even in the face of such a painful death, it is clear that Jesus Christ accepted his death with joy and love. As a result, he was given the greatest blessing in the universe upon death. The miracle of resurrection will be the greatest blessing this universe can bring to a death. The love Jesus Christ had shown with his death has become a glory that has shone for over 2,000 years as the result of the miracle of resurrection.

I don't think the miracle of resurrection is restricted to one individual alone. All humans are governed by the same laws of nature and an exception is not granted to just one person. I believe that if someone chooses to have a death that deserves the same greatest blessing in the universe as Jesus Christ did, the person will see the miracle of resurrection as well. Heaven blesses all death. Heaven blesses those who gave up on life by giving an opportunity to live again; heaven blesses those who lived their given lives to the fullest by giving them honor; and heaven blesses those who heroically sacrificed their lives to give opportunities to others by giving them the glory that will remain in the hearts of people. And the highest form of the blessing is manifested through the miracle of resurrection. That is the law of the universe that blesses all forms of death, and this law is applied to all of us.

For that reason, I want to have a good death. I want to face an honorable death after living my life to the fullest while being grateful for each moment, so that I will be left with no regret in the end. I care for my life, wishing for an honorable death for myself. I am also an allergic rhinitis patient, and I cannot say that I have a strong first chakra. So, I make every effort to care for the lives of my patients and treat them, while treasuring my own life. I give my love to the plants I'm growing, and I pledge to become a being who doesn't take the food I eat for granted by being mindful of the food that I consume each day and remembering the zest of the orange I have and the dynamic of the belt fish I ate. When I drive, I value the lives of myself and other drivers, and I suppress the instinctive urge to accelerate so that we can all live until we have peaceful deaths. I pull the plugs out to save electricity for the environment; I try to use less detergent; and I don't spare efforts to sort garbage and recycle. My endeavors helped me easily overcome minor sicknesses such as a cold, even though I had always suffered seriously from them, and my rhinitis has improved enough for me to feel comfortable.

I suggest you do the same: treasure all lives for the sake of your own immunity and your ability to act. What you need to do is to generously agree to systems that celebrate all birth and death, and start taking one small action intended to save the numerous lives on Earth. When you continue to practice activities intended to care for lives, your first chakra becomes filled with light. The results will not only show in your immune system, but they will also lead you to live as a person who takes actions and has a healthy stamina to have a joyous sex life. You never lose when you invest in absolute values. It brings you bountiful prosperity in accordance with solid principles. It is always right to value all lives, celebrate the birth of life, and choose to have a peaceful death.

The Sacred Boundary of the First Chakra

This part is about the values of birth, life, and death, and it is the sacred boundary that protects the first chakra by using the Hon-Baek-Shin-Ui-Ji energy. If you keep these ideas in mind, the first chakra will eliminate the difficulty that you have in communicating with the universe and promote recovery and expansion. I ask you to read it whenever you need the power of the first chakra. And I also ask you to spread it not just to your heart, but also to the hearts of others whose power of life is weak. Whoever you spread the value of life to, it always comes true to the ones you spread.

(1) Birth – Death

* As I was born into earth and am alive,
I had the opportunity to transform myself with the energy of life.
I am grateful for having been born as I gained the time and space to live in.

The energy of life within us is limited and therefore,
we have the opportunity to leave and finalize our life.

That is why we are fortunate to have this life that advances toward death.

As we can transform thanks to being born and finalize such changes with death,
let us now reflect our lives on the mirror of death.
I wish to live a life with no regrets in the face of death.

* We are created and born with the providence of heaven.
The opportunity was given to live and experience the providence of heaven
and feel them as if they were your own on this earth.

The providence of heaven is simple but ever wide.
The recurrence of birth and death to experience them all is inevitable,
so please know that you are amongst the blessings of Samsara.

Please know that our birth has been our own choice and hope,
and death is the mirror of life as well as the inevitability of the cycle.
The repetition of the cycle of life and death completes our experiences.

* The moment of birth entailed excruciating pain,
but we all consent to and willingly accept the pain,
and we are magnificent beings which rejoice in birth born out of pain.

Thoughts of death bring about extreme fear,
but we consent to and calmly accept the moment we need to finalize,
and we are beautiful beings that take comfort in our departure.

Since we are eternal beings in the endless cycles of life and
death,
since the joy of birth and peace of death are always with us,
the pain of birth and the fear of death cannot hold us back.

* Bless and protect the birth of each and every life.
Alleviate the pain of such birth, offer a helping hand,
And share in the joy of birth as if it was your own.

Mourn the death of each and every life and protect them.
Stay by the side so that such death does not lead to fear,
let your peace embrace the peace of such departure.

The more you embrace the birth and death of others,
the joy of birth and peace of death will accumulate inside you,
and you will learn and practice love that transcends life and
death.

(2) Life

* Let us regret how we lost our vitality and energy
as we failed to recognize how precious our life is,
and injured ourselves with harmful minds and actions.

Life gives us the energy needed to create changes to time and
space,
and a healthy body is the foundation for a life.
So let us devote ourselves to take good care of our health.

Efforts to maintain health must be balanced.
Devoted but not being greedy, sincere but composed,
that is how you should balance your health.

* The life of the earth repeats in a single, entire cycle and
therefore,

when no harm is done to nature,
can our life remain sound and whole.

We are the apex predator as well as the conqueror on earth.
Be grateful for the lives that we consume and enjoy,
and take responsibility to make them ever more meaningful.

That is how we stand responsible for the meaning of life as the apex member,
creating harmony with nature as an element of earth,
and protect the dignity and value of life by living the life given to us until the very end.

* Our biological phenomena are sometimes displayed as sadness and pain.
Such pain is the laudable efforts of life to protect ourselves and therefore,
I hereby offer my condolence to the efforts of pain that I resented until now.

Our life demonstrates miraculous self-reliance.
We adapt to the environment to mitigate discomfort, we regain our vigor no matter how tired we are,
so please pay tribute for the vitality of each of your cells.

My cells act according to my feelings and actions.
Since I am heaven and God to my cells,
let's take care of our cells with divinity and greatness.

* We have been ignorant about the life of other species,
we neglected their pain and fall,
and that is why we are in a situation where our lives are threatened.

Since all life on earth is connected as one,
there is no species that we may not love and therefore,
we must save the environment and lives that are being
threatened.

Let us love even a blade of grass, flowers and trees, dogs and
cats and animals,
willingly practice our efforts to heal the suffering earth,
and achieve prosperity for the many lives with our love.

(3) Integration of Birth – Life – Death

* I had the privilege of the various opportunities in my previous
lives that I do not remember,
and achieved many changes while living in various forms,
and so I overcome the regrets that I left in the face of past death.

That is how we fulfill the meanings given to us in this life,
exert our best so as to leave no regrets in the face of death,
and remain solely grateful to the life we live today.

Congratulations in advance, for moving beyond the cycle of
birth, death, and rebirth and reaching the state of nirvana,
through contemplations on life after death,
and accumulation of meanings that will enrich the next life if
allowed to us.

Endnote

2   Sewol Ferry: a big ferry, Sewol, went down in the water in
     2014 killing numerous passengers. Most passengers killed
     in the incident were high school juniors who were on their
     way to a school trip. This incident is remembered as a
     tragedy by Koreans.

4. The 2nd Chakra: Individual – Self Realization – Solidarity

We all create our own lives with our own consciousness (consciousness + unconsciousness). Also, the world is created by the power of collective consciousness, which is the gathering of all our consciousness. The second chakra contains an absolute value that determines the individual consciousness that creates an individual's life and the characteristics of collective consciousness that creates the world. The second chakra's individual-self realization-solidarity is an absolute value that creates and evolves our lives and our world.

We are the main players that create our own lives. Therefore, our attitude toward life and the thoughts and feelings we have as we lead our lives is important. We create our lives with those, and we also assist the creation of the world with those. We have to look closely at what kind of a being we are becoming and how we are creating our lives. Through these moments of self-reflection, we have to find and keep our own individuality that does not jump on the bandwagon of the trends of the time. Pursuing life as a being that is most true to oneself is the individualism that qualifies as a true absolute value.

It is normal that we have thoughts that are different from others. If we had the same thoughts, that would be abnormal. Thoughts have to be different, and thoughts have to be diverse. The pursuit of diversity, in which ten thousand different thoughts shine in a myriad of colors, is the absolute value that we must follow. Therefore, we must take the road where we can find and keep our own colors. We must know what we want to do and which method we prefer. We must pursue our own fashion instead of mindlessly following trends; we must study in our own way; and we must modify learned skills into the skills that are most suitable to us. Imitating the methods of others is fundamentally impossible, and even if you can imitate to perfection, you cannot expect the same results from it, because a method that works really well for others doesn't mean the method will work really well for you too.

There's nothing that interferes with the development of your skills more than comparing your skills to others. Being a medical practitioner involved in the clinical study of physical constitution, I was always uneasy in heart about the differences between my diagnosis results and the results for a percentage of the population who are diagnosed with having certain physical constitutions as reported by prominent researchers.[3] They reported that *taeyang* physiological type was rare, but five visitors were diagnosed as having that type by me. Another famous hospital director reported that *soeum* physiological type was rarer, but if I diagnosed more visitors with that type, I was worried that I misdiagnosed them. This anxiety affected my diagnosis activities eventually increasing my misdiagnosis rate. However, I realized that the diagnostic ratio that others are talking about is valid only for them because they followed their own diagnostic methods, and that it was meaningless to me. I was able to improve my accuracy rate beyond my expectations once I reinterpreted the diagnostic skills I'd learned in my own way. In the end, you have to make everything you do fit into your individuality. Only then can you create the life you want, because the individuality that was given to you is the optimum condition for your soul to achieve the desired self-realization.

Besides, the process of transforming what you've learned into your own way is quite interesting. It's really fun to find your way even when you study. When you transform your learned skills in your own way, you can even temporarily feel like you've become a great person. Even when you play, it is much more fun when you play by finding something that is fun to you than when you follow and play along with others. At first, it is easy to imitate others, but it is not fun anymore if you continue to do so. Everything becomes fun to you only when you color everything that comes to you in your own color, while still thinking about what you can do better than others and what you really like to do. I hope that you will color everything that comes to you with your own colors. This interesting process is something that qualifies as an absolute value that you should never let go of.

The process of fitting into your individuality is the right thing to do and it corresponds to absolute values. Also, the process of others adjusting to fit into their individuality is always the right thing to do as well. If you have reached a level where you can teach something to others, you are likely someone who has transformed what you have learned and made it your own. You can never reach a level where you can teach others if you keep imitating or following others only. However, you cannot demand that others do something the same as you while you yourself are transforming the method to fit your individuality. Those who learn from you should be able to do what you like to do to acquire something like you did and become someone who can teach others. It is out of the question that you should not complain or be disappointed by others for not doing exactly as you told them and taught them to do. If your student is finding joy in what he does in his own way, you are obliged to encourage and support him instead.

Yet, it is still very important to let others know what you have learned. Instead of thinking, "They will do whatever they want to do even if I teach them this," you must think, "I hope that what I've learned will be advanced to become something different," when you teach them. When you share what you've learned with others, express your thoughts, and find a path that you can take with like-minded others, you are on your pursuit to realize the second chakra's individual-self realization-solidarity value. For example, even though I do not expect others to practice the same pulse taking method that I've acquired while seeing patients, I can say that, when you communicate with others who are involved in physiological diagnosis through pulse diagnosis and form a solidarity with them, you can get a more efficiently advanced diagnosis as a result. In other words, it opens a way to diagnose patients more easily. The shared determination to use pulse for physiological diagnosis evolves into a collective consciousness, which in turn evolves into a bigger energy. While diverse thoughts and methods are being encouraged and exchanged within that collective consciousness, you become capable of developing your own method.

The most important reason we should express our own individuality while at the same time forming an alliance is because we are all under the control of the collective consciousness (consciousness + unconsciousness) even though each of us is creating our own lives. In order to complete a life that you want, you need the support of the collective consciousness.

Mothers in Korea are sick of the excessively competitive enthusiasm for education, yet, they do not dare to drop out of that competition, all because they are not supported by the collective consciousness. They feel bad about their children being sacrificed by over-heated competition, but they sign up their children to private after-school academies and force them to study hard because they are afraid that their children will fall behind others. I myself was determined not to send my child to private academies since elementary school like other mothers do and I would never make my child stressed over school studies. But it was so difficult to keep my determination. Concerns from people around me was one of the reasons, but on a more fundamental level, I kept feeling worried despite my determination. I kept asking myself, "Is it really okay not to let my child study harder?" Eventually, this anxiety got the best of me and I would end up putting my child under the stress of studying.

The power that amplifies my anxiety is the controlling power of the collective consciousness that we have all created. Of course, I wouldn't have been swayed by collective consciousness if I didn't have even one percent of anxiety about child learning. You can get to be controlled by collective consciousness over the things that you don't have. But if you have even a slight amount of anxiety that resonates with you, that anxiety is amplified by collective consciousness. It is the controlling power of the collective consciousness that can blow up my small anxiety to twice its size. It is too difficult for an individual to overcome this anxiety alone. The controlling power of the collective consciousness, which is constantly transmitted through unconsciousness, is what creates an amplification of anxiety beyond my will. To break away from this collective consciousness, what we need is the power of solidarity, which you form with like-minded people, along with your individual efforts. In other words, a new sense of group is necessary.

I desperately needed solidarity with like-minded parents in order to give my child the opportunity to choose his own learning. I used to find solace from the blog of the writer Oh Soh-hee[4] whenever my beliefs became shaky. On her blog, I could see replies written by mothers who were going through the same trouble as I did, and I was relieved to find out that I was not the only one struggling. Yet in our society, the collective consciousness about giving our children the right to choose their own learning is weak. As a result, parents are in need of a place where they can consciously find solace, but if this solidarity grows, parents might not need to consciously search for solace.

In order to become parents who are not swayed by the destructive consequences of competitive education, we must form solidarity with our respect for our children as a common denominator. There are parents who force their children to study harder and there are parents who don't want to stress out their children over study, but their love for their children is the same. It is not the difference between who loves more and who loves less. In order to break down the collective consciousness of competitive education, respect for the children and determination not to force our children to do the things that they don't want to do should become the common denominator, instead of a general love for our children. With regards to their lack of patience or emotional control issues, the older generation points out that they are weak because they were spoiled by their parents. But it is not because they were spoiled by their parents that they are weak. The underlying cause is the problem of oppression, because they grew up while being forced to do things without understanding why they had to do the things that they were forced to do.

Children who are respected for their choices and individuality and understand why they are respected will surely live happier lives than children who are not, because it is a path of absolute value that preserves the value of individual-self-realization-uniformity. In our society, children are growing up without being respected for their choice of learning, forced to take extra lessons in private academies for prior learning, and go through the boring process of having to study what they've learned already. And these extra lessons for prior learning makes life feel tiring and boaring, thereby hindering children's self-realization. When they are subject to repeated tedious and arduous learning from an early age, they don't learn how to achieve a sense of rewarding. Parents should now unite their minds to respect their children's individuality and choices and raise them to apply to studies autonomously, so that they become liberated from the prior learning lessons that make life boring and tiring. When children who have learned how to achieve a sense of rewarding on their own become adults, they will achieve self-realization with strength, which is the opposite of weakness. They will lead rewarding and satisfying lives while sharing their self-realizations as members of society.

In Korea, the power of the second chakra that deals with collective consciousness is great. Even in recent years, Koreans achieved democratic change of power by holding peaceful candlelight rallies[5] with the power of the second chakra with which they are born. During the Taean oil spill, a large number of volunteers rushed to clean up and made the miracle of saving the beach. Now is time for parents to gather their minds with that same power that they are born with. Korean parents have the power of the second chakra that will unite them to respect their children's individuality. Before we produce more generations who have been raised brokenhearted due to academic oppression, we must grow a collective consciousness that respects our children's right to choose their learning learning and their individuality. In lectures and programs about good parenting, co-parenting, self-initiated learning, and creativity, the speakers are preaching to parents to acknowledge children's subjecthood. The first step to forming solidarity is for parents to join their power and participate in these efforts. As a result, children who grew up while being respected will be able to lead happy lives, and the collective consciousness created by competitive education will disappear into the past.

Korea is a country with well-developed second chakra. In his book *Happen To Be Koreans*, the psychologist Dr Huh Tae-kyun explains six psychological characteristics of Koreans, which include subjecthood, relationalism, and family expandability. These three characteristics clearly reveal the individual-self-realization- solidarity value. Koreans treasure their relationship with others around them and love to be together. When choosing food menus, they prefer to coordinate their choices with people who are with them, and they prefer to plan and have fun with others instead of alone. And they tend to be mindful of what happens as the consequence of human relationships. Because they treasure relationships so much, they consider others as their own family members, try to show their responsibility for society as they do to their families, and hope others do the same. In particular, the historic March 1 Independence Movement[6] as well as the street cheering during World Cup matches and the candlelight rallies that denounced the government's corruption are a few examples that show us how powerful the power of solidarity is in the characteristics of Koreans.

But we don't ignore individuals. In our national character, we have a well-developed self-praising culture. Dr Huh Tae-kyun explains that a "party-on-me culture" that is pervasive in our society is what makes Koreans uninhibited to boldly stand up to become the center of a crowd. Koreans consider their influence in this relationship very important, and they confirm and manifest their presence. In addition, Koreans always judge the situation from their own perspectives. For example, they follow or violate traffic laws in accordance with their own judgment, and they demonstrate well-advanced citizenship by voluntarily cleaning the streets, cheering for national teams, or large-scale candlelight rallies.

Koreans also have a sense of solidarity strong enough to extend the concept of family to a greater range. In addition, Koreans have the subjecthood that allows them to surreptitiously or in any way possible reveal their presence in a relationship. In other words, the ideal tendency of having the value of the second chakra to circulate into a circle is shaped into a universal national characteristic of Koreans. Koreans' such power made such a rapid growth possible. Korea is the only country to have achieved its current democracy after going through a period of military dictatorship within such a short time in history. Korea is the only country on the planet that has transformed itself from an international aid recipient to an international aid provider. We made all these miracles possible with the desire to reveal our presence, and the commitment to share the miracles together. The second chakra's individual-self-realization-solidarity value is an absolute value we need to change the world. Until now, mankind has evolved by changing the world with the power of the second chakra.

Only when you realize your desire to reveal yourself can you grow up, and only when you have the power to be together can you change the world. If something has to change now, you have to reveal yourself and unite with someone. We cannot invade each other's free will, but the collective consciousness we created together has control over everyone. And the power of collective consciousness does not increase by addition; it increases exponentially. It is with this principle that we are controlled by collective consciousness. According to a report about a statistical analysis of all forms of anti-government protests from 1900 to 2006 released by the American professor Erica Chenoweth, no regime can hold out if 3.5% of the population continuously and steadily hold non-violent rallies. The power of just 3.5% of the population to change the country is in the law of exponential amplification.

But there is an important point here. That is, the power to change the world has to be in the form of non-violent activities. The preposition of non-violence is important because it is a way to cherish an individual even within a group setting. Using violence is possible only when you don't value an individual. It is impossible to change the world if you don't value each individual. That is the reason the method of terrorism cannot change the world as they wish to. Besides, since terrorism runs counter to the current of the universe by undermining the absolute value of life, its cause disappears as a meaningless thing.

Behind terrorism, a greater collective consciousness is formed when the entire global community comes together to mourn over the senseless and brutal loss of precious lives. No terrorist group has a collective consciousness that is greater than this collective consciousness. Those who pursue violence may share the same idea about violence, but they carry out violence with different objectives. Some turn to violence for personal revenge, some for religious reasons, and some for mental problems and fun. A collective consciousness cannot form when all these different minds come together. Besides, it can never surpass the numerical superiority of people who mourn over the loss of lives. How can anybody stop the minds of the people from all over the world who come together to mourn after reading the French truck terror story in newspapers! United minds – no matter how small each mind may be – become a collective consciousness with an immense power by the law of square multiplication.

The reason the desire for change comes out in the form of violence is because everybody has ideas that are different from others. When different ideas clash, it turns into violence and the desire to change the world fails. In order for a world-changing collective consciousness to be formed, people's minds have to become one, even though they have 10,000 different ideas. It doesn't matter if people think differently from one another. All that counts is for them to unite as one mind – a mind that wants to grow further, a mind that wants justice to be realized, a mind that feels sorry for lost lives. The aspiration that comes from the united mind changes the world with the law of square multiplication. When everyone unites as one mind, they don't clash even if they have different thoughts from each other. When some protesters turned to violence at the candlelight rallies, numerous others stepped out as one mind to restore peace. The non-violence that was maintained in that way prevented the path of harming individuals and eventually changed the world. The power of the second chakra is a collective consciousness created by a united mind, and it becomes the power that changes the world when it is in the direction of pursuing both individuals and solidarity.

Thus, it is advantageous to move forward as a self-governing country if a country wants to grow. The unity that respects the autonomy of each province and brings together the power of each province becomes the foundation for realizing the absolute value. The US is a united coalition that respects the autonomy of each state. The US successfully formed a huge coalition of states that accounts for almost half of the continent while respecting the autonomy of each state, and now it has grown to become the richest nation on Earth. China is just as big as the US and succeeded in forming a coalition of states, but China falls short in terms of respecting regional histories and diverse ethnic groups that are scattered throughout its vast territory. China could become the new center of the world if it can achieve unity that respects all peoples, instead of insisting on unity with the Han Chinese people at the center. The wind of constitutional revision is blowing in Korea, but I hope that Korea will choose to be a country of local decentralization. Fortunately, many insist on moving toward this absolute value. The universe will respond to us with abundance and well-being if we achieve a nation that realizes the values of both individual and solidarity.

As of now, mankind's greatest sense of solidarity remains only on a national level, but it is time to move beyond that national level. Mankind must now move on to solidarity as a community on Earth bound together by a common destiny on Earth. The first step for that journey has been taken already. Though not as powerful as I wish it to be, we have the United Nations (UN), and the European Union (EU) is also gaining its ground. But we are only reeling in the face of this journey. Britain has chosen the Brexit policy, the US has declared protectionism, some wealthy regions within one country have demanded separate independence for themselves, and homophobic politicians are emerging as stars in countries around the world. Exclusivism that is not the same as demand for autonomy is a choice that goes against the absolute value. That is a choice that cannot help us achieve affluence and prosperity. Perhaps we will face many difficulties for some time as a result of choosing exclusivism. Those difficulties are inevitable until we realize that those are the consequences of our decision to choose exclusivism and choose to be changed again. The response of the universe to the choice that goes against the absolute value is always the same: It leads to hardship that shows us that it is not the right direction.

However, the response of the universe to the choice that corresponds with the absolute value always leads us to happiness. Therefore, we now have to move beyond the nationalism and move forward toward the solidarity of all mankind, all earthlings. Mankind has reached a point where we have to think hard about how to share the excess material resources of the planet. We have more than enough food on Earth, but too many people are still starving to death. Mankind will continue to achieve materialistic growth into the future, but we have to develop systems and technologies to share those materials with all. Since mankind has experienced the failed socialism that suppresses individual's self-realization in its past history and felt the need for a free market that emphasizes individual's self-realization more, it is time that we need to experiment with self-realization and solidarity that covers the entire planet. We must develop systems that bring mankind together as one, while at the same time respecting each country's autonomy and culture to preserve individualism in that experiment. If we fully realize the absolute value of individual-self realization-solidarity on this planet, the universe will respond to us with the prosperity of all mankind.

I hope we don't remain undecided long standing before this gate. I hope we will open a system in which all mankind will become one, while respecting the autonomy of each region. When it happens, we will eventually achieve the evolution of the world as a response to our pursuit of absolute values. The evolved world can push us to move beyond our solidarity on Earth to the point where we have to think about this galaxy because of advanced technology. The more we evolve, the bigger the scale of our solidarity will grow because each individual becomes more precious.

In the book *Conversations with God*, the author discusses "highly advanced beings" found among the other objects in the universe. According to the author, these highly advanced beings become fully aware of themselves through their indirect experience of love while watching us the earthlings, who are still in a low level of evolution. The sense of solidarity that these highly advanced beings have is in a cosmic level that goes beyond one particular planet. Therefore, there's no such thing as an alien invasion, because the respect for individuals and solidarity of the beings who have advanced their consciousness to go beyond one planet is more than we can imagine. If we make the best of our second chakra and bring about the evolution of the world, we can achieve the evolution of the Earth that necessitates us to expand our solidarity into space. It is thrilling just to imagine what the world that we have to embrace the galaxy as a part of our solidarity would be like.

The Sacred Boundary of the Second Chakra

This is the sacred boundary that protects the second chakra by using the power of the Hon-Baek-Shin-Ui-Ji with the individual-self-realization-solidarity value. If you keep these ideas in your mind, the second chakra will eliminate the difficulty you experience in communicating with the universe and promote recovery and expansion. I hope you will read this part whenever you aspire to change your life and the world. I would appreciate it more if you would pass it on to other people's hearts, because whoever you pass on self-realization to, it always will be realized to the subject who passes it on to others.

(1) Individual – Self-Realization
* I regret forgetting the fact that I am the master of my life,

not knowing the power of my emotions and thoughts that I gained,
and unwittingly filling my life with dim and gloomy colors.

I myself should always be the master of my life.
My life was the joy as well as pain of realizing myself,
so let us take a moment to contemplate on the emotions and thoughts that formed my current life.

I dream about what I wish to fill my life with moving forward.
With intense effort of filling it with what I desire and emptying what I do not wish to fill it with,
I will fill my life with the light that I desire from now on.

* I regret the confusion of the past, of not knowing that my character was given to me from heaven,
of not reflecting on what God plans to do through my colors,
and not being able to grow accordingly.

I now reflect on the meaning of traits I have,
and believe that God is always with me in my predetermined realization,
so I can dispel whatever fear there may be, and continue to realize the meaning of my fate.

Ultimately, I will fulfill the realization predestined by God,
and leave the glory and peace of my share in this world,
so that is how I will serve as the beacon that lights up the world.

* I regret failing to recognize my existential value in relationships,
not having the courage to show my light and talents,
failing to become the existence that I desired.

Let us now start fulfilling ourselves while remaining true to ourselves,
by trusting and loving ourselves that seems almost foolhardy,
and by dreaming and practicing what I wish to become in this relationship.

I will definitely realize myself and disclose all the lights I have,
through confirmation of my existence value by remaining true to myself,
and becoming the existence that I genuinely wish to become.

* I repent presuming that people with character traits different than mine were odd,
treating them with disdain, criticizing them,
and unconsciously trampling on their existence value.

From now on, let us accept how people live in different ways,
respect and cheer for the character traits that are different from ours,
and bless them so that their character traits may shine.

By blessing the realization of various character traits,
remembering that each and every one of them are needed in this world,
we support the diversified evolution of the human kind.

(2) Solidarity – Self Realization
* I regret being ignorant of the solidarity that I belonged to.
I feel ashamed at stepping back from problems,
passing them onto others and expecting others to solve them while I benefit from them.

I regret that our solidarity tried to enjoy our achievements only between ourselves.

I feel ashamed that we begrudged sharing with others,
caring only about ourselves and our well-being.

From now on, I shall actively seek the role I should play for my
solidarity,
endeavor to willingly share the fruits of our solidarity with
others,
and pave the way to live and share with many more.

* Let us recognize the remorse of disgracing our solidarity,
by failing to recognize the meaning of the fate of our relations,
selecting people and picking sides based on empty and secular
values.

Recognizing that it is the cosmic fate that we exist together,
let us build the values and faith we should protect
while sympathizing, thanking, forgiving and blessing one
another.

We create the small steps for the progress of the world,
by creating the glory and peace of our solidarity,
while honorably keeping the values and faith we built together.

* I regret allowing my light to gradually fade away
because of the expectations and pressure from the surroundings,
neglecting myself and giving up on my dreams.

Finding the way to keep my will despite pressure from the
surroundings,
and finding the way to bring benefits to the surroundings while
keeping my will,
the scope of self-realization continues to expand through
conflicts.

Therefore, whichever relationship I may be in, I shall treasure, care and protect myself,
never mistreat any relationship, exert my best,
and continue to expand the value of my existence the way I am.

* Let us comfort each other for failing to recognize the hearts and efforts of the people we were with, thereby,
giving rise to misunderstandings and mistrust,
and forming the relationship of complaints and resentment.

Even if members' opinions differ from mine,
let us believe that they have the same heart and goals,
and try to become united in faith.

When we trust and love the people we are with,
our lights will resonate and amplify within our solidarity,
which will lead to a relationship that makes each other shine more brightly when we get together.

(3) The Integration of Individual – Self-Realization – Solidarity
* I overcome my lack of efforts to be together,
having difficulty revealing myself and accepting others,
as I wasn't being true to myself in the past.

Now as I reflect on what it means to be me,
and with whom and how my light can be shared,
great joy is achieved during such course of transformation toward delightful relationships.

I truly congratulate the evolution of the world created by the combination of everybody's light,
as we remain faithful to our true selves,
and help each other shine.

Endnotes

3   I treat with the traditional Korean medicine classifying humans into four physical constitution types: taeyang-taeeum-soyang-soeum.

4   Oh Soh-hee: a Korean travel writer, she is famous for her essays about traveling third world countries with her young son.

5   Candlelight Rally: a peaceful outdoor protest against the corruption of the Park Geun-hye administration, it took place on a continuous basis on a large scale every Saturday. This rally was the main driving force behind the legal impeachment of the president.

6   March 1 Independent Movement: a peaceful protest for the nation's independence that took place in 1919 when Korea was colonized by Japan. It contributed to growing awareness to independence after it spread throughout the country despite persecution and oppression by the Japanese colonial government.

5. The 3rd Chakra: Analysis – Communication – Synthesis

The third chakra is where we come to face the truth as the beings who were given life, create our own lives, and change the world. The third chakra where the truth is revealed to us is found at the pit of our stomach, which is in the middle part of our body. Truth begins with a mind that differentiates everything from me and oneness in which we discover all – including myself – is one.

We need a process of analysis to correctly understand what kind of phenomenon this is. Analysis is the process of disassembling and dissecting the fact that there are several elements in the phenomenon. So the closer the analysis is physically to the phenomenon, the better. However, the mind of observing the phenomenon must not be separated. As you can see, you can see all the elements contained in the phenomenon and analyze them objectively. In the course of a study, it is very common to take a step back and discover what was not found when buried in the study and get complete results. Objective analysis begins entirely with observing one step away.

The place where we humans live is a relative realm where all beings are separated; the place where all things remain as beings as themselves is an absolute realm. Since we are absolute beings who live in the fiction of space and the time of a relative realm, knowing our truth as absolute beings requires us to look at us after separating us from all things that are relative. And the truth of our lives can be seen only when we look at our lives as objects that are separated from our lives. We can see the true presence of God only when we look at God as being an object separated from us. We can see our true selves only when we separate ourselves from ourselves, and we can tell what colors we are only when we look at ourselves as being separated from others. The analytical skills that separate like this help us to build the discernment because it allows us to observe everything as absolute beings.

The reason we don't recognize the truth is because we can't separate ourselves on our own as we let ourselves be buried in the relative realm. As long as we fail to observe life while separating ourselves from our lives and allow ourselves to be buried in that condition, we cannot see the truth about why our lives ended up being what they are now. When we don't know what made our lives what they are now, we lose our subjecthood and eventually we become overpowered by the weight of life.

The same is true of God. The Creator God must be looked upon as an object separated from our selves. And we have to analyze what kind of being he is to be able to make such a vast and perfect creation. For I am the Creator of my life, and unlike me, God is the Creator of all beings in the world including myself, and that means I must deduce with a cool head of discernment how great his omnipotence may be. If you don't discern God with such a cool discernment, you will make the mistake of considering God as being a similar existence as yourself, and an imperfect being who, like yourself, gets angry, punishes others, and expects to be revered. We have been making errors by underestimating God the Creator to be on our level and mistook him as a being who will punish us and expects to be praised by us. And the reason for this misunderstanding is because we have not been able to differentiate God from us.

Also, you have to keep yourself in distance to see who you really are. You cannot see why you have certain feelings and act in certain ways if you let yourself be buried in your current feelings and behaviors. If you keep your mind far away from yourself and observe your actions from a distance, you will see the reason why you are doing what you are. And I am also another being, depending on the location and situation. Depending on the situation and role, I may be other than speaking in other voices, and I will change forever over time. You can fully understand yourself when you can thus put yourself in time, situation, mind, and behavior and analyze it.

You have to differentiate others from yourself to understand others as well. You need to know how they are different from you and how that difference causes what misunderstandings. If you can't differentiate yourself from others, you make the mistake of judging others based on you. If somebody is slower than you, you judge him to be lazy; if somebody is faster than you, you judge him to be hasty. If somebody makes a choice that is different from yours, you will judge him to have made a wrong choice; if somebody works less than what you can do, you will misunderstand that he didn't do his best; and if someone worked more than you, you will praise him to be impressive. But if you look at that someone separately from you, you can see that he has a working style that allows him to work slower than you, but he adds new things to his work while paying attention to detail. You can see he has an ability to react faster than you, and how he is doing his best within the limits. You feel that all things about him are speaking his individuality and are natural, and you stop comparing yourself with him. You can avoid a conflict caused by misunderstanding when you can understand him under full analytical skills.

You must be able to separate yourself from the world for the sake of understanding the world as well. But it's not easy. We are often swept away by the turbulence of the world and getting buried in the lives in the relative world. That's why people sometimes need "temple stays" to stay away from the world. When you are so far away, you have the discernment to judge what is important in the world and what is useless. Sadly, however, most of us have daily responsibilities. We cannot simply stay away from life or the world physically whenever something happens. Therefore, we must learn how to create the power to discern from the daily turbulence.

To live by the analyzing power in the world, it is good to understand the law of acceleration. The law of acceleration is explained that when a force is applied to an object, the object moves in the direction of the force, and it moves with an accelerated force. The greater the force, the stronger the acceleration, and the heavier the object, the weaker the acceleration. The same law applies to us too. When the winds and the waves of the world hit us, we are pushed by them, and the stronger their force, the greater the acceleration and the consequential turbulence. It's easy for us to be swept away and buried in that way. But the heavier your heart is, the less likely it is that you will be swept away. Moreover, if you can create a force that counters the winds and the waves of the world, you can weaken the force of the world that is pushing you. In this way, we can grow our ability to analyze by reducing the rate of acceleration that troubles us.

Then how can you make your heart heavy? In the English-speaking countries people often say, "I'm OK" and "It's going to be OK" when they are in a chaotic situation. These two expressions contain the key to raising our weight and weakening the winds and the waves of the world. When the winds and the waves of the world shake us, the belief that you're going to be okay creates a heavy weight in your heart. The belief that you are going to be okay does not mean you are all fine. It is about acknowledging that the emotions you feel and the thoughts that pop in your minds in those situations are natural. It is about believing that even though the current emotions and thoughts make things difficult for you, it is not wrong to feel difficult, and this turbulence is my share to endure. Therefore, I'm fine no matter what pressure I am under. Whatever I may feel and think, it is all natural and not abnormal. With "I'm OK," we can become a heavy rock in the world.

It is all the better if you can create a force that counters the winds that shake us. Everything is a passing process, so, this, too, will pass. Everything will surely be all right. The belief that it will get better, and the belief that everything is a passing process weaken the force that shakes us. In fact, life is a series of events anyway, and things keep happening continuously, and you solve one problem only to face another. All things till our death are just a process and there is no conclusion. You can say "it's going to be OK" only under the presumption that this is not the conclusion. In fact, we have managed to live this far because we have been okay in life no matter what has happened. Everything turned out okay and that is the reason mankind could have survived this far and continued to evolve. Things that happen in the world constantly give us opportunities to become okay. They give us opportunities in our after lives, if not in this life. That's how everything eventually turned out okay and it will continue to be that way. That is the reason the human civilizations and all lives could have been evolving this far. Telling yourself "It's going to be OK" creates a powerful force that counters the worldly winds and waves and weakens their forces.

The idea that I'm fine now and this situation is okay from now on gives us room to observe the phenomenon; we take a step back. With that margin, objective analysis and judgment are possible. And now we can make the right decisions about what is important and not important in this process and what to do. In the West, they have objectively analyzed phenomena and developed research, and as an academic result, they have developed society. The sources of that analytical power are exactly "I'm OK" and "It's going to be OK." Against this solid inner side, in the opposite headwind, they approached the truth with unburied decency in the world.

On the contrary, in the Orient, based on the oneness of the world, we have integrated multiple directions and developed research. In Chinese medicine, the same words describe other phenomena. For instance, when expressing the progression of a disease, we use "Tae-Yang, So-Yang, Tae-Eum, and So-Eum" to express the size of yin and yang, but these words are also used to describe the human constitution to distinguish meridians. Such a tendency can usually be observed in Eastern philosophy and science. Words used in the same way describe the oneness common to all phenomena. It concretely explains various medical phenomena with the rule of change of yin and yang, the oneness. Oriental research reiterates terms such as those that have been studied on the basis of the oneness nature of all beings.

This universe works by one principle. The "Conversations with God" explained that one perfect being spilt into several beings, creating the world. In Eastern philosophy, the origin of all things in the universe is displayed as "Taegeuk"[7], and they think that all beings have exactly the same principle of "Taegeuk." Since one being was divided, it means that they are all the same one in the end, and because Taegeuk expanded into a big bang and the universe was born, it means that everything is Taegeuk. That is, both explanations are based on the principle that all beings are any existence.

The feeling of touching the truth is not a joy in learning new things that I didn't know. It was a joy to say, "Oh! That was it. Of course it is." The truth suddenly realized to the question "Why didn't I know it?" is not unfamiliar at all. That is because we all have the truth of God. I didn't know the truth because it was in our lives to take out and confirm one by one while living, but forgot because of the distance between the soul and the heart. When we communicate with my soul or with God in constant reflection, our minds remember the truth one by one. At the same time, I can be more aware of the fact that it is my god.

Also, we are all different, but in the end, we are like. We each live with other limits. Some people are better than me, others are less impatient than I am. But no matter what the difference we are, all of us are the same in that we live our best to the best of our limits. The best of the person who works much more passionately than I am is the same of the best of me, and the best of the lazy person than me is also the same. However, they live in the same best, only the limits of each are different. There is only one reason why we do our best. We are all loved and loved beings, but we are doing our best. There is no one who does not want love, but no one does his best.

Everything in the world returns to one logic, "the best of the current level for love." And all natural phenomena are linked to the oneness of "Taegeuk." Therefore, all areas can be integrated with each other. Acupuncture, diagnosing by the principle of tissue anatomy and treating it on the principle of meridians, has been developed, in which the integration of Eastern and Western medicine is partially carried out. The philosophy of Yi Je-ma of classifying the world into four elements was the key to diagnosing the human body and gave birth to Sasang constitutional medicine, integrating philosophy and medicine into one. Like making an excavator that imitates the appearance of an insect, biological research may be mechanically integrated, leading to the development of new equipment. As a retaliatory definition of "eye for an eye, a tooth for a tooth," the will of Allah to guide one's karma is to give mercy while releasing the karma of the previous life, which touches the will of the Buddha, at his own expense. The will of the Buddha to guide you to your dreams is similar to Jesus' words that you can reach God with just love. Since all religions guide humankind on the same path as one source, religion integration is quite possible.

In this way, a new place of understanding will be opened to understand the oneness of the world and integrate various fields. In the new chapter of understanding, more truth can be spread to the world. New treatments will come out, more convenient ones will be developed, and various ways will be done to make human beings happier. Since we are each and every one of us, the truth of happiness that more people can enjoy is opened in the process of integrating the stories of the world into one.

We instinctively pursue the truth. This is because the chance of happiness is hidden in the truth of the world. It is necessary to integrate one by one, which is usually used for the opportunity of happiness, to have achieved the classification one by one by fierce and careful analysis. This is because the truth of a single item is not very meaningful. In addition, the origin is straightforward, but if you do not understand it, there is no reason to see the truth. In order to find out what to apply specifically, it must be supported by a thorough analysis. The truth of happiness is opened as long as the analysis and integration must be combined.

For that purpose, communication is necessary. Each person needs to communicate correctly, analyze each other correctly, discover commonalities, and maintain a true relationship without misunderstandings. If interested parties do not communicate with each other, they can analyze how their understandings are involved, find a way of coexisting integration, and avoid the foolishness of eating each other's advantages. Research in various fields must be communicated so that the above analysis enables more integrated research, opens up new theories, and develops good products that various businesses must communicate with. Can be done. Communication is important to guide analysis and integration at the same time.

Communication is smoother in Western Europe than in the East. Communication between ages and groups without difficulty in using honorifics is easier and the culture of discussion is well developed. Based on these communication skills and analytical powers, in Western society, various theoretical systems have been established and played a role in guiding the development of humankind. On the other hand, in the Orient, it is difficult to communicate between ages and classes due to the honorific culture. Therefore, the conflict between generations and hierarchies is fierce. Bossy culture, which is often observed in Korea and other Eastern countries, is a phenomenon that is separated by social truth without communication.

It is a relative evaluation, as there are also systems that impede communication in the Orient. The relative evaluation, completely contrary to analysis-communication-integration, directly interrupts the way the truth unfolds. Relative evaluation is about ranking based on comparison with surrounding others, and it connects each existence without identifying each individual. At the same time, it is a denial of the oneness of all beings, and there is no room for communication because each rank is determinism.

Relative evaluations create a seemingly fair illusion. However, unfair expediency and special favoritism prevail in society where relative evaluation is accepted as natural, and there is no room for communication. As a result, indiscriminate criticism and distortion of opponents are rampant because of complaints about unfairness. On the other hand, the more sensible the culture, the more natural the absolute evaluation is perceived. Absolute evaluation is a way to discern and assess each being's existence, and to give the individuality of each being room to communicate, eventually bringing everyone together. Therefore, absolute evaluation conforms to absolute values and leads to truth that can be fair to society. Our society must break the illusion that relative evaluation is fair. It is a perfect illusion that the relative evaluation is fair. A fair society unfolds through absolute evaluation.

Until now, South Korea has taken the relative evaluation as a matter of course when determining school grades. As a result, the ordering of workplaces, regions, and cultures is taken for granted. Moreover, even how to consume popular culture now is done in relative evaluation. A product that gathers teenagers who dream of idols, ranks them every week by voting, gives them the opportunity to make their debut, and promotes products with member photos that sell more (ranking system), which may make their fans fight each other.

It is sad to imagine how these children who have grown up exposed to the pop culture subjected to such relative evaluation and non-communication will end up creating an unfair society as a result of lack of good communication. We must break away from the relative evaluation before a greater tragedy hits us. Now we must protect our children from a culture that is pervasive of relative evaluation. This is a responsibility that we, as an older generation, must fulfill before we pass on this society to our next generations.

On the other hand, even in the Western world, we can observe the sadness of lack of integration power that is far from the truth. That might be attributed to racists. They have no discernment in the thoughts of each race, refuse to communicate between races, and do not see the oneness of the dignity of all human beings. The human truth moves away and lives in lonely anger. They can live in happier truths if they can see the eve of dignity, but it is painful to reject the truth of integration.

In Korea, there is a social system that realizes the absolute value of the third chakra very well. Korea's health insurance is a system that communicates with discerning judgment and beautiful oneness. It was possible for citizens to agree to set insurance premiums according to their income level because individual citizens saw the entire system by separating themselves without being buried in their health and income. If they couldn't discern themselves, they wouldn't have agreed to the system, complaining, "Why should I pay so much when I'm healthy?" However, the majority of our citizens agreed to the income-based premium as if it was a matter of fact, and they demand the government set a premium that more closely adheres to the principle. As a result, our health insurance system became a system by realizing a communication that unites the people by circulating and redistributing social wealth. Being one of the medical practitioners, I am grateful for and proud of this righteous oneness, which communicates wealth in the process of healing the sick.

The dog trainer Kang Hyung-wook[8] is a good example that shows the power of the third chakra. The way he helps improve the relationship between dogs and their owners, believing in that there are no bad dogs in the world, is founded upon analysis and synthesis. First, he distinguishes dogs and people before trying to understand the dogs' unique expressions and characteristics. And in interpreting the minds of dogs, he understands the oneness that love is the most important thing to dogs, like humans. Based on that mind, they communicate with the dogs and correct their dogs' problem behaviors. In any field, using the power of healthy third chakra in your work is like embodying the truth in that work.

The field in which I personally hope to open up a wide range of communication is traditional medicine and modern medicine. South Korea is in the state of a dual medical system. Traditional medicine is recognized as a medical practice and is supported by the national health insurance system. In the process of extending human life to the amazing development of modern medicine, most traditional medicines in the world have disappeared. Among them, Chinese and Korean medicines survived. It was possible to continue to develop because the academic system had been firmly solidified over the long history. And in Korean medicine, there are many possibilities that lead health to human beings living in the age of longevity. As the possibilities expand, it is necessary to communicate with modern medicine, which accounts for the majority of the current medical system. China and Korea are almost the only countries on the planet that have such conditions.

Despite these good conditions, the statements made by the Korea Medical Association and the Association of Korean

Medicine exchange with each other make me sad. This is because the statements are full of exclusions. It's hard to even find an attempt to find out who you are, let alone integrate. While we try to communicate, we are worried, and we are worried about it, we will analyze it once we try to investigate it, and in the process of such analysis, discover mutually beneficial advantages and pursue academic integration. It guarantees that if Korea's dual health care system seeks the absolute value of academic analysis-communication-integration, it will play a major role in the development of human medicine.

Cancer is the largest coral reef for humankind to open the era of longevity. Chemotherapy is rapidly evolving into first-generation chemical anti-cancer drugs, second-generation targeted anti-cancer drugs, third-generation immunochemistry, and fourth-generation metabolic anti-cancer drugs. The treatment rate increased with the development. However, the individual differences associated with chemotherapy are too large. Research is actively underway in the medical community to find a biological mark that can distinguish the difference between the large therapeutic effect on some patients and the weak effect on other patients, but it is still clear. There are those who have no good results. Research isolated by the medical community alone has yet to find a way.

However, there is something in common with those who increase duration of life while treating cancer that has progressed to metastasis. This is exactly the point that completely changed the attitude of life. It may vary from person to person whether they changed in any direction, but they changed their attitudes in life on the verge of death. Perhaps this difference may be an important factor in treatment response rates. Therefore, I personally hope that the research of chemotherapy will promote the integrated research of medical psychology and philosophy. It may discover the specific cause of the treatment rate for which the biological mark could not be detected.

Finally, the area I want to communicate with is religion. The existence purpose of all human beings is the Trinity. There are many difficulties in practicing love and reaching the Trinity in a difficult life, and humankind has created and developed religions in an attempt to overcome the difficulties. Mankind has protected love while overcoming many difficulties thanks to its religion, and even in long history, we have not forgotten what our purpose is. So all religions guide the way in favor of love.

Therefore, if you analyze it from the perspective of "How do they practice love when observing other religions?" you can know the true meaning of the religion. Even though all religions have little by little doctrines that interfere with love, there is no doubt that any religion has a platform of love. However, we cannot communicate with each other because we ignore the oneness of such religions and we try to analyze the false doctrines of other religions. Interreligious interruptions threaten human peace. Because when religious beliefs are violated, human beings are willing to go to war.

The more ways to go in the Trinity, the better. You don't have to go on one road at all. So in the doctrines of other religions, I try to guide or analyze some love and dream of taking advantage of what my religion did not, and integrating it with interreligious communication. When interreligious integration takes place, peace will come to mankind, where the false doctrines that hinder this love will be misaligned and lost.

The power of the healthy third chakra pursues smooth communication in this world. For smooth communication, analyze the situation one step away, realize the truth that everything is one, and do not waste it in the process of sending and receiving. The power of the third chakra allows us to see the truth in the relative realm surrounded by fiction. Academic, technical, cultural, and artistic truths are unfolded by the power of the third chakra. Even in some fields, the truth of that field can be achieved only when we discriminate and analyze, so as not to be confused by virtual images, communicate to overcome distance, and make integration that discovers the oneness.

Discerning and separating myself from everything, appreciating the beautiful single flow, and the hand that reaches out to that beautiful flow – these are always the right things to do. The right choice of this absolute value will unfold the truth before you and allow your lymphatic and emotional energy to flow unobstructed, giving you the power to live with light, refreshing body and mind.

The Sacred Boundary of the Third Chakra

This is the sacred boundary that protects the third chakra by using the power of Hon-Baek-Shin-Ui-Ji with the value of discernment-communication-oneness. If you keep these thoughts in your mind, the third chakra will eliminate the difficulty of communicating with the universe and promote recovery and expansion. I hope you read it for the truth when your body and mind are heavy, and life is troubling. And when your body and mind are light, I hope you will read them as your loved ones, remembering that, to whomever you convey absolute values, they will be always be realized to the one who spreads them...

(1) Analysis – Communication

* When we were immersed in a situation,
we were trapped in the grumbles, remorse, self-conceit and greed for life,
and we were unable to judge what we had to do.

Now let's avoid getting buried in the situation, take a step back and observe.

We will be able to better understand the causality of what's happening,
and realize how we can reduce trials and errors.

Take a step back and slowly reflect on the life you tread.
You will learn what it is that is crucial to your life
and live a fulfilling life filled with only the things you need.

* Unlike us, God is omnipotent and has no regrets,
and unlike us, is omnipotent and is love itself.
God always replies to us with truth full of love and joy.

In the multiverse (parallel), all possibilities are stored as digital (binary) information,
and the signals of the multiverse that we light up with our choices at each moment assemble in our spirits
to unfold in the form of analog phenomena in the 4-dimensional (3-dimensional space+time) world today.

That is why we need to understand the language of the universe (binary system) in order to communicate with God.
The signal that lights up love and joy is God's "yes", and the signal that turns them off is "no".
When we follow God's "yes" signals, we can approach the truth.

* As I did not try to properly understand myself,
as I did know why I was having such thoughts and emotions,
I have been swayed by emotions and thoughts I did not desire.

In our subconsciousness, the residues of our past emotions accumulated and are waiting for compensation.
The more the emotions that were not solved, the more there will be uncomfortable thoughts,
which prevent joy today and continuously hinder happiness.

That is why if we take out the pains in our past, forgive what need to be forgiven and reflect on what need to be reflected on, you'll feel yourself growing more comfortable.
So for your own self, do not let any lump of unresolved emotions remain.

* I did not spare more time to ponder on the true meanings of others' words and actions,
and was quick to strike back with the same kind of words and actions,
which built up misunderstandings that disregard each others' true feelings.

Now in order to properly understand the words and actions of others,
if you take a step back and observe not their actions but their hearts,
you'll discover that their hopes are not so different from yours.

We are all beings that want to love and be loved.
The other person simply does not know how to love and be loved,
so communicate slowly with love and you'll be able to clear the air.

(2) Synthesis – Communication
* My thoughts, feelings and efforts shape my life.
The strongest of them all are the feelings created by the subconsciousness.
I am creating my life based on the power of my subconsciousness.

Our thoughts, feelings and efforts shape this society.
The strongest of them all is again our feelings.

We are creating the world based on the power of collective subconsciousness.

Revenge is the norm in a society full of anger, and exchange is the norm in a society full of joy.
Remembering that each and everyone's heart determines the directions for the human kind,
I shall try to fill my life with joy.

* God divided himself to create us,
and filled us, the cell nucleus of himself, with all the truth he had.
We are a small and compact part of God, and God is in all of us.

Spirit starts off as a 1-dimensional existence (string) in the 10-dimensional time and space when beginning a life as a human[9],
and is completed as a 11-dimensional (universe) in the 20-dimensional time and space when the Trinity is achieved.
Our growth is the evolution of dimensions and the expansion of the universe.

That is why what we do onto ourselves is what we do onto God,
and what we do onto our life is what we do onto the universe,
so please do not forget that we are creating the universe together with God.

* Myself in the past pushes me in the present with wisdom gained from experiences,
and the feelings and intuition about myself of the future help hasten my choices today.
The current me holds myself of the past and of the future.

We obtained various experiences in all the places where we were born and raised,
and we all have different experiences based on our times (age), environment, gender and occupation,
but all such experiences combine to complete the actions I take.

Myself contained in each and every moment of life since the beginning of the existence flows into the soul to become the nature,
and all the experiences of various lives remain as inborn actions,
now I am constantly changing my nature and actions with my heart.

* Let us realize that hating someone breeds hatred,
and that not only hurts others but also ourselves,
that we become united in such hatred which brings pain and suffering.

Let us realize that loving someone breeds love,
and that not only makes others but also us happy,
that we become united in such love which brings happiness and joy.

Share your heartfelt desires with others.
Continue to experience that what you have done onto others is what you have done onto yourself,
that we are united as one every moment, and love one another.

(3) The Integration of Analysis – Communication – Synthesis
* I overcome getting trapped in each other's situation,
because of failure to notice the common essence everyone has,
and failure to learn how to communicate.

By examining them one by one through analysis,
and discovering the one essence that leads to all,
I am happy and grateful to see the doors open for communication
without misunderstandings.

Since I can communicate one truth to various places,
and apply them accordingly with accurate analysis,
I would like to send my congratulations to the world (me) for
the diverse realization of the same truth.

Endnotes

7   Taegeuk: a word meaning the start of space for all things in
    the Orient.

8   Kang Hyung-wook: A dog trainer who has a good
    understanding of dogs and is recognized by the general
    public as the dog's president.

9   String Theory: A physics theory proposed to replace the
    standard model. The theory that all particles consist of
    strings or small rings. String theory requires a space of
    ten or more dimensions, not a three-dimensional space
    (written by Paul W. Zitzewitz. The Handy Physics Answer
    Book. Visible Ink Press Publishing).

6. The 4th Chakra: Faith – Hope – Love

"Faith-Hope-Love." This is such a famous definition of absolute values. Thanks to this Bible verse, few would dispute that this is about absolute. However, it is strange that faith and love are conflicting values. They have been a pair for so long that we feel they refer to the same thing. But, as I explained earlier, they are contrasting because faith is directed at something that is not love, while love is directed to the existence itself, and circulates with hope as the pivotal center.

The Bible tells us that love is the greatest of these. Faith is necessary to keep love, and hope is necessary to foster more love. Since both faith and hope are necessary to love, that makes love the greatest of these. Therefore, I am going to focus on stories about love in the absolute value of the fourth chakra that runs through our heart. If I may present my conclusion first, I am going to talk about how only love is eternal, and the essence of all things that exist forever is love.

Do you believe in the fact that everything is love; all things other than love are only illusion, and only love is eternal? It is not easy to believe because we are surrounded by many things that are not love, but if you seek truth by the power of the third chakra, you will see that the essence of all beings is love, and the reality where all things that are not love are lost in vain. Now, I am going to talk specifically about how of all things that happen to us, only love is eternal; how the things that are not love are only illusions; and therefore, all things that exist are love.

First, I will talk about karma between souls. Between us there is a complex intertwining of dark karma, such as hostility to each other, guilt-consciousness, and bright karma, such as gratitude and blessing for each other. We can make the dark karma that followed each disappear by understanding the phenomenon and sincerely apologizing or forgiving it. If you give apology and forgiveness to your unconscious mind, you will experience that the whirlwind of emotions from the karma are no longer blowing. You will be surprised to see how they can easily disappear only through one condition of sincerity.

But as we appreciate each other, the connected karma of love exists forever and does not disappear. Of course, new wounds can appear to the one you appreciate, thereby making the person close heart and build hatred. Then, the gratitude of the past is overshadowed and disappears from the scene. It is as if it is gone. But if you brush off this newly appeared hatred with sincere apology and forgiveness, you can feel the gratitude of the past being restored and stay where it used to be. That's why it's easy to recover a relationship with someone you are thankful for, because gratitude was only hidden, not gone.

Human relationship is destined to entail conflict. Everyone experiences marital crisis at least once, and your relationships with coworkers are destined to have repeated conflicts. What makes you mend a broken relationship and recover the original good relationship despite those relationship crises are the links between gratitude and blessing. If you had a relationship where each party was grateful to the other, you can reconcile and recover the good relationship as if nothing had happened even if you had a relationship crisis and became hostile to each other. It is because the karma of gratitude does not disappear regardless of changes in situation.

But in a relationship that is not connected with a great karma, the relationship crisis means an end to the relationship. To sustain a relationship after the disappearance of hostility and guilt, you have to link the cords of gratitude and blessing. Only when he and I have a lasting bond of love, can the consciousness under the control of unconsciousness change. A connection of love that is changed in this way remains where it always is instead of disappearing. It becomes the power to always embrace each other and serve as the driving force to protect the relationship in times of crisis.

On the other hand, hostility always disappears depending on how we make up our mind. It is thanks to this that mankind has been able to develop together without being destroyed. We were able to survive instead of being destroyed despite numerous wars, tyranny, and ruthlessness, all thanks to the law of the universe, in which the karma of love, which connected at least once while completely eliminating dark karma between us, remains forever. Not only have we survived, but we also have been evolving because the karma of love has remained forever and the power that binds us together has been maintained.

The same goes for myungsu(命數), or the "destiny number" in English, that builds up as the result from love. Myungsu is a change in the body and mind that improves as we define ourselves as love and actually practice love. Once improved, myungsu will never decrease again within one lifetime. Therefore, the ability to love easier than others can also last until the end of life once myungsu is improved. If I improve my myungsu by defining myself as love only to go through a mental change later and reverse my original thought and think it's not love, the improved destiny rate of our body, or myungsu, remains the same. So, when I decide to love again, I can admit love just as I did before. Also, if you improved your myungsu by practicing love, and then it turns into an aggressive trait as the result of something, myungsu still remains the same. And when you make up your mind to love again, you can love with the ability you had before. Once enlightened, the result of love never disappears, even if you falter temporarily. The result of love remains forever in our existence and in the universe.

However, myungsu will not roll over to next life. But just because it does not roll over to the next life doesn't mean it disappears in vain. Even if your life ends when your myungsu is 50, you start again at zero in the next life. However, it is much easier to increase the number to 50 than in the previous life. When you see some people who are determined to improve myungsu, you can notice that they easily improve the number at a faster pace. These are people who have experienced that level in their past lives. In their souls, more precisely, in their ninth chakra, the experience of love remains, and their love remains in the universe forever. So, it is easy for them to improve myungsu. Although myungsu does not roll over, it doesn't mean the experience of love itself is gone forever.

Besides, the phased completion of the expansion of myungsu brings about eternal changes that apply to all lives. Suppose someone completed the second phase of myungsu expansion in this life and increased myungsu to 30 during the third phase of myungsu expansion before his life ended. Then, in his next life, he is born as a being where Hon and Baek are combined and Shin and Ui are combined, and he starts at zero, which is the beginning of the third phase of expansion. The integration of Hon-Baek-Shin-Ui-Ji that we completed through love is a permanent result and it is never to be separated. Completing the love experience in each phase signifies that you will experience a new love as a perfectly new being. In the end, you achieve a result that lasts through all lives. The result of the love we have achieved in this way remains forever.

Myungsu may improve only to take a fall again when your mind is directed against love. This is not because myungsu is being cut off; it happens because there appeared an anti-myungsu(反命數) that counters myungsu. An anti-myungsu refers to the pathological consciousness that is most adverse in Hon-Baek-Shin-Ui-Ji. The anti-myungsu of Hon is hatred. The anti-myungsu of Baek is a grudge. The anti-myungsu of Shin is denial; the anti-myungsu of Ui is lie; and the anti-myungsu of Ji is irresponsibility. When we fail to overcome the pain that can be overcome at the level of our growth and take actions marked by hatred, grudge, lie, injustice, or irresponsibility, an anti-myungsu is formed in our unconsciousness. The anti-myungsu makes our mind and soul become distant, and our mind moves away from the control of the soul. Then, we end up suffering from uncontrollable emotional confusion and hardship.

However, anti-myungsu disappears without a trace when we change our mind. You may hate somebody and tell yourself, "I hope he will suffer as much as I do." But if you change your mind, turn the hatred around, and tell yourself, "I should not hate him. I'm sure he had a good reason," the anti-myungsu will disappear without a trace. The distance between the soul and the mind is restored to its original position and psychological difficulties will be eliminated. The anti-myungsu disappears completely without leaving any lingering trace.

Thinking and practicing love leaves lasting consequences, but the law of the universe is that the opposition of love always disappears without a trace. Myungsu, or the destiny number that is built up as a result of love, continues throughout life without being cut down. Even if you start again in your next life, the love is recorded in the universe forever, giving you the resilient power to build myungsu all over again. In addition, the result of completing a phase of love gives us a lasting change of being reborn as a new being. On the other hand, anti-myungsu, which is the opposite of love, is just an illusion that vanishes helplessly at any time when we changed our mind. The hostility and guilty conscious we hold against each other is also an illusion that vanishes without trace, and the gratitude and blessings we give to and take from each other has been driving our evolution as an eternal power that lasts throughout all lives.

Love is forever in all things that surround us, but things that are not love vanish helplessly. This fact proves that our true essence is love. In our Hon-Baek-Shin-Ui-Ji, there coexist physiological and pathological consciousnesses. Of these two, the physiological consciousness that corresponds to love exerts its power with the existence itself – in other words, soul, mind, and body – at its foundation, but the pathological consciousness which is the opposite of love, is based on the space where our trinity – soul, mind, and body – is unfolding. Therefore, love can stay for us for eternity, but not the things that are not love; they vanish helplessly depending on the changes in space.

We are essentially one-bodied beings in the absolute realm, but in the relative realm, we are in an imperfect condition where there is space between the soul and the mind and between the mind and the body. My actions don't match what I have in my mind, and my mind is not in sync with my soul, and this disparity makes it difficult and uncomfortable for us. However, this sense of disparity (space) is reduced by our efforts and eventually disappears. The more we expand myungsu, the narrower the gap between these three entities. All things that are not love disappear due to the narrow gap, and the change in the existence itself that has made this gap narrow continues. Myungsu, which is a product of love, as well as physiological consciousness, gratitude, and blessing exist forever and pathological consciousness caused by the in-between space, hostility, guilty consciousness, and anti-myungsu can be completely extinguished by spatial changes. So, even if we have pathological consciousness, our true nature is love. When we look at ourselves, we have to look at the true nature, not space.

The completion of a human (forth phase completion of myungsu), where the scattered Hon, Baek, Shin, Ui, and Ji become integrated, signifies the disappearance of space in the mind and body. First of all, as Hon-Baek-Shin-Ui-Ji merge one by one, the space in the mind disappears, leaving no room for pathological consciousness to settle. All anxiety, disappointment, doubt, and indifference disappear from the inside and a sense of inferiority lingers around. In the sixth chakra where Hon, Baek, Shin, Ui, and Ji integrate, there are a hypothalamus and pituitary gland that comprehensively control the body. Consequently, the integrated mind is fully realized in the body, and the distance between the mind and the body disappears. As a result, the power factor forms a whole number one in the affirmation of unconsciousness.

The final fifth completion signifies that Hon, Baek, Shin, Ui, and Ji are enveloped in spiritual light as the mind, body, and soul become united. The pineal body, where Hon, Baek, Shin, Ui, and Ji are integrated, is a third eye, and it is a spiritual communication channel. In other words, the soul's light envelops Hon, Baek, Shin, Ui, and Ji in the spiritual communication channel, as the space between the mind and the soul disappears and the two become a united whole. Now, the pathological consciousness cannot remain even outside Hon, Baek, Shin, Ui, and Ji, and all that is left is love. The last remaining dark karma that was connected to the outside also disappears because it has no means to connect with the outside, and all that is left is a karma marked by bright light. Consequently, the spirit's free will is fully realized and the trinity of spirit, mind, and body can always form one unity. Now that the relative space is gone, no illusions can break in. You become a being that has fully realized in the form of your true original existence.

Just as all presences are eternal with love, and what is not love is an illusion that disappears at any time, so are good and evil – good whose true nature is love and what exists eternally, and evil that is a wind blowing between the gap on the true nature. The true substance that exists forever determines the composition of the space and creates the wind blowing into it. Therefore, good always regulates evil, and evil is created or silenced according to the will of good. So, the good that determines space is the one that controls evil, and the evil is only the passive realm that is under the control of the good. All we need to do is understand the good as the self-regulated realm and observe the evil, which is the passive realm, just as a phenomenon.

What we feel as evil is like the rain and the wind that comes and blows in the spiritual space and unconsciousness. The wind blowing in a personal space was created by ourselves, and the wind blowing in a shared space was created by our collective consciousness (consciousness + unconsciousness). We may feel cold and troubled because of this rain and wind, but we will never be melted and disappeared by them. The law of nature is, the wind will blow and then disappear, and the rain will come and then stop. If we become drenched and disheveled by the rain and wind of evil, we can simply dry and clean up ourselves. We can turn over and calm down the rain and wind that we create, and with regards to the rain and wind of collective consciousness, we can fiercely look after love and find a cover to avoid it.

However, the bigger the space, the stronger the rainstorm blows. Strong winds blowing in a wide space can turn into something like a tornado, and sometimes collective consciousness can turn into something like a hurricane. Even if you are possessed by the devil like in the exorcism films, instead of driving away evil, you have to calm down the hurricane with a group or big love and restore the distance between the mind and the soul. The evil phenomenon that happens in a certain physical space is just a storm created by many people's negative consciousness. What you need to do is turn it into a breeze with many people's affection for the place.

The anti-social personality disorder that we see in the recent atrocious crimes seems to be a perfect example of evil because these criminals don't feel any remorse. Even if someone showers them with love, that somebody will feel an impregnable barrier to the acceptance. That is because most of their chakras have turned into an empty space after rotating in the direction that is opposite to the natural law. Their basic skeleton is love, just like ours, but their chakras are making a reverse circulation, causing love to spin off instead of being embraced. That's why most of their space is empty. Inside an empty space, there is always a blowing wind. That's why they seem to be the existence of evil. For them to be able to hold love, their chakras must restore its right direction of circulation. This subject will be discussed with specific methods in the following chakra restoration part. When the chakra cycle recovers, a given love can be embraced inside. When you send a big love in that situation, they can begin to recover their true selves. When you fill an empty space and calm down the wind, the good foundation frame will reveal even in the beings that seem to embody the perfect evil.

The idea that life is a war between good and evil is a childlike idea of fighting an imaginary enemy in the windy air. There are still a few who name that windy air, evil, and treat it as a tangible being. Now, space should be seen as space, and the force felt in the space should be seen as the rainstorm we have created. We are the true entities that exist in the windy space of collective consciousness that created together. We are the subjects who control the wind blowing between the space within us and the space of the world, and we can make the distance between our souls and the minds narrower or broader. If you build up love inside yourself, the space for rainstorm disappears and the light breeze blows. When our collective consciousness creates a friendly wind, the rainstorm around us subsides. Evil can never beat good. From the beginning to the end, good dominates evil.

Given that, there is no way for me to deny that this world was created solely for the purpose of experiencing love...Given the fact that love is the only thing that leaves eternal traces and results how can we claim that its sole purpose is not love? So, you can believe it: God the Creator always loves you, and he only loves you. There is no reason for him to punish you, put you in hell, and make you disappear without a trace. When we choose the wrong way and suffer, God constantly taps us and tells us to turn around and look at him because he is not in that direction. He never punishes us if we go the wrong way, and he taps and waits for us with an infinite love and earnest desire for us to turn around and look at him. And when we wholeheartedly turn around, he only embraces us with bright light, because we are part of him, and we are his life...And when you are struggling to overcome your limitations, God is steadfastly supporting you, with love, earnestly wishing for you to finish the road till the end... We just have to believe in God's love and move on. Nothing can destroy our very existence. Therefore, you are, and we are, the existences of wholesome love. It is a perfect love that can expand forever, with the promise of eternity, and gives us opportunity forever. We may love all beings with a firm faith, because your eternity only wants love, and you can be most happy with your only purpose that is love...

The Sacred Boundary of the Forth Chakra

This is a sacred boundary that protects the fourth chakra by using the power of Hon, Baek, Shin, Ui, and Ji as the value of faith-hope-love. As a love for love, the fourth chakra will smoothly communicate with the universe and promote healing and expansion. You can read it at any time to increase the power of chakra when you don't see the road. And I hope that you will spread it to your loved ones, because that love will surely make you happy.

(1) Faith – love
* I repent not having faith in the power of my efforts,
begrudging the results of my life,
and giving up, thinking that all my efforts are useless.

Since efforts certainly leave traces in life,
believing that they will pay off in any way someday,
I try harder everyday based on such beliefs.

As my efforts gradually accumulate every day,
the time I have lived and will live become more priceless,
and based on such beliefs, I do my best to love my life as much
as I can.

* Let us overcome the misunderstanding that the world is unfair
and random,
believe in the fairness and correctness of all karma in the cosmic
time,
and believe that this universe works only for the purpose of
experiencing love.

It was our misunderstanding that God judges and punishes,
so let us believe in his omnipotent love,
and that God cannot help but to love us, who are a small part
of himself.

I firmly believe that we are given a fair chance based on our
own karma,
are always given omnipotent love from God,
and promised the eternity and integrity of existence.

* It was a misunderstanding that we were a sinner punished for
original sin,
remember the fact that we were created with God's love and
blessings,
and believe that we came to this world in order to love.

Although there are weaknesses in me that prevent me from
loving and loving only,
and I get swayed by things that prevent me from loving,
I still believe that my nature that pursues love does not change.

I constantly evolve as a bigger and brighter being of love

through the choices of love I make through many trials and errors,
I am confident that one day, I will be able to practice love and only love.

* I understand that those who did wrong, sinned and hurt me in the past,
were unable to care for me only because they could not handle themselves,
and that they did not have ill intentions to trouble me.

Those who make me uncomfortable with undesired love today,
I understand that they are only trying to care for me from their part,
and I believe they are doing so out of good will.

All humans are created with love and blessings,
and so trust that they are doing their best within their limits just like me,
and pave the path for love within that trust.

(2) Love – Hope
* I console the pain that rendered me powerless,
as I was disappointed about the opportunities of today,
and giving up hope that there will ever be a good opportunity for me.

With the hope that I will one day have that chance,
waiting for that moment, sparing no efforts,
I live everyday prepared for that moment.

Even when I am at a loss not knowing when that chance will arrive,
since I always exert my best while loving what I can do now,

new hopes arise in each and every effort I make.

* With the hope that God will save me from this pain,
I overcome the fear I face today,
and keep marching on the road that lies ahead.

With the hope that God will lead me to happiness,
I take the challenge for love today,
and create the path to happiness.

Since God guides all existences in this world including me to love,
the universe keeps engaging in the expansion of love,
and I live everyday with hope in this world that God presides over.

* I have many regrets looking into my past,
but I pat myself on the shoulders for all the hard work I've done,
and love myself so that I can become a better me.

In order to love myself as I am,
I appreciate myself for being excellent today, soothe my frustrations,
and try to empower myself to push the envelope further.

Dreaming of a better self moving forward,
loving yourself every day the way you are,
and you'll find yourself shining big and bright.

* Having high expectations about others based on your greed,
and getting disappointed that they did not meet your expectations,
and falling out of love, would you call it true love?

If you get exhausted and wounds pile up because of the love you're in,
and the efforts to recover love continuously get torn apart,
is it right to keep that kind of love?

In order to continue loving someone, there must be hope.
That is why you can get rid of your greed and rekindle love with the slightest hope,
and banish the lingering affection and sadness to put an end to the love that does not accompany the slightest hope.

(3) Integration of Faith – Hope – Love
* I overcome all the pain of the past,
of not being able to foster hope due to lack of faith,
of not being able to love due to lack of hope.

Earnest hope based on strong faith,
and sincere love based on earnest hope,
I have only to thank all the love that I have today.

Since there is no moment without faith, I am always full of hope,
and since there is no moment without love as I am always filled with hope,
I congratulate the completion of whole and sound love.

7. Spiritual Health

Man deals with the problem of mind – among the soul, mind, and body – as a psychiatric treatment. Psychoanalysis and psychology have revealed much about the human mind. This has allowed us the medical benefits with regards to the symptoms that show when we have mental issues, pathological mechanisms, and even treatments. But there are real spiritual problems that cannot be resolved by psychological treatment alone.

Spiritual energy is the fundamental energy that awakens love. In order to love properly, spiritual health is necessary. Since spiritual problems are associated with mental health, those who suffer from them recover through psychological treatments, and because they are different from psychiatric problems, they often encounter limitations with psychological treatment alone. In order to properly understand spiritual health, one must understand the relationship between good and evil, as well as possession and the shields of mind.

1) Possession

When we imagine spiritual matters, we often think of some lifeless souls harassing living humans. In fact, that's what happens on a daily basis. Among these phenomena, when a dead soul is strongly influenced, it is called possession. There are souls that do not leave Earth after death. Then we must know why these souls remain after death. Only then can we understand by what principle possession occurs and how we can cope with it. There is a reason for this phenomenon, and it is similar to a natural law.

First of all, when your life expires and you die, the conscious energy and the spiritual energy of the moment of death will leave your body. It is this phenomenon that people who have experienced near-death describe about themselves floating in the air and looking at their bodies. As conscious energy and spiritual energy converge, they naturally break free of Earth's gravitational field and return to their homes in the universe. This process is described in detail in Michael Newton's *Journey of Souls*. However, there are spirits that cannot leave Earth's gravitational field in this process. Failure to leave after death is due to certain conditions, which fall into four categories.

First, when the karma that must be fulfilled at the end of one's life exceeds the maximum that can be fulfilled in a single lifetime, the spirit cannot break free from Earth's gravitational field.

Second, when the karma that is to be received at the end of a life exceeds the maximum that can be received in a single lifetime, the spirit cannot escape Earth's gravitational field.

Third, a strong denial of oneself, a denial of one's permanence, a strong denial of one's own wrongdoing, and a strong denial of one's past life keep the spirit from leaving Earth's gravitational field.

Fourth, strong denials of the Creator keep the spirit from leaving Earth's gravitational field.

If any one of these four conditions is met, the spirit cannot pass on. This is like a law of nature that applies equally to all.

Not being able to leave Earth due to the burden of karmas to receive or fulfill means that human beings are born on condition that at least all karmas can be resolved in at least one lifetime. Everyone who lives now on Earth as a human being has come to this world under this condition to resolve all karmas in this life. Otherwise, we would not have been born again as human beings and exist as spirits that wander around Earth. When the spirit relieves its karma and reduces it enough to fulfill it within a lifetime by relying on the consciousness energy while wandering like that, the spirit can leave Earth and return home in the universe like in any other death.

Since a spirit has no life, it has no energy to create something. So, it cannot directly pay back or receive karma. It has to borrow and rely on humans' conscious energy. Souls who could not leave Earth are the same spiritual beings, eternal beings, and the reality of love as we are. However, they must have their karma lighter in order to leave Earth's gravitational field and return to the cycle of the universe, and therefore they are asking us, humans, for help.

Spirits with a heavy karma to repay amplify emotions by remaining next to a human who goes through a process similar to the situation in which it has to apologize. When the human holds regret and remorse in heart, the spirit takes a little bit of that energy and reduces its karma with it. This is possible because in-between karma is a domain of all. For example, if you repeatedly get angry with your children and then regret it, it may be the result of an amplification of the feeling that you are sorry because of a spirit that is sorry for not having fulfilled its responsibility with love. It amplifies the feelings of the person who causes the same feelings as its regrets and waits for them to regret and reflect. Fortunately, if a person is sorry for what he has done, the young-ga can take a part of that sorry feeling. However, if the affected person recognizes the possibility of a spirit and understands the regret and remorse that it is holding, the spirit can absorb the entire consciousness energy instead of taking just a small part of it, and use it to reduce its karma by a big margin.

Conversely, in the case of a ghost with a lot of karma to receive, it amplifies that feeling to a person who can experience the same feeling in the situation in which he or she should be apologized to and waits to be consoled and able to let go. For example, if you keep wanting to give an excuse to your innermost thoughts for nothing, or you are excessively uncomfortable when you are even slightly misunderstood, you might have a ghost who hurt his or her feelings attached to you, and wishes to be consoled and apologized to for the hurt feelings. If the affected person consoles themself and forgives the one who was misunderstood, the spirit gains that mind little by little and gradually reduces the karma. If the affected person notices the possibility of a ghost being attached to him and personally consoles and forgives the ghost, the karma of the ghost can be reduced significantly, because the in-between karma is a domain shared by both of them.

Ghosts who remain on Earth through the third and fourth mechanisms cannot repent for themselves because they don't have life either. The ghosts who remain in denial to themselves amplify depression and lethargic feelings in living humans. And they go through a slow process of recovery by gaining the living person's efforts to remain strong despite of depression and to love themself. For example, if you feel lethargic and don't find any joy in what you do, a ghost who has lost its sense of presence in a life of lethargy may be attached to you and amplifying your feelings. In this case, if the living person recognizes the presence of the ghost and personally consoles the ghost by telling him, "You are a being of eternal love," you can release your depression rather easily.

Ghosts left on Earth in denial to God amplify negative tendencies. This is because humans find God when they think that something is going wrong. If you get upset for no reason, things don't go well, and negative thoughts build up in your mind, it could be the God-denial ghost stirring up those problems next to you. If you reach out to God and pray even in this situation, the ghost can gain a little from your heart. You can get out of that situation more easily if you send comforting messages to the ghost about how the ghost is one with God just like you are one with God.

We sometimes experience the problem of repeating strange feelings about a situation. It can be getting annoyed at our children for no apparent reason, regret over past mistakes that keep coming up to your mind, repeated sense of victimization for no good reason, or becoming lethargic or negative for no reason. Such repeated emotions and thoughts may be a sign that a ghost who wants help is around you. After I understood the impact of this ghost, I would ask, "What pain do you have?" and concentrate on it when the discomfort of my emotions was repeating for no reason. And then in a heart-moving imagination, I was able to feel, "Ah! This was your pain!" I frequently experienced how I could get over certain emotions when I personally gave my apology to a ghost that needed to be comforted and apologized to or repented for a ghost that had debt to pay. The examples I share here are just part of my such experiences.

I was able to realize the wisdom of life through the influence of these ghosts. Now, after I do my contemplation, I'd add to them to take everything if they need my thoughts. Hoping I could help the ghosts relieve their pains greatly...And sometimes when I hear people telling me about what's bothering them, I tell them to treat those bothering thoughts as if they belong to other people. I'd ask, "What comfort and forgiveness do you need?", imagine the lives of others who are likely to have those pains, and advise them to comfort themselves as if they are comforting others if they find any resonance in their heart from these thoughts and persuade themselves as if they are persuading others. This process can sometimes result in faster recovery than normal efforts.

The spirits that affect you from your side do not cause a pathological phenomenon. It is a routine phenomenon that is affected by a ghost, although it cannot be definitively called "possession." Ghosts can't amplify feelings or thoughts that you don't have in the case of ghosts that affect you from your side. If anything, certain existing traits grow stronger temporarily. Not being affected by the problem you don't have means the emotions amplified by ghosts are ultimately your own emotions.

It is just your emotion that is amplified. Problems associated with emotions that you overcome and the wisdoms you gained by yourself are not affected by ghosts. Therefore, the process of healing the pain of a ghost was also the process of my own growth.

But what we commonly call possession is a case when you experience continuous pain. Your personality changes and, sometimes, even your life is ruined. These ghosts go beyond affecting you from your side, and they place themselves deep in your unconsciousness or consciousness. Ghosts can directly infiltrate into the minds of people only when the possessed persons have karma to be paid entangled with those ghosts. In other words, the possession becomes the process of removing the karma. Thus, unlike the possession that affects you from your side, there is a difference of showing continuous symptoms for a long time because of the karma. The relational karma that has to be resolved between ghosts can be classified into the wounds in mind that are connected to each other's Hon, Baek, Shin, Ui, and Ji, and the physical pain that is connected to each other's lives. And since all karmas are manifested in the form of reciprocal justice, the symptoms you suffer from possession go in parallel with the pain you gave to the ghosts.

First of all, the karma in the mind settles in the person's unconsciousness and causes emotional transformation. The person emotionally feels the pain he gave to the ghost and shows signs of changing personality. For example, anger control disorder or fear-stricken anxiety disorder is the karma of Hon and Baek; endless sadness, wandering sorrow disorder or annoyance from self-pity is the karma of Shin; reclusive personality change that makes you withdraw with intense resentment is the karma of Ui; and the lethargic inability to feel interest represents the karma of Ji. In other words, the feelings associated with Hon, Baek, Shin, Ui, and Ji each occur in unconsciousness and persist for unexplained reasons. And while most of these wounds are concentrated in one thing, sometimes there are many different types of wounds piled over. This intrusive emotion-changing type of possession can be relieved by apologizing for the respective pain. Of course, anybody other than the directly involved party can resolve it.

Up to here, there is little difference from the general release of karma in the mind. But possession is a bit different. Possession refers to the situation when a ghost is directly penetrated into an object's unconsciousness or consciousness. This means that ghost and object have become one existence. Thus, when you acknowledge and empathize with your own incomprehensible feelings, it resolves karma with an apology-like effect. Essentially, the most important condition of apology is empathy. When you say, "It must have been hard. Of course, I understand it could happen," that becomes the foundation of genuine apology. Therefore, it's enough just to empathize with your feelings. Even if you cannot apologize because you did not realize you've been possessed, the emotional possession can be healed simply by sympathizing with your strange feelings. It is possible because the two are one being.

Second, karma that is connected to each other's lives intrudes on consciousness, not on unconsciousness, influencing thought and causing changes in behavior. This is because you have to control your consciousness to change your life. And it creates a change of thought and behavior that will create the same difficulties as the pain inflicted on the ghost's past life. Therefore, a persistent condition resulting from abnormal habits or delusional disorders often indicates that your consciousness, instead of unconsciousness, has been intruded upon. For example, a delusional anxiety disorder that constrains sexual guilt may be a karma from having suffered from sexual abuse in a previous life. Health concerns which make you become obsessed with any phenomenon in the body is often a karma from constraining the body. There are also types that cause behavioral changes rather than delusions, and sudden moving toward alcoholism is often the karma that forced the possessing ghost to a life-threatening addiction in the past life. Also, the disorderly behavior that pushes oneself into sadistic pain and danger could be the karma that has caused pain with violence.

Possession, which makes life so difficult, can be cured by paying back the physical karma. But a ghost is not living a life. You cannot pay it back with physical return. Therefore, the only solution is making efforts to change one's own life for the better. In order to fix your twisted life, you need awakening and practice to add strength to your chakra. And these efforts become a positive energy to the chakras of the ghost, and it will become a force that will be reflected on your next life. The ghost that intruded on consciousness and possesses the object is in a state united with the object. Therefore, all the love that you send to yourself that acts and thinks strangely is ultimately the love you send to the ghost. In particular, the karma is drastically reduced when you are filled with the highest values of chakra, such as empathy, gratitude, forgiveness and blessings.

It is about feeling sorry for your strange habits and behavior; forgiving yourself and being grateful for the efforts to overcome it; and blessing for things to work out well. You empathize about sexual guilt, agreeing that it is understandable, forgive yourself, try to learn the warmness of sex while feeling proud of yourself about it, and pray for you to enjoy the sex of love. Feel sorry for having destroyed life with addition and forgive its restrictions, be thankful for small efforts to do something about it and bless the life that is pulled out of addiction. Possession does not go just by loving the strange you. This is also possible because possession is a state in which you became one with it.

If I may share my symptoms of possession, I have had some problems with concentration and impatience since my late teens. When I was working alone, I couldn't concentrate for long, and I would easily wander off to different thoughts for a long time before I returned. My work was quite inefficient because I was full of unnecessary thoughts especially at critical moments. Then I became impatient, and I would procrastinate over my work for the lack of concentration until I got the work done in a hurry. In the process of improving my myungsu and overcoming my shortcomings, these two issues remained unresolved. I made efforts to grow the third chakra associated with concentration, but my concentration problem showed little sign of changing and I easily became impatient. Then I thought it was because of possession for having taken something important in somebody's life in my previous life, made the responsibility heavier, and brought about crisis, and I started sending my apology and gratitude to myself. I added forgiveness and blessing to them, and these two problems started to show clear signs of improvement within a short time.

"How hard is it to keep going despite the difficulty of concentrating? Yoon-jeong, heaven will feel sorry for me too. So, let's ask God to forgive my distraction, and let's generously forgive my distraction.

My short concentration is okay too. It is possible. People all work in their own different ways. People wonder why I take things so long and have doubts on me, but I can take it and empathize with them. I am making progress little by little, and if I don't give up, the world will definitely be able to empathize with my efforts later. Eventually, the world will fully understand my slow work process and forgive me. So, let's try hard to forgive the stimulus of the world that interferes with my concentration.

After all, I can achieve something big by adding small concentrations, and I've worked really hard until that happens. Yoon-jeong, even God forgives me and all my distractions, saying that I've worked hard and encouraging me. So, I have to warmly comfort and forgive God, telling him it's okay, because he had to shake me for the wholesome completion of my work."

"I may not concentrate well, but isn't it grateful that I can do this work? Yoon-jeong, God will be also very happy and glad. Let's proudly bless for trying with such a short concentration, and let's be blessed by God, too.

The efforts I make with this short attention is good enough. Let's be grateful and enjoy that moment, too. If people know what great efforts I make not to give up, they will be glad, thankful, and bless my efforts. Let's not give up until the world can be grateful and bless me, and let's do it little by little with the mind that blesses the world and you.

After all, I'm proud to be doing the work gladly even with my short attention. God is very grateful and congratulating me. So, I congratulate God for having succeeded in doing this through me, and I should be grateful to him for being there with me on this journey."[10]

That's how I talked to myself and treated my possession problem that caused my distractions. Filling inside of me with sympathy, gratitude, forgiveness, and blessings was not only a method to treat possession but also a way to heal inner trauma. Since a ghost is settled deep in my consciousness, it is not much different from a trauma left within me. At first, you just start slowly from empathizing, forgiving, thanking yourself, and blessing. When you get used to it, you are advised to make it into a ritual of exchanging it with God and the world. This is the way to resolve the other karmas of the ghost and more proactively pay back karma.

Possession is not a phenomenon to be treated with any kind of spiritual power. It is the process of relieving the karma by causing and making you suffer from similar difficulties. It is the process of paying back the debt to the ghost. When you empathize with its feelings and give love to its actions and habits, the karma is quickly resolved. Therefore, even if you do not recognize being possessed, you have to acknowledge and accept how you usually act and think. Instead of trying to push away strange emotions or blaming yourself for your troubled mind, you should accept how you feel inside, and be okay with it, while embracing and empathizing with those feelings. When strange habits, actions, and thoughts persist, people usually try to get away with them, but you should bless all the process, deeply consoling, forgiving and saying it's okay, and be thankful for your efforts. You can release the karma of possession with the mind that loves you alone and by becoming one existence.

The effort required to heal depends on the amount of karma. A large quantity of karma requires a lot of effort. However, the strength of the possession varies depending on the amount of karma, the mental health of the object, and the stability of life. Even if the amount of karma is large, it persists in a level that is not difficult to deal with as long as the mind of the object is strong, and life is stable. However, even if the amount of karma is small, you can experience delusional disorders or severe personality changes when the mind of an object is weak, and life is not stable. Therefore, mental health and stability of life are important to treat possession. It is much easier to empathize with and love yourself if your mind is healthy and your life is stable.

In addition, since the ghost that possesses the object is one existence while at the same time two existences, the possession phenomenon is also the karma between the object and the ghost. If someone is suffering from severe possession symptoms due to mental and life problems, anyone who can understand the person's possession can resolve the respective karma. Because the karma between the two is their shared domain. When you heal your mind by resolving possession in that way, you can take a smooth course of treatment.

In fact, there are a lot of ghosts on Earth right now that have not been able to pass over after death. Think about it. It's been less than 100 years since we treated human rights importantly.

Looking back on our history, we can fully understand how many karmas of wounds and pains have been created in large quantities. The human race is now passing through the process of resolving the massive karma created by the past after it has begun to universally recognize human rights. And psychology and psychoanalysis are playing a major role in the healing process. Possession is a common phenomenon on Earth today. It is a problem that most people experience more than once or twice in their lives. In a spiritual relationship that has many karmas intertwined, possession is like a privilege that makes us to quickly resolve by being temporary one existence.

2) The Shields of Mind

The pineal gland is where the Hon, the lord of the mind, dwells. The pineal gland is wrapped in a shield of mind. And this shield is made by the energy of the soul. This shield gives us the basic power to withstand the external rain and winds of unconsciousness. Since birth, most people have this shield tightly protecting the pineal gland. This shield is damaged when you are hurt and shaken in your life, but it can be restored again. When we remember love and faith even in times of pain, the shield is restored. The soul again envelops the heart because love and faith are the way of connecting with the soul. Moreover, the more the number of myungsu grows with love and faith, the stronger the shield becomes. The shield of mind that surrounds the pineal gland is the means by which the soul protects the mind, and at the same time, the channel through which our soul controls the mind.

However, if you look around, there are people who gradually turn into people with negative traits when they suffer or get hurt. These are people who have failed to restore damaged shields. The more the shield of the mind is damaged, the more their traits turn negative. Because when our hearts lose love and faith, we become more and more pessimistic in heart.

Sometimes people are born without this shield at all. Then there are also people who destroy all of these shields while leading their lives. Those who were born without shields are the souls whose shields were destroyed in their previous lives. The disappearance of the spiritual energy that surrounds the heart is like living with a naked inner self in a harsh, windy relative realm. So they need to make more effort than normal people to go for love. A common feature of those who have no shield of the mind is that they are always negative and pessimistic. Personality varies greatly, but whatever personality they may have, their personalities are dominated by pessimistic tendencies. Also, because they do not look at love and faith positively, they do not feel deep joy in anything. They can do things to the extent where they find interest and have fun, but they don't feel the joy that comes from deep inside. The joy that comes from deep within is the manifestation of spiritual energy, and it is difficult for those who have lost their channels to the soul to feel it.

That means, we are born with the joy of existence guaranteed. The shield of mind is divine protection that guarantees inner joy. It is the driving force that generates positive power even in times of pain. Sadly, however, we sometimes make choices that tear down this shield. Here is the general mechanism by which the protective shield is damaged. We usually endeavor to understand the meaning of pain such as separation, betrayal, and failure, and try to subdue our emotions over them. In this process, we remember the love we have and extend our wisdom. But when pain is too much to bear, we are buried in the emotions and thoughts that bother us, not knowing what to look for in the situation. Every 18 days of failure to recover, the shield of mind is damaged by 1%. In the end, we find the right meaning, and with that meaning, we restore the damage by remembering the love and faith of Hon, Baek, Shin, Ui, and Ji.

The shield of mind is damaged by the interval of 18 days because the circle of our consciousness is six days. When we are given a new stimulus, our mind moves at its center in the order of Ji → Hon → Baek → Shin → Ui → Total every day. In my case, Ji is weak, and Hon is strong. So, when there is some confusion, I usually cannot shake it off the first day, but I can do it well the second day. If you are the type that can shake off minor situations on the first day, you have strong Ji, and if you can do it well on the fourth day, you will be a person with strong Shin. This cycle of consciousness is a law that applies to everybody.

If you still do not get out of it and are surrounded by thoughts and feelings that are the opposite of love even after 18 days of repeating this 6-day cycle three times, your shield is damaged by 1%. If you fail to get out for 1,800 days without missing a day and raise emotions that interrupt love, the shield of mind is completely disappeared. The damaging mechanism stops if only you have a few days in between to get out of the situation and the cycle begins anew. If you think of love and faith through something else, the damage is restored. And when we get out of it even though you have not remembered love and faith, the damage stops. This doesn't mean you have to recover in 18 days to avoid getting hurt. You can begin to comfort your negative feelings and realize how to make up your mind within 18 days. Even if the damage occurs, you can restore the damage if you eventually remember love and realize wisdom. The recovery process is also a way of expanding the number of myungsu. We suffer pain, wounds on the outer walls of our heart, and then overcome those pains with love, during which process we extend our myungsu.

So even if all the shields are gone, if you remember your love and faith with all your might, you can fill them again. However, the important thing is that to restore the shield, you must consciously think and embrace in your heart about

345

love and faith of Hon, Baek, Shin, Ui, and Ji. You can't restore the shield by thinking, "It happens. It's just the way it is," or through any other process of the expansion of myungsu. Only by remembering Hon, Baek, Shin, Ui, and Ji's love and faith again can you restore your shields. This is God's will to never forget love in any pain, it is the will of our souls. The only meaning inscribed in the free will of the soul is love and must never be forgotten in every step of life.

If the shield is partially damaged, you can recover by 1% by completing one cycle of the five physiological consciousness of Hon, Baek, Shin, Ui, and Ji. This is the same as the expansion of myungsu mechanism. If you think about the pain of the past and the emotions of those days are replayed, you may not have recovered completely. At this time, you can heal one by one by creating a cycle of consciousness that recalls love and faith. The thought doesn't have to be related to the specific day. The shield will be rebuilt as long as you consciously think of love and faith in anything. Of course, if you create love and faith in anything that has direct connection, you can have the benefit of expanding myungsu as a bonus, but you can restore the shield even with love and faith about other things as well.

However, the first start is very difficult when rebuilding after the shield is completely gone. This is because the connection between the soul and the mind is lost. At this time, the 29-day cycle of the moon must be completed before the first 1% brick can be raised. The moon is the star that presides over the sixth chakra that houses the pineal gland, and you have to complete one full cycle of it. After the first brick, the soul and the mind are connected, and you can recover by 1% in each cycle. When the shield is restored to 100%, one level of myungsu expansion is completed as well.

In rare cases, there are children born negative. In addition, in rare cases, some people lose their protective shields while leading their present lives. They may not have been able to recover from their pain for a long time either in their past life or present life, or they may have chosen to throw out all of their shields at once. Unlike the usual mechanism, there is a choice to lose the shields all at once.

First of all, in the first phase of myungsu, all the shield disappears when you lose all faith and love for yourself and God. It is not just about having doubts and ignoring yourself and God. If you have no love for yourself, you can't love anything, so the shields disappear because you need the process of remembering love. Also, if there is no faith in the Creator left, then you cannot take even a step toward unity with the Creator, so the shields disappear to remember that faith. Because love of oneself and faith in God are the foundation of all beings.

During the second phase of expansion, the shield disappears if you lose all your love for both yourself and God or obsess yourself only with materials and vanity. It is not just to the extent of being swept away by materials and vanity. When you learned that love is the most important thing through experience upon the completion of the first phase and you are obsessed only with vanity, the shields disappear completely to remind you that the only purpose is love. Here, the vanity includes everything that blocks love. It includes not only professional success or satisfying desires, but it also includes obsession with evil that is illusion.

During the tertiary expansion, the shield disappears when: you lose all faith in both yourself and God; obsess yourself only with illusions instead of love; or when you make conclusions based on your discrimination against people's values. It is not just about having a hard time with the difference between you and others. When you reach the conclusion that others are beings with different values even though you've learned through experience during the second completion that we are one, all the shields disappear so that you can remember that we all have the same values even though we are all different.

During the fourth expansion, the shields disappear when: you lose all your love for yourself and God; obsess yourself only with illusions instead of love; make conclusions based on your discrimination against people's values; or you completely deny the divinity of existence. It is not just about having doubts on the sanctity of existence. When you completely deny the divinity of beings even though you've learned through experience that all beings are one with the Creator and have infinite possibilities upon the completion of the third expansion, the shields disappear so that you can remember the truth that all of us are the Creator.

During the fifth expansion, all the shields disappear when: you lose all your faith in yourself and God; obsess yourself only with illusions instead of love; make conclusions based on your discrimination against people's values; completely deny the divinity of existence; or resent that the laws of heaven are unfair. It is beyond the level of suffering from pain in your heart and lamenting for being difficult. If you wholly resent even though you learned through experience upon the completion of the fourth expansion that the fair will of God is enfolding in all things, the shields disappear so that you will remember that everything is achieved by the will of God and our will.

There are choices where the beings that became one with God after the completion of the fifth expansion forsake all the shields. The shields disappear for all the above-mentioned reasons as well as when you forget that you are one human being living on Earth. Since those who realize trinity on Earth are the ones who realized themselves through their lives living as humans, you must not forget that you are the same humans as any others.

In conclusion, when we turn back completely against what we know and have done with experience, the shields disappear temporarily to go through the process of consciously recalling the results of the past experience. We remember the past experiences with the physiological powers of Hon, Baek, Shin, Ui, and Ji, rebuild the shield of the mind, restore the connection between the soul and the mind, and at the same time, take the course to expand myungsu anew.

The shield of the mind is the force and the means by which the soul guides the mind. When we move forward with choices that go away from the will of the soul, the shield of the mind loses its strength, and when we awaken the will of the soul, the shield of the mind is restored. The fundamental force that gives us real joy and experiences love is in the soul. Understanding the shield where the power of the soul is realized can help you keep your spiritual well-being.

Endnote

10 I will address the principle of this prayer in the part about the sixth chakra and trauma treatment later.

8. The Fifth Chakra: Freedom – Calling – Responsibility

We need this world in which we live to realize the only purpose which is experiencing love. We need this world that is not surrounded by love. So, to us this world is precious, and we all have an obligation to maintain and keep it. Every soul who has been given the opportunity to live as a human on Earth has a basic duty to keep it and to develop it into a place where more people and lives can thrive. Our choice to fulfill this responsibility is always the right absolute value.

Parents are responsible for nurturing and protecting children, adults are responsible for fulfilling social roles, and children are responsible for growing while learning the world as children. Because we are generally fulfilling these responsibilities, the world is running in full swing, and many souls can be offered opportunities here. Therefore, ideas and actions that regard each responsibility as meaningless are the opposite of the absolute values. In that sense, the life of religious people living in the mountains to practice asceticism is not bad, but leaving young children behind is a choice the entire universe is not happy about.

Also, we must enjoy the freedom to experience love in this world. We must defend that freedom because the only purpose we live is love. We must experience diverse love by overcoming compulsions in our lives, and we must build a world where it is easier to love. That is the reason obsessions and stereotypes that hinder freedom are against absolute value. Keeping freedom is our responsibility as well. After all, we must fulfill our responsibilities to be able to love, and we must experience love by seeking freedom choices that are not restricted by any frame.

Therefore, all responsibility given to us is the calling freely chosen by our souls. The only difference is whether we consider it a calling or a heavy responsibility. Of course, you can be happier if you consider it your calling. People who consider it as a responsibility will say, "This is hard but I must endure," and those who consider it as a calling will say, "It is hard but I must endure it well because this is what I like to do." This difference is the key to determining quality of life. Whether you consider it as responsibility or calling, life is hard for anybody by nature.

The book titled *The Janitor* by Ray Hilbert and Todd Hopkins is describing the happy calling of a sanitation worker. To the janitor who always did his job with a happy face, a young man asked, *"Isn't the job hard? What are you so happy about?"* Then the janitor answered, *"I'm sweeping a corner of the earth now."* The janitor recognized that cleaning Earth was his calling, and he was happy about his calling. Psychologist Dr Choi In-cheol introduces this anecdote in books and lectures, and he encourages us not to see our work and responsibility from a short distance, but to look at them from the universal perspective.

When you look from the perspective of the universe, you can see a calling instead of a responsibility. It is something you don't like to do, boring, and sometimes troubling to do, but if you look from the perspective of the universe, it is something that is essential to all, important, and a rewarding thing to do. When you realize the universal calling that your work has, you can feel your preciousness. Even difficult work can make you happy and bring a sense of reward. The janitor had a calling to cleanse this beautiful Earth, farmers and fishermen are in charge of an important role in the perfect circles of lives, sales and delivery workers are evangelists who connect the world into one with logistics, business management executives are contributing to the materialistic prosperity in our planet, and mothers of children are the watchers of the survival and prosperity of mankind. Nothing is unimportant and unnecessary. Therefore, once you realize your calling, there is no work that you cannot do with joy like the happy janitor.

Also, when you look at our relationship at the cosmic level, you can see that the responsibility we have to each other is the destiny where it has to be that specific soul out of numerous souls. I was destined to be a mother exactly to my daughter, not another soul. It is by no means a coincidence among many souls; it is a cosmic bond and calling where my value as a mother can shine most. Everything I play as my parents' daughter, my friend's friend, my patient's healer, is the universal destiny that makes me shine most as a calling.

Be it any kind of responsibility, work or relationship, it becomes a shining call when you view it from a cosmic perspective. When we fulfill our calls, they turn into freedom. Those who fulfill their callings are free. They are happy because they are free. That's how the janitor, Bob, was able to work always with happiness while enjoying freedom.

Responsibility for us is like a hard solid. But if you look at your responsibility from the cosmic perspective, it gently melts and turns into a liquid-form of calling. In addition, if you fulfill your calling with joy, it simmers and boils until it evaporates into the air as a free gas. The relationship between responsibility-calling-freedom is very similar to that of solid-liquid-gas in that sense. Even if ice melts into liquid water and water boils into vaporing gas, the molecular structure remains the same. Ice, water, and steam differ only in their forms, but in their essence, they are all the same. As such, our responsibility, calling, and freedom are of the same nature. In other words, it is not that we become free by escaping from responsibility; we become free when we change the form of responsibility. Responsibility and freedom are, after all, the same in essence, and the change of form is a matter of choice.

Responsibility, calling, and freedom are all absolute values. Be it responsibility, calling, or freedom, they are all the same in essence after all, so you can either do something as a responsibility, or consider it as your calling, or pursue freedom. It doesn't matter if you're treating it as a heavy responsibility rather than a calling. In some situations, it may be advantageous to you to treat it as a heavy responsibility. Responsibility is also a choice you make in pursuit of absolute value. Nevertheless, if you fulfill your responsibility, you will see your calling and eventually move toward freedom.

On the contrary, there are situations in which you have to choose freedom without fulfilling your responsibility. If you cannot really experience love in the present situation, you should choose freedom from the situation even if you have not fulfilled your responsibility. In this case, through the new pursuit of calling while being in a free state, eventually you can find a way to fulfill your responsibility.

There are times when we have to choose between responsibility and freedom, depending on the situation. But no matter which you choose out of responsibility-calling-freedom that corresponds with your current situation, you eventually have to make them circulate and create one circle. If you open a path where responsibility becomes freedom and freedom becomes responsibility, it can always be the right absolute value.

Let's take the example of politicians who chose responsibility and politicians who chose freedom in the past changing political community. During the process of the disbanding of the political party, Representative Na Kyung-won, who had urged the change of the Saenuri Party[11] during the impeachment process, remained in the Saenuri Party and chose to take responsibility for the change of the party, while Representative Yoo Seung-min left the party that had no intention to change and chose freedom to unfold his will. In the same context, Representative Ahn Chul-soo thought it was difficult to change the Democratic Party[12] and established a new party in pursuit of freedom, while Park Young-sun, who demanded changes in the Democratic

Party, remained till the end and she is currently taking charge of changing the mainstream members of the party.

We cannot say who is right and who is wrong because all of them – Na Kyung-won and Park Young-sun, who chose responsibility, and Ahn Chul-soo and Yoo Seung-min, who chose freedom – pursued absolute values. Each has made a choice that suits his or her desires, and everyone has made the right choice. Now all that remains is to find and fulfill their callings within their choices. If Park Young-sun and Na Kyung-won fulfill their callings to reform the existing party, they will have the freedom to express their will in the end. Yoo Seung-min and Ahn Chul-soo will suffer from freedom in the wild, but if they overcome the hardship and find and fulfill their callings, they will eventually be fulfilling their responsibilities as politicians in the end.

But what we need to know in the cycle of responsibility-calling-freedom is the law of conservation of mass. The volume of ice, water, and water vapors varies greatly due to changes in form, but their mass remains the same. This law of conservation of mass applies to responsibility-calling-freedom as well. The total amount of mass remains the same in any form of change during the process where responsibility turns to calling, calling turns to freedom, and freedom turns to responsibility at the end. We are given many opportunities in life and we must take responsibilities as much as we enjoy them. And we can be as free as much as we are responsible. Life can evolve into a calling only when we realize and practice the law of conservation of mass in freedom and responsibility.

The place where this law is practiced better than any others is "Google." Google guarantees freedom in how people work at the company so much that the company is considered the symbol of a dream workplace. You are free to choose the location, time, and form of your work, and you can freely coordinate your work with your coworkers. The company also has facilities to ensure freedom of various relaxation and play activities. On the other side of this freedom, however, is a supporting through performance responsibility system. Employees are obligated to fulfill their responsibilities as much as they enjoy the freedom. As the mass of freedom and responsibility is preserved in this way, employees' performance becomes a company-wide calling, and Google grows into a company that fulfills the calling of opening a new world.

Google grew fast based on freedom, and mankind made rapid materialistic growth in the freedom market economy. Ensuring freedom first among responsibility and freedom drives growth. However, our society has many stereotypes and compulsions that hinder freedom. When something goes wrong, Koreans tend to avoid it rather than find new solutions. So, there is a problem, they don't let you do it, and if there is another problem, they don't let you do that either. As time goes by, any social system becomes heavily regulated. As a result, it is difficult for companies to grow with new challenges. In order to achieve economic growth without being trapped by regulations, we must not be scared when problems arise. Before you get scared and forbid, you have to think to see if there's a new way. The social system can grow when you know how to think creatively.

In a person's life, enjoying freedom first is the driving force for growth too. So, young children must be freed first. Only then can they find interest in taking responsibility for freedom, and that interest helps turn responsibility into a calling. If they start with the responsibility that they have to carry without having enjoyed anything, then the previous sense of unfairness is added even if the freedom is given to them. Then, a greater freedom is necessary to relieve that sense of unfairness, and later when the responsibility becomes greater, it becomes harder to reach their callings because they give up on account of life being too tiring.

That is why Korean children who learn responsibility first instead of the freedom of learning feel life is hard and they give up early. If we want our children to become talents who fulfill their callings, we must first allow them the freedom of learning. We must teach them to be responsible as much as they enjoy freedom and make life a fun playground of callings. The responsibility that is acknowledged after choosing freedom becomes a calling that is rewarding and fun. Therefore, the more freedom a person has, the harder the person fulfills the responsibility in life instead of using the freedom.

But if responsibility does not follow freedom, growth stops, and confusion arises. Humanity has grown steadily for a century as a free market and is now stagnant due to its limitations. To continue to grow, we need to try to be responsible for the freedom we'd enjoyed.

Today, the plastic and vinyl waste produced by mankind is now reaching a level where Earth cannot handle it. To solve this problem, it is necessary to have a system that holds companies that distribute plastic bottles accountable. For example, companies that distribute water and beverages in plastic bottles should be primarily responsible for the collection and disposal of the waste, and consumers should be secondary responsible for sharing the responsibility. Only then can a system to safely dispose of vinyl and plastic be actively developed and used.

Unfortunately, there remains plenty of freedom to use plastics and vinyl on this planet, and no country is fully equipped with a system of responsibility. This unrestricted freedom cannot be an absolute value, and it is making Earth sick. The fundamental solution to this problem is the system that asks the distributors of plastics to take responsibility that corresponds with their action. The solution to the industrialization problem faced by mankind is to realize the law of conservation of mass with a system to take responsibility that corresponds with freedom.

The Republic of Korea has a lot of regulations, but it has a shortage of a system of asking for responsibility. This is the decisive reason there hasn't been development despite the deregulation efforts over the past decade. We have not prepared a system that asks companies that received freedom as the result of deregulation to take corresponding responsibility. As a result, the unrestricted freedom of the companies resulted in the senseless loss of precious lives in such incidents as the Sewol ferry sinking[13] and the humidifier disinfectant case[14]. In addition, there is no system in Korea that can hold them responsible as much as the freedom that caused the tragic incidents.

Countries such as the United States have laws that punish corrupt companies with hundreds of years in prison in addition to powerful punitive damage compensation. This system may seem to entail outrageously heavy punishments and compensation, but this powerful damage compensation system and heavy punishment for corporate crime is the driving force for American companies to grow by turning freedom into a calling.

What we need now in Korea is not just deregulation. There is an urgent need for a system that asks for responsibilities that match current freedoms. Korea's compensation system does not receive half of the actual damages, and corporate crime and unfair trade are subject only to a slap on the wrist punishment. The system of asking for responsibility is very poor compared to the freedom our society provides. This is because the laws of conservation of mass in social systems have not been realized, and as a result, the remaining freedom continues to damage, prevents the fulfillment of callings, and hinders growth.

Social systems can also develop only if the law of conservation of mass is observed. The system should be overhauled so that the masses of freedom and responsibility are equal. When we create a system, it must be accompanied by a system that asks for the same degree of responsibility, while ensuring as much freedom as possible. This can become the driving force for growth by turning freedom into calling. The current solution to the low growth of our society is to establish a system that asks for full responsibility along with freedom-ensuring deregulation.

Korea's volume-based waste charge system[15] is pursuing an absolute value because it does not limit the freedom to make garbage in our lives, while asking for the minimum responsibility for the waste we create. As a result of this volume-based waste charge system, we have an active recycling practice. In order for the freedom of a company's product development to benefit the world, it must be accompanied by a legal system that asks for strong responsibilities. With the freedom to develop products and at the same time a strong responsibility system, better products can be released to the world in a more elegant way. In addition, legal penalties for strong responsibility for corporate corruptions must be in place. Allowing freedom to neglect because of its contribution to the national economy ultimately hinders the growth of the company. The penal system that calls for a reasonable responsibility for the amount of corporate corruption can guarantee a transparent management of the company, grow the economy with a virtuous cycle of wealth, and open the conditions for the company to grow bigger. Realizing absolute values by giving more freedom and asking for responsibility more strongly becomes the foundation of social development because it is a system that ensures the fulfillment of calling.

It is good to think about freedom first, because giving freedom first and then asking for responsibility next can result in growth. The system should be overhauled to ask for responsibility for freedom as well. There is an exception, however, where responsibility must be chosen before freedom. In situations where there is a conflict between the absolute values of the first to the fourth charkas and freedom, you must fulfill your responsibility first and be as free as your responsibility. When a child is playing with a dangerous fire, freedom should be blocked and restrained, and cell phones and TV watching that interferes with family communication during mealtimes should be restricted, and freedom should be given after finishing a family mealtime. In order to keep life, self-realization, communication, and the hope for love, it is advisable to implement regulation first, and freedom next as a rule.

The fifth chakra of freedom-calling-responsibility is the highest chakra of life's design value because calling allows the absolute values of the first to the fourth chakras to be manifested in the world. Therefore, in the cycle of freedom and responsibility, it is wise for us to start with freedom for satisfactory growth, but in life, self-realization, communication, and love, we must start with responsibility and meet freedom next.

The freedom to own a gun is against the value of life, so regulation must come first in this case. Thus, the Second Amendment to the United States Constitution, which guarantees freedom to arm, should not precede regulations that prevent firearms from harming life. The humidifier disinfectant case in our society was also the result of the error of choosing freedom over regulation before the value of life. Child labor in underdeveloped countries should be banned because it deprives them of opportunities for self-realization. We regulate the working hours by law and keep the minimum wage, because it is to put regulations first to ensure self-realization, and then guarantee freedom within that restriction. If there is a blockage of communication between the classes in the course of economic growth, it must be regulated so that communication is not blocked.

The first thing to note when regulating is that freedom should be limited in ways to ensure absolute value will be realized. For example, there are architectural regulations designed to protect local character. When regulating building and house repairs to maintain a traditional village, a specific measure is taken to unify the unique characteristics of the village and create a synergy effect, and this measure results in increasing the value of each individual's house. This regulation is a true realization of the absolute value of self-realization. It is essential to refine the method so that absolute value is well realized instead of ending up just restricting freedom.

It is the law of the world that freedom and responsibility are constantly cycled in life and freedom-calling-responsibility is converted to the same mass. So, it makes things easier to be responsible for what we've enjoyed as much as we want to be free. However, since life is created in complex relationships, there are situations where you cannot fulfill your responsibility. If you choose freedom without fulfilling your corresponding responsibility as much as the mass you have enjoyed, then the hardship unfolds before your freedom. Through the hardships, you find new calling while overcoming your limitations, and the way to fulfill your responsibilities opens while you fulfill your calling.

Therefore, Yoo Seung-min and Ahn Chul-soo, who left the existing party, have a different amount of suffering from freedom. Representative Yoo Seung-min has secured a seed as a politician from an existing political party and has entered the stage to become a presidential candidate. Representative Yoo Seung-min enjoyed much in the existing political party and has a lot of responsibility for the party. And in front of him who chose freedom, there are as many political hardships as much as the mass of his responsibility. His Bareun Party faced the challenge of low support ratings, being dismissed by existing supporters, hardly gaining new supporters, and facing the spread of internal disappointment.

On the other hand, Ahn enjoyed little political gain from the Democratic Party, so he lacked much of his responsibility for freedom outside the Democratic Party. Thus, he did not have to struggle long enough to establish a newly formed People's Party, and he was able to grow without difficulty in securing support as a candidate for the new party. And the support he gained in the presidential election is the mass of new responsibility. It is not the end that we have achieved freedom through responsibility and calling. There comes a new responsibility that is given to free beings. The cycle of responsibility-calling-freedom continues endlessly along with life.

Although the two members had different weights of responsibility, the two members who chose freedom made the right choice. If they could not experience love in the existing party, they had to pursue freedom. There is only a difference in suffering, and their new calling is spread out under different conditions. Representative Yoo Seung-min is fulfilling a calling to regenerate the corrupt conservative forces. In order for democracy to work properly, a healthy conservative force is needed, and he accepts the calling. If he fulfills his calling while overcoming his limitations in the current hardship, he will be able to freely express his will in this political community by fulfilling his past responsibilities with the integrity of a new conservative. And all that freedom creates new responsibilities.

Ahn also has a new calling before him as a politician. He is faced with a calling as someone who became a politician with the support of the younger generation, created a political party with the support of Honam, which is the base of progressive forces, gained the support from voters with conservative tendencies in the presidential election, and as the politician who received multilateral support for the first time in Korea. The role that unfolds before him is to flexibly coordinate and buffer the conflict between generations and regions. When he fulfills this calling properly, he can shift his responsibility for the various support he receives to freedom. I wish the two lawmakers to complete the callings that are revealed before their chosen freedom.

If I may introduce my laws of conservation of mass as an ordinary individual, I have been benefiting from confirming myungsu regularly through a pendulum for the past two years. I swear that if I could not confirm my myungsu, I would not have achieved this growth. I have enjoyed the benefits of this path for longer than anyone else. Thus, the way of confirming the truth by the pendulum, and the total amount of responsibility to restore the degeneration of losing love and clinging to evil, was great. But I did not fulfill my responsibility as much as I enjoyed, and I chose freedom. Since then, I have had to suffer physically, mentally, and situationally for the pendulum of my responsibility for a while, and through that hardship I have overcome my limitations, and as my limitations have been overcome, new calling has begun to appear. I am now converting my last responsibility to freedom by fulfilling my calling to unfold the truth about growing while confirming my myungsu into a universal truth that anybody can understand. I am curious about the freedom I will have when I fulfill this call. Therefore, I dream of a future where new responsibilities and callings will unfold. I still believe that my hardships that I have chosen freedom without fulfilling my responsibility have been the best choice for me. And I understand that the pain I went through was a reasonable mass proportional to what I've enjoyed.

So, when we decide which of the responsibility-calling-freedom to choose now, it is important to know how much we've enjoyed. If you understand what you have enjoyed, you know how much responsibility you have to take. You can have the power to consider your current responsibility as your calling. Also, the hardships of freedom of your choice don't feel so unfair. A mind without a sense of unfairness guides you to overcome limitations through hardships, and having grown up that way, we can fulfill our responsibilities with new calling. That's why it's important to keep a close eye on how much you are enjoying now. If you know how to appreciate what you enjoy, you want to be responsible. That responsibility looks like a calling, not luggage. The process of fulfilling that calling can be freedom.

Find out the love, protection and growth you have enjoyed in your family relationship so far. You are obliged to be responsible for your family; my current family is my destiny love, and my responsibility to them is a cosmic calling. Find out the benefits, growth, and stability you enjoy at work. You will find the light that will light up your calling in your work life, and you will be able to make the call you want by growing beyond the limits when you want freedom from work.

When you fully grasp the mass of opportunities you have in the world and move on to responsibility, calling, and freedom, your hormones can fulfill metabolic functions that aren't lacking in fulfilling your calling. Also, your feelings will stand tall with firmness that will not be shaken by any conflict and will fill your life with sparkling creativity. This universe will cheer for your calling, and it will also take the responsibility for and support your calling, and cheer for your hormonal health, emotional strength, and abundant imagination with your fifth chakra.

The Sacred Boundary of the Fifth Chakra

This is a sacred boundary that protects the fifth chakra by the power of Hon, Baek, Shin, Ui, and Ji with the value of responsibility-calling-freedom. For your calling, the fifth chakra will freely communicate with the universe and promote healing and expansion. I would like you to read this part whenever you'd like to avoid responsibility because it is too heavy; when you are frustrated because you cannot recognize your calling; or when you wish to be free. And I also want you to read it as the ones who cheer for you, because that calling will definitely make you free.

(1) Responsibility – Calling
* I cannot escape the harshness of life,
avoiding and blaming others for the things that are happening to me.
This is because I cannot change others and they will not take responsibility for my life.

I ought to change as nobody other than myself is responsible for my life,
I reflect on what I've done that made it come to this,
recognize that I am the one to blame for them and try to take responsibility.

When you admit that you are responsible for all that's happening now,
your past can no longer haunt your future.
You can make choices with more freedom when you take responsibility in your life.

* I regret failing to notice the appropriateness and glory
of not knowing the meaning of the predestined calling,
claiming that it's not just and getting it all wrong.

The responsibility given to us is the desire of our soul,
please remember that the Creator and the entire universe support us to fulfill the calling,
and that is how happiness will unfold before you.

We become free beings in the happiness that fulfilled the predestined mission,

and grow into beings that accept bigger responsibilities as an honor,
and that is how we will continue to shape a better world.

* Let us apologize to ourselves for the self-betrayal of not believing ourselves,
failing to discover the light in ourselves that helps fulfill our responsibilities,
giving up in disbelief that it is not in my power to fulfill them.

Since the light to fulfill the responsibilities given to me is inside me,
with the efforts of self-love which brings out and grows the power to fulfill responsibilities,
let us present the joy of fulfilling our calling to ourselves.

That is how we embed the confidence of fulfilling our calling,
expand our excellence by taking on new missions,
and ultimately become free from all the responsibilities that continue to rise.

* I wish to apologize for avoiding or grudgingly accepting them, and giving them a hard time,
while struggling to accept the subjects of responsibility, saying it is difficult to even care for myself.

If I were all alone without any responsibilities for others,
life can easily become meaningless, it becomes difficult to overcome the adversities of life,
and even more difficult to fulfill the will to live.

That is why we are so fortunate to have people we're responsible for.

Through the responsibility for others, we can share deep and abundant love,
and so how can we not rejoice at being responsible for them?

(2) Freedom – Calling

* I reflect on pushing myself too hard because of the obsession that I must perform well,
avoiding because of the obsession that something bad might happen,
clinging to the results and restricting my life.

I thought I would be in trouble if something doesn't work out, but new opportunities arise,
and I thought I would be in trouble if I do something, but unexpected pleasant surprises emerge,
and so regardless of the situation, there are always options.

Everything we face in life is a process,
and there aren't really things you must do or must not do.
So let us value process over results, and live with free choice.

* I thought my burdensome fate cannot be changed,
gave up my freedom and followed what others demanded of me.
We must repent such blasphemy.

Heaven gave us respect and complete free will.
With that free will, we are to create our own destiny in the time of the universe and so,
we must learn the sacred responsibility of living with that free will.

Since our spiritual free will is inviolably sacred,

we can only be happy when we voluntarily select the path that
leads to genuine happiness,
so please overcome the fear that is blocking you and select the
path to genuine happiness.

* We did not allow freedom to ourselves in the past.
Under the illusion that whatever I do would get me in trouble,
I, myself, have been restricting myself.

Now I wish to heal the heart that restricts myself,
while remembering that we can freely try this or that,
and that we have the power to recover regardless of the situation.

So let us stop fearing hardships and freely take the challenge
for our mission.
You can look after yourself, grow and achieve,
and that is how you will be able to fulfill your responsibilities.

* We have been restricting those around us under the name of
love,
under the name of protection and the illusion that I am superior
to all of them.
Now is the time to admit our faults and apologize.

You cannot restrict anyone just because you love them.
Even the Creator does not restrict us but respects us all.
Now I know, that love is respecting the other person and
maintaining a certain distance.

Let us now practice love that frees the other person.
While maintaining such distance of love that frees others but is
reachable,
with free love that gives a warm embrace whenever he gazes at
me...

(3) Integration of Freedom – Calling - Responsibility

* I overcome losing my own freedom by responsibilities held back,

lamenting that the responsibilities given to me are too heavy,

failing to discover the meaning of the calling in such responsibilities.

Since my responsibilities are the mission that I wish to fulfill

I willingly make efforts to accomplish my mission,

and gladly enjoy the freedom from the fulfillment of the mission.

Life (world) becomes freer,

and a grander mission in the freer life (world) awaits me,

and it is truly an honor to assume more rewarding responsibilities.

Endnotes

[11]   The Liberty Korea Party: a conservative political party in South Korea.

[12]   Democratic Party of Korea: a progressive political party in Korea.

[13]   Sewol Ferry Sinking: a big ferry, Sewol went down in the water in 2014, killing numerous passengers. Most passengers killed in the incident were high school juniors who were on their way to a school trip. This incident is remembered as a tragedy by Koreans.

[14]   Humidifier disinfectant case: it refers to a case where a toxic ingredient was discovered to have been used in disinfectant that was supposed to be added to water in humidifiers, resulting in death, permanent lung damage, and other medical conditions for many users.

[15]   Volume-based waste charge system: a system that charges by the amount of garbage produced by people; it started in 1995 in Korea.

9. The Mind and the Law of Physics

So far, several laws of physics have been mentioned to understand absolute values: the law of acceleration to understand the value of analysis-communication-synthesis; the law of mass conservation to explain the absolute values of freedom-calling-responsibility; and the law of inertia for easy understanding of the reason it is difficult for us to change. I never imagined that these laws I learned in middle school would help me understand life. However, these laws of physics have helped me to come closer to a more peaceful and happy life.

"A science is shifting from matter to mind," said Fred Alan Wolf, an American physicist. I think it is so true. Energy dynamics seem to be both the laws of matter and laws of mind and soul in the relative realm. Here are two more laws of physics that are helpful to life. The book introduces classical mind-related dynamics, but in quantum mechanics there must be many laws of the soul that I haven't realized.

1) The Law of Universal Gravitation

We sometimes have an experience of recalling memories of someone and chewing on them for a long time. This phenomenon is the result of attracting each other's hearts. Between objects there is a pulling force that is proportional to the mass product of each other and inversely proportional to the square of the distance. This is called the law of universal gravitation. That is, the larger the physical quantity is, the stronger each other is drawn, and the closer the distance is, the stronger the pull. The same is true of our minds. We pull each other according to the size of our hearts toward each other in their unconsciousness and the distance of our hearts to each other.

The universal gravitation is proportional to distance. The distance of the mind does not simply mean physical distance. It means the stage in which the mind has grown and the direction of values. Suppose in the past you were close to somebody with a similar level of consciousness, but one made a rapid growth and moved on to the third stage of myungsu expansion while the other is still remaining at the first stage. Then you naturally grow distant from each other as the result of fewer common interests. Also, if the values are in the same direction, the distance between the minds will be closer. In this case, even if the growth stages differ greatly from each other, an intimate relationship is formed. That's the reason there is such an expression as "Birds of a feather flock together." People who went through similar stages of growth or share the same direction are quickly recognized and become close with each other.

In addition, the universal gravity is proportional to the physical quantity. For example, if someone near you is blaming me so hard, you keep thinking about that person. You may be worried that he or she thinks bad about you, or you may feel sorry for that person, or you may also blame that person in your mind. Whatever the case is, you keep reminding and thinking about that person. If someone has a crush on you, you also keep being conscious of that person. It may be the same affectionate feeling, or burdensome rejection, but whatever the case is, it doesn't remain unnoticed and ignored. When one party raises up the energy of the mind and thinks of you, the gravity makes you react to it in your unconsciousness.

At this time, it is possible to measure the physical quantity of each other's unconsciousness by the gravity you feel. Between the karmas connected to each other, there is a significant physical quantity of unconsciousness. So you react sensitively to the other's words and actions and chew and think about them for a long time. That means gravity is working strongly. The larger the karma, the stronger and more attracted you become to each other. In particular, in the case of karma that binds each other, the attracting gravity can hardly be ignored.

If you heard your friend's complaint and you are worried about it keep thinking about the words you haven't spoken, it could be a case where the karmas between you in addition to your love for your friend have created a gravity. If you are uneasy in heart even though the person was just a casual acquaintance, or you keep imagining unspeakable things happening with that person, you can notice the person has an unfinished karma from the previous life with you even if you don't know that person very well. We can feel karma we have with others by the law of universal gravitation.

In addition, if there are many karmas connected to each other and when a realistic crush is added to them, you may fall in love at first sight. In the case of a relationship where you fell in love at first sight, or a troubled relationship laden with love and hate, it is most likely that you fell in with the other person due to the karmas you have for each other. Positive karma creates a gentle attraction that supplements and supports each other, while negative karma creates a strong attraction by making a force that restricts each other. You must know the meaning of that strong attraction properly so that you can solve pain that restricts each other and turn that strong attraction into deep and happy love.

Explaining strong attraction as a karma of redemption may seem to destroy romance. But explaining our attraction in terms of karma is rather romantic too, because it is the soul's choice to recognize his charm and beauty that you haven't recognized in the previous life and give him the best love in the present life. This choice is a romantic thing that makes us more perfect.

The phenomenon of being attracted to each other in mind is the result of the conscious thoughts and unconscious feelings pulling each other. The source of the attraction is the level of consciousness that communicates with each other, a similar direction of life, the emotions created in the present life, and the karma's power accumulated in the past lives. In our minds there is a universal gravity that pulls each other's minds. If you have somebody who keeps attracting your mind, I hope you will dream about realizing this love with this gravity. It is clear that it is a bond of love that will make us happy, regardless of whether the karma is resolved or the history of the new one. Now, I hope that you will find the way to make your relationship happy with a full understanding about the universal gravity that our minds raise.

2) The Law of Conservation of Energy

Our lives unfold in the relative system consisting of matter. Thus, life runs in parallel with the law of conservation of mass which is the law of materials in the transformation of freedom-calling-responsibility. And our emotions and thoughts, which comprise our minds, are the energy produced by our cells. That is why the law of energy conservation applies to our minds.

The law of energy conservation is the principle in which opposite energy is converted into the same physical quantity. And our minds are converted to each other by the same amount of opposite energies. If we are frustrated with dissatisfaction in some circumstances, it can turn into dissatisfaction because we have experienced satisfaction in the opposite situation. And if we create a feeling of resentment under certain circumstances, it is possible because joy and pleasure have happened in the opposite situation. Dissatisfaction happens because we know satisfaction; we build compulsion because we know pleasure; we develop anxiety because we know peace; and we feel frustration because we know excitement. If you have never experienced contentment, peace, reward, pleasure, joy, or pleasure, it is impossible for these opposite feelings to happen in the first place.

What is the energy of the mid-point that is neither this nor the other side? For example, the midway between satisfaction and dissatisfaction is a point of nothing. That is, it is the point where the energy is zero. There is nothing at the point of zero energy. Even inanimate stones carry energy. Thus, we, the existing beings, cannot exist at the point where energy is zero. There are some people who discipline their minds and set the point where their emotions are zero as their idea. But to be at the point where the energy is zero is equivalent to extinction. It's as impossible as chasing a mirage that doesn't exist in the first place. We can only exist at points of satisfaction or dissatisfaction. To feel dissatisfied means that we were satisfied when we were not dissatisfied. Thus, our mind energy is circulating with opposite energies, just like a roller coaster. If one mind is a kinetic energy, the other mind becomes a potential energy and they switch into each other like a roller coaster that moves up and down by the law of energy conservation.

Then, you might want to dispute and claim that you've felt a lot of points that weren't really satisfaction or dissatisfaction. Or you might want to ask if I can guarantee that the beginning is a satisfaction. In order to understand the laws of energy conservation in our minds, we must know that much larger energy is formed in unconsciousness that we cannot recognize than in the consciousness that we can recognize. Unconscious feelings and thoughts are the domains that we do not perceive, but they have enormous energy that cannot be compared with the areas of consciousness we perceive. And in a situation where we pass through without feeling satisfied or dissatisfied, our unconsciousness feels satisfied with quite a lot of energy.

In order for the mind to start the roller coaster at the beginning of life, one must start with the potential energy at the highest point first. As we are born and begin to live, the roller coaster ride begins without any effort. Think about it. Even in times when we make no effort, life goes on, and the mind is filled with emotions or thoughts whatever they are. Honestly, just one minute is very long if you spend it with thoughts or emotions. The mind is always filled with something by itself. So, the roller coaster in mind rolls on itself without any additional power. That is life.

Our hard-working mind is not used as a power to drive the roller coaster up, but to change the course we drive and to change the size and shape of our mind. It helps to make the crashing tracks shorter or flatter, and to make high-rising tracks remain longer and be maintained better. It is changing the course of karma you are to drive. It also changes the size and shape of the mind itself that is running on the track. It starts as a small tetrahedron, passing through the shapes of several polyhedrons until it becomes a giant sphere so that you have a mind that is happy at all times either on downhill or uphill.

Life is like a nonpower roller coaster driving on its own. The roller coaster, which operates on the law of energy conservation, starts with potential energy. The power that makes us start from the highest point originates from the energy of the universe created by God. Therefore, the energy from which our unconscious begins is from peaceful life from a high position. Since our existence itself is love, the unconscious feelings that we take for granted are always positive emotions that are close to love. The emotions opposite to love are in the inner space (imaginary), so they cannot be completely dissolved in the unconscious, and at least some of them are perceived by consciousness. In other words, when my unconsciousness is frustrated, it is not possible for my consciousness not to notice it at all. But our consciousness may pass without knowing if our unconsciousness feels joy. And unconscious feelings that we could not recognize can always be converted to other forms of energy. This is the principle of how our emotional stress is created.

It was through my obsession with water play that I realized the law of energy conservation in my heart. I love to swim in the valleys and the sea. Perhaps I was feeling the joy of becoming one with Earth when I put my body in the valleys and the sea.

So, when I go to the sea or valley and cannot play in the water, I experience a surging emotion because the frustration becomes obsession. As myungsu expanded, it was reduced to weak frustration, but it was not completely peaceful. Then one day, on my way back home after I regretfully gave up playing in the water, I thought, "I seemed to be happier and more joyous when playing with water in nature than I had thought." And then, recalling the water I'd enjoyed playing with, I brought up the joy and fun that I had not recognized at that time, and thought "I was really happy. I had more fun than I had imagined," after which my frustration vanished.

It was a case in which the unconscious joys and pleasures that I did not recognize existed as potential energy until they switched to kinetic energy when I was in a situation where I could not have fun, and surfaced in the form of obsession and frustration. However, when I discovered the fun and joy that was in the unconsciousness and took it out into consciousness and remembered happiness, the kinetic energy was converted back into potential energy so that my mind could be peacefully placed on high ground.

When we feel irritated, dissatisfied, resentful, nervous, and lethargic, it is the proof that there was significant satisfaction, pleasure, excitement, joy, peace, and a sense of rewarding in our unconsciousness in situations when we were not experiencing these emotions. It is how it should be because energy is conserved. Positive emotions that we did not recognize are transformed into negative emotions when they are not and create stress. So being stressed is clear evidence that the positive feelings you didn't know were there, largely existed in your unconsciousness. Also, feeling a lot of stress means that people often push their unconsciousness without recognizing their daily satisfaction, peace, reward, and pleasure with consciousness.

Psychologist Kelly McGonigal advises us to abandon the stereotype that stress is bad and to be friends with stress. Stress is a signal that tells us how big a positive emotion is in our unconsciousness. Therefore, it's natural to be friends with it. Now, I want you to know when you are frustrated at heavy traffic that the pleasure of driving smoothly in light traffic is in your unconsciousness, and when things don't go well and you experience numerous unlucky events, how much deep peace you have felt when all things were going well, and be thankful for that happiness. If we bring all the unconscious happiness into consciousness with everyday stress, we can experience the truth that our peace does not exist at a point that is emotionally zero, but at a point where all things elevate into happiness.

Now realize that your stress is a blessing by the law of energy conservation, and I hope you will enjoy the happiness that presents in a high place by freely switching energy with your consciousness. If you can recognize all positive emotions that are in our unconsciousness, you will fully feel how life itself is a blessing.

10. The Sixth Chakra: Apology – Us – Receiving Apology

The sixth chakra is situated at the height of Indang, which is found between the eyebrows. This position is where the pineal gland, the third eye where soul and mind communicate, is located. The pineal gland is the channel where the Hon, the lord of the mind, resides and the soul and mind are in direct communication. That is, the sixth chakra plays the role of eye of the soul. Because the sixth chakra is the eye of the soul, it communicates with the energy of the entire universe, not with one planet, unlike other chakras. That is why the sixth chakra communicates with the moon, which is Earth's satellite. The moon is a satellite orbiting Earth. It is responsible for receiving the energy of the universe from all directions and transmitting it to Earth and collecting the energy of Earth and sending it to space. The sixth chakra communicates with the moon, Earth's satellite, allowing us to accept the energy of the universe, and send our energy into space because it plays the role of the eye of the soul.

The moon is the largest and brightest being in the night sky. Our people have a culture that celebrates the full moon and makes a wish on the moon. We pray to the moon for safety and well-being at the start of the farming season in the lunar January 15 and thank the full moon for the ending of the farming season on Chuseok, which is lunar August 15. Also, when we face something that is difficult or important, we have a culture of offering a bowl of purified water to the moon and praying for our safety and well-being. The culture has significantly disappeared now, but until just a few decades ago, women would pray on the moon about their family's well-being.

When we make a wish to the moon, we wish to avoid danger and to pass safely rather than with abundance and prosperity.

Because the moon illuminates the dark night and leads us to find our way in darkness. Such a moon gathers the energy of the entire universe and leads mankind to a path of well-being in fearful darkness. The sixth chakra is empowered by the moon to open a path for us to life in safety in accordance with the will of soul in the relative world that is surrounded by things that are not love.

Thus, the sixth chakra is the most important of all chakras. In practicing yoga that develops chakras, we recommend that you start the sixth chakra training first. The sixth chakra is a channel of direct communication between the soul and the mind, while at the same time it interacts directly with the pituitary gland and the hypothalamus, which controls the body integrally. It is the window through which the energy of the soul is transmitted to the mind, the place of the soul, the master of the mind, and the mecca of hormones that dominate the whole body. The sixth chakra lays the groundwork for our fundamental purpose of experiencing the love, mentally and physically.

The absolute value that forms the foundation of love with the strength of the sixth chakra that matters most to us is apology. To each other, apology exerts the power to settle negative relationships and situations. To yourself, apology exerts the power to heal yourself, and to God, apology makes a new beginning possible. In other words, the power to settle everything that hinders love is in apology.

For us, the absolute value of apology exists in many ways. First of all, the apology to tell you are sorry to others is one typical example. And regretful feelings and deep regrets are other examples of apology, and sympathy and comfort are expressions of apology as well. In our culture, apology and consoling are different meanings, and sorry and empathy are different meanings. But in English, empathy, consoling, sorry, and regret are all considered the same expression as apology. In Korean, "I'm sorry" and "I feel bad" are different, but in

English, it means the same. When we express our sympathy for the other's pain and wish to console them, we use many different expressions, such as, "It must be hard on you," or "What should we do?" but in English, it starts easy with just with one expression of "I'm sorry." They insightfully knew that apology, sorry, regret, empathy, and consoling are all values of apology. And the uniformed language made it easy to give and take apology. Therefore, the language that accurately expresses the absolute value of the sixth chakra is the English sentence, "I'm sorry," rather than its counterpart Korean sentence.

The objects you need to give and receive apology and build love with are the God the Creator, others, and yourself. Let's talk about apology with others first. Misunderstanding, resentment, unbelief, and guilt between each other hinder love. But if someone you've been very resentful of offers an apology to you, your resentment can go away like melting snow. When the others console you and tell you it's okay when you suffer from guilty conscious and hide, you can get over the guilty conscious. As such, if we are being apologetic to each other, we can bring down the barriers to love. We can lay a solid foundation upon which we can give and take love without any obstacles. In a relationship, apology is the foundation for starting love.

It is not a guilty conscious for others when we feel sorry for them as an absolute value. True apology is to feel and sympathize with the pain and trouble of others. Apology without empathy is not apology. Consoling without empathy is not consoling. Empathy is the only necessary condition for true "I'm sorry." So, you can apologize for any pain you can relate to. Even if you didn't do anything wrong, or you have nothing to do with something, you can apologize and console the others as long as you can sympathize with the pain of the others. If you can sympathize with someone who is struggling because of you, you feel truly sorry and do something for that person. If you sympathize with someone who is struggling next to you, you will truly comfort the person and find something to do for that person. Thus, real apology that enfolds empathy is a consciousness that heals the pain of the other and at the same time increases the value of your own existential value.

Guilty conscience to the other is not a true apology. Guilty conscience is a feeling that arises when you focus on your own shame while the empathy for the other is absent. Therefore, guilty conscience develops when you have a selfish consciousness that focuses more on yourself rather than on the pain of others. If you are really sorry for someone, you will find something for him, but if you are feeling guilty, you will hide somewhere and not want to do anything. If we feel guilty for someone, we have to work hard on something for the other person, if only for the sake of shaking it off. We have to think hard about what you will need if you were in the other's position and take action. Expanding ourselves with empathy in this way and working hard for the others is the true apology.

Also, to God, feeling sorry to him allows us to begin a new way. That is why religions emphasize the importance of penitence and repentance. Confession and repentance are prayers that bare everything of you before God the Absolute, confessing your regrets, and telling him you are sorry about that. Repentance and penitence lead us to overcome limitations while healing ourselves and help us stand in the starting point to experience love with their force. Therefore, it is best if repentance and penitence become your daily habit, because the sooner you discover and overcome your regrets, the wider the path of love experience will be.

Repentance and penitence give us the power to realize the wisdom we realize in real life. If you discover your problems and realize the wisdom to overcome them, yet you repeat the same mistakes as before in similar situations. It is not because we lack wisdom that we make the same mistake again. It is because the power of inertia is pulling you back. This inertia is the karma's energy that we've made with our last mistakes and habits. Therefore, what is needed to avoid repeating the same mistake next time is not a pledge of "I will definitely do it right next time," but a regret that, "I really regret the pain I've caused with my past mistake." This penitence can neutralize the inertia that pulls you back.

Only those who regret the past can move on and go to the desired future. This is because painful regret is the power to overcome inertia. Reflection without regret makes you repeat the same mistake every day, but reflection with true regret melts past karma and enables a new beginning. Thus, the way to realize newly acquired wisdom can be opened. If it is hard to raise bone-aching regrets, I encourage you to repent a little bit each day in the meaning of Hon, Baek, Shin, Ui, and Ji. When we have painful regrets, we think again about existence in every sense. Likewise, if you repeat the penitence of Hon, Baek, Shin, Ui, and Ji, which are the main pillars of consciousness, you will have the same power as bone-aching regrets. As you build penance in this way, the past inertia disappears, and the power of wisdom will push you forward.

The important thing in repentance is not to feel guilty. You can let your penitence begin anew, but guilt is a conscience that draws itself down into disappointment and despair. God, our Creator, does not demand guilt from us. He rather refuses it. The very expression of rejection itself is the disappointment and despair caused by guilt. True repentance is not the guilt of sinners before God, but the regret and feeling sorry for having discovered your possibilities belatedly for the love you could have made and admitting that you are overcoming your limits little by little with this feeling of sorry. The more you penitent correctly, the more you are released from the oblivion that you are a sinner. As you overcome your limitations, you feel yourself expanding, and the more you repeat such penitence, the more you realize that you are one with God. True penitence is a way that takes you closer to the truth that you are part of God and God the Creator is all of us. So, don't miss out any sorriness and regrets you feel and repent and be penitent. It is the way to remember your true self.

Finally, it is I who sends and receives apology. In fact, exchanging apology with me is the first step to realizing the absolute value of the sixth chakra. Being sorry for me starts with empathizing with my feelings and thoughts. It is about consoling me for hard work and hardships and accepting and empathizing with how upset you are now. As I empathize and comfort myself, including my own intimate mind that only I know about, I start to feel what my self wants. I realize the disappointment between me and what I want now. You can expand yourself with a sincere reflection on that regret. Then I am ready to choose and experience the love I desire myself.

If I do not sympathize with my feelings, it is difficult to love and truly sympathize with anyone else's feelings. If I do not comfort myself for my hard work, it is difficult to be truly grateful for the hard work of others and comfort them. It is hard to embrace and love anyone's disappointment unless I reflect on my own regrets and reflect with affection. People who are stingy about their feelings are very stingy to others. If you analyze those who are generous to themselves and sensitive to others, you find that they are not generous to themselves, but they cannot empathize with themselves, and they don't know what they are sorry about. These are people who have turned back on themselves because they are stingy to themselves.

If you turn your back on yourself, you become a person who criticizes others, and if you are being stingy to yourself, you become a person who is stingy to others. So, to live in love with someone, you have to sympathize with yourself, comfort yourself, and be affectionate to yourself. You make up your mind by comforting yourself by telling yourself it's alright, things will get better since it is natural to feel this way because you were shocked and hurt your feelings, you will find the way you need to take while you try to endure like this, and you will find what is blocking you from searching for the love you want and you will stand on your feet again. If you convey your sorriness to you in this way, your inner traumas are healed and the power that hinders love disappears.

The wounds that we keep in our minds can be divided into the breakdown of the shield of the mind and inner trauma. If the shield of the mind breaks down, you lose calmness. The condition of being unable to control emotions is the symptom of the shield of the mind breaking down. The calmness can be restored as you reiterate love and faith again as explained in the fourth chakra. But trauma can be sustained as an unaffected calmness because it is always there deep in the heart. Trauma means a deeply engraved inner wound.

The trauma that is mangled in heart is largely created by three principles. One is by big shock. Not being able to endure a place alone after a long isolating accident, not being able to look at fire or smoke after a fire, and not being able to talk with kids after losing a child are the symptoms of traumas caused by shock. If you have repulsion against something, that is an expression of a trauma.

Another form is a trauma formed by wounds repeatedly caused during the same routine in everyday life. There are a lot of people who endure pain as it is because they cannot sublimate continuous pain into love and faith or deal with it with a sense of rewarding. But if this endurance builds up for a long time, it creates a wound inside. People with this cumulative trauma often live looking fine outwardly and do not realize that they are sick.

Finally, repeating one's negative emotions and consciousness for a long time also forms a cumulative trauma. If you make it hard for those around you with your own immature feelings, but do not try to fix it and repeat it over and over, you will form the traumatic energy that is fixed inside. When a cumulative trauma occurs, you are often caught up in ominous imagination uselessly. And long-lasting trauma, be it cumulative or caused by shock, often results in physical pain, chronic anger or depression, nocturia, or sleep disorders.

The pain of difficult control of emotion is the wound caused when the shield of the mind that envelops the pineal gland is destroyed. Inner trauma is a wound that degrades the spiritual function of the pineal gland. Symptoms you experience when the spiritual function of the pineal gland has been degenerated are feeling rejected by something, ominous imagination, chronic anger or depression, persistent pain, and sleep disorders. The pineal gland is where Hon dwells and it is an organ that regulates sleep by releasing hormones during the day and night. Thus, when trauma begins to heal, it is well observed that sleep demand increases rapidly. With enough sleep, Hon gains the energy of the universe and restores the spiritual function of the pineal gland.

It is the sorriness of the sixth chakra that heals our trauma, deeply embedded pain. In order to heal the trauma, you have to feel sorry for yourself or others. In addition, if you cherish and appreciate yourself penitent, forgive yourself regrets and stop being angry with yourself, and bless your happiness, the effect of healing will be amplified. And it must be based on sorriness. Since sorriness is the center of healing, pain cannot be healed by gratitude, forgiveness, and blessings without sorriness. And the sorriness must be at the bottom to form the foundation of healing.

Absolute values of the upper chakra that have sorriness at the center have the power to heal the trauma. Here I introduce a prayer of healing trauma by exchanging sorriness, forgiveness, gratitude, and blessings with myself, God, and the world.

"I send myself a sad sorriness and regrets that my soul has suffered pain in my life, and I ask God for forgiveness with honest penitence. I feel the sadness of God who forgives my pain that has not yet been healed.

When I'm hurt and going through a hard time, I go through the process of warm healing by sending comfort to me and telling myself that I'd gone through a lot but it will get better; sending my consoling words to the pain of the world (the people) that I've caused, say that I'm sorry, and say that it will get better; and filling the time of healing with contemplations of willingly accepting the comfort the world (people) is sending to me. Also, I find peace by forgiving and embracing myself, feeling sorry and telling myself that it is okay to have shortcomings and make mistakes; send my forgiveness to the world (people) that have hurt me; and continuing reflection so that I will be forgiven by the world (people) for all my shortcomings. In this way, we recover our wholesomeness in warm and peaceful healing.

In the end, after I have fully recovered my well-being, I forgave all my past pains, so I am comforted by God who tells me that I've suffered so much, and I am forgiven for all my faults. Therefore, I comfort and forgive the heavens for having had to give me pain in order to heal pain with this life, because this is the healing promised to me..."

"I am welcoming with happiness the existential healing to escape pain in my life, and I sincerely pray to God to bless my healing. God answers my prayer by willingly blessing me. I also receive God's gratitude for healing and respond with joy and gratitude.

When I recover from my pain, I am only thankful to all those involved in my healing, and I reflect on myself with warmness, coolness and perseverance that would impress the world (people), and I am only so proud of myself going through that process of healing, eventually keep expanding the opportunity for my healing. And in the whole process of my healing, I follow the natural laws that are worth being blessed by the world (people), I bless myself by willingly practicing all blessings that will help my healing, and make up my mind to bless the world with my healed self, consequently making a miraculous healing within a short time possible. The healing amplifies and happens within a short time with such many opportunities.

Eventually, Heaven is happy for my miraculous healing and recovery of well-being and congratulates me, making the joy of my healing bigger. I congratulate God for having succeeded in healing me, and I sincerely thank God with all the will of my soul for having stayed with me throughout this healing process."

This prayer of healing trauma is structured to circulate in the order of the sorriness to the world and God with me at the center, gratitude, forgiveness, and blessing. The values of healing are exchanged with myself, with the world, and even with God. Because even though healing can be accomplished by just comforting, thanking, forgiving, and blessing myself, the power of healing becomes more wholesome when you accomplish healing together with the world and God instead of alone. More wholesome healing makes the miracle of fast recovery possible.

It is familiar to us to give and receive gratitude and blessings with God, but giving and receiving apology and forgiveness with God may seem awkward. Usually we think we unilaterally apologize to God and ask for his forgiveness. The notion that God is sorry for me, that I comfort God, that I forgive God, and that God asks me for forgiveness is not yet familiar to us. But there is no reason to put God as the exception in the circulation of absolute values. There is no reason to make the circulation with God a half-circulation by unilaterally conveying and receiving. Rather, the effect becomes clearer when we make the full circulation with God. God the Creator is no exception in the laws of "Give and Take."

But there is an important difference from our God the Creator. While we desperately need God's comfort, forgiveness, gratitude and blessings, God does not need our comfort and forgiveness, gratitude, and blessings at all. Even if we do not forgive God at all, he or she has nothing to lose. God is almighty and therefore needs nothing. If we have comfort, forgiveness, gratitude, and blessings, God only accepts them gladly. God only accepts our mind gladly and amplifies our healing with the effects of "Give and Take."

The absolute value of the apology of the sixth chakra is about both healing and self-expansion. Saying sorry and apologizing heals the pain of the relationship, and empathy and comfort we give to and take from each other creates an intimate expansion of the relationship. The apology that we give to ourselves and God heals the inner trauma and opens the way of love. In addition, the ability to accept the apology passed on to us is as important to healing and expansion as it is to repentance. If you accept comfort and empathy given to you from somewhere, you will heal and expand. Therefore, you need to develop your ability to recognize and accept the various comforts that are given to you.

It is difficult to heal pain if somebody sends you condolences to comfort your pain but you are displeased with the way the person is talking to you without really knowing what is going on and act picky about it because the way the person speaks is not pleasant to hear and doesn't comfort you. You will be healed if you find solace from the fact that he truly cares about you with enough gratitude. Healing and expansion happen if you even accept your own regrets and self-criticism as a penitence. We can be healed if we accept even our complaint as a comfort and find solace in the way other people show how much they care about us.

Also, those who feel the comfort of God embedded in the various things of the world are quick to recover. They are comforted by the beauty of nature and art, and comforted by the love of others, and they heal their trauma naturally. While driving they feel tears falling listening to the music they happen to get to hear on the radio; they brighten their minds looking at the flowers in the apartment flowerbed, lighten their minds by looking at distant mountains, and feel touched in their hearts at the story introduced on TV. That's how God is always comforting us. Wherever you go, there is beauty, and there is an eye that is looking at us with a caring heart. We are healed even if we accept the comfort that we find from those. Therefore, the effort to accept apology and comfort is as important as practicing apology.

The apology that communicates in the sixth chakra manifests in the form of heartfelt regret and reflection, a repentance of apologizing before God, a heartfelt sorriness, and a sympathy of pain and gentle comfort. All of these are the same expression of apology. Also, those who feel sorry for you are comforting you in whichever form of expression, and God always empathizes with us and comforts us in various ways. To accept those minds is to accept the apology.

The absolute value of sorriness is the natural way of healing of pain. In the sixth chakra, the various forms of apology we send and receive whirl, while laying the foundation for love. The sixth chakra includes the pituitary gland and the hypothalamus, and they are the mecca of hormone release, neurotransmitters, and enzymes that control all of the body's functions. Thus, sorriness allows you to have a balanced peaceful body in any love experience. That's how the power of the sixth chakra establishes the goodness with which we can experience love.

The moonlight, which softly and gently illuminates the dark night world, contains God's love for our wellness and the blessings of the universe that mark the beginning of the love experience.

The Sacred Boundary of the Sixth Chakra

This is the sacred boundary that protects the sixth chakra using the forces of Hon, Baek, Shin, Ui, and Ji with sorriness and apology. For your perfection, the sixth chakra will freely communicate with the universe and promote healing and expansion. Whatever it is that troubles you, and whatever you want to achieve, I wish you to be with the sixth chakra along with all other chakras. And if you give to those who you are sorry to, their sixth chakras will shine along with yours simultaneously.

(1) Apology

* I was foolish for failing to understand the happiness of each moment.
I regret pushing my happiness into subconsciousness so easily to create exactly the opposite feelings,
and feeling the fear, anxiety, irritation, dissatisfaction and depression today.

Thanks to the stress of today, I realize happiness failed to see in the past.
I now feel truly sorry for recognizing such happiness,
and learn how huge such happiness was.

I always remember that happiness yet to be recognized always exists,
and live everyday apologetic because of the happiness that I failed to recognize,
and so I shall not miss the happiness I can feel each moment.

* I regret and repent giving up experiences for love,

so mistaken as to believe that the world is fooling us,
enraged and in grief.

I lament fearing and resenting God, (I lament denying God).
failing to believe the omnipotence of God, who is complete love himself,
misjudging him that he judges and punishes (thinking God can't do anything to me).

Since the world exists for love and God presents complete love, and we continue to experience that we are one with God in accordance with the laws of the universe,
let us achieve peace and glory of leaving everything before God in repentance.

* I am truly sorry for hurting and torturing myself,
by reproaching myself for my mistakes and insufficiency rather than offering some comfort,
and being miserly so as to even neglect the pain I felt.

It is lamentable that you remain indifferent to the infinite possibilities you have now,
remain negligent in rediscovering yourself and therefore,
failing to disclose your natural beauty and excellence.

We were given greatness and holiness with unknown limits,
so let us trust and love ourselves without any limits,
and remain true to ourselves so that we can feel truly sorry about ourselves.

* I regret breeding hatred and grudge,
by failing to believe that there was no ill will in others' acts,
distorting their intentions in our own ways.

I am sorry for not being able to provide proper help and support,
by failing to recognize the excellent qualities of others and that
it was their best,
while reprimanding their limits and belittling their finest
qualities.

Moving forward, I hope to always trust the good will of others,
recognize their excellence and that they're doing their best,
and sympathize with everyone with love and only love.

(2) Receiving Apology

* Since the creation of life takes place in complicated
relationships,
the results of all the hard work of the past do not come by soon,
and so life apologizes for the belated results and awaits the best
timing.

So recognize the repentance of life following the belated results,
and comfort it by embracing the results you currently have,
to let life bring the best results based on its repentance…

Even if life is tough and difficult,
exert your best so as to make life feel sorry,
and may you be filled with the rewards, joy and well-being of
life.

* The universe is sympathetic and apologetic
about our soul performing its destiny for an eternity
despite the many restrictions in this relative world.

God's omnipotence expands infinitely,
and since he desires to present us greater love,
he always feels apologetic about us today.

That is why he gave us complete free will,
so let us pursue genuine happiness with such free will,
for the glory of ourselves and of God.

* I regret acting contrary to my feelings out of need and convenience,
failing to think deeply about the consequences of the occasional mendacity,
and engaging in falsehoods that are unnecessary and even harmful.

Let us realize our regrets of abandoning our true selves,
not knowing that our soul's desire and heart vary,
thinking that emotions are all that matters and not working hard to change our thoughts.

Changing our thoughts through reflection so that our hearts and souls align,
and acting frankly without fear of disclosure,
that is how we accumulate the moments of alignment to become trinity without regrets.

* Sometimes my heart ached so much,
that I ignored those who sincerely apologized.
But that hurt me even more.

In fact, I know that many cannot muster the courage to apologize, even if they are truly sorry.
That is why I intend to accept their apologies, even if they are mere thoughts about apologizing.

Now I shall accept the hearts of those who apologized with much difficulty,

and be generous enough to understand even those who could not apologize to me.
As if I have already received the apologies needed, I wish to forgive all.

(3) Integration of Apology – Us - Receiving Apology
* The apologies and comfort I received healed my wounds,
the apologies and comfort I provided healed someone else's wounds,
and as such, we were fortunate to heal each other's wounds.

Remember the wound of someone else that I has not apologized or comforted,
soothing my pain that has not yet received an apology or comfort,
I overcome the wounds that are yet to be healed.

Since we feel sorry about and try to comfort someone else's pain,
and are always willing to accept apologies and consolation,
I would like to congratulate us for healing all of our wounds.

1) The Spiritual Role of the Moon
The moon is a satellite of Earth, and it plays a role of receiving the energy of the universe and transmitting it to Earth. It also takes the energy of the souls on Earth and sends them to the whole universe. In other words, the moon acts as a medium for interacting primary energy between the universe and Earth while orbiting Earth. Of course, it is not impossible to interact without a medium, but because the moon acts as a receiver with the gravity and rotational motion with Earth, the energy of the universe and Earth can interact much more effectively in a vast and massive universe.

When the moonlight shines more toward the universe, the energy transmitted from Earth to the universe is more active.

On the contrary, if the moonlight shines more toward Earth, the energy that transmits from the universe to the Earth is more active. On dark nights when the entire moonlight is shining on the universe, there is the most intense transmission toward the universe, while on full-moon nights, there is the most intense transmission toward Earth. Therefore, if we make life plans based on the cycle of the moon, we can make changes more efficiently.

During the times when the moonlight grows smaller than a half moon, thoughts and actions of dreaming of new changes in life and building its frames can be delivered to the universe more efficiently. But during the times when the moonlight grows bigger after the half moon, you reach enlightenment more efficiently through inspection and contemplation to fill meanings on the changes you make, because this is the period when transmission from the universe to us is more active. Therefore, if you realize the meaning property and ensure internal stability, you can design the frame of a more expanded life or newly modified life.

I often search and look at the moon harder when I am frustrated in my mind. I find solace just from looking at the moon. And I reached enlightenment numerous times during the days when the moon become larger and brighter. It was particularly true when I was writing prayers. First, I come up with an idea about the basic form of a prayer. Then I write the prayer in accordance to that form. While reading this patterned prayer repeatedly, I would have clear meanings that should be embedded in the form popping up in my head. And those clear meanings would fill up well mostly during the time when the moonlight was bright. That is the reason I am guessing that the energy the universe is sending to us is more active when the moonlight grows brighter.

But that doesn't mean you have to have the cycle of the moon in mind when making life plans. We all fill the meanings we receive from the universe at any time while designing our lives with the power of our consciousness and unconsciousness and repeating trials and errors. However, based on my experience, I advise that if you make a little more efficient communication with the universe in accordance with the cycle of the moon, you will be awakened and make changes a little faster.

11. The Seventh Chakra: Gratitude – Us – Gratitude Reception

The seventh chakra communicates the value of gratitude with the sun. The sun is the only star at the center of our solar system, and Earth is a planet orbiting the sun. As Earth orbits and turns around the sun, it takes the sun's energy evenly and blooms life. We have a chance to live on this planet all because the sun is shining on Earth. Therefore, how can we not be thankful to the sun that it rises every day? The absolute value of the sun, which brightens the whole world and becomes the energy of life, and grows and prospers its life, is therefore gratitude.

The light and heat of the sun are symbols of abundance because the sun sustains and prospers life on Earth. If the culture of the Korean people looking at the moon has developed in a way that wishes for safety and well-being and emphasizes the beauty of moderation and empty spaces, the culture that worships the sun, on the contrary, develops into a magnificent and splendid culture where people wish for prosperity and abundance. That is why the absolute value of the sun, gratitude, exerts the power to bring us prosperity. If we truly appreciate and appreciate something, that something amplifies into a larger shape in our lives again. The more we appreciate and be appreciated repeatedly, the more our lives become prosperous. Gratitude, the absolute value of the sun, is the value that makes a bountiful love possible by making us achieve and amplify what we want through love experience in the relative system that is surrounded by illusions that are not love.

In order for us to experience love in the relative realm called Earth, it is advantageous to live a rich life. Of course, you can experience love in any environment and have glory and peace in any environment, but you have the physical leeway to pursue love when you have less shortage in life. Therefore, it is good to pursue maximum affluence within our social foundation. That affluence opens up more opportunities for love. Creating a comfortable life with gratitude provides a way to experience love with absolute value.

In order to achieve a happy affluence with gratitude, you can do something to be thankful in your situation. Happiness and prosperity are achieved within the circle where the gratitude leaves from you and other gratitude comes to you from somewhere. Our gratitude in this circle gives us a direction to happiness. You are headed to happiness without you even noticing it while you are thankful for the things you enjoy, thankful for the work you do, and thankful for the people who are there for you. So, if there is a way to hope, you just have to be sincerely thankful for what you have as of now. Even if it's only a little now, our happiness starts from discovering and being thankful for that.

In fact, it is not that there is nothing we have except the desire to create a new human relationship. For example, if an orphan wants a parent, he really wants a parent he doesn't have, but if he wants money, it doesn't mean he doesn't have any money. He just doesn't have a lot of money for now. Also, if you want love and consolation, you can find that every person you come across has a little bit of love and comfort to share. Although it may not be a comfort that will satisfy you, it does exist. So, we have a little bit of what we want. Therefore, you must find that you have what you want, and be thankful for the present. That sincere gratitude brings satisfaction to your present. Satisfaction is a prerequisite for happiness.

Many people think that satisfied people don't grow anymore, and they degenerate. Therefore, they also believed they could grow only when they were dissatisfied. However, the growth achieved due to dissatisfaction is bound to be temporary. You were so dissatisfied that you tried hard to get out of that situation, but once you are out of the situation, you find the result is nothing meaningful and you feel empty. I can tell for sure that you cannot continue to grow happily without satisfaction. Satisfied but not growing happens because it is a fake satisfaction without gratitude. Fake satisfaction brings about the futility of life. But sincere satisfaction brings about growth. If you are satisfied with your sincere gratitude, you feel full and want more. The yearning, which starts with satisfaction, promotes happy growth and has a continuity. That's why those who live with sincere gratitude do not stop their happy growth. If you live with gratitude, you can avoid getting lost in the direction toward happiness.

A grateful mind pushes us toward the direction of happiness that we want. In terms of the law of acceleration, the gratitude we raise becomes the energy of acceleration that pushes us, and when we are pushed by gratitude, we can move toward happiness. To create a life that we want, however, we must have sorriness in addition to gratitude. As I mentioned previously, we can move forward only when we resolve our karma that keeps pulling us back. In other words, we need the penitence of sorriness to break free from the power that pulls us from our back in accordance to the law of inertia, and we need gratitude to move forward in accordance with the law of acceleration. Gratitude and sorriness make a pair that determines the direction of life and the driving force that takes us to that direction. With these two powers, we can treat possession, internal trauma, change habits, and create the life that we want. If forgiveness and blessing are added to that direction of life determined in that way, you can experience how they will become a reality without any stumbling blocks.

Our heartfelt gratitude guarantees satisfaction and happiness. But it doesn't even guarantee affluence. Of course, if you continue to grow with gratitude, you will reach affluence, but that is a bit slow. In order to achieve affluence, you must have something to deserve gratitude. Many people should have gratitude for you. Affluence is the result of being thanked. If you want to feel affluence internally, you can do it by getting many warm thanks from people. If you want to achieve affluence in your life, you have to work to be impressed by the world. The power of affluence can be activated when you receive a lot of energy of the gratitude. A being who receives such gratitude can realize affluence and prosperity.

To receive someone's gratitude, you must impress or please the person. Impression and joy are other expressions of gratitude. Restaurants impress people with the food taste, and the best-selling books receive gratitude from readers for giving them the fun of reading and touching their hearts. As a result, affluence follows. Businessmen who make lots of money or heroes who are praised by people get their affluence and honor because they received lots of gratitude from people by impressing them and giving them joy. That's why they were given economic affluence and the prosperity of honor. It is a right choice of absolute value for us to pursue the work that the world will appreciate and to do work with enough sincerity to be appreciated by the world.

Once formed, gratitude does not disappear because it is an absolute value. It is true even if the person who caused the gratitude forgot. However, when the joy and inspiration were the result of a deception, the gratitude can disappear. For example, if you have tried a menu in a hotspot restaurant, were impressed by it, but forgot about it later, the energy of the gratitude that was formed remains forever. But if it later turns out that the restaurant had a serious hygiene problem and lied about the ingredients, the previous energy of gratitude will disappear due to the sense of betrayal. Therefore, for affluence to continue, the gratitude people had toward you should not turn bad due to a deception.

People's gratitude doesn't change as long as we do what we do honestly without being deceptive. Tricks make all existing gratitude disappear the minute they are exposed. Haven't we seen enough people who enjoyed affluency until they take a fall after having their tricks exposed? Therefore, there is no need to envy people who make a lot of money by cheating, because they are destined to take a fall and their disgraceful failure is soon to become reality.

Those who earn money steadily or maintain honor have no deceit and are not swayed by greed at least. They continue to live by the principles that have touched people's hearts or live with compassion and sharing spirits in addition to that. Being compassionate and sharing with others are the easiest ways to get gratitude from people. That's why the more we share, the richer we become. If you find what you can share with others in life in your work, and if you try to be compassionate to others, you are sure to build up gratitude from people. And for people who live that way, the opportunity to become affluent is realized in the form that best suits them.

The most common example is getting new opportunities at work. Some of the minor examples include having luck at work, promotion, and business boom. Other additional examples include finding opportunities to develop forms, technology, or materials that will impress the world, and once these developments are launched in the market, they will become so-called jackpots. There are also occasional instances of accidental affluence, such as the cases of those who win first prize in the lottery or who frequently win second and third prize, and those who become stars by chance. Winning the jackpot never happens simply by chance or accident. It is the gratitude they received for having been considerate and generous to others manifesting in reality.

You can be happy when you can be always grateful for the results given to you during the process of achieving prosperous abundance with the energy of the gratitude you receive from the world. If you appreciate the results given, the direction of happiness is kept clear, and its abundance can prosper toward happiness. You don't become happy if your abundance keeps growing but you are not appreciative of it, and that abundance becomes lost. Therefore, we can continue a happy abundance if we are grateful to the reality now and find direction to happiness; practice compassion and sharing that will bring gratitude to us in daily routine; do our best in what we do to impress the world; and have sincere gratitude for the consequential abundance and share it with the world again. The abundance you have realized by circulating gratitude can be as full and massive as possible.

But there are times when it may be hard to thank. It's hard to be grateful when the reality is too heavy. Then we can assume that there is nothing in us now as a last resort. If you want money and it's hard to be grateful for the current financial situation, let's imagine that you don't even have what you have now in your wallet and your bank account. And then when you think of your wallet and your bank account balance again, you can be grateful for having money even though it is insufficient. If you're having a hard time fighting a disease and anxious to be healthy, let's imagine a life where you are in a coma and cannot even lift a finger. Then, you'll be grateful for the body that is sustaining you at the moment. If you imagine that the person who is next to you is gone, you realize how precious that person is to you; you can see how the person is trying just as hard as you are now; and you will be grateful just for the fact that the person is with you now.

If we are thankful for the present by imagining a situation where we have nothing, we don't need to beg God to make our wishes come true when we pray any more. The prayers of the present perfect tense that you say you are thankful for what you already have now will naturally flow out of you. In prayers you sincerely ask God to make your wish come true, God lets you know that he is watching over you by giving you little answers little by little. In the present progressive form of prayers that you say to see changes happening toward the realization of your wish, God lets you know that he is with you by giving you a more powerful response. But in your present perfect tense, you say prayers to thank God for making your wish come true; he responds with a powerful reply, "You are my other self," and the creation unfolds to have our wishes realized in reality.

So, I hope you'll move on from such prayers as "Let my life be a flower filled path" and quickly pass the stage where you pray "Thank you for my life being on a flower filled path" and always stay at the stage where you pray "Thank you for my life being a flower filled path." When the gratitude remains in a present perfect tense like this, we are not afraid to share what we have with others, and we have a wider range of consideration for others. Consequently, sharing and considering will happen as naturally as it can be. We can breathe with God with a daily routine where we embrace a present perfect tense gratitude and receive gratitude from others as we move on to create a happy affluence.

But what is important in the gratitude is whether it is sincere or not. The exchange of pretense, not sincerity, leads to a counterattack of deprivation. A case in point is the negative side effect of a compliment. Compliments and joy are the most common everyday forms of gratitude. When we are grateful for what we have been given, joy flows out of us and we pay a compliment to the other person. There is a saying that goes, "A compliment makes even whales dance." A compliment that expresses gratitude can really lead to a miracle of making a whale dance, because gratitude always brings satisfaction and abundance.

A compliment has all those good effects, but it also entails negative side effects that we all should know about too. The negative effect of a compliment refers to such phenomenon as giving up easily when not complimented and the lowering of self-esteem due to the burden of a compliment. Compliments such as saying somebody is great, amazing, genius, and smart entails negative effects on some people such as lowering their self-esteem due to the disparity with reality. And lowered self-esteem affects people to become too sensitive about people's reactions to them. This is by no means an affluence. Repeatedly receiving these compliments makes you less willing to do something on your own when you are not complimented. Repeated compliments create people with poor will power and make them take actions only based on the decisions and intentions of other people. Instead of bringing about affluent will power, it results in a lack of will.

Then you may wonder: Why does the exchange of gratitude with absolute values not produce rich fruits? The reason is actually simple. This is because it is a fake compliment, not a genuine one. Suppose you wanted your child to be a good person, or you wanted your child to become independent and not need the care of parents, when you complimented your child for having done something really well. In this case, did you really think your child did well and your child showed you a great side of themself? Let's think about it over again. Frankly, it would be less than ten times that you were touched by your little child who has brushed his teeth without help. There will be a difference in the number of times, but if you continue to compliment even though you are no longer impressed by an action, the compliment will backfire. One example is a child who doesn't brush his teeth when not complimented, or who doesn't brush his teeth properly even if he is complimented.

Compliments should stop when they are not sincere. If you are no longer impressed by your child when he brushes his teeth alone, just paying attention to the fact that he brushed his teeth without help will be true love. "You brushed your teeth. Are you feeling refreshed?" This is the extent of sincerity and you have to stop here. This is true not only for children but also for adults. Compliment with genuine joy when you are touched by gratitude, and just convey attention when you are not touched or do not feel joy. That is the rule of gratitude and a way to lead to affluence.

Psychologists point out that complimenting someone for being smart or a genius is not good. Those complimenting words can put pressure on the person and rather lower the person's self-esteem. Again, what is important is whether you are serious rather than how you express it. I don't know what other parents will be like, but to be honest, there aren't many moments when my child looks like a genius and smart. It's just only a few times. But there are quite a few moments when I feel pity for my child when she tries really hard. I can feel how hard she tries when I tell her to clean her room but she is overwhelmed with the work and lies down, or when I see her struggling with a math exam practice book before a test and then in ten minutes, she gets exhausted. Among the compliments we give to our children or exchange with each other, there are not many that we will make to others for being truly great, but there are many moments when we feel gratitude for their hard work. That is the reason in a psychological sense, noticing how the other person is trying really hard and telling them, "You've really worked hard. Thanks for trying so hard" makes a great compliment. Since a certain percentage of the compliment on hard work is genuine, it can make self-motivated joyful efforts more affluent.

But complimenting with such words as smart, genius, and good brains is not necessarily a bad thing. If these compliments are sincere, those words can make the communion between each other and promote rich amplification. Sometimes I am really at my child's behavior and I cry out "Wow! You're a genius" spontaneously. While creating an artwork with my child and noticing my child demonstrating clever expressions, a strong, sincere compliment springs out unconsciously. When it happens, I quickly add another word because I'm afraid my compliment puts a burden on my child. I say, "At this moment, you are the genius of this method." I've done this just a few times, and now my daughter herself comes to me when she's satisfied and boasts, "Mom, I think I'm a genius of wave at this moment!" Gratitude, expressed with sincere delight, communicates with the other person no matter how it is expressed, and brings about a richness of self-esteem to both adults and children.

Some of the fake compliments are the ones that deceive yourself. It happens when you compare yourself with others and compliment yourself. "I have many friends who are the same age as me but take a handful of medicines. Given that, I am healthy." "I am better off than him." If you look into this mindset carefully, you'll find that it is the same expression as to say that you are not satisfied at all if you don't compare yourself with others. In other words, it is a different expression of discontent. Such fake self-compliment results in a sense of deficiency without exception. So, you become the similar shape as the others who you had compared yourself with. Even though you don't really have anything better than them.

Getting satisfaction from comparing yourself with others also goes against the value of analysis-synthesis. It is about not distinguishing yourself with others, and perceiving yourself as a being not the same with others. A true self-satisfaction is the mindset that feels proud of yourself just the way you are. When you are satisfied just the way you are and just the way you act, it is genuine satisfaction. Genuine self-satisfaction brings about affluence as well. The you that you are proud of shines brighter, and you become somebody who can do better something that makes you satisfied.

The most important thing in gratitude is sincerity. Gratitude, not sincerity, must bring about a counterattack of deprivation. That's why self-esteem falls to the bottom when famous young gifted children are exposed to the compliment coming from jealousy instead of sincerity. To not compliment and express gratitude when you are not sincere is to be considerate of others. So, let's not exchange compliments that are meant to be a consideration, not sincerity. Gratitude that is just a pretense and not a sincere gratitude does not advance to amplification in life but progresses to deprivation. The counterattack of compliment and gratitude are proof that we can never fool the sun.

The praise and gratitude that is exchanged sincerely is the value that leads to the prosperity of human relations. There are positive and negative things about relational karma. Apology destroys negative karma, and gratitude is the value that connects positive karma. So, the secret to solving problems with people who are together is apology, and the secret to creating happy relationships is gratitude. If you make the karma of the gratitude thicken, the unconscious feelings that you feel toward each other are laid out in your original love. The generous room to accommodate the other people's shortcomings gains strength, and cheers are expressed to shine on the other people's strengths. Relationships with thick gratitude can also protect love in times of crisis. Relationships where you exchange gratitude also make love prosper.

That is the reason I suggested expressing your gratitude after resolving unconscious hostility when I was explaining karma in the part about mind. This is because if you connect with gratitude as the first step while negative karma is resolved, you can start a relationship of love. I suggest thinking about gratitude for those around you before going to bed and conveying it to their unconsciousness before going to bed every day. I also recommend that you think about what your partner will appreciate and take action on it. Between them and you, there will continue a karma of love that will never disappear. Just as we start by appreciating the fact that it is with me to get what we want, the love of human relationships begins with finding that there is something to be thankful for, even a little bit. The gratitude we have found remains as the unchanging eternity between the other and you.

We need to be grateful for the basic needs of honor (Hon), money (Baek), physical satisfaction (Shin), shelter (Ui), and pleasure (Ji) in order to live a prosperous life. If I am grateful for my honor, I can do the job that will receive gratitude with that honor, and it returns to me as a bigger honor. If I appreciate my money, I can spend it on something to be appreciated and I can make more money with it again. Unfolding love that lets you have honor, money, physical health, food, clothes, shelter, and joy that are amplified in this way – that is the law of the universe that leads to the rich evolution of the world with the seventh chakra.

Our five basic needs are the ingredients to love more in more diverse ways. You cannot say some of these five desires are good, some are shameful, and some are bad. All these are the ingredients of blessing for love. People who fulfill their money and honor with gratitude will have a love that is the same as lighthouses that guide the world. If you enjoy gratitude in your physical Eros with the one you love, you can have love that gives joy and comfort to the world with a high sense of self-esteem. Good house, car, and affluent household make ingredients to share small happiness with families and neighbors. Those who enjoy fun games and relaxation can have love that shares fun and dynamics with the world. There is no desire that needs to be tabooed. Instead of criticizing people for having too much desire for love or sex, there is only a desire that is to be blessed with sincere gratitude. When you put gratitude in the desire that you diligently fulfill, all can be the ingredients of love.

Thankfulness manifests itself in the form of appreciation, praise, pleasure, gladness, and relief. We can discover and increase the variety of gratitude in every aspect of our lives. With each and every one of those discoveries, we extend the gratitude, and we dream of one day being grateful for everything we've been given and everything we can. With such full satisfaction, we always dream of being considerate and able to share. There will always be a hot and bright sun above the head of such existence, enriching everything in life, and expanding the brain to spread the wealth to the world. In an expanse of brain, ingenious ways to enrich the world will emerge. A heart so truly appreciative lets us make miracles for us. Achieving the miracle of abundance is the absolute value that this universe is expecting from us. So, don't hesitate to thank all for everything, and be thankful for everything. I hope you will make and enjoy your happiness and prosperity.

When you do, the sun will always shine on you.

The Sacred Boundary of the Seventh Chakra

This is a sacred boundary that protects the seventh chakra of the crown by exchanging thanks and using the power of Hon, Baek, Shin, Ui, and Ji. For your satisfaction and prosperity, the seventh chakra will freely communicate with the universe, promoting healing and expansion. Whenever you want to fulfill your dreams of life's abundance, share this prayer together. And I hope you will read as somebody you are thankful for, because that gratitude will satisfy them and you at the same time.

(1) Gratitude

* Looking back, I was able to enjoy the stability today thanks to the past,
and I learnt precious lessons of life by enduring the hardships of the past.
All the processes I went through in the past were grateful experiences that were necessary to me.

Furthermore, today is always a new challenge to us.
Having that sense of desperation for the time that will never come back,
we need to readily achieve the accomplishments with the passion for life.

That is how we always wish for a more stable tomorrow.
That is why when we practice the lessons learnt and are grateful for the results of today,
we will be able to create stability that is completed with maturity of life.

* I thank God for creating us with love and blessing.
Since God created this world only for the purpose of experiencing love,
it is fortunate that all existences are love and those that are not love are nothing more than a fabrication.

I thank God for always loving us and blessing us.
He lets us experience love in the fair rule of the universe,
and so isn't it happy to see the infinite expansion with our free will?

I look forward to happiness resulting from our expansion.
We acquire happiness as beings that pursue truth and glow,
we will feel with our entire body that we are a part of God and be overjoyed.

* With the efforts of the past of recognizing my faults and incompleteness,
I feel proud about the moments I frankly exposed myself to,
trying not to hide the darkness in me and to overcome it with love.

By ceaselessly trying to rediscover myself,
I become greater and more beautiful as days go by,
so let us not forget to praise ourselves for the efforts today.

That is how I become a more honest person,
and become more worthy of praise,

I will one day find that I am a little God and be overjoyed.

* I thank all the people who stood by my side in the past.
It was fortunate that we could share similar experiences and emotions,
sympathize with each other and comfort one another.

I also thank those who are by my side today.
Thanking their good will and all the best efforts,
I too, wish to help and support them.

I thank our destiny of being together.
We create the joy of becoming a more full being
by filling and complimenting each other's weaknesses and becoming united in love.

(2) Appreciated
* Please remember that our life finds relief in the hardships we overcame,
feels grateful for all the efforts we make,
and has been repaying them until today.

That is why we should strengthen our will to live,
make choices that are helpful to life,
and practice so that they sufficiently satisfy our lives.

Remember that life always repays our efforts of today,
is enthusiastic about how to repay tomorrow for my choices today,
and hastens the day we will be repaid for living a rewarding life cheerfully.

* Remember that heaven is grateful

for us fully agreeing with the rules of the universe,
accepting our fate and joining the universe.

Please know that heaven is happy
to see us fulfill our free will in the cyclic universe,
grow and expand ourselves to amplify happiness.

The happiness we magnified expands the universe,
and glorifies God,
it touches God to grant us more truth and light and life.

* I repent failing to understand the greatness in me,
failing to give out all the strengths I have that are needed by the
world,
and thereby unacknowledged by the world.

Now as I firmly recognize the beauty and greatness in me,
and unsparingly bring them out to the world,
the world appreciates it and is overjoyed.

The gratitude I receive delights me,
and I give such pleasure back to the world,
which will serve as the driving force of happiness and delight,

* I become happy when others become happy with the love I
give.
I become dispirited if others are not happy nor grateful for the
love I give.
That is why I would rather engage in love that returns with
happiness and gratitude.

Those receiving love from me will be happier feeling grateful
than not,

but sometimes they lose that gratitude if I give and only give.
In that case, it is necessary to control giving so as to let others feel grateful.

Of course since we are one, it is okay that others do not feel grateful.
But happiness magnifies when love is coated with gratitude,
so why not create love whose values are respected and appreciated?

(3) Integration of Gratitude - Us – Appreciated

* Looking back, there were many things I should be grateful for, and I enjoyed happiness from all the praises and recognition I received,
so I am only overwhelmed with the abundance of love rising out of satisfaction and joy.

Remembering the joy and gratitude that I have yet to deliver,
soothing the disappointment of not being recognized or praised,
for more abundant and colorful love, I take on the challenges beyond the limit.

Ultimately, since the path is paved for joy in everything we do,
while delivering gratitude to everything before us,
I would like to sincerely congratulate you on becoming ever more surrounded by abundant love.

12. The Eighth Chakra: Forgiveness – Us – Forgiven

The value of the eighth chakra is forgiveness, and the value of the ninth chakra is a blessing. Forgiveness and blessings are the highest values of our love experience. God, the Creator and all of us, forgives and blesses everything as it is now and forever. There is no moment when God doesn't forgive and bless everything. Forgiveness and blessing are the highest values of love because they are "the same mind" of God. Thus, the eighth and the ninth chakras, which contain the highest values, are not trapped in our bodies but exist above our heads, so that God's consistent mind and the will of our souls will always be together. Uranus and Neptune, which communicate with the eighth and ninth chakras, are also in the outermost locations in the solar system, enveloping the solar system with the greatest orbit. Just like God's consistent mind surrounds all other chakras...

Out-of-body chakras that contain the highest values serve to integrate and reflect our Hon, Baek, Shin, Ui, and Ji. The ninth chakra with blessings integrates and reflects the physiological power of our Hon, Baek, Shin, Ui, and Ji, and the eighth chakra with forgiveness is integrating and reflecting the pathology of our Hon, Baek, Shin, Ui, and Ji. In other words, the eighth chakra presides over the power of illusion that is not love, as the value of forgiveness. Among the pathological forces in our Hon, Baek, Shin, Ui, and Ji, the most opposite of consciousness of love is called anti-myungsu. We define and experience inner love and build up myungsu, and the anti-myungsu is the force that is the most opposed to myungsu. It is the eighth chakra that determines anti-myungsu.

In the human unconscious there is a binary system that turns on and off. Anti-myungsu is a phenomenon that manifests itself in the binary system and is a signal that our soul "turns on and off" to guide the mind. When we have thoughts in our hearts that are hard to experience love, our souls light up anti-myungsu as a sign that they are not in that direction. When anti-myungsu is created, the distance between the soul and the mind increases, which amplifies the pain or negative emotions that we usually had. When anti-myungsu is turned on, you become emotionally unstable and it becomes difficult to hold healthy and hopeful thoughts. Then, when we think in the opposite way to the idea that turned on anti-myungsu, that is, when we fix it with the thought that the soul wants, the anti-myungsu is turned off and extinguished in our mind. Then the distance between our heart and soul is restored to its original state, and it remains stable at the level of the person's usual emotions and thoughts. Embracing anti-myungsu intensifies the confusion of the mind and resolving anti-myungsu makes the mind comfortable. In this way, it allows us to stay on track in our lives.

The anti-myungsu centered on Hon is hatred. The anti-myungsu centered on Baek is a resentment. The anti-myungsu centered on Shin is the denial. The anti-myungsu centered on Ui is falsity or truth, and anti-myungsu centered on Ji is irresponsibility or coercion. Hatred, resentment, denial, falsity, irresponsibility are the human sins which religions have always warned us to be vigilant about. The reason for the vigilance of anti-myungsu in existing religions is that these hearts make us become distant from love. When we have anti-myungsu in our hearts, it is more difficult than usual to think and practice love. Although it is possible to extend love, you might love more painfully. So, understanding the anti-myungsu that prevents our expansion is very beneficial to experiencing love. Now let's talk about what makes anti-myungsu in specific instances.

Let's first understand hatred. Hatred is not just a feeling of disliking someone. As I stress repeatedly, we have a free right to dislike someone or something. The emotion of disliking does not block our souls, but people who have many things that they dislike find life a little more tiring. As we expand our love, we can love while leaving the disliking emotion on the things we dislike as they are. But you can't hate and love at the same time. Hatred is the desire for the other person to be painful. It is hatred when you want your partner to be sick as much as you are and suffer as much as you are and fail as much as you failed. The highest form of hatred is, after all, a curse, which is about hoping that the other will disappear.

We humans do not hate anyone without anything happening. When you are hurt, sick, and finding it hard to endure the pain, the pain bursts out in the form of hatred. So, having an anti-myungsu of hate means that you endure painful and troubling times. So, to repent on the hated anti-myungsu is to look back and heal one's wounds. The anti-myungsu of hate is extinguished by saying it's okay, you have endured a painful time, and comforted by saying the pain is now healing and you are growing, that you don't have to hate any more, and that you will not lock yourself in hatred any more.

Resentment is to blame others. You think it's hard because of him, and you think it'll be fine if he is not here anymore. In order for me to expand, you have to change yourself, but resentment prevents you from expanding because it finds problems with others, not with yourself. In fact, it is easy for anyone to have feelings of resentment. When I am busy and have to go somewhere and someone is talking to you or calling you, or cars are blocking you, you easily blame the other person or the situation. Fortunately, however, our irritated emotional resentment does not easily become anti-myungsu. It becomes anti-myungsu only when you fail to recognize you have a very important reason but you don't notice it and blame others. Or, when the other person is someone who owes you a lot but keeps being irritated and resentful without recognizing it. In these situations, it becomes an anti-myungsu and blocks our soul. Resentment, too, is the curse of the highest form of what is hoping for the other to disappear.

We humans do not easily have the resentment to become anti-myungsu. When we lose our purpose and direction in life and become confused, we resent without realizing our own important reasons. So we need to stop there for a while to extinguish the anti-myungsu of resentment. Calm down by comforting yourself as you are in the midst of confusion, telling yourself that it's okay, and thinking about the fact that the object of resentment in confusion is in fact giving you a new opportunity. If you rediscover yourself by moving out of resentment in that way, anti-myungsu disappears and you grow again.

Denial that becomes anti-myungsu means hating oneself and denying the value of being, strongly denying the existence of God, or denying love. We deny our existence when we are in despair. We think it's meaningless to keep living, and it's not worth living. Thinking that you can't be given such despair if there is God the Absolute, you fall into despair that there is no such thing as true love in this world. Or we really cannot hate the other in a situation that is too painful and hard for you, we hate ourselves too. One example is when you get hurt and angry with someone and when it gets serious, you beat yourself and hurt yourself. So, the highest form of denial is the self-cursing that you wish yourself to disappear.

The situation where you deny self and deny love enough to deny God is a situation of dark despair. The presence of anti-myungsu of denial indicates that we have experienced mental darkness with no light. Fortunately, however, darkness is not the only lasting part of our lives. When you live, you find a light in the dark that has nothing at all. The anti-myungsu of denial disappears when holding on to that little hope; you believe in love and yourself, or believe in the love of the Creator, and raise yourself up. You can also disappearthe denial in which you hated yourself instead of the other you truly could not hate by thinking that just as much as the other is a being that you cannot hate, you are a precious being yourself too.

Falsity, like resentment, routinely pervades our lives. Of course, these everyday falsehoods are not anti-myungsu, so you can rest assured. There are three kinds of falsity that are anti-myungsu: causing trouble and harm to someone; betraying their love and trust; and finally deceiving God and the universe.

We humans never try to spoil or betray others' lives recklessly. But we can turn to falsity and cause trouble to others unintentionally in order to survive when we cannot find a breakthrough in the illusion that everything is crumbling down. In this case, anti-myungsu disappears when you affectionately deal with the misunderstanding about falling and feel sorry for the person who has gone through trouble because of that falsehood. We would also commit the falsity of betrayal and create anti-myungsu when we forget the gratitude of love given to us. This falsehood of betrayal is separate from failing one's expectations. We are not obligated to live up to someone's expectations, so we do not have to live up to the expectations of others. It is anti-myungsu to lie in betrayal to the trust and love beyond mere expectation. At this time, anti-myungsu vanishes when we remember the love given to us and reflect and repent while remembering that gratitude.

Even if you're not doing false to others, breaking the vows you made to yourself and God, or deceiving yourself can be anti-myungsu. That does not mean you cannot change the vows you made. We all make mistakes and fall into delusions so sometimes we make the wrong vows. However, if you cannot keep your vows, you can reflect on it by changing it slightly to fit the reality. If you change your vows capriciously without such reflection, the pain of anti-myungsu arises in the gap between the reality and resolution. In addition, sometimes pretending to be okay in situations where pain and wounds continue becomes the anti-myungsu of falsehood. Such falsehood amplifies one's meaningless pain. In such instances, mustering up the courage to become more honest to others can help relieve pain and make the anti-myungsu disappear.

It is rare but the truth, which is the opposite of falsity, can be anti-myungsu too. If you tell the truth and give someone an unworthy confusion, it becomes anti-myungsu. Revealing the truth is mostly a healing process, so you don't need to hesitate. So, the lie that hides without revealing the truth is often anti-myungsu. Nevertheless, the case where the truth becomes anti-myungsu applies to those who can bear the truth of pain alone. That means they fully overcame pain caused by the truth, and it also means it is more beneficial to resolve the situation in other ways without revealing the truth. It is a sign of self not to make another pain with a pain that you've overcome already, and it is also a sign to guide you to a wiser way. When you understand these meanings, you can resolve the anti-myungsu of truth.

Irresponsibility that becomes anti-myungsu means not having fulfilled man's most sacred responsibility. The most basic is family responsibility, and the responsibility that you have because you are aware of ethics is related to anti-myungsu. The family is a sacred group because it is the foundation of the human race. So family responsibility should never be forsaken. Our responsibility that we must keep because we are aware of ethics does not imply social constraints, such as legal violations. Those that become anti-myungsu include discarding wastes knowing their harmfulness or witnessing a scene of crime and ignoring it and not even reporting it because they are acts of disregarding what all humans have to do.

In fact, most of us instinctively strive to fulfill our family and ethical responsibilities. Then, when faced with important responsibilities at the moment of exhaustion, we sometimes choose to ignore them and create anti-myungsu. If we look at not fulfilling ethical responsibilities, we are mostly overwhelmed by the tiredness of life and became insensitive when we create anti-myungsu of irresponsibility. So, having an anti-myungsu of irresponsibility also means there was a time of exhaustion and lethargy. Therefore, anti-myungsu extinguishes by doing what can empower your exhausted self – feeling sorry for the past irresponsibility and making a life of fulfilling responsibilities.

There is one more thing to know about irresponsible anti-myungsu. In addition to anti-myungsu not fulfilling their responsibility, it is also possible to create an irresponsible anti-myungsu by acting improperly or forcing others into unfair action because you mistake it for a responsibility. We usually recommend to others what we think is right and good. Sometimes we think it is a responsibility beyond a recommendation to make others do as you say. But if the action is against the will of the other soul, it becomes an irresponsible anti-myungsu. For example, it is an irresponsible anti-myungsu if a child dreams of becoming a painter and cannot bear not being able to paint, but you take the painting away from the child and force the child to study, or when you preach a religion but trample the will of the other soul. It is because we should not break someone's free will claiming that our action is a responsibility.

So far, we have addressed five types of anti-myungsu that hinder our expansion. When anti-myungsu occurs, the soul is separated from the mind, which causes psychological difficulties. Anti-myungsu of hate and resentment amplifies fear and anger, and denial of anti-myungsu amplifies disappointment and self-regret. In addition, anti-myungsu of falsehood amplifies dissatisfaction and doubts about others, and anti-myungsu of irresponsibility amplifies depression and lethargy. Because anti-myungsu is formed mainly when we are wounded, weary, and ill, we take for granted that we are losing our true nature. And if we overcome the pain and regret the anti-myungsu we had, or reverse the thought, it dissipates naturally. Sometimes you get anti-myungsu and get rid of it quickly, saying, "I just had an extreme thought." As such, anti-myungsu repeats occurring and disappearing itself many times in life to anybody. And in general, it doesn't hold that long. You can see many types of anti-myungsu lasting long only when the direction of life is completely wrong. Even in such a way, regaining the direction of life can make all anti-myungsu disappear in a moment.

Occasionally, anti-myungsu can be missed naturally without regret. Long after the anti-myungsu disappears from memory, the psychological difficulties are diminished. Instead, the unconscious anti-myungsu is well expressed as a physical pathological condition. This is because we think back and wonder "Have I lived wrong" when you are sick and troubled for long. This condition was not caused by anti-myungsu for no reason. It is a natural condition of the patient's health, and it is usually a condition that can be well recovered from with treatment, but due to the energy generated by anti-myungsu, you suffer from a slow recovery process and increased pain. These symptoms are obvious relief when acupuncture points to the anti-myungsu treatment, confirming that the symptoms worsened with anti-myungsu. In this case, as well as physical treatment, the patient should try to remember his anti-myungsu and reverse the consciousness to make the treatment easier.

Not remembering the unconscious anti-myungsu does not mean that you need to be treated. When the person who has anti-myungsu chooses understanding and forgiveness unlike the last time in a situation similar to that of the anti-myungsu, the last anti-myungsu disappears. So those who have anti-myungsu in the unconscious experience a similar situation over and over again. Through repeated experiences, we eventually choose to grow and destroy the last anti-myungsu.

Since anti-myungsu is a phenomenon that is turned on and off in our consciousness, the extinction of anti-myungsu does not mean that you have overcome all internal pains. The presence of anti-myungsu means that our mind has a part that is opposite to the soul, and the disappearance of anti-myungsu means that the mind has restored the pace of soul's direction. If we were wounded and turned on anti-myungsu with some thought, the distance between the heart and the soul falls far apart and it is difficult to find a way to recover from the wound. When anti-myungsu is turned on, it is likely to return to its place despite several healing efforts. Only after the anti-myungsu thoughts have been reversed and extinguished can the smooth process of healing and treating one's pain become possible. In other words, anti-myungsu is the starting point of the internal healing process that takes a long time, and it is the part that should be first resolved from the long pain.

The disappearance of anti-myungsu has a triggering effect on the long course of healing. So, if we start to heal our inner pains and if the process is too hard, we need to find out what kind of ideas created anti-myungsu. Only then can you start a smooth healing. In addition, there is a difficulty that comes back once during the healing process. At this time, it is necessary to check whether the new anti-myungsu is turned on during the healing process. Only then can the healing continue to produce as much effort.

In addition, anti-myungsu guides not only in wound healing but also in daily growth. Even if it is not a big hurt or pain, anti-myungsu is turned on in thoughts that hinder our growth. Then you will continue to face your troubled inner self. If you do not recover with the process of caring and comforting yourself, you may suspect anti-myungsu. After finding and extinguishing anti-myungsu by turning on an opposite thought, we can know where our souls are going. In this way, we can clearly see the direction of happiness through anti-myungsu.

The most important thing to know about anti-myungsu is that the whole process of having and disappearing anti-myungsu is not the result of God's unilateral judgment. In conventional religion, God allegedly judges our sins, but in fact, anti-myungsu is the result of an agreement between God and our souls. On the path led by God, my soul becomes my anti-myungsu only if this mind agrees to become an anti-myungsu. The disappearance of anti-myungsu can only be extinguished if my soul agrees to disappear based on the laws of the universe. God and we are one being, and God respects us perfectly, so the creation and extinction of anti-myungsu is the will of God and the result of the free will of our soul.

When our soul agrees, that is the confidence that we can overcome the anti-myungsu. The pain we cannot overcome is not anti-myungsu. This does not mean that the hardships that come to us are easy to forgive. The process of forgiving our hardships and overturning anti-myungsu is very difficult, cumbersome, and sometimes painful, but it is clear that we can. We can list countless numbers of people who show how many have raised themselves up from great suffering. They and we remember clearly how hard it was for them and us to overcome hardships in our lives. We must always remember that it is us human beings who have done such hard work.

So the standard of anti-myungsu varies from person to person. For some, it is resentment not anti-myungsu, but for others, it is resentment that is anti-myungsu. The criteria are determined according to the status of Hon, Baek, Shin, Ui, and Ji synthesized by each of the eighth chakras. As Hon, Baek, Shin, Ui, and Ji expand to reduce negative space, anti-myungsu is determined based on more stringent criteria. Thus, a person with high growth at the fifth expansion may have anti-myungsu of mixed Hon and Baek even with some criticism or just lack of compassion. Anti-myungsu is determined at a level one can overcome and is necessary for growth. So anti-myungsu is always a fair result. It is the law of the universe of fairness, to which our souls may agree, as the standards best suited to each apply.

We accept forgiveness from God by repenting about anti-myungsu. Unless we realize ourselves and reverse our thinking about anti-myungsu, our souls block and don't accept divine forgiveness. The pain caused by anti-myungsu reflects the will of the soul. Our soul is a way of leading our consciousness. It is a way to ask yourself why it is so difficult, and in turn, to reverse the anti-myungsu so that the will of the soul is reflected in life. According to this law, we forgive the situation that caused us pain, forgive ourselves, and sometimes forgive God, and accept God's forgiveness. This is the principle of extinguishing anti-myungsu as a value of forgiveness. Forgiveness, therefore, is a higher-dimensional love that leads us to light.

Forgiveness is a high level of love in our relationships as well. Forgiveness, like sorriness, destroys hostility and guilt in relational karma. Although the effect is the same, forgiveness is high because sorriness is the solution to the cause and effect of hostility, but forgiveness is to be resolved by love not bound to causality. Forgiving others can free you from hostile feelings and start new relationships. So, it is always right for us to forgive all.

How can we always achieve the right forgiveness? The most obvious way is to benchmark God's forgiveness. God is all of us, and He is always forgiving everything. Forgiveness is always such a mind of God and is always presently in progress. God does not refuse to forgive us just because we took a long time to be penitent, nor is He being miserly with forgiveness just because our sins are too great or too much. God has already forgiven us even when we are not penitent with anti-myungsu. Our souls do not accept God's forgiveness, but choose the way of penitence for ourselves, and when it is done, we open ourselves to receive God's forgiveness.

So, the first condition of true forgiveness is always to forgive everything. True forgiveness, whether he reflects on his faults or not, forgives without regard to conditions for forgiveness. We are all one being, and the essence of all beings is love and part of God, so we are all worthy of forgiveness. Whatever fault the other person has, or how faulty the other person is, forgiving first is true forgiveness following God. To forgive in the first place makes you at peace.

But even if God's forgiveness is always present, it doesn't mean God just let it go as if nothing happened to it. God provides us with forgiveness and He also gives us the opportunity to find out what is wrong. When anti-myungsu occurs, God provides such opportunities by giving us the difficulty of separating the mind and soul. If they are not resolved and forgotten in memory, God continues to signal and gives us opportunities. Thus, He guides us to recognize ourselves, think again, and push the limits. God's forgiveness leads us to overcome our own limitations.

Therefore, the second condition of true forgiveness is giving the others the opportunity to recognize and rethink their fault. Our proverb says, "You may hate the sin, but do not hate the person." Forgiveness is all about being sincerely compassionate to the wrongdoers while at the same time giving the person a chance to be responsible for his fault. So, if someone deliberately cheated you, you can truly forgive him by being compassionate to him but while at the same time reporting him to the authority so that he has a chance to take his responsibility. If you are being compassionate to him but do not give him the opportunity to fulfill his responsibility, it is only a half-forgiveness that doesn't give him a chance to change. True forgiveness is about doing our best effort in the process of holding somebody accountable for his fault and remaining compassionate to the person till the last moment. Thus, it is the rationality of forgiveness that leads him to the path of transformation.

But the other person's fraud or theft may be the result of desperation, not intentional. We must distinguish well whether the fault is intentional or out of desperation, and it is compassion that makes us capable of distinguishing them. If you are sincerely compassionate to the person and want to forgive him, you can see the difference between intention and desperation. If he was intentional, you should lead him with an opportunity to take responsibility, but if he deceived you out of desperation, you should forgive him by embracing his desperation together. It is a form of true forgiveness that the priest embraced the desperation of Jean Valjean, telling others "This is what I gave him," when Jean Valjean was caught stealing something in *Les Misérables*. The forgiveness becomes the power to change Jean Valjean. When we are desperate, God is always with us and forgives and embraces our desperation. Those who have not forgotten this always grow while feeling God's forgiveness.

True forgiveness is the path that eventually leads the other and me to the light. When the other person does not know his or her fault, we give them the opportunity to take responsibility to know it, and when the other person falls into desperation, we embrace their desperation and save them with light. And we grow through that process. The key to forgiveness lies in growing in love. Only the pursuit of change with love is forgiveness as an absolute value.

So, in the process of forgiving, as we tolerate and wait patiently, the other person grows and changes, and so do we. In the movie *A Monster Calls*, there are adults who don't punish the boy who plays the leading role for committing a violent act due to the internal wounds. The main character boy asks, "Would you not punish me?" but, understanding that the child is having a hard time, the adult tells him, "What will it do if I punish you?" and covers up the boy's wrongdoing and forgives the boy. And the boy closes fierce inner conflict and gets up on his own.

In my youth, I used to rebel against my teacher, play mischief, and behave badly in a catechesis class. Nevertheless, the teachers always put up with me and waited for me. It seemed to me that thanks to that, I could believe Jesus' words – verbatim – that all things would be fine with love. The forgiveness I received as a child kept me from the confusion experienced in my adulthood. The process of understanding someone's fault, embracing it, and waiting for the person to change can be the process of forgiveness, because you grow with love by being sincerely compassionate to others, and that love becomes absorbed to others until it brings about changes in others.

If the process of tolerating and accepting does not change me or my partner, it is sadly not forgiveness. In this situation, forgiveness can rather happen by being honest and pouring out your pain and troubling emotions to the other person, so that he will have an opportunity to look back on himself while you relieve the pain of your wounds. This is a forgiveness as an absolute value because I am less sick, and he achieves a growth into love. The process of releasing my pain can be a forgiveness, as long as you always have the heart to embrace the other person. If I open my pain and communicate honestly, I can find his pain that I could not find and accept it and forgive it. You can forgive while accepting it. You can forgive him and embrace his efforts if he sees your pain and tries to change anything. If you try to endure him or no matter how your patience runs out and you reveal your emotions, and if he doesn't show any sign of making efforts to change, respecting his choice and liberating yourself by leaving him can be forgiveness. Forgiveness always leads to a change of love.

There is a society in our humanity that realizes this true forgiveness. It is the prison system in Northern Europe. For members of society in Northern Europe it is agreed that it would be natural to forgive offenders. It provides a healthy welfare environment for criminals who are separated from the world to ensure their maximum human rights and to look back on themselves. If they couldn't forgive these offenders, it would be impossible for them to even think of providing them with comfortable facilities where they could find new opportunities while being separated from the society.

Occasionally, when Nordic prisons are introduced to us through media reports, we often see people leaving comments on their replies to the reports, pointing out the comfort of their welfare facilities and questioning, "What's the point of sending them to a prison?" It is a testimony that forgiveness of criminals is not common in our society. In fact, a prison is not really meant to be a facility intended only for punishing criminals. Prison is a civilization of mankind that reflects the absolute value of the third chakra, and it is where criminals are expected to come closer to their truth while being separated from the society where they'd committed their crimes. For that reason, the prisons in Northern Europe are a social system where the absolute value of analysis-integration and the absolute value of forgiveness are realized. Forgiveness that is given naturally in Nordic society is the driving force for criminals' reformation. The world's lowest recidivism rate is the natural effect of forgiveness.

True forgiveness makes me peaceful and gives the best opportunity for me and others to change. I sincerely support you to forgive all those who have wronged you with the heart praying for your peace. With a heart of blessing for changes to happen to those who have done wrong, I hope you will muster the courage and generosity to provide them with opportunities for penance. If you have any anti-myungsu remaining, I sincerely wish you to extinguish it all with the power of penitence and forgiveness for your splendid expansion. I pray that you truly forgive and accept forgiveness and fill your eighth chakra with light. Thus, in the greatness of the eighth chakra, dreaming you'd be full of the infinite insights of soul, I await the day when we look after God and forgiveness will happen naturally in us.

The Sacred Boundary of the Eighth Chakra

This is the sacred boundary that protects the eighth chakra with the power of Hon, Baek, Shin, Ui, and Ji as a value of forgiveness. If you read this prayer for your expansion, the eighth chakra will freely communicate with the universe and give you peace. Share this prayer with you when you struggle to be free from anti-myungsu. Please read it as if you are all the others who you want to forgive and be forgiven. It will increase the power of true forgiveness between you and them.

(1) Forgiveness
* Looking back on my life, there are moments that I regret that constantly recur to me.
Would things be different if I made different choices back then?
I now wish to overcome the fear that pressed me back then.

The difficulties today are opportunities to let go of the regrets of past lives.
By accepting such difficulties as the fault of my own and forgiving them,
I make better choices with a firm and courageous heart.

All the choices I made in the past were the best I could within my limits.
That is why I overcome my limits each moment,
and hope to make the best choices that I will not regret.

* We face tasks and people in this life we instinctively dislike,
because of the karmas we did not forgive in the past lives we do not remember.
The instinctive attacks made in such situations were the revelation of the pain of past lives.

It is the laws of the cyclic universe that we once again have the opportunity to forgive and therefore,
heaven only wants us to forgive and become free,
but we did not know this and reacted to those situations aggressively.

It would take quite a while to soothe the pain of the past lives if we chose instinctive revenge.
But if we generously forgive, we'll soon learn that we become comfortable.
Feel the peace relieved from the pain of past lives by forgiving the repulsion you feel today.

* Forgiving the pain of the past relieves us,
so forgive with the love you have for yourself for your own happiness,
so that the happiness of forgiving is revealed to the world as your light...

The hardships today were given to you as you can overcome them,
so forgive everyone as befits your true abilities.
Express your greatness and beauty by forgiving.

As we are beings rejoicing in and ultimately capable of forgiveness,
it is only appropriate that we forgive everything.
In the end, we grow into beings that forgive everything like God.

* I will now forgive those who hurt me.
Sympathizing with their internal pain of hurting others,
wishing that they do not make the same faults, I forgive them.

There are people who offended me but did not apologize,
but I understand that those are their limits, the best they can do,
I truly feel sorry for their inability to apologize and forgive them.

We all have different standards in life,
but we are ultimately walking on the same path,
I understand that they are just like me at a specific moment in
eternity and forgive them.

(2) Forgiven
* I regret making my own life tough to live
by not reflecting on the causality of life, remaining complacent,
repeating the same faults and mistakes, undergoing the same
kind of difficulties, and receive forgiveness.

Since the spirit we bring to our lives does not create harmony,
please realize that life balance has not been made,
complement the lack, remove the excess and get forgiven.

By actively correcting my faults,
and pursuing a harmonious life so as not to go too far or fall
short,
I wish you a peaceful life forgiven about everything from life.

* We face unexpected misery and pain in this life,
because of the unforgiven karmas of our past lives we do not
remember.
Through undeserved hardships, the faults of the past lives were
forgiven.

Since regaining the opportunity to be forgiven is the rule of the
cyclic universe,
heaven only wants us to be forgiven and be free,
but we fail to recognize this and suffered at the coincidental
misfortune.

It will take quite a while to be forgiven for all the faults of the
past lives with today's suffering,

if you sympathize with the people who hurt you and the situation, you'll soon feel comfortable.
I truly hope you are forgiven with sympathy after apologizing for the faults of the past and become peaceful.

* I reflect on being stingy with forgiveness while reproaching my fault,
ignoring them and remaining stingy at admitting my faults,
and expressing the distorted self trapped in the sense of guilt or shamelessness.

From now on, I start shaping myself so that I am suitable for forgiveness
by admitting my mistakes and faults,
while generously forgiving faults based on faith in my possibilities.

In the future, I shall always reflect on my faults, forgive myself, and live so as to be worthy of forgiveness,
I shall present to myself the peace of overcoming my limits.

* I reflect on the foolishness of ignoring the people I hurt,
refusing to apologize by not admitting my faults,
and thereby, not being forgiven.

Even if I did not have the intentions,
they could have been hurt by my words and acts.
Let us muster the courage to be forgiven with sincere apologies.

If we sincerely apologize and receive forgiveness, we will feel very relieved.
Others' pain will be healed, I will be relieved of resentment and frustration,
and you'll think you were right to apologize.

(3) Integration of Forgiveness – Us – Forgiven

* I have been generously forgiven for quite a lot of faults and mistakes,

and generously forgave someone else's faults and mistakes,

I feel very fortunate about the peace achieved by our forgiveness to date.

Remembering the faults of mine that are unforgiven until today,

soothing the pain that still did not forgive,

for the peace I have yet to achieve, I take on challenges beyond the limit.

Ultimately, I do not resist forgiving anymore,

I am forgiven about everything,

and so I sincerely congratulate us on our complete peace.

1) Forgiveness in the Movie *Secret Sunshine*[16]

A question was asked to the audience in the movie *Secret Sunshine*. What if the perpetrator who harassed me received God's forgiveness without my forgiveness? In summary, the protagonist suffers after losing her son to a murder, until she was afflicted and rose with the power of religion and went to forgive the killer. The killer, on the other hand, says with a calm look that he repented with tears and was forgiven by God. The main character curses heaven and breaks down. I want to analyze this painful hypothetical setting in light of the generation and destruction of anti-myungsu and the weight of karma entangled in a human being that I'd experienced. Analyzing this may feel like a lack of humanity (less human). Nevertheless, I can say with confidence that what I realized about anti-myungsu and also about karma was possible because of my humanity. If this is a bit unfamiliar, please read it generously

To guess the killer's anti-myungsu, the denial that cursed the world and decided to abduct, the falsity that deceived the child in the process of kidnapping, the hated murder, and the irresponsible anti-myungsu of having forsaken the responsibility of protecting the child as an adult would all have occurred. Nevertheless, the killer was able to be calm because he was really forgiven by God. The process of sincere repentance before God opens up one's soul to accept God's forgiveness, which is always given. It makes its existence peaceful.

This does not mean that all the murdered karma disappears. The anti-myungsu of God's agreement has been extinguished, but the physical karma that has brutally damaged life is linked to this world and the dead child, and the wounds of the heart given to the dead child remain. In addition, there is a karma in the hurt and life of the protagonist who suffers the loss of a child, and a new karma in Hon and Baek, which in turn hurts the protagonist who tried to forgive him. And the pain greatly distorted the life of the protagonist, and the physical karma between the two was aggravated, and the karma that disturbed the way of forgiveness would be connected with the world.

In conclusion, to God, to those involved, to the world, these three directions of karma are conditions of life that can be happy only if the soul of the killer takes time to resolve itself. And finally, God and the soul of the killer would again judge, saying first that he was forgiven without apologizing to the protagonist who suffered his crime. Forgetting the sorriness for the victim is the loss of the essence of last repentance, forming a false and irresponsible anti-myungsu in his heart. Because he made a repentance before God false and threw away the responsibility to apologize. The film does not reveal what happened to the killer after the interview with the protagonist, but perhaps he would again suffer psychological distress from anti-myungsu and realize how to accept God's forgiveness again.

And the heroin, who suffers from the anti-myungsu of the curse of heaven, can destroy the anti-myungsu with a small hope. The soul opens oneself and accepts God's forgiveness, which is always given by the desire at least to be happy, to love, or to be loved, without forgiving the killer. It can be so peaceful.

This is the reasoning I realized as a process by which I have made and solved anti-myungsu, and a process that solved karma that came to me. Our karma is connected in three directions with God, the world, and others. The mental karma with God is myungsu and anti-myungsu. The whole process of my myungsu expansion, anti-myungsu creation, and extinction is achieved by the agreement of my soul and God. The physical karma with God is the genes of each and the inescapable fate and Saju[17]. These physical karmas are the best condition for my soul to relieve all karma in this life.

It is divided into two karma which are connected with other souls with mind and life. The wound of the heart becomes the karma that binds each other's hearts, and the conveying love becomes the karma that connects light to each other's hearts. What harms life becomes karma that binds each other's life, and what benefits our life becomes karma that connects light to each other's life. The karma connected to the world is also divided into the group consciousness (consciousness + unconsciousness) that creates the world and the karma connected to the physical world, which are further divided into the karma that connects the redeeming karma with the light. Wherever the karma heads, the karma of darkness redeems our souls, and the karma of light frees our souls.

Either my actions or my heart, this universe records everything. Since God is all of us, happiness opens up, giving us the opportunity to be forgiven and repay debts to everyone involved in the pain I have made. Karma does not just perish because God fully respects us. It is God's love to always forgive, wait for respect, and give us the opportunity to be happy. Since God is the God who creates and presides over everything, and I am the god who creates my karma and presides over me, the love between god and God now unfolds in our way of life.

Endnotes

16   *Secret Sunshine*: a Korean movie released in 2007. The leading actress won the best actress award at the Cannes film festival.

17   Saju: Saju refers to the time, date, month, and year of birth. It is used to tell the fate of the person in the East.

13. The Ninth Chakra: Blessing – Us – Being Blessed

The ninth chakra, the last to introduce, is a chakra that contains blessing. In the dictionary, "blessing" is defined as an act of wishing for and being glad about the happiness of another person or another person's future, or an act of praying for happiness and being glad for it and celebrating it. Being a value directed toward happiness, blessing is the highest value of love that is located at the highest of all chakras, and that is God's constant state of mind. God always wants us to be happy and He seeks our happiness.

Therefore, the goal of our lives is to be happy. It is not about getting rich or becoming a great person. It is about reaching the blessing that is at the top. Love is the meaning of our existence, and our only goal of life is happiness. We exist and live to be happy with love. Therefore, the most important proposition in our lives is: "Can I be happy with the love I choose?" As long as we are happy, we have achieved our goal.

However, the happiness in this case is not just about feeling good. We can laugh and be happy; we can cry in pain and still be happy; and we can be angry and happy at the same time. Happiness is a feeling of fulfillment that we feel when we are fully connected to ourselves, our lives, the Creator, the world, or someone. We feel fulfilled by connecting with ourselves when we shed tears of true comfort in times of sadness. We feel fulfilled through others when we witness injustice and express our solemn anger to stop the person committing the injustice and make the person repent for his wrongdoing. We feel exciting fulfillment just from having fun with a friend and think of something together simultaneously. We are that kind of being who becomes happy when we are connected to something or somebody through love.

Therefore, it's worth trying something even if it is hard and painful, so long as it makes us happy. Perhaps, we will grow and feel happiness in that pain. And it is also okay to let go of everything, if we cannot be happy no matter what. We will eventually find a new happiness despite any social prejudice and doubts. The Creator only wishes you to be happy, prays for you to be happy, and congratulates you on your happiness. Since happiness is our ultimate destination, blessing is the power that rules this world. Therefore, there is no being in the world that is not blessed. Every object and being contains God's blessing because nothing can exist as an exception without the will of the Creator.

I have explained the Hon-Baek-Shin-Ui-Ji and introduced absolute values so far because I wanted to guide you to the way to happiness with God's blessing. We feel happiness from time to time as we lead our lives. Sometimes we become lost and miss happiness, but soon we find our way and recover happiness again. This process repeats continuously. However, we can make happiness last if we understand mind and absolute values, because we can be happy when we realize absolute values with the power of our minds. That's how we build our myungsu and move forward toward our trinity, while remaining in blessing, which is God's constant state of mind.

In our daily lives, blessing manifests itself in the form of congratulation and well-wishing. Congratulating on birth and birthdays is a blessing on life and existence; a hundred-day praying for our child is a well-wishing for our child's happiness; and passionately cheering for our team in sports games is a blessing of victory we send to our team. Blessing also manifests itself in the form of commemoration. Our tradition of holding ancestral rites on the day of our ancestors' death is our blessing on our ancestors' past lives and well-being; commemorating our wedding anniversary is our blessing on the relationship we have with our spouse; commemorating the founding of our company or school is our blessing on that organization; and commemorating national holidays such as the National Foundation Day and Liberation Day are our blessing on history. Lovers celebrate their 100th day of dating to bless their relationship, and we celebrate a baby's 100th day and first birthday to bless the beginning of life and future life. We also hold a big feast to celebrate and commemorate special days such as a 100th day after birth, the first birthday, a wedding, and a 70th birthday, all of which are days that can be full of blessing in our lives. It is to get together to celebrate and commemorate those special days and shower those days with blessing. In this sense, funerals are also events that are meant for us to pour our blessing to those who have concluded their lives.

As such, mankind has been exchanging blessings, which is God's constant state of mind, by congratulating and making well-wising on special days. We have developed various cultures to earnestly give and receive blessings, and we have always exchanged many blessings at monumental moments in our lives. The blessings we have exchanged form a karma that fills the relationship between us with love. Blessings and gratitude are values that fill the space in the relative world that is surrounded not by love but by delusions, and blessing, in particular, is the driving force that helps our relationship to reach happiness and glory.

Therefore, I hope that, when we celebrate something, we put our earnest blessing into it instead of just taking it for granted. Let's cheer for the relationship of love by sending an earnest blessing on his birthday to fill the blessings he can shine for a year, and by earnestly blessing a couple and their relationship on their wedding anniversary. I hope you will not forget that blessing comes first before you criticize food at the wedding and the first birthday party you attend. Since these events are our civilization that has developed to fill this world with love,

I hope that we will fully appreciate the significance of those events.

Recently, however, the sincerity of blessings has become significantly tarnished as we care more about the format and financial aspects of big events that we celebrate. It is ironic that the more enriched our lives become, the more tarnished the significance of our big celebrations. Therefore, our blessings must be directed at daily routines instead of being directed only at our special days. Just like the way that God's constant state of mind is. When we bless each other in our daily routines, it would be the manifestation of our mind that wishes others to be even a little happier than they are now. And that is also an act of wishing for their happiness and benefiting the world. Therefore, the various thoughts and actions we do to wish for the happiness of others are a form of blessing, and even the various thoughts and actions we do for others to overcome their misfortunes are also a form of blessing.

It is a blessing to wish for a habitual thief to stop stealing from others, and it is also a blessing to wish for the one who has wounded you to stop hurting others. Let's bless the spouse who keeps snapping at you out of tiredness to take a good rest; congratulate a child who took his first step and stopped feeding from the bottle and say how proud you are of him; cheer and encourage your child not to forget his greatness when he is discouraged over bad school performance; help and bless your troubled coworker to persevere; bless and stop evil-doers so that they can stop committing evil acts; and build daily routines where we wish everyone around us to do better in their lives. Since blessing is the highest value of love, we can bless everything in every situation.

For that reason, the opposite of blessing is to believe others have no hope and cursing at them. We easily think of others as being hopeless, saying, "He has no chance to improve himself because he's hopeless," "I have no hope of getting better," or

"That person is sure to fail in business because he's being so unkind." These are a form of cursing. In general, we think that cursing is about having an elaborate ritual to harm somebody. But cursing is not always that extraordinary. Anything that is clearly the opposite of blessing is a curse. The curse that you hold on someone is passed on to the person's unconsciousness and feeds on the person's power to become happy, while feeding on your own energy of the 9th chakra and putting a curse on you as well.

So, we must live while staying alert in order not to hold a curse in heart. Curses that you hold without you even realizing are gnawing at your happiness. "That pathetic loser never tries to do anything, and anybody can tell how much he'll suffer from numerous errors and trials going forward. I hope those sufferings will help things get better, but who knows...", "How can they run a business while being so rude and unkind like this? They should experience losing customers to learn a lesson", "How the hell is it possible that nothing that I do ever works out? Perhaps I'm destined to have luck in the later years of my life. I am determined to persevere until then." These cannot be exactly defined as blessings, but at least they show how you control your mind so that you don't hold curses on others at least.

Thinking that all existences are in the process of growing helps to avoid curses and keep blessings. No matter how pathetic and evil a person is, and no matter what situation we are in at the moment, we are all beings that are infinitely growing in the time of the universe, we are all in a different stage of growth, and we are going through a different process of trial and error in our growth. There is no one who does not change, and there is no one who does not grow. We can keep our happiness by blessing growth with that belief in mind.

Blessing is the highest concept along with all love. Therefore, it embraces our everything from the top of our chakras. Neptune, the planet of blessing, also orbits farthest in our solar system while embracing all the planets in the solar system as well. God the Creator being us all, He always blesses everything, and there is nothing that is out of His blessing, and there is no moment that does not hold His blessing. Blessing is the highest point of absolute values that is there in every moment.

You might suspect that, if God blesses every moment, is God's blessing really in the pain of life? Can you say that there was really a blessing from God in the moment you were sexually assaulted? Is it really possible for God's blessing to be in the pain of losing one's child in an accident? Can a permanent disability really be God's blessing? If I say that God's blessing was with them even at such moments and occasions, it would make those who are barely living through the moment of pain and suffering feel betrayed by God. They'll say that you don't know because you haven't been through it. Such a reaction is so natural and correct. But those who forgave the moment of pain eventually discover God's blessing that was there in that moment.

There was a famous American boy named Matthew J.T. Stepanek who suffered from muscular dystrophy. The boy watched his brother and sister die of the same disease, and his mother, who was taking care of him, was also suffering from the same disease, and he himself suffered from the same disease until he died from it at the young age of 14. Matthew had realized his existential value as a person by writing poetry since he was three years old and left poems that convey courage, hope, and peace to us during the short 14 years of life. There's something he said in an interview.

I could have asked myself, "Why me?" But this is what I think. "Why shouldn't it be me?"

Thinking that it was okay because there was no reason it shouldn't have been him, Matthew truly forgave his life and forgave God. And he left us a collection of love poems, *Heartsongs*, while enjoying the glorious blessings he received.

Now there are countless tragedies and brutal crimes that are being committed on this planet, and there are countless people who are suffering from extreme pain as a result, and there are people who have to live a taxing life because of physical disability. I'm sorry and sorry again to tell them that the pain they suffer is enfolding God's blessing. Nevertheless, I say God's blessing is in many human sufferings, hoping that you will forgive me. I hope you will forgive your life and God who is all of us who have given you the pain, and I hope you will forgive me for daring to say such a thing to you while being somebody who is living a comfortable life. I sincerely hope that you will discover God's blessing that is given to you as your share through forgiveness, and I sincerely hope for everybody to enjoy it.

You can find the blessing if you forgive even a situation that you cannot accept as a blessing. Given that, the difficulties that we experience commonly in our daily lives are blessings without a doubt. When we look back on the past in our respective lives, we realize all those troubled moments are left in our hearts as beautiful memories. Everything becomes our memories – the times when we had financial difficulties, or the times when we broke up with our first loves. We feel memories as a faint happiness because now we fully realize that the past was a blessing. After years later, we finally realize we were blessed in those days, even though we didn't realize it back then. The situations we experienced as a result of economic difficulties were happy daily routines, and that hardship was the blessing that made us stronger now. We now feel beauty and innocence from our past selves that were hurt and cried with the pain of failed love, and that pain was the blessing that made us grow up a notch.

Moreover, there are many people who bless the world through the pain of the past that cannot be considered a good memory. A good example is the case where victims of sexual assault take the lead in the initiatives designed to help prevent sex crimes and also help other victims heal. They try to make their pain disappear from this world while at the same time do something for the world to make a difference. They refuse to remain in the pain of the past, and instead they move on toward blessing. They live while blessing today with the pain of the past.

We realize today that things that happened in the past were blessings. And what happens today will probably be remembered tomorrow as a blessing. Even if it is not a memory, we will try hard to make it through today with today's blessing. Wouldn't it be better to just accept today's daily life as a blessing if today is the day we will accept as a blessing someday? We will be convinced and remain standing strong if we are thankful for the blessing of peace if today was a day of peaceful routines, persevere hardship believing that it is a blessing intended to make us strong if today was a day of hardship, and firmly believe that, if today was a painful day, we will eventually understand the meaning of its blessing someday. If we consciously and repeatedly acknowledge that everything that happens to us is a blessing, the gap between the times we feel the present blessing as a blessing narrows. Then one day, we will reach a point where how we feel about today becomes the same as how we feel about the memories of the past. We will feel the present pain while at the same time our hearts become soaked with the meaning of its blessing. We will live while fully feeling how all the processes we live in are blessings.

Blessing is the Creator's constant state of mind and the highest form of love. Therefore, the life that blesses other absolute values that make us experience love is the most perfect form of life. Let us celebrate birth and bless death, while rejoicing that we are given the energy and time to love. Let us bless the plants we grow at home, bless the ants' nest we see in the playground, and practice and take action on adding even a small amount of strength to protect this nature. Let us bless this planet by using things that are less harmful to nature and investing generously in things that are beneficial to nature, even if it costs a little more. The life and death we will bless are always around us, and there is no life we should not bless.

Let us help new parents become happy parents, bless children in puberty for their discovery of their true identity, and bless the self-realization of those who are with our nephews who had just taken their first step into society. Let us work while wishing for the prosperity of our workplace, do something to add strength to our children's schools and our neighborhood to develop a little more, and vote while blessing for the prosperity and development of our country. We always have the solidarity and companions to bless because we are always with someone, and there is no self-realization that should not be blessed.

Let us cheer for the process of separating ourselves from our daily lives, rejoice in communicating with each other, and bless our daily lives of discovering our wholesomeness. Let us leave messages and comments that benefit the world in social media, YouTube channels, and other websites. Let us root for the study of analysis and integration that sheds light on the truth of the world, and celebrate the achievement of literature, art, and science. Let's share our happiness with our competitors because we are all moving forward toward the same goal and let us compete with others while celebrating the paths that are different from the path we are pursuing. Since we always live in the pursuit and realization of our truth, blessings are always needed so that our truth can be love and joy.

Let us rejoice in the love we are sharing now, and let us pray that the hearts that cannot love now will be directed toward love. Let us bless our only wish that everyone only wants to love, and let us accept every opportunity in life as a blessing of love with that wish. Let us make every effort for religious reform, hoping that the religions that lead us with love will be reborn as a more wholesome love, while using and sharing countless knowledge and wealth in the world to love others. Let us do all this while wishing for us to remember and never forget in any moment that our only meaning is love...

Let us take heavy responsibility as a calling, and let us sincerely pray that we can become free by fulfilling our calling. Let us console the irresponsibility that blocks responsibility, overcome the compulsion that blocks freedom, and bless our lives. Let us give those who are tired with heavy responsibilities a blessing of rest, sincerely congratulate those who have fulfilled their calling, and bless those who are bored with freedom with new responsibilities. Let us add strength to social reform so that people can work more comfortably instead of accepting working hard as being normal and let us bravely challenge the way to become a society full of joy and fulfill its calling. There is no one in the world who has not given a calling, and there is no calling that should not be blessed.

Let us support and bless the feeling of sorrow and regret so that we can achieve world peace by sincerely apologizing and accepting apologies. Let us celebrate the gratitude we give and take, so that we can move forward to abundance and prosperity with gratitude. Let us earnestly pray for the whole process of forgiveness, so that we may eventually bless even the pain through forgiveness. Finally, I sincerely congratulate, bless, and pray for our happiness and the glory of this world.

We are the beings who wish to live while blessing every absolute value in our daily lives. The chakra structure that puts blessing at the top proves it. So, it's enough for us to take our blessings out of our heads to embrace our everything with blessings and to live while blessing our everything.

The Sacred Boundary of the 9th Chakra

This is the sacred boundary that protects the 9th chakra using the power of Hon-Baek-Shin-Ui-Ji with the value of blessing. If you read this prayer when you want your myungsu to expand, the 9th chakra will facilitate the expansion and healing while freely communicating with the universe. I ask you to read it with respect to all those you wish to bless and be blessed from, because then, the true blessing will be there forever between you and those people.

(1) Blessing

* So as to not let our lives of the past in vain,
repenting the faults of the past, blessing the efforts to date,
let us feel happy for the lives that we are shaping today.

So as to not cower before worries about the future,
while preparing for the worst case scenarios and designing optimal outcomes,
let us live a life faithful to what can be done today.

This moment is a miraculous moment in which everything is possible.
Since we can create a meaningful past and future with the choice we make today,
let us shape genuine happiness faithful to this moment.

* I would like to congratulate us on the growth we achieved in the past life.
Since our growth further glorified God,
I bless God with our growth.

Even today, we strive to love in our life.

The rules of the universe are shaped only for the purpose of love,
I would like to bless this world with the karma of love I create.

God the Creator of this universe is always waiting for our blessing.
Therefore, I shall continue to shape the karma of love and never cease to grow,
to achieve happiness that will eventually add to God's glory and the creation of peace in the universe.

* Losing our true selves because of the many wounds in life,
but with the blessing of self-love that continuously consoles and cares for ourselves,
we have been protecting and healing ourselves.

That is how we arm ourselves with the blessing of self-esteem,
bring out our light into the world,
and further brighten the world.

With self-love which heals me and self-esteem which protects me,
I continue to discover the greatness and holiness I hold,
and so I simply bless the infinite possibility I have that will light up the world.

* I am truly sorry to those I could not wish the best luck to among my past relationships.
I made the hasty conclusion that things will not go well for them,
and I truly regret cursing them, which is the opposite of blessing.

Those who I could not understand must simply want happiness like me.

As desperate as I am in wanting my own happiness based on
my choice,
I truly hope they become happy with their choices.

Since we are all existences of infinite possibilities,
we do not know how someone would grow and change.
That is why I hope glorious growth makes everyone happy.

(2) Being Blessed
* Looking back, I have been provided with much opportunities.
There were opportunities of fortune and opportunities of
misfortune,
and I only regret failing to fulfill the meaning of blessing in
such opportunities.

The opportunity I have today is a blessing too good to lose.
If I do not do anything, this opportunity will be of no use,
so I accept the blessing of life by enduring and attempting at
everything.

We are creating the opportunity for tomorrow with the practices
of today.
Tomorrow's opportunities will be just right for the choice I
make today,
and shaping my own life as such is a true blessing.

* Making efforts to identify the logic that is appropriate for
myself,
and selecting the right path in my life to be blessed,
will guide me toward living a life of predestined happiness.

We were blessed to receive only love and respect from God,
we can wholly experience love with such blessing,
and enjoy the blessing of expanding the existence (myungsu).

We are a part of God as it was in the beginning, and now, and ever shall be, world without end,
with his truth, emitting his light, and since we are his life,
we rejoice in the fact that God's divine protection and blessing are always with us.

* I regret failing to recognize the light in me and thus,
was busy trying to hide it,
not being able to be confident about the blessings that were in my way.

The light I have is the existential essence bestowed by God,
and my darkness is the space of possibilities in which I can expand,
and my light increases the possibilities to disclose my true self.

My true self that was revealed brightly fills the inside with joy,
and creates delight that brightly lights the world,
so I transform everything that comes to me into blessing with joy and delight.

* I have been blessed from many in the past.
Thanks to the people who pointed out my faults and guided me toward the good path,
I was able to create better changes.

Even today, I am blessed by many.
In the comforts, praises and encouragement that things will go well,
I muster strength and grow.

I am where I am today thanks to the blessings from many.
I would not have been able to be this happy alone.
I sincerely thank everyone who blessed me in any way.

(3) Integration of Blessing – Us – Being Blessed

* Looking back at the kind of blessings I received,
and what kind of blessings I delivered and left to others,
I feel happy, fortunate and good for all the happiness I fulfilled.

Reflecting on what kind of blessing I failed to deliver
and what kind of blessings that I received but failed to recognize,
for the happiness I could not open, I take on challenges beyond
the limit.

Ultimately, accepting everything in life as a journey toward
happiness,
it is only right and just to bless everything,
and so I truly congratulate the existence of happiness around
us at all times.

14. Sorriness – Thankfulness – Forgiveness – Blessing: Relational Karma

The five values of the lower chakras are the values that design life, while the four values of the upper chakras are the values that exchange and fill the world. Sorriness and forgiveness achieve peace by healing the pains of the world, and thankfulness and blessings fill bountiful prosperity and brilliant glory. Therefore, sorriness, thankfulness, forgiveness, and blessings determine the relationship karma that exists between us. And as I said before, the space between you and me being the space of everybody, anyone other than directly involved parties can create a new relationship karma. So it is effective to use this when praying for someone or for the world. For example, if we are praying to resolve political conflicts in our society, it is difficult to pray for conservative rightists and progressive leftists – who have been deeply conflicting with each other over the past 50 years – to change, because we cannot violate their free will. But the conflict between progressives and conservatives can be changed. You can change their conflict by gathering the hearts of more people than the involved parties to resolve the negative karma between them and linking them to the positive karma.

So, the key to prayer for world peace is to target the conflict. We can change the karma between them by delivering prayer to the other group by standing in the position of one group in a conflict relationship, and by delivering prayer to this group by standing in the position of the other group. The karma between them can be transformed when we deliver sorriness and thankfulness to each group by standing in each of the involved party's position and collecting many hearts that send forgiveness and blessing to them until their power becomes stronger than the power of those groups. And then the changed relational karma becomes the power to evolve the world.

It may seem awkward at first to stand in the position of some other group, but it is absolutely possible by starting with remembering those who are close to us, such as family, friends, and neighbors, and also by remembering how they are the same people as us, and therefore the same mankind. It surely is possible because we have been one being from the beginning of time.

In the past 50 years, conflicts that left wounds on each other have been deepening between the progressives and the conservatives. The conflict between the stubborn conservatives and the radical progressives must be healed in order for us to prevent this conflict reaching the confrontation that we have seen in history between the political factions known as Western and Southern People[18], which ultimately brought down the Joseon dynasty itself. For this reason, I want to share and recommend prayers for a new relationship karma between them. Those who belong to these political camps might find it difficult to agree to these prayers. However, I believe that there are many moderates who truly feel sad about the political situation of this country and generously embrace the minds of each political camp. And I also believe that there are quite a lot of open-minded people in both the progressive and conservative camps. I hope that they will gather their hearts and heal the space where this conflict has left wounds.

I dedicate This to the Respectful Conservative Elderlies

* I send my words of comfort to the pain and limitations you must have felt when you had to choose only one way under the pressure of totalitarianism after the war. I want to express how sorry I am for the historical pain that made it difficult for you to see various possibilities while being trapped in one choice.

I thank you for having achieved the evolution of the world with firm commitment and by never giving up while unfolding your glory, and having passed on a world to us, where we can now see various possibilities.

I sincerely hope that you will overcome the historical limitations left by the war, and free choices will be with you as a blessing in the future. I also bless you so that you can enjoy the freedom of making political choices, so that you won't be trapped in totalitarianism ever again.

* I apologize for mistakenly thinking that your greatness has been tarnished due to the corruption committed by the conservative regime, and I sincerely ask for your forgiveness.

I remember the history where your brilliant light has become the light of the world, and I am thankful for that. I hereby send my grateful blessing so that your great light will continue to light up the world, and I hope that you will be the light of the world till the end.

* Please realize that, when we dream of reform, our hearts are the same as the hearts you add when you wanted to develop the world during the past history, and please recall your past days and bless the reform we are dreaming of today.

I would appreciate it if you can send us affectionate blessings so that we can achieve what we dream just like you did in the past.

I dedicate This to the Respectful Progressive Leftist Generation

* I apologize with my heartfelt regret for the despair and anger you must have felt when others blocked your opportunities while accusing you of being "commies" by mistaking your challenge and hope for the changes in the world for being totalitarian.

Nevertheless, you challenged us older generations with tireless commitment and gave us an opportunity to break away from totalitarianism. I am thankful to you for that.

Sincerely hoping that you will keep moving forward with a freedom that will not let you be trapped in current experience and thoughts, I am sending you my blessings.

* I send my words of comfort to you and ask for your forgiveness for the barriers we have created so that you could not overcome those barriers and your challenges repeatedly failed, weakening your hopes during the process.

Accepting how we, who live together with you, really need your commitment to reforming the world, I want to thank you for your willingness to challenge.

I hope that your will of reform will be empowered, like us who never gave up.

* Believe that the reform you are trying to practice with love is reflecting the same commitment we had to keep love from the horrors of the war, I send you blessing with gratitude to your efforts of love.

And I would appreciate it if you send us the blessing of love by considering the repetition of history that what we are today could be what you will be in your future.

* God, who is all of us. I pray that you will fill the gap between all those who are heartbroken due to the political realities of this country with such apologies, forgiveness, thankfulness, and blessings.

There are countries on this planet that are struggling with political conflicts like we are, and some countries are struggling in pain due to the deepening conflicts that escalate into civil war. I sincerely ask you to join to pray in order to send apologies and forgiveness to the pains that exist among them, and to add the power of peace in that space.

The civil war in Syria began when the dictatorial regime oppressed the people's aspirations for democracy, but when the religious conflicts in the Arab region brewed and exploded, it changed into the skirmish between the Sunnis and the Shi'a clans. The Shi'ite-regime, the Syrian government, defines rebels as radical groups, but these rebels represent the Sunnis, the majority group in the country, and the territory is mostly seized by the Islamic State, which is mostly Sunni who took the civil war as an opportunity. In the Arab region, confusion inevitably recurs in the course of social evolution, and during this time of confusion, two religious groups conflict with each other, persecuting and slaughtering each other, thereby hindering social evolution. In this way, the karma between the two religious groups is steadfastly hindering evolution in the course of history. If this karma is resolved, the growth and peace of the Arab region will become strengthened. That will eventually bring peace to the nearest Europe, and open a road to peace for the entire world because the world will become free from terrorist threats.

Of course, conflict and confusion in the Arab region cannot be attributed only to the problem of hostile karma. There are tangled up physical karmas caused by war and massacre, and it is also a reflection of the collective consciousness created by society. However, when the relationship karma is resolved, the restrictive feeling of being pulled into each other can be eliminated, thereby creating a condition where they can evolve rather lightly. So, I recommend we send sorriness and forgiveness to the two religious groups whenever we come across the Arab situation on the news and on the internet and send our thankfulness and blessing on their behalf. I pray that the war will end, and peace will descend on the Arab region with the hearts raised by the whole human beings who come across the news about the Syrian civil war. I hope that humanity will continue to accumulate in this area and that miracles will happen.

First, let me briefly introduce the conflict between Shi'ites and Sunnis. This conflict has a long history of 1,400 years, so it has a complicated history. After the death of the founder of Islam, Muhammad, the country became divided into Shiite and Sunni due to the difference in their opinions about selecting a succeeding leader, caliph. The Shi'ite means 'Siat Ali' and it indicates a follower of Ali, and they only acknowledge Ali, Muhammad's own blood, as being authentic. The Sunni means the people who follow the practices of the Muslim community, and Sunni insisted on electing a leader by election. In the beginning, Sunni grabbed hegemony and elected four caliphs by election, but when his blood Ali became the caliph, Sunni became afraid that they would lose the hegemony. They carried out assassinations and operations against the Shi'ite, thereby signaling the hostile relationship between the two religious groups. Currently, the majority of Arabs are Sunni, and the Shi'ite are the mainstream in only a few countries, including Iran and Iraq. On the contrary, in Bahrain, more than half of the population are Shiites, while their political leaders are Sunni. For this reason, when Syria and Bahrain's domestic conflicts were added to the neighboring countries that were divided into Sunni and Shi'ite groups, the whole situation blew up into a civil war. The terror group ISIS that is a cause of concern these days is a militant group established by Sunnis who have been persecuted and harassed in Iran and Iraq where Shiites are the majority. I sincerely hope that you will join to pray for them with the minds of Shiite and also with the minds of Sunni. We can practice the wholeness where we can be both minds, because we are separated from them.

From Sunni to Shi'ite

I send my apology to you, who is Shi'ite.

I apologize for having failed to respect you in the will of Allah and having oppressed you as a minority.

I'm sorry for undermining your greatness who tried to keep your will while being pushed around as a minority.

I apologize for the retaliation committed by our fellow Sunni who had been persecuted in your land.

I sincerely apologize for the hardships of life you have experienced due to their retaliation.

I deeply regret the past history when we didn't love you as our Arabic brethren and rejected you.

Also, we forgive all of you who are Shi'ites.

We acknowledge the religious pursuit that is different from ours because we respect you with the will of Allah.

We forgive your thoughts of not noticing the greatness of us as we expand into the majority in the Arab region.

We forgive the persecution of life against us, Sunnis, who lived in your area.

We forgive the past history when you didn't love us as Arab brothers and rejected us.

Now we bless you who are Shiite.

In the will of Allah, we respect your religious beliefs and bless you to advance with dignity.

We send our blessing to the strength you have kept as the minority in the Arab region.

We sincerely wish for your happiness and well-being.

As Arab brothers, we bless you with our love.

From Shi'ite to Sunni

We send our apology to you, who are Sunni.

We apologize for not having respect for you in the will of Allah and having considered yours as a false religious belief.

We are sorry for not having recognized the greatness of you as you grow into the majority in Arab.

We sincerely apologize for the persecution of life that has been inflicted upon you who lived in our region.

We regret our history in which we did not love you as our Arab brothers and rejected you.

We also forgive you, who are Sunni.

With the will of Allah, we acknowledge your religious belief and we forgive you.

We forgive your thoughts that did not recognize the strength of us who survived as a minority.

We send forgiveness to you for the hardships of life we've experienced in the process of being pushed back into a minority.

We forgive the past history in which you did not love us as Arab brothers and rejected us.

Now we bless you, who are Sunni.

With the will of Allah, we respect and bless your religious belief.

We acknowledge and bless the greatness of you who have expanded into the majority in the Arab region.

We pray that you, Sunni, who belong to our society will have a happy and good life as well.

As your Arab brothers, we bless you with our love.

* Absolute Being (Allah), who is all of us and who is Shi'ite as well as Sunni. Please fully fill the gap between all those whose hearts are broken due to the religious conflicts in the Arab region with such apology, forgiveness, thankfulness and blessings.

I ask for forgiveness for writing this without knowing their specific pains as a third party who doesn't belong to Islamic culture. I was encouraged to write this because I believe there are many who will fill my shortcomings. I hope that this shared spirit will calm the rain and wind that is sweeping against the spirits of the Arab world and become the sun and the breeze that can warmly dry their wet and tangled souls.

Endnote

[18] Two political factions of the Joseon Dynasty, the Western and Southern People, are blamed for weakening national power by abusing their power for political revenge against each other.

15. Diagnosis of Nine Chakras

The nine chakras have their dominant areas in our mind and body. We can deduce the state of each chakra by checking the state of these dominant areas. For example, we can identify the first chakra by checking the state of the immune system and we can tell the fifth chakra is weak if somebody is having trouble due to ambivalent emotions. The physical problem is mainly caused as a response to the external appearance of a chakra, while the mental problem is mainly caused by the shallow depth of a chakra. And the color of chakra has the greatest effect on the body and mind.

I want to share the condition of my chakras here so that you can use it as a reference to diagnose your chakras. And you can tell what you lack in your life based on that condition. You can move forwards to become a more wholesome being by filling in what you are lacking.

First, my first chakra is weak. The first chakra dominates the immune system, and I had frequently cold symptoms as a child. Beginning from my mid-20s, I had suffered chronic allergic rhinitis symptoms, which continued to aggravate as I got older. After finding the purpose of life, my condition improved a lot and there is little discomfort in everyday life, but it is also allergic rhinitis that reacts first when my condition is not good. Looking back on my life, I realize I could not practice the preciousness of life well. I often bought flowers and plants only to abandon and kill them, and I did not fulfill my responsibility to love my pet animals. I was also rather indifferent to the birth and death of those around me. The fact that my first chakra is weak is the result of my past lives, not just this life, but even in this life, but I have lived without practicing well for life.

Besides, I am very weak in action. The behavioral ability in everyday routines is also weak, but in an emergency, it is worse.

In a gravely dangerous situation when my daughter almost fell from somewhere high as a toddler, I had an episode of tension immobilization that almost paralyzed my whole body and I could not move. All I could do was scream. Fortunately, the child was safe thanks to my other family member who rushed to us after hearing my scream, but I had to suffer from a guilty sense for a long time because I blamed myself for having frozen at a time when my child was in grave danger. This was an episode that showed me how my chakra was not deep.

But now, I try to use disposable products and detergents less, and I live deeply appreciating the beauty of life. I bless the gratefulness of life when I observe the beauty of nature, the softness of babies, and the elders who endure pain. My clinic being situated in the suburbs, I often come across roadkill animals. I send my comfort to their deaths and blessing for their rebirth, and I always pray for those whose job is to remove them to remember the beauty of life and to live courageously in the face of death. In this way, I grew my first chakra to improve my immunity and enhance my behavioral ability.

When I see patients, I realize there are quite a number of people who are suffering from allergic and autoimmune-related symptoms. All of these patients need to increase the power of their first chakra by practicing actions to value life while expanding their external growth. This is because the first chakra is the key to the fundamental treatment of immune-related disease. Also, those who have problems with their sexual sensibility must deepen the depth of their first chakra as well.

My second chakra is also rather weak. I think that of all my nine chakra, the second one is the weakest of all, and it's probably the smallest chakra of all as well in terms of all aspects of appearance, depth, and color. The basis for this diagnosis is my autonomic nervous system reaction and forgetfulness. My forgetfulness is so severe that there is no comparison to it. My forgetfulness made me ruin my works, be late for appointments, and caused me numerous other problems. My employees and family members who are around me must have experienced many inconveniences because of my forgetfulness. Fortunately, I don't have emotional bipolar tendency, but those who suffer from bipolar disorder should reconsider the value of individual - self-realization - solidarity.

My peripheral parasympathetic nerve reacts sensitively even in slightly cold weather, causing the blood vessels of the limbs to contract and become as cold as a sheet of ice. So, in the winter, I often find myself in an embarrassing situation where I am advised by my patients to take a herb medicine. Then I also easily develop the opposite sympathetic hyperplasia, which leads to a burning sensation due to fatigue. When I become nervous of being with others, the tension causes my sympathetic nerves to become hyperactive until my face turns red, the voice trembles, and the eyes become red. I do pretty well with presentation but the hyperactive sympathetic nerve is difficult to control. In my case, the autonomic neurological symptoms appear in a fluctuating manner in the cardiovascular system, but I often come across people who complain of the autonomic neurological symptoms such as excessive sweating. Other typical symptoms of the autonomic nervous system disorder include chill that follows sweat drying up too quickly even due to a gentle breeze, and an occasional sense of being sucked into the ground.

Looking back on my past, I realize I have a strong individualistic tendency, but I have not been good at sharing my thoughts with others at all. When meeting other people, I was often there with a feeling of floating around rather than being fully there and assimilating with them. I have a friend who is the opposite of me and actively participates in any gathering while being very social, but she also complains of the symptoms of autonomic nervous system disorder. Although she has great powers of solidarity, she cannot find a way of self-realization in it and does not realize her preciousness. Chakras cannot remain in good shape if one pursues only one side of an absolute value as well.

My third chakra is fairy big and healthy, but it also has a chronic regretful problem. First of all, I have rarely suffered from edema or swelling because I have such a good lymphatic circulation that I didn't even have swelling issues after childbirth. When the lymphatic circulation becomes weak, you often experience not only swelling, but also chronic myofascial pain, body aches, and headaches, but I quickly recover even when I develop muscular pain and I rarely suffer from flu because of circulation disorder. I occasionally experience headaches, but even then, I recover quickly. I had depression when I was in a desperate situation, but as soon as the situation was resolved, I quickly recovered. In fact, the more difficult it is to separate yourself from the situation, the easier it is to get yourself caught in pain and depression.

When I think about it, I had good concentration until I was a teenager, and when I was studying, I did pretty well on subjects that required classifying, dividing, and comprehensively figuring out conclusions. Even when developing a treatment, I have a good ability to put together various theories, and I am good at picking out the ancient oriental medicine theories and readjusting them into modern theories. And I lead my life believing that people are all similar. Perhaps that's because I have been growing my third chakra in good shape through numerous lives.

However, I have some issues with my ability to discern rather than my ability to concentrate, which makes me lose discernment and flutter in the early stages of some situations. In addition, I experience symptoms of circulatory disorders in the upper respiratory tract and pelvic cavity once every while, along with cramping pain behind the ear. Although I have no complaints about this level of symptoms, it seems to be telling me that I have less than perfect third chakra and its functions.

I was born with a weak fourth chakra, but this is the chakra that I have grown significantly in this life. The fourth chakra dominates the cardiovascular system, and in fact, I have had a clear sign of a low blood pressure problem since I was a child. My highest blood pressure was rarely over 100, and in childhood, I often felt dizzy due to orthostatic hypotension. The autonomic nervous system reacts more sensitively in the cardiovascular system than sweat, and it is also the effect of the fourth chakra that is smaller than others. High blood pressure, migraine due to vasospasm, vascular disease such as cluster headache, arteriosclerosis, and dementia and paralysis are also symptoms that are mostly affected by the fourth chakra. For that reason, the most important key to preventing dementia and paralysis in an aging society is to increase the power of the fourth chakra with love, hope, and faith.

When I was young, I had a lot of anxiety before taking tests. I studied harder because of this anxiety, but I remember that studying motivated by anxiety did not give me a sense of achievement. In addition, my propensity to regret past behavior due to the lack of my spontaneity had dominated my life up until my early 30s. I had some physical and mental difficulties because my fourth chakra was slightly weak in terms of its size and depth.

In this life, I kept growing the power of my fourth chakra with a strong belief that God the Creator always loves me. Later, I expanded my belief and believed that no existence is not enough to be loved. Thanks to that belief, I have almost no sign of hypotension now, and the symptoms of flare and redness caused by autonomic nerves have improved compared to the past. The spontaneity that shows while I see my patients has grown significantly, and I overcame the anxiety over life surprisingly well. Perhaps I've been doing well with the circulation of hope and love that has been initiated by faith.

I was born with the fifth chakra as healthy as my third chakra. Thanks to that, I have never had a hormonal disorder. The most common hormonal disorders known to us are hyperthyroidism, hypothyroidism, diabetes, and polycystic ovary syndrome. Fortunately, I have a regular menstrual cycle and it indicates I don't have a disorder in sex hormones, and even though I have nodules in the thyroid gland, this organ is also functioning normally. And diabetes is rare in my family history. Lately, hormonal diseases have been on the rise, perhaps as a result of society growing more complex and an increasing number of people fail to recognize their calling, find their responsibilities burdensome, and lose their freedom.

I am most thankful to the power of my fifth chakra because it gave me rich imagination. I am good and find it fun to put my imagination to trivial things and come up with hypothesis. I also find it amazing that as I grow older, and as my responsibilities grow stronger, my imagination is becoming richer.

In fact, I cannot say that I have done well to realize the values of responsibility, calling, and freedom throughout this life. First of all, the total amount of responsibilities given to me is not very large. I have only one child, and my parents have supported me for a long time, so my responsibility for life is very light. That is the reason it was not difficult for me to fulfill my responsibilities. Thanks to my light life responsibilities, I have the freedom to do almost anything I want to do. Perhaps I might have been given a free life in this life because I've worked hard to fulfill my responsibilities in my past lives, and thanks to that, I was given fun callings through the fifth chakra in this life.

What you must know regarding the fifth chakra is the ambivalent emotions. Whatever you do, there are always conflicting processes involved. Those with weak ambivalent emotions have a strong tendency to deny all other points if one point is correct. The person who thinks of only one possibility is one example of weaker fifth chakras. I like the bi-literalistic integration, and my experience tells me that even if I encounter a result that is contrary to what I had in the past, I easily accept the results from both the past and present. However, if you look around, you will see many people who deny the result of the past or neglect the result of the present when they are faced with a result that is the opposite of the result from the past. I feel sorry whenever I see how they lose one side completely.

However, if the fifth chakra becomes weaker than that of constraint, the power to select and decide something goes down to a level where it becomes ineffective. You cannot make any selection because you are afraid that you'll get yourself into a big trouble if you choose this or even choose that. Fear is a typical emotion that you get when you fail to integrate ambivalent emotions.

If the fifth chakra becomes so sick that this tendency reaches an extreme point, you may develop a tendency in which you become violent or emotionally disturbed until you start acting out recklessly. There are people who commit violent actions or emotional abuse and do something good again as if nothing had happened. When you see people like that, you are sure to feel that they control people as they like to, and they seem very evil. However, these are the people whose fifth chakra is so severely damaged that they can only develop two extreme ambivalent thoughts and they are not capable of integrating them in between at all. They are not capable of acknowledging that their extreme thoughts are hurting others. People whom we usually think to be evil are the ones whose fifth chakra is in a really bad shape.

I think I was born with a normal sixth chakra, but it is making a robust growth through this life. The sixth chakra is the most important chakra in the integration of body and mind, and I can't say confidently that I was born healthy because my natural balance is not good. But that doesn't mean that I was sick due to any serious imbalance, and it is hard to say it's a big problem because I sleep well at night. Besides, I can say that I've been quite healthy since I have been good in logically following causal relationship since I was a child, but on the other hand, I cannot definitively say that I've been healthy because it has not been easy for me to control anger.

The recent increase in people suffering from anger control disorder or committing unprovoked violent crimes indicates that there is an increasing number of people who have problems with their 6th chakra. As the number of people who need to apologize goes up, there are many people whose power of the 6th chakra is growing weaker. The sixth chakra being a chakra that comprehensively integrates mind and body, those who are unable to control themselves, both physically and physically, should reflect on the sorriness of their 6th chakra and practice appropriate actions.

The effect of the 6th Chakra on the physical body is revealed through the hypothalamus and pituitary hormone. But these hormones control the entire hormones in the body and, therefore, it is difficult to explain through a single symptom. However, there are two symptoms that I believe require the treatment and recovery of the 6th Chakra through my spiritual experiences. The first is sleep. When the energy of the 6th chakra needs supplementation, one requires more sleep. This is because the Hon(魂) goes out into the universe for a longer period of time to recover the 6th chakra. In addition, when energy confusion occurs in the 6th chakra, sleep disorder takes place. During this time, the Hon(魂) cannot go out into the universe, which aggravates emotional confusion. Sleep issues are a symptom that requires a lot of self-reflection. If the power of the 6th chakra recovers through self-reflection, sleep issues will be resolved naturally.

Another symptom is nocturia. Nocturia refers to the symptom of waking up in the middle of the night because of urination. When healthy, antiuretic hormone increases in the pituitary gland to reduce the amount of urination, and when the secretion of this hormone drops, nocturia takes place. Therefore, the repetition of nocturia is the symptom of the body with weakened 6th chakra due to hypopituitarism. As for myself, nocturia occurs when I do not realize what I ought to do. When I realize what I ought to do and practice it through self-reflection, nocturia miraculously disappears. In addition, nocturia comes naturally with aging. This is a natural aging process following the decrease in the secretion of hormones, and the weakening of the 6th chakra due to traumas piled up over a long period of time. Elderly is the time where self-reflection of looking back on one's life is required the most. Fierce self-reflection helps complete life well, and maintain the healthy functioning of the pituitary gland.

I was born with the seventh chakra in a fairy good shape. The seventh chakra that fills gratitude dominates the nervous system, and since I was young, I was pretty good at figuring out my surroundings and having good sense about what to do. Since the sixth chakra determines judgment on causal relationships, it is involved in rational reasoning, and the seventh chakra being there to determine overall judgment, it is involved in the decision-making power and good sense of surroundings. But when I was little, I didn't know how to really appreciate it. Rather, I was full of complaints and dissatisfaction. Even though I started to appreciate it only as I got older, I was able to keep my seventh chakra in good shape. I think it was the result of my previous lives. Perhaps in the beginning of this life, I might have lived while eroding the power of my healthy seventh chakra.

In addition, the development of the seventh chakra leads to the development of our mirror neuron system, which enhances the sympathetic and indirect experience abilities and enriches the sensibility of life. So, if your emotions are dry and your understanding is poor, you can overcome the problem with the value of gratitude. In addition, if you have neuron-related diseases such as dementia, Parkinson's disease, dystonia, schizophrenia, and behavioral disorders, it becomes easier to heal and manage them when they realize the value of gratitude.

I was also born with a healthy eighth chakra, which contains the value of forgiveness. As a child, when my mother was very angry with me, I was good at sincerely asking for forgiveness without attempting to give excuses. Sometimes that attitude resulted in more severe punishment for me. There was a time when I was on my knees asking for forgiveness with sincerity without trying to find out who was right and who was wrong when my misunderstanding put somebody in a difficult situation. That person turned himself around and became his original self after being touched by my sincerity. As I grew bigger, I noticed that I was really good at asking for forgiveness with sincerity compared to most others. There were times when I wondered if that was because I was being too submissive, but now, I know that it was the power of the eighth chakra.

Another moment I feel the power of the eighth chakra is when I quickly recognize my anti-myungsu. I easily can recognize anti-myungsu from my mental state and I rather quickly realize what has caused my anti-myungsu. And I'm good at finding out the meaning of why it's anti-myungsu for me. Thanks to this, I was able to speed up my expansion.

With this power of my eighth chakra, I was able to discover a way to treat physical disorders caused by anti-myungsu and I am using my discovery for treatment. I see many people who have difficulty in forgiving and being forgiven. The process of forgiveness and overcoming the difficulties remains as a force of the eighth chakra that never betrays and leads me to a path of happiness.

I was born with an ordinary ninth chakra, but I've grown it significantly recently. Myungsu expands quickly for those who have a large and healthy ninth chakra that contains the value of blessing. In the days when I was sharing my confirmation of myungsu with many people, I was able to see people growing at a particularly fast pace. These are the people with a very healthy ninth chakra, which oversees the expansion of the mind and soul. In my case, my speed of myungsu expansion is just average: it is not too fast or slow. However, since the completion of the first round of myungsu expansion, my myungsu expanded faster than before. I'd experienced how my insights into truth have improved to an unrecognizable level after my myungsu expanded in that way. It was the result of holding onto the value of blessing while weathering the storm that hit my life at the time. The process of blessing anything speeds up the expansion of the mind and soul.

Chakras contain all the love our souls have experienced for an eon of time. So, the condition of our chakras contains not only the results of this life but also of all lives we have lived through. Therefore, there is no reason to be disappointed in the present life just because they are weak now, nor to be proud of the present life just because they are healthy now. All you need to do is just know the present and see what you can do well, dream how you want to change your life, and take action to make it happen.

However, there is something you need to know in the process of understanding your chakra. Among the heavy karmas that keep our souls in the relative realm is the one connected between us and the world. The world we live in is being created by the power and actions of collective consciousness (consciousness

+ unconsciousness) that mankind has been accumulating for a long period of time. The collective consciousness that creates this world has been created by what we did, thought, and felt while living the many lives we have lived through. There are still many collective consciousnesses in the world that prevent absolute values from being realized. That is the reason we have life-threatening terrorism and murders, societies where people cannot fulfill their callings because freedom is suppressed, and revenge instead of forgiveness is widely prevalent. Many of these pains that exist in the world are the result of reflecting the collective consciousnesses that mankind has been accumulating.

Thus, the karma between us and the world is determined by what power we have added to the collective consciousness and behavior that creates the world. And the karma between us and the world is connected to our own chakras. In my process of expanding myungsu, I was able to grow the first and second chakras rather slowly and had experienced allergies and difficulties in expanding my social skills even though I grew my fourth and ninth chakras significantly with the same amount of effort, and the reason was because my karma that went against the values of the first and the second chakras was deeply intertwined with the world. That meant I was the one who had added power to the collective consciousness that treated life recklessly or abused lives at some point in my past life. Also, I was the one who sought selfish greed in a shared solidarity, suppressed individuality of others, or hindered people's concerted efforts to evolve the world.

Considering how my third chakra is well developed but is continuously causing chronic problems, I think I may have re-created heavy karma after achieving a big expansion. The karma that is connected to the third chakra has been distorting the truth of the world while being obsessed with the conditions of life or disrupting the cycle of becoming one through communication. Just like a racist. The karma that is connected to the fourth chakra is associated with interfering with spiritual purposes by breaking faith and desire for love. For example, it is similar to forcing a sense of original sin or inducing a war of good and evil. If it's the karma of fifth chakra, it may have something similar to suppressing freedom, interfering with calling, and imposing undue responsibility, or, on the contrary, abandoning responsibility, refusing calling, and turning freedom into hedonistic indulgence.

The pain of the sixth is probably the karma of having chosen brazenness over sorriness. Brazenness amplifies the pain of the world and hinders healing. The seventh might be the karma of having chosen arrogant greed and futility over gratitude, and of having created relative despondency and inequality to hinder affluence. The eighth is the karma of having chosen revenge rather than forgiveness, or having intentionally repeated it even though you knew it was wrong, consequently undermining the chance of forgiveness. In the nineth, the karma of having chosen curse over blessing could lead to darkness.

These karmas make it difficult for chakras to expand into lights despite our efforts. In order to grow freely, we must sincerely repent to the world for our past wrongdoings and try to pay off our debts to the world to resolve the karmas we have with the world. And the karmas that are connected to the world also go through the process of resolving all the pain before reaching the Trinity. Therefore, the faster myungsu expands, the faster we meet our karmas.

In general, we have thought that the results of having lived as good and hard-working beings are determined posthumously. The reality, however, is that the results of our lives are always a "work in progress," and they are reflected on our minds and spirits, as well as on our bodies and lives. I have lived my life with a weak immune system, and it was the result of my choice. My inability to trust people and share my thoughts made my autonomic nerves experience difficulties. Thanks to my efforts to believe in love, I was able to break free from low blood pressure and anxiety issues, and thanks to my efforts not to neglect my responsibilities, I became lucky enough to discover a fun calling.

There has never been a judgment over the practicing of religious teachings, and it does not happen after our death. It is going on currently and dominating us through chakras. Our souls, together with God the Creator, judge and dominate themselves at this moment. I have unfolded my nine chakras for you like this. Now, I want to ask you: How are your chakras doing?

16 Restoration of Chakra

The surface of our chakras is circling in a whirl. The direction and speed of the circling are determined by the karmas between us and the world. In the beginning of time, the soul was created to circulate in the direction of the natural way of chakras bearing love. The karmas that conform to absolute values strengthen the cycle further so that love can be embedded into chakras better. On the contrary, the karmas that go against absolute values become a force that circulates in a reverse direction, thereby slowing the speed of the circulation and reducing its range. As a result, growth becomes slow despite efforts to expand the chakras. But if the karmas that go against absolute values become bigger and the range of their reverse circulation expands, the light contained in the chakras can flow out and the interior can gradually become void. In the end, when most of the surface circulates in a reverse direction, we might experience the tragedy of not being able to recognize the love given to us at all, or not being able to hold any love at all. Even though this is a rare case.

Therefore, in order to restore the cycle of chakra, we must heal the karmas that we have with the world. The awakening shield of each chakra I have introduced earlier is protecting the chakra while expanding the depth and restoring internal circulation. And the way I am about to introduce you now can restore the surface of charkas back to the original cycle by resolving our karmas with the world. The karmas that are connected chakras are also divided into two groups, one associated with mind and the other associated with physical behaviors, just like relational karmas. First of all, a genuine apology and forgiveness are needed to resolve the karmas that are connected to our minds. However, it is easy to express our sincerity with regards to the karma of this life because we have memories of it, but it is difficult to express sympathy over what happened in previous lives because we don't remember them. As a result, it needs our imagination.

Looking back on the past history of mankind, many things have been done against absolute values as if they were nothing serious. It is us (our souls) of the past lives who had done all those things. We became what we are today after having expanded little by little due to reincarnation, but it's not that we are not those of the past. Therefore, studying history, reflecting on the regretful things of the past, and sympathizing with the pain of those days through movies and books is also a good way of healing the pain of collective consciousness over past wrongdoings. In addition, if we acknowledge and imagine that we are the ones who had caused the pain and apologize for it with empathy, we can heal the pain of the world more actively.

In my case, I apologize for the restoration of my personal chakra, but I tend to apologize and forgive both for the restoration of others' chakras. I apologize to the world that suffered pain on behalf of the responsible people, and forgive their limitations at the time when they had no choice but to do so on behalf of the world, with sorriness that sympathizes with the pain, and understanding the heavy weight of forgiveness...

To raise empathy, I imagine linking symptoms caused by chakras with absolute values. For example, my rhinitis has caused me to repeatedly experience lethargy and difficulty in conducting daily activities, so I think I have been doing things that caused pain and lethargy to life for a long time. Therefore, the inconvenience I suffer from rhinitis is the process of receiving physical forgiveness for that, and the act of actively treating the symptom is the process of my physical apology to the world. And the difficulties I faced in finding a publisher to work with me and making a colleague who will study my therapies together with me are the processes of being forgiven for the physical karma that made me distort the truth and disturb evolving together in solidarity, and my efforts to continue challenging despite those difficulties are a process of conveying my apologies.

Physical karma connected to the world can be resolved through physical pain. And this can also be resolved without physical pain. This karma came into being while causing harm to the world, and therefore, it can be resolved by giving out to the world. Those who strive to resolve their pain and do something good for the world end up resolving a huge amount of karma, and can escape pain. In addition, there are many instances where those who practice good deeds in daily life suffer less pain of physical karma. On the contrary, it is not easy for those who resent their destiny, shrieking why, to escape pain. If you face hardships with a mindset that is hard to be forgiven, you have to go through as much wounding as you have given the world.

All karmas are realized in the form of a retributive justice, which makes it possible for you to recognize your karma of your previous life based on your physical pain and hardship. The pain I suffer now is the pain I brought to the world in my previous lives. We deduct a substantial amount of physical karma through the body. Therefore, you can guess which physical karma your illness and symptoms are entangled with by figuring out how your disease and symptoms are closely connected to the physical responses of which chakra. For example, immune system-related diseases are connected to the first chakra; chronic pain, with the third chakra; and hormonal diseases, with the fifth chakra. And in the case of more serious incurable diseases like cancer and Parkinson's, many chakras are physically intertwined together. When you have the problem of life that is hard to resolve, you can understand it better if you think about what value it is connected to. You can break free from that hardship the fastest possible if you stop feeling resentful and feel grateful and sorry instead, all based on what you find from that process. In that way, you can solve both mental and physical karmas that are connected to the world.

Besides, since this karma exists in a space between you and the world, anyone who finds anyone's as well as yours can be involved. Practicing good deeds for someone and praying for the world can help resolve that person's physical karma. Praying for the world is an especially effective way that can be practiced wherever and whenever you want. Since the world is created by the power of collective subconsciousness, adding beneficial thoughts and emotions for the world to the collective subconsciousness counts as a good deed. Therefore, I recommend you to say this prayer of chakra, which adds more energy to the absolute values, for yourself or those who are suffering. If we reduce physical karma with the prayers of chakra, the collective subconsciousness that disturbs the absolute values will lose power, and we will be able to usher in a world where the absolute values are implemented.

However, it has to be a sympathy for the pain and never be a criticism of the past. Frankly, none of us are in a position to blame anyone. If you look into the chakra of each person, everyone is entangled with the karma of having pained the world. The beings that don't have this karma do not come to this world. Along with relational karma, karma that goes with the world is the gravity that makes us stand on our feet in the relative realm. There may be differences, and some may have more than others and some have less than others, but ultimately, the difference is not significant, and we don't know what kind of karma we've been building for an eon of time. Therefore, we cannot mindlessly criticize other people's karma.

Even if the law of karma is made up of retributive justice, nobody can tell you "Suck it up because it's all your fault" except yourself and God. No one else can decide or judge another person's karma. Your karma unfolds after being determined by a perfect agreement between yourself and God the Creator. So, you are the only person who can complain about your karma. Recklessly judging others' karma is to violate the free will of other souls, and it is also a blasphemy against God who unfolds the way.

The mind we can hold while looking at the karma of others is to bless the soul that has agreed to resolve it, and to be thankful for the person's efforts to endure hardship, because it is thanks to the person who resolves his or her karma that there is an opportunity to change the world, and we can get a better opportunity in the changed world. We are all evolving this world into a better place while resolving our karmas in that way. Therefore, with regards to the karmas of others, we must sympathize with each other's limitations that had to be that way and apologize and forgive the world that suffered pain as the consequence. With that mind, we can even restore someone else's chakra.

Also, restoring someone else's chakra is the fastest way to heal the physical karma connected between the other person and you as well. The relational karma connected to each other's lives can be resolved in any way that will improve the lives of the parties concerned. Restoring someone else's chakra is the way to restore the person's life. Besides, it is more effective than the Rosenthal effect. It demonstrates clear effect even if you try just once, because there is a space we know as relationship. Therefore, the physical relational karma can be quickly resolved. In our chakras, there is a way to solve various karmas at once.

Currently on Earth, there are numerous karmas that have been created at a time when we could not acknowledge human rights. People who live with lighter karmas should reach out with the hands of love to those who carry lots of karmas. Only then can the piles of karmas quickly resolve, and this Earth can evolve peacefully. I think that adding strength to their chakras even though they are continuously creating heavy karmas can be compared to using your next month's data in advance.

Advanced use to restore chakra is always justified because it is the law of the universe that, even though they are headed to the opposite of happiness at the moment, ultimately they are destined to head toward happiness in a certain future – sometime in their next life if not this one, and if not even in the next life, sometime in the life that comes after the next life.

Now, I will introduce a way to heal the pain of chakra more meticulously. As you might have expected, it is about thinking about the meaning of the five pillars of Hon, Baek, Shin, Ui, and Ji with regards to the pain caused to the world. All wounds can be healed without exception when you apologize and forgive the pains of all five pillars with regards to your pain and difficulties. Chakras can swirl in the direction of the righteous direction and become stronger if you connect the thankfulness and blessings of the world to each chakra in addition to it. When it comes to the restoration of chakra, the essence is to exchange sorriness and forgiveness with the world to heal counter-circulation and to exchange gratitude and blessing. Connecting to your current physical pain and imagining a happy future, I hope you will pray toward the world or the individual who will resolve karmas.

1) The Restoration of Each Chakra
(1) Birth – Life – Death

① Contriteness - Forgiveness
* Since I created or neglected miserable death and obsequious birth without dignity,
discriminated birth, got disappointed by death, lose the joy of life,
at the start and end of life, get exhausted by breeding difficulties, and left one alone so as to get the heart pierced by terrible loneliness...

Apologizing to the world for being cruel to the cycle of life as such,
I have been asking for forgiveness to the world with my life which endured the fear of life and death.

* Crushed the dignity of life, breaking the wholeness of nature, undermining vitality by being harsh on my body,
inflicting pain on other life rather than love,
trampling on the noble will to live or recover...
Apologizing to the world for causing violence and oppression to life as such,
I have been asking for forgiveness to the world with my physical pain.

* With God's will and the will of all lives in this world,
that allowed us to desperately seek ways to heal the pain of losing lives to illness,
consistently confirming that recovery takes place despite injury and exhaustion,
preventing causing harm to each other by growing compassion for life,
and extending life as generations are repeated,
the world has always been pitying and forgiving our heartless violence and cruelty of not caring for life and nature.

② Gratitude - Blessing
* Since glory and peace were achieved by protecting the dignity on the way to birth and death,
joy was not lost on the way to not only birth but also death,
creating stability and presenting cozy comfort at the beginning and end of life,
and was together with abundant love at the beginning and end of life...

That is how I have been blessing the world with my efforts for birth and death,
and I always feel grateful to the world for giving me the opportunity to be born and live.

* Since the value of life was blessed, the wholeness of nature followed,
greatness of life enjoyed by the good management of health,
love given to other lives,
and the noble will to live and recover blessed...
I have been blessing the world by caring for many lives,
and I feel grateful to all lives I was with on earth that helped me live.

* With God's will and the will of all lives in this world,
that create whole nature with the dignity of all lives,
allowing lives to evolve ever strongly through fierce competition for survival,
not easily giving up lives that are in pain and caring for them,
allowing them to become stronger as generations repeat,
the world has always thanked and blessed our efforts for birth, death and life.

(2) Individual – Self Realization – Solidarity

① Contriteness - Forgiveness

* Since it was a disgrace trampling on noble values and faith,
incitement of shame by oppressing confidence,
thoughtless refusal by rejecting others' unique characteristics,
and generation of lethargy by not allowing others to live by their characteristics...
Apologizing to the world for my ignorance that caused each other's loss of light,

and with difficulties that were neglected from my role, I have
been asking forgiveness to the world.

* Since the relationship was filled with doubt and betrayal and
not love,
lethargy presented by not being together but being alone,
and as such, each transformed into scattered grey,
and regression of the world made by breaking solidary with
selfishness...
Apologizing to the world for breaking solidary by stoking up
division,
I have been asking for forgiveness to the world with the
loneliness of being alone.

* With God's will and the will of all in this world,
that teach that it is easy to get neglected when one is not
confident about oneself,
intertwining fates so as to relieve misunderstanding and
distrust,
making one get involved in shameful deeds, when the direction
of life is lost,
preventing one to live a stable and comfortable daily life,
the world has always been pitying and forgiving out regress
while neglecting each other and getting scattered in different
directions.

② Gratitude - Blessing
* Opening the way to let honor shine with noble values and
faith,
having confidence and letting our unique characteristics shine,
providing assistance so that others' characteristics could shine
more brightly,
I have been lived joyfully and gloatingly day by day...

That is how we blessed the world based on mutual respect so that each other can shine,
and I feel grateful to this world for allowing me to reveal my existence value with my role.

* Overcoming doubts, filling relationships with belief and love of holding hands together,
establishing stability through fellowship,
becoming more brilliant in a stable fellowship,
hearts were gathered to help the world evolve to the next level...
I have been sending blessings to the world with my efforts of protecting and developing solidarity as such,
and I thank all relationships for giving me the opportunities to grow together.

* With God's will and the will of all in this world,
that help find one's special characteristics by doing what pleases oneself,
making one strive even more to gain others' recognition and support,
preventing one to become dissatisfied with things as usual as instructed and thereby,
helping one nurture honorable values and beliefs,
the world has always been thanking and blessing individuals' self-realization that shone ever brightly and the evolution of the world.

(3) Analysis – Communication – Synthesis

① Contriteness - Forgiveness
* Dignity was disgraced by getting trapped in the distortion about money and honor,
safety of existence at risk by getting trapped in the distortion about the body,

surrounding people pushed away by getting trapped in the distortion about materials,
and the will to live weakened by getting trapped in the distortion about work and rest…
That is why I apologized to the world for my distortion of truth as such,
and I have been asking for forgiveness to the world with the resentment of being misunderstood or not being understood.

* Misunderstood others without listening intently to others,
exaggerated or hid my story and enabled misunderstanding,
allowed my life to become aloof from the flow of the world,
and created misunderstandings and speculations in the world by distorting the truth and being deceived by lies….
That is why I apologized to the world for the communication difficulty I caused that disrupted the understanding of integration,
and I have been asking for forgiveness to the world with the difficulty of not being able to confess my story and having nobody listening to me.

* With God's will and the will of all in this world,
that prevents one from overcoming difficulties when one goes against God's will (the way the world works),
making one repeat mistakes when one fails to know accurately about oneself,
making one get deluded by having arbitrary judgments about others,
giving things to worry about until the misunderstanding and distortions of daily life are solved,
the world has always been pitying and forgiving our communication difficulties that created misunderstanding and distortions.

② Gratitude - Blessing

* Since dignity was pursued by having discernment of money and honor,
the joy of existence enjoyed by having discernment of body,
rewarding feeling and happiness created by having discernment of work and rest,
and the convenience and abundance of material discerningly used to share love....
I have been blessing the world with my analysis which revealed reasonable truth in details,
and feel grateful to the world that showed and informed me of various stories.

* Since principles of the world was realized through various experiences and learning,
understanding about others made while listening to others,
being understood from others by frankly telling them my stories,
and things learnt from the world practiced one by one in my life...
I have been blessing the world with my comprehensive thinking that pierces through the essence of various aspects,
and I felt fortunate to have the truth in the world that is making it function as one.

* With God's will and the will of all in this world,
that let one find happiness with joy and love when one follows God's will (the way the world works),
making one learn accurately about oneself while constantly going through disappointment and confidence,
making one ask others and not fall into delusion and thereby,
understanding and solving the problems of daily life.
The world has always been rejoicing and congratulating us for our revelation of concrete truth and comprehensive essence through our communication.

(4) Faith – Hope – Love

① Contriteness - Forgiveness

* Not believing in God's love because of the misunderstanding that heaven punishes us,
based on mistrust that unjust evil prevails in the world,
believing that all my efforts are useless,
not having confidence about myself because of mistrust,
and did not love because of doubt that others have dark desires...
I have been apologizing to the world for my mistrust that blocked the road to love
and asking for forgiveness with situations where I could not be trusted and I was suspicious.

* Not knowing God's omnipotent love and rather blaming him, getting easily disappointed about myself because of failure to see my potential,
not giving love to others because of disappointment from unreasonable expectations,
and lived loosely without making any efforts with disappointment in my life and the world...
I have been apologizing to the world for my disappointment (despair) that undermined love
and asking for forgiveness with situations where I had to endure the continuous disappointment (despair).

* With God's will and the will of all in this world,
that makes one lose the purpose of life and stray when one doubts God,
making one not want to live when one can't even die when desire for life is lost,
making one unable to love anyone properly when one does not love oneself,

making one long to be loved by somebody in loneliness,
the world has always been pitying and forgiving us who could
not love properly while failing to trust and getting disappointed.

② Gratitude - Blessing

* Believing that God does not punish but loves us,
believing in the reasonable rules of life and the world,
believing that someday, my efforts will bear fruit,
believing and loving myself for my good will and best efforts,
I also believed that others were doing best with good will...
I have been blessing the world as such with my faith of protecting
love,
and I thank this world for having trusted me.

* Not losing hope by relying on God's omnipotent love,
having hope about myself based on my potential,
growing love based on hope that the opponent does the efforts,
I have consistently made efforts, with hope about life and the
world and waited for my chance....
I have been blessing the world with the hope I nourished,
and thank this world for having showed me hope.

* With God's will and the will of all in this world,
that make one feel God's love the more it pursues the purpose
of existence,
making it all the more fun to live when one cherishes one's own
life,
making one love someone else more the more one loves oneself,
and allowing a life being loved by others,
the world has always been touched and blessing us for all our
efforts made while having faith and dreams in love.

(5) Responsibility – Calling – Freedom

① Contriteness - Forgiveness

* Since I felt irritated for the responsibility of daily routines,
threw away the fateful meaning of the responsibilities given to me,
gave up saying it's not my business,
and ignored the subject of responsibilities...
Apologizing to the world for my irresponsibility of making the world a tough place,
I have been asking for forgiveness to the world with my heavy and burdened life.

* Since freedom of daily life was restricted and bound by unjust format,
freedom to express one's thoughts and emotions oppressed,
the freedom to love to one's heart's content blocked,
the type and methods of mission strictly restricted and interrupted...
Apologizing to the world for my obsession that made the world a difficult place,
I have been asking for forgiveness to the world with my life in which freedom is being oppressed.

* With God's will and the will of all in this world,
that make one not wish to work the more one procrastinates and make work pile up,
making it hard for one to withstand difficulties without responsibility for someone,
making one lose confidence by easily giving up,
and not easily allowing opportunities until negative thoughts disappear,
the world has always been pitying and forgiving how we gave up irresponsibly, failing to create changes due to obsession.

② Gratitude – Blessing

* Since responsibilities for daily life were taken,
the fateful meaning of the responsibilities given to me realized,
life endured with confidence that it's my business and that I can do this,
and loved the subject of responsibility...
I have been leaving blessings to repay the world by ultimately fulfilling my responsibilities,
and I really love this world that continuously had something that I could do.

* Since changes in daily routines are created with various possibilities,
the freedom to expose anyone's thoughts and emotions
and the freedom to love to one's content protected,
and challenges continuously taken in various aspects to fulfill the mission of existence...
I have been blessing the world with my efforts at freedom that lightens life,
and thank the world that allowed me this freedom and expansion of freedom.

* With God's will and the will of all in this world,
that makes us want to have fun after working hard,
leading us to find the sense of mission for the things we are doing now,
enabling us to encourage ourselves to do well,
allowing us to get recognized and congratulated by the things we worked hard for,
the world has always been feeling gratitude and blessing us for the changes we created while fulfilling our responsibilities to the end and taking challenges freely.

(6) Sorriness – Us – Receiving Apology

① Contriteness - Forgiveness

* Since I chose shamelessness over apologizing despite my faults,
rubbed the wounds of the people wounded by me,
exacerbated the confusion in my life,
made heaven pity me as such,
and ended up hurting myself...
Apologizing to the world with sincere contriteness at my foolish shamelessness,
I have been asking for forgiveness with the course of my life that kept on getting twisted.

* Since I ignored sincere apologies and condolences,
failed to heal my wounds,
created the pain of rejected hearts,
refused the healing of heaven as such,
and ended up with a miserable life...
Repenting with strong regrets about my cold-hearted rejection,
I have been asking for forgiveness to the world with the time of an uncomfortable heart and body.

* With God's will and the will of all in this world,
that rub our wounds
as we continue to resent the heavens and oneself,
making the wounds between everyone deepen
when we resent life, the world and those around us,
the world has always been pitying and forgiving us who were in so much pain as we failed to apologize or accept apologies properly.

② Gratitude - Blessing

* Since I sincerely apologized for my faults,

those I wounded were healed,
confusion in my life removed one by one,
I was able to protect myself as such,
and heaven was relieved...
I have been blessing the world with my sincere apology and contriteness,
and I thank this world for letting me realize my faults and insufficiencies.

* Since sincere apologies and condolences were accepted,
one's own pain healed,
the joy of sincerity being accepted created,
the healing power of heaven accepted,
and my life shaped stably...
I have been leaving pacifying blessings to the world with my warm embrace,
and I thank everyone who apologized and comforted me so that I wouldn't get hurt.

* With God's will and the will of all in this world,
that do not let our pain heal
if we fail to feel sorry for the heavens and ourselves,
not relieving pain in all our relationships
if we fail to recognize our faults to life, the world and those around us,
the world has always felt relieved and blessed our compassion that healed pain by giving and accepting apologies and condolences.

(7) Gratitude – Us – Receiving Gratitude

① Contriteness - Forgiveness
* Since gratitude for daily life lost, life trapped in complaints,
fateful opportunity permitted by heaven unrecognized,

opportunities that came to me missed because of failure to realize my possibilities, regretted,
and indiscreetly stingy to neighbors...
Apologizing to the world for my arrogance and discontent that made the world heartless,
I have been asking for forgiveness to the world with results that fell short of my efforts.

* Since life was made harsh because of greed and vanity about life,
deficiency and ignorance of others disregarded,
made heaven resent with one's own achievement,
and ultimately made one's own abundance shrink....
Apologizing to the world for my greed and vanity that impoverished the world,
I have been apologizing to the world with the deficiencies in my life.

* With God's will and the will of all in this world,
that leave us in destitute
if we continue to hold complaints about the heavens and ourselves,
making us live in a heartless world
if we complain about life, the world and those around us,
the world has always been pitying and forgiving us struggling in deficiency due to greed and vanity, living in destitute due to arrogance and complaints.

② Gratitude - Blessing
* Since I was satisfied with what I enjoy in my daily life,
rejoicing and enjoying myself,
sharing and rejoicing with neighbors,
and tried to repay the world and God as much as I feel grateful...

I have been blessing the world with my satisfaction and joy that make the world flourish,
and thank this world which is the source of all opportunities offered to me.

* Since the rewarding feeling was created by practicing sharing and help in daily life,
others' insufficiencies and ignorance satisfied,
the satisfaction of heaven magnified,
and ultimately made one's abundance flourish...
I have been leaving blessing that replenishes the world with my sharing and help,
and I thank this world which has given me sharing and caring.

* With God's will and the will of all in this world,
that prevent us from further evolving
if we fail to recognize gratitude to the heavens and ourselves,
not allowing joyful situation
if we fail to thank life, the world and those around us,
the world has always been feeling relieved and blessed how we achieved prosperity by joyfully sharing with and caring for others.

(8) Forgiving – Us – Being Forgiven

① Contriteness - Forgiveness
* Shaming the opportunity to be forgiven by justifying faults,
I neglected others and left them in pain with my justification,
rejected the forgiveness God always offers,
made myself fall into the abyss where it's so difficult to become forgiven,
and created cold-hearted life and world with sarcastic smiles....
Apologizing to the world for my selfish justification,

I have been asking for forgiveness to the world with my life that feels so cold-hearted.

* Thinking that I cannot be the only one in such pain,
I filled the inside with darkness while being controlled by pain,
pushing others to perhaps greater pain,
and that is how we all hurt our Creator,
and created a merciless life and world...
Apologizing to the world for my foolish revenge,
I have been asking for forgiveness to the world with my life that feels so harsh.

* With God's will and the will of all in this world,
that make us suffer in pain
if we continue to attack the heavens and ourselves,
making this world fall into a swirl of confusion
if we do not stop attacking life, the world and those around us,
the world has always been pitying and forgiving our revenge and selfish self-justification that shattered peace.

② **Gratitude - Blessing**
* Realizing my fault, genuinely repenting, apologizing,
and enabling others to forgive me with my apology,
I accepted the forgiveness that the Creator always offers,
and entered into peace of being forgiven,
which ultimately created peace in my life and the world....
I have been blessing the world with so as to prevent confusion in the world with my hard-earned forgiveness,
and I truly thank all in this world for forgiving me.

* Since I chose forgiveness for my pain,
filled my inside with light of forgiveness,
presented others the stability of being forgiven,

comforted our Creator as such,
and made life and the world feel warm....
I have been blessing the world so that it becomes peaceful with my fierce forgiveness,
and I felt fortunate that my forgiveness stabilized the world.

* With God's will and the will of all in this world,
that do not let us overcome our limits and our faults
if we don't forgive the heavens and ourselves,
not allowing peaceful situations
if we don't forgive life, the world and those around us,
the world has always been taking comfort in blessing the peace we achieved by overcoming our faults and exchanging forgiveness.

(8) Blessing – Us – Being Blessed

① Contriteness - Forgiveness
* Since I failed to understand which direction was the blessing from God,
deluded by things that disturb my happiness,
refused the blessing of others,
and rendered happiness in daily life meaningless...
Apologizing to the world for my foolishness of refusing genuine happiness,
I have been asking for forgiveness to the world with my life's mishaps.

* Thinking that others who gave me a hard time will be ruined,
isolating myself thinking that I am such a miserable being,
causing harm while thinking that life and the world are foul,
I betrayed God by betraying the providence of the universe that is all about love...

Apologizing to the world for ultimately moving toward curses which are the opposite of blessing,
I have been asking for forgiveness to the world with my life's miseries.

* With God's will and the will of all in this world,
that make our misery continue
if we get caught in ominous thoughts about the heavens and ourselves,
not allowing us to even budge an inch because of the ominousness of the world
if we do not stop cursing life, the world and those around us,
the world has always been pitying and forgiving our limits that led to misery, intimidated by ominous thoughts.

② Gratitude - Blessing

* Realizing that my destiny is the conditions of happiness agreed with God,
contemplating on what would truly make me happy,
thanking the fact that I am being blessed by others,
I tried to magnify the happiness daily life presents,
I have been blessing the world with my choice that leads to genuine happiness,
and I thank the waves of the world that ceaselessly surged so as to magnify my happiness.

* Wishing that people around us are healthy and happy,
treasuring and comforting ourselves,
leaving benefits while thanking life and the world,
I pursued the glory of God by following the providence of the universe which is all about love,
I have been blessing the world with my efforts of sharing and spreading happiness,

and I felt truly grateful to this world for embracing my blessings and rewarding with blessings.
* With God's will and the will of all in this world,
that prevent happiness
if we do not exchange happiness with the heavens and ourselves, not allowing a happy world
if we do not exchange blessings with life, the world and those around us,
the world has always been taking comfort and blessing the growth of our happiness that glorified the world.

17 Change in the Route of Chakra: Fulfillment of Dreams

We all wish to fulfill our dreams as we live. Life is more enriched when you have dreams than when you don't, it is not easy to give up dreams easily once you get them, feel excruciating pain about frustrated dreams and yet start nurturing different dreams again. This is because life is more enriched when you have dreams than when you don't. And that is why it is human nature to strive to fulfill dreams. People have different dreams, but having dreams are their destiny, taking on the challenge is a choice they make, and the results create a new and different destiny.

Since the world is composed of materials, we need tools to fulfill our dreams. If you wish to become a successful businessman, you need to have a business item, if you wish to become a bestseller writer, you need to have a manuscript, and if you wish to serve the world, you have to have something to give whether it be actions or materials. Thinking alone does not fulfill dreams. However, it is energy that determines the use of materials. Even the best of the best product will not be used by people if it doesn't contain bright energy, and if so, it is rendered non-existent. Materials must have bright energy to be able to make use of it, and only then, it becomes valuable. This is just like how many are attracted to the beautifully shining diamond, and people wish to have it, and it becomes a priceless jewel. Ultimately, the essence is energy, and energy is created by thoughts and emotions. That is why mindset is very important in fulfilling dreams.

Those who fulfilled dreams say that the driving force between their success is positive thinking and confidence. Many self-development books emphasize on mindset, that our thoughts and emotions shape the reality. And that is indeed true. However, as so many experienced that positive confidence about dreams is not easily converted into the reality today, this proposition deteriorated into a subject of ridicule. How did this come to be?

We need to look more closely at the universal aspect of our lives. This is because we can achieve our dreams only if you understand the principles of life. Our life is influenced by the element called destiny to a certain degree. Issues like "what kind of parents we meet, which country we are born to" influence the bigger frame of life, and this is determined by the destiny given to us. Furthermore, destiny is set for individuals at many decision points in life. And based on such destiny, the flow of life also has the basic route of karma. Life is like a roller coaster and so it repeats the ups and downs. In the Eastern culture, we call it saju palja (fortune and destiny), and there are many instances where much of the saju palja largely coincides with life. I would like to emphasize once more that destiny exists. However, destiny constantly changes depending on our thoughts. That is why we can say that our mindset shapes the reality.

To put "our mindset shapes the reality" more accurately, "each and everyone's thoughts and efforts slowly changes the predetermined route of karma." This is not to say that when you start a business at the downhill route of karma, having positive expectations will make your business successful, but you can create the change of making the slope of the downhill road less steep. That is why mere positive expectations cannot change the course itself, but can only change the degree. That is why people get disappointed by the truth in self-development books.

In order to change the route of karma more conspicuously, you need something more than simple positive emotions. You need a new resolution and practice to live differently from the past. You cannot expect your life to change while living the same way you did in the past and therefore, you need resolution and practice that you'll live differently.

First of all, you need to promise yourself that you'll not repeat what you've been doing in the past. Efforts to move away from the past such as "I should not be full of complaints as I was before," "I should not speak ill of people no more," "I should not be lazy," "I should not allow others to mistreat me," brings the end point of the route of karma; in other words, the turning point of life closer to today. A new life is only possible when you stop what you've been doing wrong.

Next, you should promise yourself to attain a new attitude to life and practice. Efforts to create new changes such as "I should exercise regularly," "I should try new marketing strategies," "I should develop the habit of taking notes," "I should take short moments of reflection at the end of each day" create a longer and higher slope of an uphill road.

As such, we are living today while changing our lives of each moment, little by little. And destiny is different for every single person. For some, there are a lot of level grounds and uphill roads, and for some, downhill roads occupy more than half of life. That is why there are some people whose destiny easily responds, while for some, the downhill road is so long that no matter how hard they bring the turning point closer to the present, it is still far away. Some people may not feel rewarded at all because although the steep slope has become gentle, it remains a downhill road.

If you are still trapped in a harsh reality despite so many efforts to fix the wrongdoings in the past and attempts at a new change, I would like to let you know this: You are doing an excellent job of changing your destiny, the slope of the downhill road has become significantly even, and the turning point in your life is now a step closer to you.

Even as I write this, I am still treading on the downhill road of destiny. I strived and tried very hard, and so now my inner side is full of changes, but there is not even a slightest change being made to my life. "What on earth have I done in my previous life that is creating this unchangeable downhill road? I must have lived off of the world, preying on people," "I wouldn't have held on so much to this road if my stomach is full and my back is warm. I am making the best choices in life." If I failed to achieve this inner growth on this long downhill road, I don't know how deep down I would've plunged. And I have confidence. I have confidence that my efforts are bringing the turning point of life that lied afar, and that the uphill road in my future is becoming higher and higher...If I have readers reading my book, then the downhill road in my life must have stopped and I have gone through the turning point of life. And I believe that day will come.

There is no life with a never-ending downhill road. And there is no life with a never-ending uphill road. Always check whether you are making the right efforts and believe in the changes of destiny. You can level the downhill road in your life and you can create a higher uphill road in your future...Let us strive a bit more to raise the karma of our destiny higher.

Route of Chakra

Are we making the right promises and efforts? In order to shape the destiny in the direction I desire, accurate and right efforts are necessary. I hereby introduce prayers that can change the destiny of chakra with the absolute values of chakra. Through these prayers, you can check whether your efforts are moving in the direction that is right and proper to make the universe respond.

(1) Birth – Life – Death

① Contriteness - Forgiveness

* Since I shall not neglect miserable death and servile birth that lost dignity,
remove discrimination against birth, overcome the sadness of death, and safeguard the joy of life,
relieve pain so as to not get tired at the beginning and end of life,
and stand by the side as to prevent the dreadful loneliness at the beginning and end of life....
I reaffirm my resolve to the world that I shall not leave any cruelty in the cycle of life,
asking for forgiveness to the world about my life that endures the terror of life and death.

* Since I shall not indiscreetly break the dignity of life and the wholeness of nature,
not recklessly use the body so as to prevent the weakening of the body,
prevent inflicting pain and not love on other lives,
and strive not to interfere with the noble will to live and recover...
I reaffirm my resolve to the world that I shall in no case exercise violence and suppression to life,
asking for forgiveness to the world for my physical pain.

* The world will continue to pity us and open the way to forgiveness for the violence and cruelness of not caring for life and nature that still remain
all with God's will and the will of all lives in this world
opening the way to heal illness for us, the more we treasure life,
presenting the self-regenerating power for the pale life to gain vitality,
enabling us to save failing lives with warm care,
retrieving dying lives and preparing them for a new life.

② Gratitude - Blessing

* In order to be born in welcoming greetings and put an end to life in nostalgic farewell,
creating solid dignity that does not dwell on life and birth,
always accepting birth and death as joy,
I shall live so as to mark natural beginning and end of life with my will...
I shall bless the world with my efforts for birth and death,
and always feel grateful to the world for giving me the opportunity to be born and live.

* Using the energy this earth provides with the greatest efficiency,
maintaining health until the end of my life,
revitalizing other life with energy based on love,
I shall create reality with the will to live and recover...
I shall bless the world by caring for many lives,
and continue to feel grateful to all lives I was with on earth that helped me live.

* The world will continue to feel grateful for our sustained efforts for the birth, death and lives, and constantly gave its blessing
all by God's will and the will of all lives in this world
showing the dignity of the earth through the whole cycle of nature,
enabling evolution favorable to each and every life,
promoting healthier evolution of lives with love,
making one become the healthier, the more the body is trained.

(2) Individual – Self Realization – Solidarity

① Contriteness - Forgiveness

* By preventing disgrace of trampling on noble values and faith,
not inflicting shame by recklessly oppressing self-confidence,
not indiscreetly refusing others' characteristics,
I am going to remove the lethargy of not living by the unique
characteristics...
Asking for forgiveness to the world for my role which is
neglected by the surrounding,
I reaffirm my resolve to the world that I shall not indiscreetly
disregard anyone.

* In order to prevent the regression of the world which breaks
solidarity with each other's selfishness,
I affirm my resolve so as to not indiscreetly doubt or betray
others,
not leave one helpless deprived of the backing of others
and I am going to strive so as to not let the scattered individuals
turn grey...
Asking for forgiveness to the world for my loneliness of being
alone,
I reaffirm my resolve to prevent the dissolution of the world by
valuing each and every person.

* The world will continue to pity and pave the way for forgiveness
for our regression resulting from neglect and division
all through God's will and the will of all in this world
making one gain an opportunity to be recognized in society
with a dignified attitude,
enabling one to collaborate by resolving distrust and
misunderstanding,
making one go through trials and errors and allowing the
identification of the directions in life,
consistently providing the opportunities to recover the honor
that fell to the ground by discovering faith.

② Gratitude - Blessing

* Revealing the value of existence everywhere as being absolutely needed,
bringing out the light of others hidden in the dark,
filling the world with joy of living based on individual characteristics,
I shall become the lighthouse that lights up the world with noble values and beliefs...
That is how we will bless the world based on mutual respect so that each other can shine,
while feeling grateful to this world for allowing me to reveal my existence value with my role.

* Building up a great deal of faith and love for each other,
sprouting hope knowing that we have each other's back,
creating brilliance by collecting various lights,
hearts will gather to help the world evolve with glory and peace...
That is how I shall continue to protect and develop our solidarity and bless the world
while thanking all relationships for giving me the opportunities to grow together.

* The world will continue to offer gratitude and blessing for each of our self-realizations that shines in collaboration and the evolution of the world
all with God's will and the will of all in this world
making one rise up with joy when one's characteristics shine,
making one more rewarding and joyful when taking the lead in one's own life,
making one enable stronger satisfaction when being acknowledged and supported by others,
making one create unwavering honor when continuing to protect dignified values.

(3) Analysis – Communication – Synthesis

① Contriteness - Forgiveness

* Since dignity will be recovered by correcting the distortion about money and honor,

security of existence protected by correcting the distortion about the body,

preventing people near me from feeling uncomfortable by correcting the distortion about material,

and stability of life found by correcting the distortion about work and rest...

Asking for forgiveness to the world for my resentment of being misunderstood or not being understood,

I reaffirm my resolve to not distort the truth of the world because of thoughtless misunderstanding.

* While distinguishing falsehood and truth so that misunderstanding and speculation do not occur,

giving enough chance for others to speak so that I don't misunderstand,

preventing others from misunderstanding me because of my exaggeration or concealment,

and efforts made to prevent my life becoming isolated from the flow of the world...

Asking for forgiveness to the world about the difficulty of others not listening to me and me not being able to disclose them to anyone,

I promise to the world that I shall not make a single-minded judgment by being trapped in communication difficulty.

* The world will always pity and forgive our distortion that still misunderstands in communication difficulty

all through God's will and the will of all in this world

making one search for God desperately when in fear and misery,
making one reflect back on oneself when losing confidence,
making one necessitate conversations to resolve misunderstanding,
leading one to correct distortions by testing one's thoughts through actual performance.

② Gratitude - Blessing

* By the power of discreet fortune and fame, raise everyone's dignity,
by discreet distribution of the world's resources, deliver them to everyone in need,
by the power of discreet physical body, renew the existing records,
by the discreet daily life, I shall create rooms to try anything I desire...
I shall continue to thank the world for showing and informing me of various stories
and bless the world by revealing the detailed truth through my realistic analysis.

* Understanding without repulsion anyone's stories,
not having any hesitation to reveal and let myself be known,
finding enlightenment in everything in daily life,
I shall deliver the truth of joy and love to the world...
I shall bless the world with my comprehensive thinking that pierces through the essence of various aspects,
and I continue to feel grateful to the truth in the world that is making it function as one.

* The world will continue to rejoice and congratulate on the discovery of the comprehensive essence and detailed truth through our communication

all with God's will and the will of all in this world
making one understand God's will while pursuing genuine happiness,
making one seek the expansion of existence through balanced reflection on oneself,
making people understand of one another more deeply through steady conversations,
allowing the discovery of new truth through various practices.

(4) Faith – Hope – Love

① Contriteness - Forgiveness
* Since I shall overcome the mistrust that God will punish us,
not thoughtlessly mistrust the world just because life is tough,
not give up thinking that all my efforts are useless,
overcome mistrust about myself by stopping thinking that I am not good enough,
and not breed doubts that others have dark desires...
Asking for forgiveness to the world for the various situations that I can not be trusted and I am suspicious,
I promise the world that I shall protect love by protecting faith.

* Since I will remember the omnipotence of God so as to not resent God,
see my potential so as to not get disappointed about myself,
not retrieve love out of disappointment from unreasonable expectations,
and strive to not live loosely because of disappointment about life and the world...
Asking for forgiveness to the world for the continuing disappointment,
I promise the world that I shall not easily give into despair for love.

* The world will continue to pity us and open the way to forgiveness for us who are unable to love properly by not trusting and getting disappointed
all with God's will and the will of all in this world
making miracles occasionally so as to not forget the existence of God,
making one not want to die so as to not lose the will to live,
making one feel desperate so as to not let go of the love for oneself,
making people get attracted so as to not lose love for others.

② Gratitude - Blessing
* Believing that God and I am one being,
believing that the universe always operates for everyone,
believing that living until this day is a miracle that we achieved together,
as if it is only natural that we trust and love ourselves,
I shall believe that it is only natural that we love others...
I will bless the world by protecting love with my faith,
and continue to thank this world for trusting me.

* Infinite opportunities open up as I always have hope in myself,
sending hope that is right for others as is for me,
creating a hopeful world with such hopeful life,
I shall make God see hope in me and protect me...
I will continue to thank the world that provides hope,
and bless the world by nourishing love based on my hopes.

* The world will continue to appreciate and bless us for our faith in love and dreams about love
all with God's will and the will of all in this world
compelling us to turn on love by God's omnipotence,

making us to shine brilliantly the more we are confident about love,
making us to build warm solidarity the more deeply we love,
making one replenish the will to live with the rewarding feeling and joy of love.

(5) Responsibility – Calling – Freedom

① Contriteness - Forgiveness

* I shall not get irritated for the responsibilities of the daily routines,
not throw away the fateful meaning of the responsibilities given to me,
not give up saying it's not my business,
and not ignore the subject of responsibilities...
Asking for forgiveness to the world for my heavy and burdened life,
I reaffirm my resolve to not make the world a harsh place through my irresponsibility.

* Since I am not going to restrict the freedom of daily life, bound by unjust format,
not to oppress freedom to express one's thoughts and emotions,
not to block the freedom to love to one's heart's content,
and not strictly restrict and interrupt the type and methods of mission...
Asking for forgiveness to the world with my life in which freedom is being oppressed,
I reaffirm my resolve to not make the world a difficult place to live with my obsession.

* The world will continue to pity and forgive us for irresponsibly giving up and failing to create changes because of our obsession all with God's will and the will of all in this world

enabling the rewarding feeling of living by continuing the tough daily routines,
enabling one to not give up easily with responsibility for anyone,
making one become more self-confident the more one achieves by not giving up,
paving the path of destiny to make the impossible possible.

② Gratitude – Blessing

* Deeming daily responsibilities as joy of life,
willingly taking on challenges for a bigger mission for the world,
fulfilling them with confidence,
I shall share deeper and wider love through bigger responsibilities...
I shall continue to welcome things I must do that are spread in this world
and fulfill my responsibilities to create the blessing of repaying to the world.

* Doing things freely in daily life without leaving any regrets,
freely controlling my thoughts and feelings,
being able to deliver genuine love in all kinds of ways whether it be warm or cold,
I shall make sure that all the deeds I do are according to God's plan...
Feeling grateful to the world that gradually expands freedom,
with my efforts for freedom, I shall create the blessing of lighting up life.

* The world will continue to thank and bless us for the changes we achieve by freely taking on challenges and fulfilling our responsibilities to the end
all with God's will and the will of all in the world
providing the joy of daily routines with interesting exercises and plays,

enabling the acceptance of fateful mission with a strong sense of mission,

enabling the existence to shine ever brighter by accomplishing the mission,

making people around gather the more the missions are accomplished.

(6) Sorriness – Us – Receiving Apology

① Contriteness - Forgiveness

* Realizing that shameless attitude of not apologizing for my faults hurt myself more,

not indiscreetly rubbed the wounds of the people wounded by my shamelessness,

not exacerbated the confusion in my life,

and promised that I will never make heaven pity me...

Asking for forgiveness to the world for my life which keeps on getting twisted,

I reaffirm my resolve not to act shamelessly about my faults.

* Not forgetting that ignoring sincere apologies and condolences will result in the neglect of one's own pain for a very long time,

accepting the sincerity of those who muster up the courage to apologize,

not refusing the healing of heaven as such,

and promising to myself to ease the anguish of life...

Asking for forgiveness to the world for my uncomfortable mind and body,

I promise the world that I shall not coldly refuse the apologies and condolences that were offered to me.

* The world will continue to pity and forgive us, suffering from pain and not being able to properly apologize or receive an apology

all with the God's will and the will of all in this world
making us to tend our wound
while not indiscreetly blaming heaven and oneself,
making us to tend all wounds between relationships
while not indiscreetly blaming life, the world and people
around us.

② Gratitude – Blessing

* Never giving up to apologize for my faults,
not leaving anyone wounded because of me,
never repeating the same mistake again,
growing myself as such,
I shall always follow the will of the heavens...
I shall continue to thank this world that allows me to realize my
faults and insufficiencies
and bless the world with sincere apologies and processes of
contrition,

* By making all kinds of apologies and condolences offered to
me effective,
treating my pain so that none remains,
liberating others' spirits from the heavy karma,
making good use of the way the universe operates as such,
I shall create a smooth life without any hitch...
I shall continue to thank this world that presents the
opportunities of condolences and recovery,
and leave pacifying blessings to the world with my warm
embrace.

* The world will continue to feel relieved and bless our sympathy
for exchanging apologies and condolences while healing pain
all with God's will and the will of all in this world
enabling us to heal our pain

while exchanging contriteness with heaven and myself,
enabling us to heal pain between all relationships
while exchanging contriteness with life, the world and people
around me.

(7) Gratitude – Us – Receiving Gratitude

① Contriteness - Forgiveness
* In order to not lose gratitude for daily life and get trapped in complaints,
remain awake so as to not miss the fateful opportunity permitted by heaven,
realize my possibilities so as not to miss opportunities that came to me and regret,
I am going to not be indiscreetly stingy to neighbors…
Asking for forgiveness to the world for the results that fell short of my efforts,
I reaffirm my resolve to the world that I will not indiscreetly breed arrogance.

* So as to continue to pave the path where one's abundance never disappears,
not live a harsh life trapped in greed and vanity about life,
not disregard deficiency and ignorance of others,
and not make heaven resent with one's own achievement…
Asking for forgiveness to the world for my deficiencies in life,
I promise that I shall not impoverish the world with my greed and vanity.

* The world will continue to pity and forgive us for delaying prosperity and getting trapped in greed and vanity by arrogantly breeding discontent
all with God's will and the will of all in this world

enabling us to alleviate our impoverishment
by shaking off discontent about heaven and myself,
enabling us to break down the harshness of the world
by shaking off discontent about life, the world and people
around us.

② Gratitude - Blessing

* Continuously making efforts as I can be satisfied with my
efforts and performances in daily life,
doing my best as I always feel grateful to the opportunities the
world offers,
caring for relationships as they are always ever precious,
I shall take pride in myself for such endless growth...
I will continue to thank this world that offers opportunities to
me
and leave blessings that make the world flourish with my
satisfaction and joy.

* Sharing and helping become my natural daily life,
and nothings feels like a waste as I would do for others what I
would do for myself,
as such, attracting the energy of the universe to make the world
prosper,
I shall become an existence that shines ever brightly...
I shall continue to thank this world that gives me help and
caring
and bless the world so that the world can become more abundant
with my sharing and caring.

* The world will bless us and continue to be touched by our
composure of joyfully sharing, being considerate of each other
and pursuing prosperity
all with God's will and the will of all in this world
enabling our brilliant growth

while exchanging gratitude with heaven and oneself,
enabling us to open a delightful and abundant world
while exchanging gratitude with life, the world and people I
am with.

(8) Forgiving – Us – Being Forgiven

① Contriteness - Forgiveness

* So as to not miss the chance to be forgiven by justifying faults,
thinking about the pain that others would suffer with my
justification,
repenting so as to not reject the forgiveness God always offers,
saving oneself as such from the abyss where it is difficult to be
forgiven,
I am going to confront head-on with the cold-heartedness of my
life and the sarcastic smiles of the world....
Asking for forgiveness to the world for my life that feels cold-
hearted,
I reaffirm my resolve to not create a sarcastic world with my
selfish justification.

* So as to not make my pain spread anymore,
I shall strive to not fill my inside with darkness even in pain,
and not think it is fair that others suffer the pain I suffered,
soothing the pain of our Creator as such,
I am going to end the ruthlessness of my life and the world...
Seeking for forgiveness to the world for my life that feels so
harsh,
I reaffirm my resolve to not disrupt the world with my foolish
revenge.

* The world will continue to pity and open the path for
forgiveness for our revenge and selfish justification that still
shatter peace

all with God's will and the will of all in this world
making us to calm our pain
by stopping attacks on heaven and oneself,
making us to calm the confusion of the world
by stopping attacks on life, the world and those around us.

② Gratitude - Blessing

* As I overcome all the faults I did in my life,
I am going to be forgiven by everyone who suffered because of me,
not be leaving any confusion in my domain in this universe,
and become an existence that is not retrained by anything...
Continuing to feel fortunate that there are still opportunities to be forgiven in this world,
I shall bless the world with my ceaseless efforts to be forgiven.

* As I overcome all the hardships in my life,
I am going to become an existence that can forgive everything,
nobody will be restrained by me,
and I shall create peace across my domain in this universe...
By readily accepting the world that needs my forgiveness,
with hard-earned forgiveness, I shall present the blessing of calming the confusion of the world.

* The world will continue to appreciate and bless the peace we created by overcoming our faults and exchanging forgiveness
all with God's will and the will of the world
leading us to overcome our faults and limitations
by exchanging forgiveness with heaven and myself,
leading us to open a peaceful world
by exchanging forgiveness with life, the world and those around us.

(8) Blessing – Us – Being Blessed

① Contriteness - Forgiveness

* So as to not fail to recognize which direction is the blessing from God,
strive not to be deluded by things that disturb my happiness,
not indiscreetly refuse the blessing of others,
I promise not to render happiness prevalent in daily life meaningless...
Asking for forgiveness to the world for my misfortunes,
I affirm my resolve to not lose genuine happiness with my foolishness.

* Not thinking that even those who give me a hard time will be ruined,
reflecting on myself so as to not isolate myself in self-pity,
remaining vigilant so as to not inflict harm thinking that life and the world are foul,
I will not betray the providence of the universe which is all about love...
Asking for forgiveness to the world for the miseries in my life,
I reaffirm my resolve so as to not move toward curses unwittingly, which are the opposite of blessings.

* The world will continue to pity and forgive our limits that lead
to misery because of being daunted by ominous thoughts
all with God's will and the will of all in this world
enabling us to put an end to our misery
by stopping ominous thoughts about heaven and oneself,
enabling us to do away with the ominousness in the world
by stopping cursing on life, the world and those around us.

② Gratitude - Blessing

* As I am going to use my misfortune and misery to serve as the foundation of happiness,
organize relationships so that they are beneficial to me whether they be good or bad,
protect my happiness in whichever situation I may be in,
I shall make sure the universe guarantees my happiness....
I shall welcome the waves of the world that ceaselessly surge so as to magnify my happiness,
and reaffirm my resolve to the world to always make choices that lead to genuine happiness.

* By continuously growing my happiness,
filling my daily life with little but important happiness,
laying the foundation for people around me to be happy,
I shall make God smile saying "it is good"...
I promise the world that I shall strive harder to share and spread happiness,
waiting to repay all the blessings I received in the world.

* The world will continue to rejoice in and bless it for becoming glorious with the magnification of our happiness
all with God's will and the will of all in this world
making our happiness to spread
while exchanging blessings with heaven and ourselves,
making us to open up a happy world
while exchanging blessings with life, the world and people around us.

18 Kundalini: Humility – Greatness

Kundalini that penetrates nine chakras bears greatness and humility. Greatness and humility are not the ingredients of love, but the absolute values that you get as a result. If we choose absolute values and experience love with the power of Hon, Baek, Shin, Ui, and Ji but we don't awaken to both humility and greatness at the same time as a result, it means that the love experience is somewhere lacking or going in the wrong direction. So, you should look carefully into humility and greatness, which are a result of love.

Humility is the value that comes from the relationship with the other person we love. The more we love someone, the humbler we become. Since you can share more love with the other when you are humble, it is natural that the more you love, the more humble you become. Also, since you can be with more people when you lower yourself, it is natural that the more you love more people, the lower you put yourself in. Therefore, becoming humble in relationships with others as a result of love is also proof that you are on the right path.

However, you should not forget that humility is the value that appears in your relationship with the other person. You don't have to belittle yourself in order to stay in a lower, humble position. For example, if someone praises you, gratefully accepting that praise is the result of a true love. If you are truly grateful for the other person's praise, you cannot but become humble in front of this person who gave you the compliment. You cannot be arrogant to the person, because you are grateful for the affectionate attention the person has shown you, and for the person's greatness in recognizing you. Therefore, it is true humility to accept the praise given to you by the other person with gratitude while lowering yourself.

It is common in our society to refuse to accept the compliment given to us by others and deny it, but it is actually not humility. It's rather an act of degrading the other person's point of view and affection to your own level. Suppose someone praised you, "You're so elegant and beautiful," and you replied, "No, I'm not. It's too much exaggeration." In this case, you have degraded the other person's aesthetic point of view and affection for you to the level of your self-esteem that doesn't make you feel beautiful. In other words, it is not the humility of raising the other person and lowering me, but the result of bringing the other person down to your position. If you truly love someone, you wouldn't want to bring the person down. If you truly love someone, you believe in the person's sincerity, which you might feel is exaggerated, and accept it with gratitude, feeling the person's love for discovering your beauty.

Therefore, if you love humbly, you will see the greatness of existence itself. The other person, who has discovered your elegance and beauty hidden by mediocrity, thinks about how great the person has realized the truth of beauty. The more you love, the more you discover the greatness of all beings – the greatness of all beings, including yourself. You find that we can love like now because we are great, and you discover that we regard love as happiness because we are great. The more you experience the truth that there is no limit to love, the more you feel the truth that the being, as the subject of love, is great.

However, greatness – the result of love – is not a relative but an absolute greatness. It's not something that is great and beautiful compared to someone, but it's something that's great and beautiful in itself, and it's something that everyone has in common in terms of having infinite possibilities. Conclusively speaking, when you fully experience love, you become humble in front of others by lowering yourself, and you discover the greatness of others while the being shines greatly in itself.

Therefore, looking pessimistic at existence while feeling relative superiority is a clear sign that you did not love properly. If you love properly, you can never have a relative sense of superiority. You feel relative superiority only through experience, not love. Relative superiority eventually leads you to regard others as inferior beings, and as this view grows bigger, you regard all beings, including yourself, as beings full of sins and limitations.

If you keep comparing yourself to others and become arrogant, you should know that it is a sign that there is a lack of love in your experience. In that case, if you find out where love is lacking and fill up the lacking gap, then naturally arrogance will disappear, and humility will take its place. If you feel intimidated by yourself or you feel someone is pathetic and inferior, this is also a sign of a lack of love somewhere in your experience. As expected, if you fill your love properly, you will naturally discover the greatness of all beings, including yourself. Relative humility and absolute greatness serve as the clearest compass for our love.

If you build humility and greatness inside as a result of love, you can fully understand and love yourself. We reject part of our minds, deny them, and press them down unconsciously to create inner shadows, because we don't understand all of our own minds. And shadows form a force that interferes with love. But when we build up humility as a result of love, we have the power to acknowledge and accept all our minds. If we can be truly humble, we have the power to admit childish thoughts, instinctive desires and sometimes cowardly minds. We can naturally regard that those minds are part of our sincerity and acknowledge them.

If you build greatness as another result of love, you will have the power to see where the dark minds come from. The childish, instinctive, and cowardly ideas are in touch with the spiritual desire to love more. The childish desires to be recognized by others and the cowardly imagination you have for those who don't recognize you begin with the spiritual will to wish many people happiness with the love you want to give to the world. By recognizing the spiritual will of such a dark mind and embracing the mind with love, you can unfold greatness to overcome.

Therefore, because there is no shadow in the inner world of the people who have achieved oneness with God, they can always humbly lower themselves before others, always shining on their own, and always bringing out the greatness that shines from others. Relative humility and absolute greatness are always expressed in them, because those who became the incarnation of all true things can fully live the present moment while experiencing love.

The reason why the result of this wholesome love is expressed with humility and greatness is because greatness and humility are the breath of the soul. Just as the human body alternates between inhalation and exhalation for life, the cosmic breath for the soul to exist is greatness and humility. Just as we cannot live without breathing for a moment, our souls can also exist in this universe with the breath of greatness and humility. Therefore, in the love experience that reflects the will of the soul, the breath of the soul is revealed, and as a result, greatness and humility are expressed.

Due to the breathing of the soul, we are repeatedly facing the moment that we become great and we need to be humble. We remain in the imagination where we become arrogant in a situation where our possibilities are unfolding, and then we face the situation where we find our limitations and humbly repent. And at the end of this humble repentance, our greatness begins to unfold again. This repeats constantly in life. Just as we can't keep breathing in or breathing out only, we can't keep being great and we cannot keep being humble, because greatness and humility are alternating breathing.

If we understand the breath of the soul and keep our minds and lives in line with this repetition, we will be glorified in peacefulness. So you have to prepare for the breath to turn into humility with gratitude at the moment of joy when your potential unfolds, and prepare for your new possibility at the moment when you hold yourself up with humility. If you repeat this, you will eventually complete a breath of greatness and humility within the same situation. This is the way to go with the breath of the soul.

Also, we must distinguish by the breath of the soul which is the illusion of the relative realm and which is the real truth of the absolute realm in our daily lives. The relative world we live in is made up of matter and illusion. The material and conceptual condition for experiencing love in everyday life is illusion. And the beings and absolute values in it are real. We must recognize this reality and do our best, and we should not be tempted or buried by illusion in order to live a life where the will of the soul is realized. However, we should not ignore illusion as being meaningless. We must humbly do our best in this illusion, which is a condition of love experience, as we are the souls who have accepted the constraints of matter. You can get the opportunity to realize absolute values with the humility in everyday life, because you cannot get the opportunity to realize absolute values when you are not being humble to illusion. And we can also unfold our greatness with all our hearts to the real things we have discovered.

Regretfully, however, we tend to go beyond the efforts to become humble and wholeheartedly become tempted while we take care of our bodies, decorate our homes and cars, manage our reputations, think about playing, and concentrate on managing our finances. If you are tempted by the illusion, you cannot recognize the absolute values contained in it. The daily routine of taking care of the body contains the absolute values of taking care of life, self-realizing, and loving oneself.

Decorating house and car has hidden real things that fulfill responsibilities and calling, provide comfort to life, and share abundance. Finding delicious food contains the absolute value of prosperous life and pleasantly communicating with those who share it. The real reason for managing reputation and finance is to communicate with the world, achieve peace of apology, and achieve prosperity of gratitude. That's why we have to do our best in this illusion. When you do your best, you can reveal greatness with all your heart because absolute values contained within illusion manifest themselves. But we become exhausted by being buried by illusion instead of humbly doing our best. As a result, we cannot reveal greatness because we are forced to make a reluctant choice with irritated mind with regards to absolute values that are contained in it. In this way, our daily life is taking the complete opposite direction from the breath of the soul.

In order to match everyday life with the breath of the soul, we must humbly do our best to the condition of the illusion, and take the breath of humility while appreciating the result. We must do our best, but we must be humble not to be carried away in mind. A humble mind gives us a room to be content with the results, while making us willing to accept what we have to do, so that we can be tirelessly eager and discover the real things contained in it. The repeated dish washing also has absolute value for life and fulfilled responsibility. There is absolute value hidden in all our daily lives. It's just a matter of finding it or not. If you keep getting carried away by the illusion, don't run away, and humbly think about the absolute value contained in it instead. You have to breathe greatness with all your heart with regards to the absolute value you discover in that way. Greatness can gush out only when you do your best with all your heart. And giving your heart to absolute value gives you joy, not exhaustion. In this way, we can reveal the greatness of humbly striving in our daily lives and devoting our heart to the absolute values inherent in us. This is how we live while taking the breath of soul.

Please look back at your daily routine and think about how much it matches the breath of your soul. If life is tiring for you, you lack a moment that matches the breath of your soul, and if you are living a quite comfortable and happy life, it means you are living a life that is quite consistent with the breath of your soul. Matching everyday life with the breath of the soul is the result of the expansion of your myungsu and at the same time a condition for the continued expansion of the myungsu. As we move closer toward the Trinity, the distinction between daily illusion and reality become more and more noticeable, and you can surely realize the corresponding breath of humility and greatness. The result is, of course, full happiness.

This universe breathes with greatness and humility for the coexistence between the condition of illusion for experiencing love, the absolute values that are real, and being. As a result, we and the world are made up of sacred dichotomy. Since we are great beings who experience love humbly, our Hon, Baek, Shin, Ui, and Ji grow while integrating two extremes. You must humbly trust and follow God and live with a great free will (Hon), recreate karma with humility as a great observer of the karma (Baek), and humbly protect your nobility in the greatness of giving yourself to the world (Shin). In addition, you must humbly accept the difference of others so we all become one as a being with infinite possibilities (Ui), and we must understand the greatness of beings while doing our best in life with humility, knowing that all processes are happening just because that's what we want to happen (Ji).

Also, since this universe is a stage for greatness and at the same time a place where we should humbly experience love, our chakra, which communicates with the universe, circulates and its two extremes come into a circle. So, greatness and humility revolve around the centripetal value of chakra. If you realize the greatness of life, you have no choice but to be humble before life. In order to achieve great self-realization, you must be humble in our being oneness. When you humbly listen to others' stories, you find a great oneness that is common with everyone. When you realize that the wish of love is the source of a great power, you have the humility to regard even a small wish as love. You start with humility that upholds the triviality of everyday life by calling and reach the result of completing a great calling. You can humbly apologize to everyone with the greatness that you can bear sorriness to everyone. With humility that can appreciate everyone, you can unfold greatness that is appreciated by all. With the greatness of forgiving everything, you can exercise the humility of asking for forgiveness from all. You have a great love that blesses everything with humility that accepts everything as a blessing.

Chakra contains a perfect idea of what we will experience love with, and Kundalini guides us through the breath of humility and greatness whether the love we experienced is wholesome. As we are all great spiritual beings, we humbly accepted this path of living on Earth as human beings. Now, I hope that you will believe in the greatness of this universe and humbly abandon yourself to the laws of this universe.

Awakening and Expanding Kundalini

When you lead a busy life and work fiercely, you may feel doubts as to whether you are "living well" and sometimes you may lose the directions to pursue in life. Kundalini is energy that reflects the results of life, so you can take stock of your life until today using the prayers of Kundalini. By reflecting on "how I lived my life" and reading the prayers of Kundalini, you'll learn where you lost your path. You can regain the directions to a healthy life. Read the following prayers while filling your mind, and take stock of your life.

(1) Birth – Life – Death

① Modesty
I regret failing to notice how precious this living moment is.
If there is no energy from life, there can be no love, no growth and nothing that I can do,
and so living every day feeling grateful for being alive is right and just.

I truly repent destroying the complete nature of this earth.
Since we humans can maintain a complete life in the harmony of the ecosystem,
humbly following the way nature operates is right and just.

I regret being insensitive to things that harm my health.
Now, striving to limit things harmful to the body and nurture healthy habits,
the humble habit of moderation for health is right and just.

I apologize for not enduring the slightest inconvenience for other lives.
As we are threatening the lives of other species thinking only about our own conveniences,
enduring inconvenience for other species is right and just.

② Greatness
I regret failing to notice our lives' power of adaptation and resilience.
Now, astonished by the power of life which becomes stronger with training,
the efforts to build up health and stamina are right and just.

It is a pity that I do not understand the earth's magnificent evolution process.

Now, praising the amazing evolution created in eternity
having the confidence that all lives will evolve to become greater
beings is right and just.

I regret failing to see the beauty in my physical body.
Failing to see the beauty and focusing only on the shape leads
to damaging health,
seeing the beauty and making a healthy body is right and just.

I repent oppressing the nature of other species and utilizing
them for humans.
Utilization of nurturing the congenital nature was beneficial to
humans as well as the species,
discovering the method to nurture the nature of other species
and utilizing them is right and just.

(2) Individual – Self-realization – Solidarity

① Greatness
I regret not thinking hard about the ultimate goals of life.
Without an ultimate goal of life, it is easy to lose one's way in
unexpected situations,
and so establishing an ultimate goal of life so as to not get lost
in this long life is right and just.

I reflect on myself whether I stopped the evolution of the world
as I was afraid of changes.
The world evolved while suffering labor pains for changes,
accepting changes boldly and seeking development are right
and just.

I reflect on being unnecessarily self-conscious and being ignored
by others.
Lowering yourself too much may make others ignore you,

having the panache so that others can't look down on you is right and just.

I regret always blaming others for the conflicts that arose in relationships.
Not forgetting that relationships are built together,
and reflecting on what would have been better for others is right and just.

② Modesty
I regret growing weary because of goals that were hard to achieve, neglecting the reality.
Realistic dreams are achieved by changes that accumulate,
and so upgrading achievable goals and realizing them is right and just.

I regret seeking secular reputation of the world.
Secular reputation is like a mirage that is swayed by situation.
Following the will of God that is an unwavering standard is right and just.

I regret trying to (authoritatively) focus too much on myself in relationships.
Authoritative thinking breeds shamelessness that does not know contriteness or gratitude,
and so feeling contriteness and gratitude in horizontal relationships is right and just.

I repent believing that everything will go well if I do well in the conflicts arising in relationships.
Now as I realize that all relationships are built together and not alone,
determining the direction of relationships considering the responses and efforts of others is right and just.

(3) Analysis – Communication – Synthesis

① Modesty
I regret pushing aside small problems and making them grow.
Before such huge problems erupt, there are always danger signals,
and so not procrastinating and solving small problems is right and just.

I reflect back on having the delusion that I am where I am today all thanks to my choices and efforts.
I now understand that my destiny until today unfolded in the flow of the world,
and so responding humbly to the surrounding circumstances and the changes in the world is right and just.

I regret blaming my surrounding for the strange feelings that bother me and deeming them as a jinx.
True self sent signals that bother one when it desires a change because of the frustration felt inside, and so
filling in my insufficiencies by taking my responses as the signal is only right and just.

I deeply repent arrogantly insisting in front of others that only my arguments are right.
Now, humbly listening to others' opinions,
the course of reaching an agreement while coordinating each other's opinions is right and just.

② Greatness
I regret losing bigger opportunities by being greedy about insignificant things.
When you became less greedy, the more you recognized truly important matters,

and so removing little greed and drawing a big picture as we live is right and just.

I regret living so small-mindedly, trapped in the frame of the mundane world.
Now, as I view things from the perspective of the universe and feel the omnipotence of God with my entire body,
understanding the appropriateness and possibilities of all things is right and just.

Think once again how small-minded you have interpreted yourself.
Since we matured with pain and approached bigger happiness, and so interpreting the pain as possibility of happiness is right and just.

I repent that misunderstandings piled up because I fail to have frank and open communication with others.
As the more open-minded I communicated, the better I understood each other,
clearing the air with frank communication and understanding each other are right and just.

(4) Faith – Hope – Love

① Greatness
I regret giving up easily because my life did not turn out the way I wanted.
In the face of death, there is always more regret of "I should've done more" than "I shouldn't have done it",
and so believing in your will and making efforts so as to not leave any regrets are right and just.

I look back on how I got discouraged, saying that there is no hope in this world.
Since the world is always changing,
thinking that one day there will be hope is right and just.

I regret living in the dark because of lack of hope in myself.
Believing that I become a better person each passing day,
having hope in yourself and living an optimistic life is right and just.

I regret not doing best for love that I wish to be in and can be in again.
As remorse pierces you when your beloved person leaves you because of your too much thinking,
courageously loving and leaving no regrets when you are together is right and just.

② Modesty
I regret getting disappointed easily as I was impatient with results.
Rather than pursuing an unfeasible plan, repeating a reasonable amount every day,
changing life hopefully with the small and steady efforts is right and just.

Believing that the rules of the universe are fair and reasonable,
humbly accepting one's destiny,
and not resenting any more is right and just.

It was bound to fail as even I did not believe in myself and yet I tried to believe and love others.
Now as I realize that I should love myself in order to love others accordingly,
efforts made to first believe and love myself are right and just.

I regret mistreating those who believed in and loved me.
Since being loved is valuable happiness that cannot be replaced, realizing gratitude for those who believed in and loved me is right and just.

(5) Freedom – Calling – Responsibility

① Modesty

I regret trying to have too many formalities by creating frames in our lives.
When trying to fit into frames and formalities, sincerity could be lost,
and so having simplified formalities that maintain the meaning of life are right and just.

I regret getting into a lather of criticism saying the world functions pathetically.
Since the world goes on by the efforts of so many who do their best on the tasks given to them,
feeling grateful for the efforts of many and doing the best on my tasks is right and just.

I regret not asking for help although the work given to me was too much to handle.
In order to fulfill one's responsibilities, sometimes one needed to lower oneself and seek help and therefore,
lowering oneself to receive the support one needs is right and just.

I regret having complaints that others do not work as hard as I do.
We all do our best albeit differences in our capabilities,
and so having faith in others' efforts and helping them accordingly is right and just.

② Greatness
I look back on deeming my deeds were meaningless.
If there is no sense of mission, you only rush to avoid your responsibilities when there is a problem,
and so having a sense of mission in the things you do is right and just.

I regret pursuing only money and fame, and not working to make this world a better place.
The world always became a better place through unknown new challenges,
and so new and creative challenges for the world are right and just.

I regret losing confidence and failing to unleash my talents.
Without trying different opportunities, it is difficult to find out your talents and capabilities,
and taking on challenges to pave the way to unleash your talents is right and just.

I was easy to blame unskilled workers but failed to teach them properly.
We all became skilled workers after going through the period of being a beginner,
and so giving enough opportunities, teaching and time to become a skilled worker is right and just.

(6) Apology – Us – Receiving Apology

① Greatness
I reflect on how I wasted my time, failing to notice the value of the time given to us.
Then I shall be sorry about putting off tomorrow what I have to do today,

setting our hands on the things we should do now and not putting them off is right and just.

Overcoming my pain so as to make even God pity me,
Embracing and healing the pain of others (the world) so as to make even God feel apologetic,
and advancing toward holy beings that accept the apology of God is right and just.

I regret neglecting my own pain.
Unhealed pain persistently burrows into subconsciousness to make negative changes,
and so proactively attending to and healing your pain is right and just.

I regret not apologizing for my faults and distantly feeling sorry.
It was precisely because of that which caused so much pain to others...
Apologizing properly for someone else's pain is right and just.

② Modesty
I regret failing to muster up courage to stop when I felt I should have.
If you don't stop, it becomes more difficult to stop as you've gone too far in the wrong direction,
and so stopping without hesitation when you have the chance to stop and reflecting on yourself is right and just.

We will only feel apologetic if we know how much God loves us,
and so I humbly repent my resentment of the past in front of this whole universe.
Repenting in front of God and seeking the essence of existence is right and just.

I truly regret not feeling contrite, dismissing my fault as nothing serious.

Dismissing your fault as something trivial will make you insensitive and lead to bigger faults,

and so truly feeling sorry regardless of the severity of your fault is right and just.

I truly regret not being ready to accept apologies when they were made.

If you are not ready, you cannot resolve conflicts even if apologies are made,

and so being always prepared to accept sincere apologies is right and just.

(7) Gratitude – Us – Gratitude Reception

① Modesty

I reflect on my attitude of getting easily disappointed at dis-satisfactory results and feeling arrogant at over-satisfactory results.

Humbly accepting dis-satisfactory results and remaining humble at over-satisfactory results,

feeling humble gratitude for whichever results you achieve and remaining unmoved is right and just.

Thanking God for creating me,

thanking God for always being with me,

and willingly following the natural course of love created by God are right and just.

I truly regret feeling superior to others.

Letting others down to feel comfort (satisfaction) is a type of selfishness,

and so feeling grateful for who I am now is right and just.

I reflect on imprudently patronizing on others.
Indiscreet goodwill serves as an obstacle to the growth and happiness of others,
and so exercising moderation so as to prevent indiscreet goodwill is right and just.

② Greatness

I regret not being able to fully enjoy life, complaining everyday that life is too tough.
Hardships of the past are memories today but I failed to notice the joy I hold,
and so taking the time to enjoy this moment is right and just.

Loving myself so as to make even God thank me,
loving someone so as to make even God touched,
and creating my own happiness the universe will welcome are right and just.

I regret floundering in inferiority complex, comparing myself to others.
Growth created out of inferiority complex is doomed to stop when you encounter someone more talented than you,
and so recognizing yourself for making the effort and pursuing consistent growth is right and just.

I regret belittling other people's efforts just because they failed.
Failure can also serve as the basis for bigger growth,
and so giving a chance to those who learnt from their failure is right and just.

(8) Forgiveness – Us – Forgiven

① Greatness

I regret falling down to my knees because of the hardships of life.
Life was a repetition of ebbs and flows,
and so strengthening one's will through hardships is right and just.

I regret destroying myself, resenting the heavens for inevitable misery.
Accepting that my misery is also my destiny that I should experience and overcome,
overcoming my misery at last and getting forgiveness from the entire universe is right and just.

Since I am a holy being that wishes to forgive all,
and since I am a great being that can forgive all,
forgiving all is right and just.

I repent taking out anger on others while exchanging wounds in conflicts.
Pain stopped when someone stopped attacking,
and so forgiving others first and reaching out to reconciliation are right and just.

② Modesty
I think once more about the delusion that I am the one and only suffering.
People all lead different lives but there is no exception that it is tough and harsh,
and so enduring the burden of life given to me is right and just.

I regret believing that I am the victim and that everyone should go easy on me.
If you remain in the role of a victim, you unwittingly give others a hard time,

and so forgiving all to prevent further pain and overcoming them is right and just.

I regret trying to blame my surroundings without reflecting on my own faults.
Thinking once more whether my acts could really be justified under the circumstances I was in,
fixing my mistakes in whichever situation I may be in and expanding the boundaries of my limits are right and just.

I reflect back on resenting others because they did not forgive my wrongdoing.
Whether to forgive me or not is entirely up to them,
making efforts until the end so as to heal the wounds that I caused is right and just.

(9) Blessing – Us – Being Blessed

① Modesty
I regret failing to realize how precious things I enjoy now are.
Happiness taken for granted and whose meaning unrecognized is doomed to disappear,
and so attaching the meaning of happiness to the things I enjoy today is right and just.

I greatly regret losing the purpose and objective of existence being swayed by the illusion of life.
Since we are spiritual beings that came to this land to experience happiness based on love,
living a life that is faithful to the spiritual purpose and objective is right and just.

I reflect on myself thinking "I should endure and endure" for others.

Devotion based on love leads to happiness and sacrifice unilaterally demanded only breeds misfortune,
and so letting go of one-sided sacrifice and not giving up on efforts for happiness is right and just.

I reflect on taking others' efforts for granted.
Reflecting on the troubles they had to endure,
and making sure their blessings are not wasted is right and just.

② Greatness

I regret sacrificing happiness today for happiness in the future.
Since happiness today serves as the foundation for future happiness,
appreciating happiness I feel at each moment in life is right and just.

I regret failing to see my destiny agreed with God as a blessing.
Now, as I accept whichever fate that befall me as my share,
the sacredness of deeming life's triumphs and tragedies as blessings is right and just.

Since I am a holy being that wishes to bless everything,
since I am a great being that can bless everything,
blessing everything is right and just.

I repent for my jealous mind and behavior of someone else's happiness.
They achieved happiness by overcoming the hardships I have not experienced and with efforts I have not seen,
and so sending sincere congratulations to others' happiness is right and just.

Kundalini's right and just path is the only way we have to go and want to go for happiness.

Epilogue: Search for Truth through Unconsciousness

There is something I really want to add before I finish writing this book: the principle with which the active power of the human body responds to our questions with truth and lies. In the good deed club that I'd belonged to, we asked the number of our myungsu to unconsciousness and confirmed the yes-or-no response with a pendulum as we pursued the growth of mind. For example, I asked "is my myungsu thirty?" and received "yes or no." Then we asked questions from other areas to the unconsciousness and confirmed the responses and believed those answers were the truth. And the result was disastrous, as shown in the epilogue of Part 1 of this book.

The active power that responds to a thought is the body's natural response. Someone else can also discover and confirm and experience the same trial and error as the good deed club did. In order not to repeat this disaster, I think we must honestly reveal the pain of trial and error we've experienced. In addition, I think it is the responsibility of the person who has experienced it before to leave a note about the principle that was discovered in the process.

Muscle testing is known before the pendulum test as a way to check the active power of the human body. Muscle testing is a method developed by an American chiropractic physician named George Goodheart. It contacts the patient with the body's responding points, drugs, and food necessary for treatment and tests the strength of the patient's muscles. A response that strengthens the patient's muscles is beneficial to the patient and the response that weakens the patient's muscles is not beneficial to the patient. Dr David Roman Hawkins has extended this muscle testing to the search for truth. Dr Hawkins found that muscles responded differently – either to strengthening or weakening – to the thoughts that people had within. In addition, it confirmed that the true truth was unfolding in response to the strengthening of muscles, and he proclaimed that the result is the way our unconsciousness responds to the truth of the universe.[19]

As explained in Part 1, the observation of the rotation of a pendulum is another method of the same principle of checking the active power of the human body, just like muscle testing. So, a pendulum-based search for truth is in line with Dr Hawkins' search for truth. But there is one thing Dr Hawkins overlooked in his search for the truth of unconsciousness: the results of muscle reactions are not always based on the truth. The active power of the human body is merely an expression of whether or not it corresponds to the unconsciousness of the subject party. And our unconsciousness is vast and touches on many truths, but not always. In our unconsciousness there are many negative realms that overshadow the truth, and often it fails to reach the truth.

There is an important difference between doing a medical test for medical reasons and doing a muscle testing to search for truth. The existence or absence of the active power that unconsciousness sends to a certain thought is expressing if it is valid to the unconsciousness of the involved party, but the existence or absence of the active power that unconsciousness sends to the medical contacts is expressing "good or bad." And the expression of good or bad is good or bad for the limited situation at the time of examination and good or bad determined by combining the unconsciousness of the patient and the therapist who performs the test. Our unconsciousness is always an open door, enabling us to communicate with each other without any barriers. When conducting muscle testing for medical treatment, the good or bad of the patient to treat and the treatment system of the examiner are combined into one, and active power is formed in the most ideal stimulation in the current combination of the two. Therefore, even if the same patient is tested by a therapist with a different treatment system, different results may be produced. In other words, the active power is best formed in the patient and therapist combination.

Since this medical muscle testing expresses likes and dislikes for specific situations, it is rare to see the phenomenon of holding consciousness accountable for the outward manifestation of unconsciousness. Therefore, there is no big problem in using a muscular test that features medical contact for anyone through practice. But in truth exploration, there is a phenomenon in which consciousness is held accountable for its outward manifestation of unconsciousness. This phenomenon is a common reaction to all acts of bringing out unconsciousness to consciousness. Hypnotherapy, muscle testing that responds to questions, and observing the stillness (no) and rotation (yes) of a pendulum when asked a question while holding it in your hand are all ways to communicate with your own unconsciousness. And as I mentioned in Part 1, communicating with your own unconsciousness involves the risk of having your unconsciousness attacking you. In fact, a more accurate expression than an attack is a signal. The signal that tells you that your consciousness hasn't found the meaning of the answer given by unconsciousness, or hasn't found any significant meaning, perplexes you.

This perplexing and sometimes painful signal also means for you sometimes to realize why the answer is true at times, and sometimes to recognize the darkness that obscures yourself and why the wrong answer was given to you. The answer to a pendulum or muscle testing is simply a binary language with the expression "Yes or No." The meaning of the answer is an area that must always be interpreted as the party's free will. Therefore, we have to realize whether the answers we get from the pendulum or the muscle testing are true or false, and why they are true or false, and we have to practice the meaning to eliminate the signal that our unconsciousness is sending. With regards to the results of hypnotherapy, we also need to realize the meaning and practice.

Therefore, revealing one's unconsciousness to the surface is a process that requires very strict observation into oneself. For this reason, asking unconsciousness about our daily life inevitably takes too much physical time for insight and can be burdensome. Perhaps for those who have not gone through the third stage of expansion, they might have to cling to only insight and prayer all day long like a monk. Of course, if you do this process right, you will make a quick voyage toward human perfection, but for those who are not monks and live normal lives, the better everyday choice is to live on their own consciousness.

Nevertheless, finding truth to observe the active power of the human body is too important for mankind to give up, because during the process of communicating with unconsciousness, we can reach the truth of the vast universe. If we understand the principle of our unconsciousness reaching the truth, the truth finding through muscle testing and pendulum can sufficiently spark the evolution of mankind. It can be made into a blessing for mankind. It is up to us to decide whether this way will be disaster or blessing. If you look at the results so far, it started as a blessing in the early days, and became a disaster that left a lot of pain, went through chaos where unconsciousness did not understand the principles of unconsciousness reaching the truth, and remained a disaster that left many pains. Therefore, here I am introducing the principle of the unconsciousness I found reaching the truth.

First of all, in order for unconsciousness to reach the truth of the universe, the number of the first-stage myungsu has to be at least 75 or higher, and you must know that there is a step-by-step distinction in reaching the truth depending on the stage of myungsu expansion. Having the number of 75 or higher in the first stage of myungsu expansion means that consciousness has grown to the point where it is not overwhelmed by unconsciousness. It also means the power factor that is formed by unconsciousness has reached 0.19 or more, being able to reveal the effective power. Before that, it is very difficult to reflect on one's unconsciousness because not only is it difficult to clearly distinguish the effective power whether or not, but also because consciousness is overwhelmed by unconsciousness. This means that those who are about to complete the first stage of myungsu, in which they experience how love is the most important, can manifest their consciousness and start exploring the truth.

Therefore, unconsciousness can reach the conceptual and abstract truth beginning from 75 or more in the first stage of myungsu. Conceptual truths include the logic of time and space such as the theory of relativity, the conceptual system for classifying life, and the conceptual system for classifying the world. Other conceptual truths include: myungsu, anti-myungsu, relational karma, chakra, Hon-Baek-Shin-Ui-Ji, the principle of space composition, the principle of karma, and philosophical reason. In other words, a theoretical system that classifies or abstracts a phenomenon is a conceptual truth. Therefore, Dr Hawkins' consciousness energy levels that are divided from 0 to 1,000, myungsu, and relational karma correspond to conceptual truths.

Beginning from 75 or higher in the second stage of myungsu expansion, you can explore personal truths as well. Personal truth means individual's private truth, such as personal fate, life problems, and specific relationship. Those who know by experience that there is no distinction between self and others are qualified to reach the personal truths about personal relationship or fate, such as: "What does my relationship with him mean?"; "Why does this phenomenon repeat to me or you?"; "How did his myungsu improve and by what?"; and "What caused this relational karma?" In his book *Power vs Force*, Dr Hawkins said that since all truths are recorded in space, the problem of finding the real culprit of any incident is possible through muscle testing. However, since the truth of these individual incidents constitutes personal truth, the power to reach the truth begins when the myungsu of the second stage of expansion reaches 75 or higher.

Beginning from 75 and higher at the third stage of myungsu expansion, you can explore material truths. Material truths involve the classification criteria of matter, not life. Since the system of distinguishing certain phenomena, including life, belongs to the conceptual truth because they are made of human ideas, the system of classifying materials, such as elements, atoms, molecules, electrons, and protons, is material truth. In addition, the law of universal gravitation, which is a scientific law of matter, as well as the law of conservation of mass, and the law of conservation of energy, are material laws and therefore are included in material truths. On the other hand, the theory of relativity being a theory about time and space, it is a conceptual truth. Other methods of selecting and making specific materials that correspond to material truths include: "Which items should be chosen?"; "What prescriptions should be used for treatment?"; and "How should it be made?" This is because those who know their own and others' divinity are eligible to know the truths of the material world.

There is a step-by-step distinction in the truths that can be reached according to the stage of myungsu expansion. If you ask for personal or material truths in the first stage of myungsu, the true and false probabilities of the formed answer can be either positive or negative. Occasionally, if the questioner who is grabbing a pendulum has put forth considerable efforts in relation to the question, he or she may form a true answer to the material truth at the first stage of myungsu. But he or she may not have enough power to reach the truth. Therefore, you have to understand the stage of truth that you can explore according to the stage of myungsu expansion. It is estimated that Dr Hawkins had been heading for more than the completion of the third stage of myungsu completion since he started the muscle testing. Therefore, most of the unconscious responses must have reached the truth of the universe. However, it should be noted that there are differences in how you can reach the truths depending on the stage of expansion, because most of mankind is undergoing the first stage of myungsu expansion.

Secondly, the question you ask your unconsciousness should always be corresponding to absolute values. Because the design of the universe consists of absolute values, truth is naturally always about absolute values. When asked about something that does not correspond to absolute values, there is no answer to give from the perspective of the universe. In that case, answers are made up by your own unconsciousness. If you ask which stocks you should invest in, or when and at what price you should sell your house, you will only get answers made up by your unconsciousness as it pleases. When unconsciousness wants to be greedy, greedy answers will come out, and when it wants to lose, losing answers will come out. If you continue to ask these questions, answers that will attack yourself will be formed. It is an expression of your unconsciousness' intention of not wanting you to keep asking because it is a life that goes against the free will that was given by the Creator. The question of choice in life should be judged by your own consciousness, not by asking your unconsciousness.

Also, if you repeat a question that goes against absolute values, it rather forms an answer that goes against the value. For example, if you ask questions that don't show your life's gratitude for food, it will rather lead you to form an unhealthy answer to remind you to be thankful to it for your life. If you ask questions that show you are being selfish in human relationships, it will also form an inhuman answer so that you will realize you are going the wrong way. If you repeatedly ask with ideas that go against absolute values, it will show clearly wrong answers that are contrary to absolute values to tell you that you are asking wrong questions.

Third, when collecting a piece of information, valid results can be achieved when it is in the area where a lot of information has been accumulated previously. In this universe, all information that a humanity experienced to date is stored. Not only the information that has been established by the humanity as a proposition through experience but also unconscious information that has not become a proposition are all stored. The exploration of unconsciousness serves as a useful means to pull out such unconscious information and transform them into a proposition. At this point, the important thing is to ask with an accurate conception. This increases the accuracy of the data. However, if it is a new area where information has no standardized group, then the answer a pendulum can provide is completely random. That is because valid data do not exist in this universe. In an area where the standardized group is small, information that has a wide margin of error is confirmed through the pendulum. That is because the amount of valid data is small.

For example, let's assume that we are using the answers provided by the pendulum to more systematically organize the efficacy of a herbal medicine that has been used for a long time. The herbal medicines recorded in Chinese Herbal Literature have the information of countless numbers of people administering them in a long history stored in the universe. Not only the information that exists as a proportion but also information that has not been transformed into a proportion are all recorded in the existing Chinese Herbal Literature. Therefore, a more accurate and systematic organization is possible through exploration of the unconsciousness than what has already been revealed. However, when trying to explore a completely new treatment method, the answer of the pendulum is not very valid. That is because there is no data in this universe to refer to. New principles or methods cannot be opened by exploring the unconsciousness, and can be revealed in the world through general methods such as experiencing directly and propositionalizing. However, if some new principle is somehow connected to the existing data, then it is useful in finding a quick application method through exploration of the unconsciousness.

In the exploration of unconsciousness, errors can easily be made when asking whether one can make judgments on their own. Therefore, when anaylzing information, one must have reasonable doubts. When collecting information, one can observe that errors are made in the information that the researchers know for certain. Such errors are never created randomly. This is a phenomenon that tests the subjecthood of the researcher when the researcher unconditionally accepts the results of the pendulum. If one fails to detect and modify the errors, then more errors will be created in the course of information collection and ultimately, create random errors. One must have subjecthood when exploring the subconsciousness.

Fourth, the questioner's chakra should be in a healthy, well-developed state to facilitate communication with the universe. Each chakra is a channel of communication that reaches the truth of the universe with absolute value. Thus, when the questioner's chakra is weak or damaged, the truth of the universe cannot be delivered to the questioner. If a wrong answer is formed to a question that corresponds to an absolute value, it is a sign that the questioner's chakra is weak or problematic. In the case of such a wrong answer, it can serve as an opportunity to check one's chakra and fill one's own shortcoming.

The truth of the universe that each chakra guarantees is as follows.

The 1st chakra contains the absolute value of birth-life-death. It can explore the life phenomena about death and birth and the life phenomena about reincarnation, and it can also explore the cycle of life that takes place on Earth. In addition, it can explore the truths about the human body and other living things in the field of life sciences and medicine. The logic associated with life energy, such as physical constitution classification and classification of life, is attributed to the 1st chakra.

The 2nd chakra contains the absolute value of individual-self realization-solidarity. It is a force that touches truths such as problems in human relations, relational karma, psychological research for self-realization, and social science. In particular, relational karma can be identified by dividing a current antagonistic relationship into figures from zero to 100. In other words, the size of wound can be confirmed in terms of physical volume, you can see which among Hon, Baek, Shin, Ui, and Ji the karma is associated with. Also, the karma of physical relationships, not the wounds of the mind, can be confirmed by the power of the 2nd chakra. However, confirmation of unconsciousness is not absolutely necessary because you can fully see what kind of wound it is as long as you understand the hostile karma with your head and heart.

The 3rd chakra contains the value of analysis-communication-synthesis, and it communicates with the fields of society, science, art, and philosophy. In other words, it can explore the theoretical system in any field. In medicine, it is the 1st chakra that identifies who is in which constitution, but the theoretical principle of classifying the constitution is explored with the power of the 3rd chakra. The identification of karma in human relationships is due to the 2nd chakra, but the domain of psychology and social science is based on the 3rd chakra. In other words, the pursuit of essential truth is unfolded through the 3rd chakra. So, the 3rd chakra includes most areas of academic exploration of truth. However, it is limited to uncovering pure logic, and the practical implementation method does not apply.

The 4th chakra contains the value of love-hope-belief. It becomes a channel for exploring religious and spiritual truths. The absolute God, Hon-Baek-Shin-Ui-Ji, the chakras, the principle of the universe composition, and the evolutionary stage of the soul open through the 4th chakra, because they are the principles that teach us that love is our only purpose. In addition, those that are associated with life phenomenon in reincarnation are associated with the 1st chakra, but the spiritual principles are based on the 4th chakra.

The 5th chakra contains the values of responsibility - calling - freedom. It lets us know about the composition of personal life and the nature of the world. It can explore the way individuals discover calling and how they move toward freedom, and it can explore the principle about how the world develops through calling. In other words, specific methods such as social system, application of science and technology, and expression of art are in line with the value of calling. Therefore, the methodology for actually applying the academic logic identified through the 3rd chakra can be opened by the 5th chakra.

The 6th chakra is where all the answers to the truths come together. The answers formed by eight other chakras communicating with the truths are expressed through the 6th chakra. Because Hon that leads all mind is in the 6th chakra, and since the active power created by unconsciousness begins in the pineal gland where Hon is, it is the 6th chakra that determines the answer. Therefore, when the 6th chakra is unhealthy, errors can be formed in any truth exploration. The health and stability of the 6th chakra should always be ensured in the quest for the truth of unconsciousness.

The 7th chakra, which contains gratitude, also plays a role of guiding the questioner in the right direction in the exploration process. Therefore, you can check the health status of each chakra with the power of the 7th chakra. Also, since it serves to protect the truth from going the wrong way, it serves as the basis for checking whether the question you are going to ask is necessary or not for you now. In order to lead you to the most necessary quests at present, it doesn't make any response to any additional question when you are in a wrong direction or wrong quest, and it would raise power to move you again only when you find the necessary direction. This can be fully achieved only when the 7th chakra is healthy.

And another thing to remember is that in your quest for exploration of unconsciousness, you may face a collective consciousness (consciousness + unconsciousness) that obscures the truth. Collective consciousness cannot be fully overcome by an individual. Therefore, if the storm of the collective consciousness is strong, errors can occur, and the unconsciousness of the questioner is bound to get wet and tangled. In that case, if the 7th chakra is healthy, it protects itself by keeping the pendulum fixed or by creating a cough or stomach ache that cannot grab the pendulum. At this time, the questioner must decide whether to stop promising the next time you will grow further or continue the quest regardless. If you continue your quest, you should thoroughly arm your chakra and consider the possibility of error in your exploration. And after completing the exploration, a recovery is needed to fix the wet and tangled unconsciousness. The process of recovery is to repeatedly hold sorriness, gratitude, forgiveness, and blessing in your mind, just like healing a trauma.

This is because the truths that mankind has yet to unravel have a collective consciousness that prevents the story from being revealed. Therefore, facing painful collective consciousness is inevitable in order for us to open up a new truth. The relationship between the previously mentioned myungsu and the human strength, and the myungsu of intellectually disabled is the result obtained from the unconsciousness exploration through the pendulum. Since one has faced a collective consciousness wounded in association with myungsu and disability, one needed some significant time to recover afterwards. In my personal opinion, I think the fundamental logic is true, but I leave open the possibility of error in specific parts.

The 8th chakra contains the value of forgiveness. It becomes the power to confirm anti-myungsu, because it aggregates the areas that are opposite of love in Hon-Baek-Shin-Ui-Ji. Like relational karma, anti-myungsu can also be confirmed by the numbers from 0 to 100. If my anti-myungsu counts two, that means there are at least two major actions that I've done for anti-myungsu. Therefore, I need to remember those two actions and repent for them. In addition, it is possible to identify which of the five types is anti-myungsu, and it is also possible to check if they have been expired. Although the process of directly confirming it at an early stage when your understanding of anti-myungsu is not enough is useful, you can awaken and discover on your own if you understand anti-myungsu, and you can notice it expiring with your repent.

The 9th chakra contains the value of blessing, and since it aggregates the areas of love in Hon-Baek-Shin-Ui-Ji, it becomes the power to check the number of myungsu. You can check it with the numbers from 0 to 100 in each stage and find out what stage it is at, and you can also check each energy level of Hon-Baek-Shin-Ui-Ji with the numbers from 0 to 100 as well. Verifying myungsu is also very useful as a guide in the early stages of understanding the myungsu extension. However, it can be replaced with the measurement of human body factor, and if you fully understand the expansion of myungsu, you can feel yourself growing up without having to check the figures yourself, and when you complete one stage of expansion, you can realize that you have been reborn anew.

In the first period of use of the pendulum, it began with confirming myungsu and anti-myungsu. Then after a period of chaos and disaster, it was no longer possible to confirm myungsu and anti-myungsu with a pendulum, and it was because the 8th and 9th chakras of those who grabbed the pendulum became damaged and weakened. It was a natural result of the fading significance of forgiveness and blessing, because evil must be punished in the conception of a war between the good and the evil.

To reach the truth, the chakra must be large, healthy, deep, and shine brightly. This point is very important. Therefore, in order to explore unconsciousness, you must go through the process of fully controlling the health of the associated chakra along with the 6th chakra. If you meet a collective consciousness that blocks the truth, you should control it more thoroughly. In order to fully control the chakra, you need prayers that add light to the chakras, along with the previously introduced awakening shields and Kundalini prayers. A prayer that adds light consists of a structure of apology, gratitude, forgiveness, and blessing, as the trauma healing in the 6th chakra. Prayers that add light to each chakra will be introduced in the next volume to be written in the future.

Fifth, the mind of the questioner has to be based on the physiological power of Hon-Baek-Shin-Ui-Ji. In the early stage of holding a pendulum, you easily repeat the same error of asking the same question because you are not sure if the answer you formed is correct or not. However, if you repeat the same question out of suspicion, it causes confusion in the body's production of active power, resulting in ambiguity or error in the movement of the pendulum. When you learn a muscle testing, those who believe in the reaction of their muscles learn the technique easily, but those who repeat the same question, suspecting if it actually works or not, fail in the end. Therefore, you have to ask clearly with the mind that believes in you, the mind that believes in the Creator and the universe, the mind that believes in our lives, and the faith in others.

Also, you must ask with sincere love for yourself and others, with the mind that loves the Creator and the universe, and with the mind that loves our lives. If you ask questions while you doubt and resent others, distrust yourself for what you can do, and are afraid of being punished by the Creator and the law of the universe, you will be blocked by the pathological power of Hon-Baek-Shin-Ui-Ji and cannot reach the truth. You should organize questions and structure them with a heart that loves all and explore the truth of unconsciousness. For that reason, it is better to start after engraving love and faith in your consciousness with the awakening shield of Hon-Baek-Shin-Ui-Ji with regards to the exploration of unconsciousness.

Sixth, if you have achieved the answer to the question, you should experience love with it. For example, if you have identified someone's myungsu or anti-myungsu, you should practice love with that answer. If you have identified someone's karma, you should practice love to resolve that karma. If you have explored the truth about something, you should find a way to share it together so that the truth can be used for someone's or everyone's love experience. And if it's an answer that you can't experience love no matter how you interpret it, you should know it's a wrong answer. Since the only purpose we have to explore the truth of the universe is love, the real truth must be interpreted as a way of experiencing love. It must be true to its sole purpose of exploring the truth.

This means that you should not ask your unconsciousness when there is no purpose in experiencing love. Therefore, you hold the pendulum only when you need an answer of unconsciousness to experience the love you wish to do. You should not do the muscle testing for experiencing love you don't wish to have, even if you are curious about it. If it's a love experience that you want to do, but you can do it on your own even if you don't have an answer from your unconsciousness, you'd better just do it on your own. Therefore, you should use the pendulum and muscle testing only when you meet two conditions: when you want to do it, and when you absolutely need it. You should always experience love when you get an answer manifested by unconsciousness outwardly.

Finally, there are a few other things you need to know in the quest for the truth with your unconsciousness. First of all, when you ask questions to your unconsciousness, you must think inside. Since thinking while talking is the intermediate frequency of the audible area, it doesn't effectively generate active power. Since thinking inside is clearly divided into high frequency and cursing waves, it can reveal whether it is active power or not. When you do an actual test and ask such questions as "Am I a human?", you can see the pendulum doesn't move if you ask by vocalizing the question, but it rotates when you think the question inside. This phenomenon is caused because active power changes depending on the frequency. Therefore, you have to think in your mind instead of talking when you do the muscle testing because it follows the same principle.

Also, the more specific questions are refined and the more limited the range is, the better. Since the only response to active power is "on or off," the answers are likely to be prone to error if the question is ambiguous or too comprehensive. And no matter what answer you have formed, it is better not to regard it as a solid conclusion but to accept it as the answer to the process toward truth. It is because truth exists at a high level, but if your consciousness is at a level that is too far from it, a positive answer is formed within a range where it can present direction, even if it is not a solid truth. In the future, when your consciousness grows to a higher level and becomes closer to the truth, you can understand the direction of the answer and modify it toward a clearer truth.

As previously explained, you may not reach the truth and encounter error if the collective consciousness blocks the truth, because you cannot fully overcome the situation with your individual power alone. In this case, it is necessary to explore by making an actual authentication because it produces a result of a mixture of truth and error. Another reason why you should regard the answer from unconsciousness as a process rather than a conclusion is this collective consciousness. The truth that mankind has not uncovered now is because there is a collective consciousness that prevents it from being uncovered. Therefore, when you uncover something new with the exploration of unconsciousness, there is almost always a situation where some errors are formed, and the questioner's unconsciousness gets wet and tangled. That is the reason an actual authentication is necessary.

In some cases, unconsciousness of some individuals, not collective consciousness, collides. When confirming something about someone, mine and that other's subconsciousness create the answer together. If there are no problems in the subconscious emotions, the answer is created based on the truth, but if there are many subconscious emotions that cover the truth, then an answer that hides the truth is created. If it is a problem of selection, then the answer is created based on the agreement formed by their subconscious emotions. Such subconscious agreement is not a selection about right or wrong, but is a mere reflection of the subconscious state. The problem of selection is not relevant to the subconsciousness in principle, but please refer to this point mentioned as there are instances where you cannot avoid the subconsciousness that speaks to you when you lift up the weight.

Another case would be conflicts arising when several others oppose, with love, the truth that you wish to explore. In this case, partial error can be formed. However, the conflict between personal subconsciousness can be overcome unlike collective consciousness. And the key to this is genuine love for others. When you truly love the people who you are curious about, and embrace their hearts which oppose you with love, then conflicts between individual subconsciousness can be overcome.

Sometimes intentional wrong answers are formed. Even though it is rare, intentional wrong answers are given to broaden the range of truth or love experience. In this case, the wrong answer opens up a new possibility and eventually you can realize that the wrong answer was an opportunity for you. Intentionally wrong answers may be created at times. Although rare, intentionally wrong answers are presented to expand the domain of truth or experience of love. In such cases, new possibilities will be opened from such wrong answers, and you get to realize that the wrong answer was an opportunity for you. At times, you may also feel a huge amount of pain. In particular, wrong answers are presented for questions that constitute stages of change for a bigger frame, and the path to truth is discovered while enduring the pain. This is perhaps because truth that is beyond the existing limits cannot be known without pain of equivalent significance. In conclusion, the presentation of intentionally wrong answers by my subconsciousness is a challenge of sort. It is a challenge that leads to truth of a different dimension. Forgive the pain of wrong answers, learn the path toward truth, and have faith that it will turn into blessing, and you'll reach the truth of a whole new dimension.

The last thing to consider is solar power. All light is electromagnetic waves. In the case of light, electric and magnetic fields are consisting the wave. Among them, solar power improves the body's active power because it creates a wave that has a great influence on the body's magnetic field. Walking in the sun when we are depressed makes us feel better and brighter, and bright and sunny days give us the power to shake off all worries. This is the result of the increased active power of the human body after the solar power strengthens the magnetic field that is raised by Hon-Baek-Shin-Ui-Ji.

For that reason, you must avoid sunlight in order to explore the truth of unconsciousness. It is because active power is easily formed under sunlight, increasing the possibility of errors of affirming falsehood as truth. When you explore the truth through a pendulum, it is rare to have a problem caused by the error of pendulum not rotating in reaction to the real truth, but several problems arise due to errors where the pendulum rotates in response to falsehood, expressing it to be true. Therefore, for the strictly reliable results of truth exploration, it is better not to hold the pendulum for two hours around noon, when the solar energy is the strongest, and avoid being directly under sunlight or avoid the time when the sunlight comes indoors directly through the window. This condition applies the same to the conditions under which power factor is measured or muscle testing is performed. However, it doesn't matter if it is the indoor light as long as it is not sunlight.

You can see that you don't have much time to explore if you exclude outdoors, four hours around noon – two hours each before and after noon – when you are most affected by the sunlight, indoors that is affected by direct sunlight around sunset and sunrise, and the night hours when you go to bed. It shows that it is not desirable to pursue the truth of unconsciousness as your main job, and that it is natural to allow it only on occasions when it is necessary for the truth exploration.

Accordingly, there is a limit to the total amount of truth that a person can approach. This amount is calculated using the same method used for a car battery. The battery would charge automatically if driven safely and naturally, but it would be consumed if driven meaninglessly or wrongly. Therefore, in order to keep the amount, you must ask questions that are only reasonable and organized. Exploration of truth should be approached in a restrained and refined manner.

These are the principles of reaching the real truths by pursuing truth holding a pendulum that reveals your unconsciousness outwardly. These are also the principles of reaching the real truths through muscle testing. Comprehensively speaking, in order for our unconsciousness to reach the truth of the universe, we must achieve more than 75 in the first stage of myungsu expansion so that our consciousness grows enough not to be overwhelmed by unconsciousness. It is also necessary to explore the truths while understanding the difference in stages until you reach the real truth depending on the stage of myungsu expansion. You always should ask questions that meet absolute values, and the questioner's chakras should be large, deep, and bright. And we must explore the truths with faith and love for everything. Lastly, we have to practice and experience love with the answer we have formed. If the answer we have formed is not the way to experience love, then we must recognize the lack in our chakras is the reason we cannot reach the truth, or the answer was formed by the hidden pathological power of our Hon-Baek-Shin-Ui-Ji. By doing so, we must overcome this by filling our chakras and Hon-Baek-Shin-Ui-Ji with the light of love, and love ourselves with that wrong answer.

In conclusion, if you have achieved a true answer, share it with others and experience love, and if you have achieved a wrong answer, experience loving yourself with it. Always experiencing love with an answer from unconsciousness – this is the righteous way for those who try to hold a pendulum and reach the truth of the universe before the law of the universe and the almighty God. Also, this is the righteous way for those who wish to reach the truths of the universe through a muscle testing to protect and love themselves. If this righteous way is not followed, the massive unconsciousness will signal to awaken your consciousness that is being irresponsible before the truth, and when this righteous way is followed through, the massive unconsciousness will bless your consciousness that is faithful to love.

The pendulum is just one tool for us humans, just like smartphones and computers. It is a tool that outwardly expresses our unconsciousness and allows us to open the truth of love – no more, no less than that. I don't expect the truth exploration through pendulum or muscle testing to become a common way of exploration right away. But this path has already begun: It has been presented to mankind, and how it will be made is entirely dependent on our hands. Perhaps it might become a universal truth exploration method for mankind by the time most of us mankind is headed for the third stage of expansion. Until the day when this path can become a universal truth exploration for mankind, it is my hope that all the disasters that have so far been made by the exploration of unconsciousness will be healed, forgiven and preserved wholesomely.

The Sacred Boundary for Exploration of Subconsciousness
* In order to communicate well with subconsciousness, various conditions must be satisfied
and time and efforts should be invested in advance.
Since this is not an easy task, I should prepare enough beforehand.

Since we have to endure tough situations and consume much energy during exploration,
I should control so as to not overwork, heed caution so as to avoid risk,
and balance my will well.

Although it may be tough, this is certainly what I wish to engage in.
By investing my time and efforts willingly and controlling so as to fit with the situation
I shall continue exploring subconsciousness joyfully and proudly.

* Epiphany was achieved easily as I began exploring subconsciousness.

Such fortune was possible, thanks to God, the Holy Spirit and attending to my spirit.
I extend my sincere gratitude for such hard efforts.

But it is only natural that such fortune continues on.
Inevitable errors can only lead to confusion and pain.
During the course, it was very fortunate that the natural course led me here.

Now as experiences build up, I can understand the details of the natural course of this exploration.
While thoroughly examining how I can communicate with the truth with absolute values,
I shall strive to equip myself with properness so as to touch upon the truth.

* The fortune of obtaining the truth easily on this path at the beginning
was partially because of the innocence and love I had.
As such, I was able to start on this path.

I went through various confusion and wounds because of the errors caused by subconsciousness,
but I am proud of myself for enduring such course and standing still firm to this day.
I was able to grow by exploring subconsciousness and I will continue to grow.

Now I know. All errors were made possible because of the darkness in my subconsciousness
While letting my greed, self-conceit and dependence down
I shall strive to explore with my innocent love, belief and will.

* I tried to exercise love when getting to know someone through my subconsciousness,
but I repent not being able to exercise pure love.
I promise myself that I shall not rashly invade others when I am not pure love.

I failed to think deeply about the main agent of pain when I felt difficulty exploring.
From now on, I will reflect on the pain of numerous many whenever exploration feels difficult,
and sincerely hope that the answers I discover heal their pain.

In addition, it is not my own achievement that I found the right answer to the truth I sought.
It must have been the power of so many that helped me touch upon such truth.
Moving forward, whenever I am able to clarify the truth, I shall thank everyone for their efforts.

* I ask for my forgiveness for what I lack in the exploration of truth in subconsciousness.
Asking about what I already know, and asking without clearing my thoughts...
I shall overcome them by growing into a more mature explorer.

I feel grateful for everything I was able to enjoy on this path
and although it is difficult, I am truly intrigued and amazed by this exploration.
I shall continue on with due gratitude.

Please congratulate everything that was enjoyed on this path.
I shall not forget the past where this exploration was on the wrong track,

and strive so that this exploration can be established as a tool for happiness.

Endnote

19   Refer to the book *Power vs Force* for answers to your questions about muscle test.

O-BOOKS

SPIRITUALITY

O is a symbol of the world, of oneness and unity; this eye represents knowledge and insight. We publish titles on general spirituality and living a spiritual life. We aim to inform and help you on your own journey in this life.

If you have enjoyed this book, why not tell other readers by posting a review on your preferred book site?

Recent bestsellers from O-Books are:

Heart of Tantric Sex
Diana Richardson
Revealing Eastern secrets of deep love and intimacy to Western couples.
Paperback: 978-1-90381-637-0 ebook: 978-1-84694-637-0

Crystal Prescriptions
The A-Z guide to over 1,200 symptoms and their healing crystals
Judy Hall
The first in the popular series of eight books, this handy little guide is packed as tight as a pill-bottle with crystal remedies for ailments.
Paperback: 978-1-90504-740-6 ebook: 978-1-84694-629-5

Your Simple Path
Find happiness in every step
Ian Tucker
A guide to helping us reconnect with what is really important in
our lives.
Paperback: 978-1-78279-349-6 ebook: 978-1-78279-348-9

365 Days of Wisdom
Daily Messages To Inspire You Through The Year
Dadi Janki
Daily messages which cool the mind, warm the heart and guide
you along your journey.
Paperback: 978-1-84694-863-3 ebook: 978-1-84694-864-0

Body of Wisdom
Women's Spiritual Power and How it Serves
Hilary Hart
Bringing together the dreams and experiences of women across
the world with today's most visionary spiritual teachers.
Paperback: 978-1-78099-696-7 ebook: 978-1-78099-695-0

Dying to Be Free
From Enforced Secrecy to Near Death to True Transformation
Hannah Robinson
After an unexpected accident and near-death experience, Hannah
Robinson found herself radically transforming her life, while a
remarkable new insight altered her relationship with her father, a
practising Catholic priest.
Paperback: 978-1-78535-254-6 ebook: 978-1-78535-255-3

The Ecology of the Soul
A Manual of Peace, Power and Personal Growth for Real People
in the Real World
Aidan Walker
Balance your own inner Ecology of the Soul to regain your
natural state of peace, power and wellbeing.
Paperback: 978-1-78279-850-7 ebook: 978-1-78279-849-1

Not I, Not other than I
The Life and Teachings of Russel Williams
Steve Taylor, Russel Williams
The miraculous life and inspiring teachings of one of the World's
greatest living Sages.
Paperback: 978-1-78279-729-6 ebook: 978-1-78279-728-9

On the Other Side of Love
A woman's unconventional journey towards wisdom
Muriel Maufroy
When life has lost all meaning, what do you do?
Paperback: 978-1-78535-281-2 ebook: 978-1-78535-282-9

Practicing A Course In Miracles
A translation of the Workbook in plain language, with
mentor's notes
Elizabeth A. Cronkhite
The practical second and third volumes of The Plain-Language
A Course In Miracles.
Paperback: 978-1-84694-403-1 ebook: 978-1-78099-072-9

Quantum Bliss

The Quantum Mechanics of Happiness, Abundance, and Health
George S. Mentz
Quantum Bliss is the breakthrough summary of success and
spirituality secrets that customers have been waiting for.
Paperback: 978-1-78535-203-4 ebook: 978-1-78535-204-1

The Upside Down Mountain

Mags MacKean
A must-read for anyone weary of chasing success and happiness
– one woman's inspirational journey swapping the uphill slog for
the downhill slope.
Paperback: 978-1-78535-171-6 ebook: 978-1-78535-172-3

Your Personal Tuning Fork

The Endocrine System
Deborah Bates
Discover your body's health secret, the endocrine system, and
'twang' your way to sustainable health!
Paperback: 978-1-84694-503-8 ebook: 978-1-78099-697-4

Readers of ebooks can buy or view any of these bestsellers by
clicking on the live link in the title. Most titles are published
in paperback and as an ebook. Paperbacks are available in
traditional bookshops. Both print and ebook formats are
available online.

Find more titles and sign up to our readers' newsletter at
www.o-books.com

Follow O books on Facebook at **O-books**

For video content, author interviews and more, please subscribe to our YouTube channel:

O-BOOKS Presents

Follow us on social media for book news, promotions and more:

Facebook: O-Books

Instagram: @o_books_mbs

Twitter: @obooks

Tik Tok: @ObooksMBS

www.o-books.com